THE LIBRARY
ST. MARY'S COLLEGE OF MARYLAND
ST. MARY'S CITY, MARYLAND 20686

084403

COGNITIVE DEVELOPMENT AND EPISTEMOLOGY

COGNITIVE DEVELOPMENT AND EPISTEMOLOGY

Edited by

THEODORE MISCHEL

DEPARTMENT OF PHILOSOPHY
STATE UNIVERSITY OF NEW YORK
AT BINGHAMTON, NEW YORK

1971

ACADEMIC PRESS
New York San Francisco London
A Subsidiary of Harcourt Brace Jovanovich, Publishers

COPYRIGHT © 1971, BY ACADEMIC PRESS, INC.
ALL RIGHTS RESERVED
NO PART OF THIS BOOK MAY BE REPRODUCED IN ANY FORM,
BY PHOTOSTAT, MICROFILM, RETRIEVAL SYSTEM, OR ANY
OTHER MEANS, WITHOUT WRITTEN PERMISSION FROM
THE PUBLISHERS.

ACADEMIC PRESS, INC.
111 Fifth Avenue, New York, New York 10003

United Kingdom Edition published by
ACADEMIC PRESS, INC. (LONDON) LTD.
24/28 Oval Road, London NW1

LIBRARY OF CONGRESS CATALOG CARD NUMBER: 71-169083

3-23-78

MAY 26 1978

PRINTED IN THE UNITED STATES OF AMERICA

CONTENTS

PART I. COGNITIVE DEVELOPMENT AND EPISTEMOLOGY

Genetic Psychology, Genetic Epistemology, and Theory of Knowledge

BERNARD KAPLAN

PART II. BASIC ISSUES IN THE PSYCHOLOGY OF COGNITIVE DEVELOPMENT

A. The Development of Physical Concepts

The Development of Physical Concepts

HARRY BEILIN

Comments on Beilin's "The Development of Physical Concepts"

JOHN H. FLAVELL

From Praxis to Logos: Genetic Epistemology and Physics

MARX W. WARTOFSKY

PART II. BASIC ISSUES IN THE PSYCHOLOGY OF COGNITIVE DEVELOPMENT

B. The Development of Moral Concepts

From Is to Ought: How to Commit the Naturalistic Fallcy and Get Away with It in the Study of Moral Development

LAWRENCE KOHLBERG

Moral Developments: A Plea for Pluralism

R. S. PETERS

PART III. THEORIES OF COGNITIVE DEVELOPMENT AND THE EXPLANATION OF HUMAN CONDUCT

LIST OF CONTRIBUTORS

Numbers in parentheses indicate the pages on which the authors' contributions begin.

WILLIAM P. ALSTON, Department of Philosophy, University of Michigan, Ann Arbor, Michigan (269)

DAVID P. AUSUBEL, Educational Psychology Doctoral Program, City University of New York, New York, New York (357)

HARRY BEILIN, Psychology Department, Graduate Center, The City University of New York, New York, New York (85)

PETER C. DODWELL, Department of Psychology, Queen's University, Kingston, Ontario, Canada (365)

JOHN H. FLAVELL, Institute of Child Development, University of Minnesota, Minneapolis, Minnesota (121)

D. W. HAMLYN, Department of Philosophy, University of London, London, England (3)

BERNARD KAPLAN, Department of Psychology, Heinz Werner Institute of Developmental Psychology, Clark University, Worchester, Massachusetts (61)

WILLIAM KESSEN, Department of Psychology, Yale University, New Haven, Connecticut (287)

LAWRENCE KOHLBERG, Department of Education and Social Relations, Laboratory of Human Development, Harvard University, Cambridge, Massachusetts (151)

NORMAN MALCOLM, Sage School of Philosophy, Cornell University, Ithaca, New York (385)

THEODORE MISCHEL, Department of Philosophy, State University of New York at Binghamton, Binghamton, New York (311)

R. S. PETERS, Institute of Education, University of London, London, England (237)

CHARLES TAYLOR, Department of Philosophy, University of Montreal and McGill University, Montreal, Canada (393)

STEPHEN TOULMIN, Department of Philosophy, Michigan State University, East Lansing, Michigan (25)

MARX W. WARTOFSKY, Department of Philosophy, Boston University, Boston, Massachusetts (129)

PREFACE

Philosophers often conceive their task as the analysis of concepts. While they do not always agree on just what is involved in conceptual analysis, at least part of the task consists in bringing out features of some of our concepts by examining the implications of the ways in which these concepts are used. But such analyses do not occur in a vacuum: their point can be seen only against the background of questions and issues which they are designed to illuminate. Thus the analysis of cognitive concepts, of the ways in which "belief," "knowledge," "cause," etc. are used, may be designed to shed light on questions of epistemology (the branch of philosophy traditionally concerned with the analysis of the nature and justification of human knowledge). Again, by analyzing cognitive and other psychological concepts, philosophers have hoped to illuminate conceptual issues in psychology.

But the use of concepts is something that also interests the psychologist. For the attempt to deal with human behavior as if thinking and the use of concepts made no difference is now being abandoned, and empirical investigations of "conceptual behavior" and "cognitive processes" are the cutting edge of today's psychology. Further, psychologists do not regard epistemology as a purely philosophical preserve: the ways in which children come to acquire that knowledge of the physical and social world which adults take for granted is investigated empirically by psychologists, and some of them (for example, Piaget) would argue that these investigations have important implications for epistemology.

The acquisition and use of concepts, the growth and development of knowledge, clearly are areas in which the interests of philosophers, concerned with conceptual analysis and the theory of knowledge, seem to overlap with those of psychologists interested in cognitive development and "conceptual behavior." This makes it plausible to suppose than an attempt to break the insulation between these disciplines—an insulation hardened by the fact that psychology's relatively recent separation from philosophy has made its practitioners anxious to ignore philosophical issues—might be of some value for both epistemology and cognitive psychology.

The papers in this volume were written for a conference which attempted this, a conference which the editor planned with the help of Richard Peters and Stephen Toulmin. At a conference held in Chicago in 1967, the three of us had been involved in an initial attempt by a small group of psychologists and philosophers to explore broad issues relating to the conceptual framework needed for the explanation of human actions [see T. Mischel (Ed.), *Human Action*, 1969]. Our impression was that this exchange had been sufficiently fruitful to warrant another conference at which a more sharply delineated topic could be explored by a group of this sort. After consultation with colleagues in both fields we decided on the topic and on the participants for this conference, which was held at the State University of New York at Binghamton, September 18–22, 1969.

Since the Chicago conference had indicated that many of the central issues in the explanation of human actions are connected with questions about the ways in which language, thought, and purposive, rational behavior develop jointly in the child, we decided to use Piaget's theory of cognitive development as our point of departure. We thought that this might give us a common ground from which to explore broader issues relating to cognitive development and epistemology. In particular, we thought it might be useful to start some joint exploration of questions like the following: Can the adult's use of concepts be fully characterized in abstraction from the developmental processes through which concepts are in fact acquired? Through what kinds of psychological processes and/or sequences are concepts acquired? Are there invariant sequences in cognitive development, such that the acquisition of the "operations" (rules, strategies) characteristic of a given stage are prerequisite for later stages? Are claims for invariant sequences in concept development based on empirical or conceptual grounds? What general form can a theory of cognitive development appropriately take and how does its conceptual structure differ from that of stimulation–response theories? What can such "genetic" theories contribute to our understanding of the adult's use of concepts? What can theories of cognitive development contribute to epistemology?

David Hamlyn and Stephen Toulmin were invited to prepare papers dealing with the relevance which the genetic study of concept development may have for the analysis of concepts. Is a "genetic epistemology" possible? What can a theory of cognitive development, like Piaget's, contribute to epistemology? Bernard Kaplan was invited to serve as commentator on these issues. This general topic was intended to set a framework for subsequent discussion and appears as Part I of this volume.

We then moved to an examination of some of the specific issues in intellectual, moral, and emotional development with which a theory of cognitive development must deal. Harry Beilin prepared a paper on the development of physical concepts (for example, object, space, time, causality) while John Flavell and Marx Wartofsky served as commentators for this topic. Moral development was the topic for papers by Lawrence Kohlberg and Richard Peters, with Bill Alston acting as commentator. Bill Kessen and Ted Mischel addressed themselves to motivational issues in cognitive development, with comments by David Ausubel. The results make up Part II of this volume.

Finally, we sought to assess the adequacy and relevance of this genetic–developmental approach for an understanding of adult cognitive behavior. Peter Dodwell and Charles Taylor were invited to prepare papers dealing such questions as: What can a theory of conceptual development add to our empirical understanding of adult human behavior? Is a theory of cognitive development, such as Piaget's, necessary for understanding the thought and actions of adults? Part III of this volume contains these papers and Norman Malcolm's comments on this topic.

Preparation of first drafts prior to the conference made it possible to devote the conference sessions to detailed discussion by the entire group of issues raised by the papers, discussions which were led off by the commentators. In light of these meetings, the participants then revised their papers or commentaries for publication. In many cases these revisions were extensive, and in some cases postscripts were also added to deal with issues that arose in discussion. As a result, there are numerous cross references between articles in this volume, and these are indicated by italics.

The high degree of mutual understanding and relevance which developed at this conference was, we believe, very unusual for attempts at interdisciplinary discussion. We hope it is reflected, at least to some extent, in this volume. Our aim in publishing these essays is not only to point up critical issues raised by Piaget's important theory of cognitive development, but also to promote further interchange between philosophers engaged in conceptual analyses of knowledge and psychologists engaged in empirical investigations of cognition. For whatever the "right" view of the relation between these disciplines may turn out to be, and whatever the position one may take on other, related issues discussed in this volume, it is at least clear that such discussion can be interesting and stimulating for investigators in both of these disciplines.

The conference from which this volume resulted was supported jointly by Grant GS-2557 from the National Science Foundation and by the State University of New York at Binghamton. We are grateful to them for making this conference possible.

Part I

Cognitive Development and Epistemology

EPISTEMOLOGY AND CONCEPTUAL DEVELOPMENT

D. W. Hamlyn

I. The Status of Genetic Epistemology

Piaget has invoked the term "genetic epistemology" to describe his theory of intellectual development in the individual.[1] The term is in some ways a curious one; it does not entirely reveal its meaning, and it may well be that many philosophers in the Anglo-Saxon tradition would consider it to be incoherent. It savors somewhat of what Locke called the "historical, plain method," which he used to "inquire into the original, certainty, and extent of human knowledge." Many, if not most, modern philosophers would reject such a method of clarifying what is involved in the concept of knowledge. Questions about the genesis of our ideas, if by this is meant the genesis of ideas in the individual, are questions for psychology, not epistemology. But of course whatever term Piaget uses for his theory, he would also hold, and it would usually be held by others, that his investigations are a branch of developmental psychology. Hence the kind of objections to genetic epistemology that I have hinted at might be thought to be terminological only, and for that reason not worth serious consideration for more than a moment.

Still, Piaget does think that his theory has philosophical implications, and there are indications that he would not draw such a hard-and-fast line between psychology and philosophy as I have been presupposing. He opposes his theory, for example, both to empiricism and rationalism (or "apriorism," as he calls it) (Piaget, 1969, Chapter 8), and associates these philosophical theories with certain well-known approaches to psychology—associationism and Gestalt theory, respectively. Indeed, he says of these

[1] B. Kaplan points out that Piaget, in his *Introduction à l'épistémologie génétique* (1950a), defines genetic epistemology as the study of successive states of a science as regards its development, and thus distinguishes between genetic epistemology and the psychology of intelligence. This raises many questions about Piaget's attitude toward the thesis that there is a parallelism between ontogeny and phylogeny, but I cannot think that Piaget in general excludes the study of intellectual development in the individual from genetic epistemology.

theories that the first is "geneticism without structure," while the second is "structuralism without genesis." These are not bad slogans to sum up the views in question, and I think that he is quite right to see in them essentially philosophical points of view (see Hamlyn, 1957). His own position seems to be meant, from this viewpoint, to be a kind of Kantian reconciliation of the opposing theories, though a reconciliation that can be achieved only by the recognition of new elements, in particular the recognition of the importance of the active role played by the individual. (Apart from the Kantian influences, there are here, perhaps, shades of the reaction of M. de Biran to the empiricism of his day. Indeed, Piaget sometimes contrasts his own view with that of de Biran; see, for example, the last chapter of *The child's construction of reality*, 1955.) A reconciliation between opposing philosophical views can itself be nothing less than a philosophical point of view, and I do not think that Piaget would deny this. Hence my point about his not drawing a hard-and-fast line between philosophy and psychology. Some of the questions that he raises about the origins of our ideas are meant to be questions in the same tradition as that asked, for example, by Hume when the latter asked about the source or origin of our idea of cause. Causality, Piaget says, is "seen to originate in action" (Piaget, 1969), and in saying this he seems to be putting forward a perennial answer to this question. Yet, in his case, the answer is supposed to rest on empirical evidence. Is this or is this not confusing? Many philosophers would say, I think, that it must be, and I am of their number. The ways in which an individual may come to an understanding of a certain notion are various, depending on his prior understandings, experience, and so on. We may be able to say something general about the conditions which are normally necessary for a given form of understanding; but a story of this kind will be about the criteria for being properly said to have the concept in question, not about the origins of the concept, about the ways in which it is acquired by individuals. This in turn makes it necessary to ask questions about the status of Piaget's account of the ways in which conceptual development in general takes place. This is a point to which I shall return—not necessarily to dispute the facts, but to ask what is to be made of the facts so described.

What I have been suggesting so far is that Piaget's approach has philosophical implications and presuppositions, and that it may be necessary to sort out what is acceptable and what is not. This will involve asking which questions are genuinely philosophical and which are not, for the most important part of trying to assess any theory is determining which questions are being asked. Only then can one go on to determine whether the questions have been properly answered. I have already hinted, for example (and I cannot claim to have done more than this), that questions about the conditions which are normally necessary if one is to be said to have a certain form of understanding are different from questions about the origins of that form of understanding. I have also suggested that the former kind of question is a genuinely philosophical one. As far as concerns the second kind of question—that about origins—I have allowed that questions about the development of a given form of understanding in an individual may be genuine psychological questions, but I have suggested that questions about the development of forms of understanding in people in general should be considered for the time being as of undetermined status. It will be part of our task to settle the question of their status. If it were the case, for example, that people always came to a certain form of understanding in certain distinct and determined environmental conditions, this would be a very interesting psychological discovery, although it might raise many other questions in its train (questions so different as that about the criteria for being said to have this understanding and that about what there is in these environmental conditions that explains the acquisition of the understanding under consideration). But Piaget's discoveries are not obviously of *this* kind, and it is this among other things that raises the question of their status. It is also not obviously clear that questions about intellectual development are analogous to questions about physical development or even to questions about the development of such psychological factors as personality.

Thus, if it turns out that genetic epistemology is relevant to epistemology as it is usually taken by philosophers, this may be because genetic epistemology is, if not a branch of philosophy proper, at least intimately and closely involved with it, whether in an acceptable way or not. This would have obvious consequences for the status of at least this branch of genetic or developmental psychology. It might, however, be held that my premises are incorrect, and that I am wrong in thinking that philosophical questions about the nature of a certain form of understanding and about its conditions and criteria are utterly divorced and distinct from psychological questions about the conditions in which such understanding develops in individuals. It may be that if a philosopher thinks that the question of what it is to have a concept can be illuminatingly discussed independently from questions about the acquisition of that and other concepts, he is wrong. If so, cooperative enquiries on the part of philosophers and developmental psychologists are not only desirable, they are necessary. It is to this question that I must now turn. (If it is implied in what I say that I think that the questions which I have mentioned can be illuminatingly discussed independently from each other, this should not be taken as also implying that I am quite against cooperation between philosophers and psychologists. One form of cooperation, for example, may consist in a joint sorting out of the questions that they are asking.)

II. Conceptual Development and Conceptual Understanding

A suggestion that the supposition on which I am working is wrong was made, in effect, by Toulmin (1969) in his contribution to the first colloquium of this kind. He suggested that "the analysis of concepts cannot be divorced from a study of their genesis in quite as sharp a way as philosophers frequently suppose" (Mischel, 1969, p. 36). Toulmin (1969, p. 83) claimed that "We may accordingly conceive a possible collaboration between philosophers and psychologists, designed (*a*) to analyze our concepts, and at the same time (*b*) to show how they are acquired." And in his conclusion (Toulmin, 1969, p. 102), he raised the question, "Can philosophers, after all, hope to 'analyze' concepts without considering their ontogenies as well as their finished structures?" And he makes use of the notion of a "standard ontogeny" in this connection. At the risk of appearing ungracious both to him and to the psychologists whose cooperation he invites, I would like to examine and challenge these claims.

It is best to start from the question which Toulmin himself started from, "What is a concept?" or better in this context, "What is it to have a concept?" To have a concept is to have a certain form of understanding; to have a concept of X is to understand or know what it is for something to be an X. (To this extent understanding is a form of knowledge, and a thesis about concepts and understanding can properly be part of a theory of knowledge.) The knowledge of what it is for something to be an X can be manifested in a great variety of ways, although the range of ways in question will to some extent be delimited by the kind of concept that X is. Toulmin is therefore quite correct to be critical of Geach's view (Geach, 1957) that the knowledge in question is the knowledge of how to use relevant words (though it has to be admitted that this is Geach's initial suggestion only and that the final view presented by him presupposes a complex theory of judgment which is only analogically based on the making of statements). Many concepts of course could be had only by language users, since in order to have the understanding in question we need the means provided in language for symbolizing the complex relationships involved. It would be quite wrong, on the other hand, to rule out understanding completely where there is no linguistic ability. If knowledge of what it is for something to be an X is clearly manifested in behavior, there can be no reason to refuse the attribution of the relevant concept. To this extent there can be no objection to the attribution of concepts to animals. I am not, of course, saying that it is always clear whether the knowledge involved in the concept *is* manifested in the behavior, and I am not, for that reason, suggesting which concepts *can* be attributed to animals. I am saying only that there can be no objection in principle in attributing concepts to animals, as long as we are willing to attribute to them other things which presuppose that knowledge, for example, perception of the world in certain ways, since perception of something in a certain way presupposes understanding of what it is for something to be like that.

Toulmin's first thesis is, therefore, that to know what it is to have a concept, we need to know what is involved in having the understanding or knowledge which the concept embraces. The understanding may manifest itself not only in language use but in a variety of forms of life, to use Wittgenstein's expression. (Whether or not Wittgenstein meant that expression to be taken in the relative and culture-dependent sense that Toulmin gives it is another matter to which I shall return.) It is, however, the second thesis that is the important one for present purposes. This is that to have a full knowledge of what it is to have a given concept we need to know how it is acquired. Toulmin takes Wittgenstein to have held that one can gain a better understanding of what it is to have a given concept by considering how we acquire it, how we learn the connected "language game." Whether this is a correct interpretation of Wittgenstein I do not know, and for present purposes it probably does not matter. It is clear enough that light *can* be cast on a concept by asking how it is typically acquired; the question is whether an understanding of what it is to have that concept *requires* us to ask how it is typically acquired. For that is what is implied by Toulmin's thesis about full understanding in this context. It surely cannot be the case that there is any *one* way in which a concept must be acquired. People acquire concepts in a variety of ways, and although we may be able to say what must be true of them if they are properly to be said to have acquired any given concept, we cannot insist that they do not have the concept unless they have acquired it in some particular way, or even the way that people typically use. To suppose otherwise is to confuse the routes to understanding of a given matter with the conditions under which alone that understanding can exist.

The justification that Toulmin (1969, p. 80) offers for his thesis (and as far as I can see the only justification) is contained in an inset passage of his paper. The first sentence reads "All scientific experience indicates that one cannot analyze the criteria for recognizing when a process is *completed,* in a final and definitive form, until the actual *course* of the process has been studied." It is difficult to know what to make of this claim, and in any case where scientific experience is concerned I am in the position of one who rushes in where angels fear to tread. Yet I would suggest that the claim begs the question when applied to the putatively parallel question about the understanding of concepts. It assumes first that we have the right to speak of a process in this connection, or rather it assumes that there is a single process such that grasping a concept or set of concepts is its completion. It seems to me that there might well be many processes of acquiring a given concept or even none at all. People can acquire understanding in different ways, and there need not be one or any process which leads to the understanding. If that is so, how can an understanding of what it is to have grasped a concept presuppose as a matter of necessity an understanding of the process of acquiring it? I am in any case inclined to dispute the claim as a general truth about processes. Does a knowledge of the criteria for recognizing when a journey is completed entail studying the course of the journey? Surely I may know what it is to have arrived somewhere without any knowledge of the actual journey.

It is another matter the other way round. I cannot know the details of a journey unless I know what its end is and thus what it is to have arrived. This is a conceptual truth turning on what it is for something to have the relation of means to end. I cannot for this reason know what is involved in the acquisition of a concept of a certain kind unless I know what it is to have that concept. It is the same truth that underlies the Aristotelian claim that things have to be understood in terms of their *telos* or end. If something is construable only as a means to an end, then it is unintelligible except in relation to that end. Any deviation from the process to that end is therefore readily construable as a blind alley. The end in the case of concept acquisition is a common human understanding; it is only given such a common understanding that we can speak of *the* concept of X. Objectivity in understanding does not entail that people should necessarily and always be agreed in that understanding; if it did have that entailment, the growth of new understanding against the current of tradition would be impossible. But objectivity in understanding presupposes both the *possibility* of common human agreement and the fact that it is the norm that what is commonly agreed is objective. This is implicit in Wittgenstein's well-known remark that "if language is to be a means of communication there must be agreement not only in definitions but also . . . in judgements" (Wittgenstein, 1953; see also Hamlyn, 1971). This in turn brings out the importance of the social in any consideration of concepts and the understanding. As I have commented on a previous occasion (Hamlyn, 1967), there is a considerable underestimation of the social in Piaget's thinking. He tends to think of the growth of knowledge and understanding as a matter between the individual and his world, as a product of interaction between subject and object. (This is implicit in Piaget's heavy reliance upon the notions of assimilation and accommodation, but see also Piaget, 1969, Chapter 8.)

Given this common understanding, we can view the learning process as a set of necessary steps towards it, and we are liable to see earlier stages in its light. That is why the philosophical operation of sorting out what is involved in the understanding of a given concept is relevant to an assessment of a theory of concept acquisition and development. It is easy for example, and perhaps in some ways right, to think of children as incomplete adults (just as it is possible to think of animals as incomplete human beings). In this light a childlike way of thinking may appear defective, even misconceived, but very much in the way that a mistaken belief on the part of an adult may be thought misconceived. Piaget gives the impression of thinking in this way in connection with what he calls the horizontal displacement of structures. The same kind of operations, involving structuring of the world, may be involved in the understanding of such things as conservation of substance and volume; yet they may appear in children at quite different ages, appreciation of conservation of substance occurring at about six, that of volume at about ten. What then of a child who thinks that when water is poured from a shallow, broad glass into a deep, narrow one it changes in amount? It is easy to say that this is a misconception on the part of the child, because within *our* system of concepts we know how the situation should be viewed. Yet it is not in any ordinary sense a false belief, since where a certain kind of understanding has not developed it is inappropriate to speak of belief at all (compare Toulmin, 1969, p. 84, and Hamlyn, 1967, pp. 33–34). At the same time, this should not be construed simply in terms of the idea that the child has not at this stage acquired a certain concept, as if there is just something missing at one time that will be present at another—as the idea of the horizontal displacement of structures may suggest. For it is not the case that the child knows well enough what water is, but simply fails to appreciate that it retains its volume when poured from one kind of vessel into another. The child is seeing the world in terms, rather, of a quite different set of concepts; the concept which goes for him with the word "water" is not our concept at all, and we have no right to suppose otherwise.

Likewise, we have no right to suppose that during the development of the scheme of concepts in question the connection between the concepts of water and, say, volume, is anything like that between the concepts of water and, say, mass. That is to say that we have no right to suppose that there are bits of understanding—the understanding of what water is, the understanding of what volume is, and the understanding of what mass is—so that we can compare and contrast the relations that hold between them in a linear way. The child's understanding of what water is will be quite different on the occasions when he does not know or appreciate that water poured from one vessel into another of a different kind remains the same water, when he appreciates this but does not appreciate the constancy of volume, and when he appreciates all of these things. Hence there is danger in speaking of a concept of water as if a child might have this by itself without other connected concepts of the kind which I have been considering. To have a concept is not an all-or-none affair; there are degrees of understanding and degrees in the complexity of what is understood. Conceptual development is as much as anything an initiation into a web of understanding which may be more or less involuted at any given time. Piaget's use of the term "structure" in order to speak of conceptual relationships implies a kind of ordering of elements, such that the relationships can be repeated at different levels or between different concepts. This does not seem to me an adequate picture of the understanding or of what having a concept is, and may be a carry-over from the atomism inherent in the associationism against which he is reacting. It is perhaps part of what is involved in the attempt to strike a compromise between that "geneticism without structure" and "structuralism without genesis" to which I have already made reference. But if having a concept of X is knowing what it is for something to be X, it should be apparent that such knowledge is not and cannot be an all-or-none affair, and that it is not formed out of fixed and constant units of understanding, so that we can without qualification speak of identical or similar structures, as Piaget does.

Hence the implications of the idea of horizontal displacement of structures (to say nothing of what may be even more misconceived—the idea of vertical displacement of structures, according to which there may be structural similarities or identities between different levels of the mental life) are likely to be very misleading. Conceptual development is unlikely to be a matter of progressive steps towards a goal that we can take for granted because it is the accepted goal. The child has to learn that some theories and ways of taking the world have to be rejected, because they do not work. What "working" and "not working" consist of in this context is of course an extraordinarily difficult matter to make clear; to give an adequate account of it would be to give a complete theory of education which I for one do not feel competent to give. At all events, the child does not have to systematize phenomena for himself; there are social pressures and influences, generally accepted standards and norms of what is right and correct. It would equally be wrong to ignore the role of feeling and emotion in the process. I mention these points because they are both factors which Piaget seems to me to underestimate. Thus, at a given time a child may, just like an animal in its own way, see aspects of the world in ways which are not simply like ours but defective; the child may see those aspects of the world in ways which are radically different from what is adult and accepted, and in ways which are suited to its needs, its emotional attitudes, and its interests. It is only our final conception of how the world is, the one which constitutes the norm of how the world really is, the one that is agreed, that makes the child's thinking appear just a stage in the development to that goal. It may, however, be both less and more than this. It may be less in that it does not constitute a stage in a process towards that goal; it may be more in that given the child's needs and interests it serves his immediate purposes admirably, and is in that respect not defective at all.

Why, then, if I stress the dangers of thinking of the child's concepts and of his way of thinking as merely incomplete versions of ours, do I also say that we can view the learning process as a set of necessary steps to its final goal? The truth is that we can view it in this way, and indeed must do so, insofar as we think of it as a *process* at all. Here I am taking what Toulmin said about processes in the passage which I quoted earlier, and accepting as necessary one half of it. It is a necessary truth that the stages of a process must be seen in terms of its goal if they are properly to be seen as *stages*. It is a further question whether we are entitled to speak of a process at all. Why should we think of the development of thought as a process of this kind? Surely children's thinking, like the development of human thought in general, involves not a steady progression towards a goal, but, among other things, the occasional pursuit of what from the point of view of the goal may turn out to be blind alleys, but which from a more local and different point of view may sometimes look like illuminating and satisfying discoveries.

III. The Nature of Piaget's Theory

In the light of what I have said so far, how is one to regard Piaget's general theory, his genetic epistemology? There are two sides to this. On the one hand, there is the wealth of observation and experimentation—something which is nothing less than remarkable. A great mass of well-attested empirical findings has resulted from the observations and inquiries of Piaget and his colleagues. If such things as the age norms are sometimes disputed, I do not think that the immediate findings enshrined in what might be called the case histories are a matter for dispute. On the other hand, there is Piaget's theory and the fact that so many of his books bear titles (in English) like *The child's conception of physical causality* (1930), *The child's conception of the world* (1929), *The child's conception of geometry* (1960), and *The child's construction of reality* (1955). If what I have said is right, these titles suggest that questions are being begged—how seriously it is impossible to say, except as the result of a detailed investigation which I cannot undertake here. (The title, *The child's construction of reality* is particularly interesting. Does the child *construct* reality? All by himself?) It is of course vitally important to be told that children do not think just like adults, and in this respect Piaget's work is enormously important; I have no wish at all to deny this. But since my concern is with the relevance of Piaget's theory to epistemology, it is important for my purposes that the *status* of that theory should be made clear. If different stages in the development of thinking in the child can be distinguished, and if these are stages of a process leading to an adult and objective way of thinking, it is society and the educational system that ensure that this process is gone through. These, as I have emphasized enough already, are not factors that loom large in Piaget's thought. Rather, his genetic epistemology might be construed as an account (perhaps in part a phenomenological one) of the progressive freeing of the individual from the chains of perception as a result of activity (operations) on his part. This emerges strongly from Piaget's *The mechanisms of perception* (1969), which is for this and other reasons an extremely important book for our present purposes. It is a book which, while not being in the direct line of other studies in genetic epistemology, provides a theoretical framework for those studies, both psychological and philosophical. It is a central thesis of the book that perception is not the clue to the nature of the world that it is sometimes thought to be. Perception is likely to be responsible for deformation in our view of the world. Objectivity comes through intelligence, which is active. Objectivity, he claims (Piaget, 1969, p. 364), "is constructed on the basis of, and in proportion to, the activities of the subject."

These suggestions raise many questions. What, for example, *is* perception on this point of view? How do the activities of the subject give rise to objectivity, and why does objectivity depend on these? Piaget's answers to these questions are, I think, essentially Kantian. The acquisition of knowledge presupposes an interaction between subject and object; an interaction which is also implicit in Piaget's use of the concepts of assimilation and accommodation, as I have suggested elsewhere (Hamlyn, 1967, p. 38). What is fundamentally wrong with the rival theories of empiricism and apriorism is that they do not allow for such an interaction; they lay all the weight on the object and subject, respectively. But Piaget thinks that the falsity of these rival philosophical positions can be shown not only by philosophical argument but also by an appeal to the facts. This is the reason for the extensive use of experimental evidence in *The mechanisms of perception* (Piaget, 1969). Yet, as must be the case if the facts are even to appear to support a philosophical theory, the facts have to be incorporated in an elaborate framework of theory. There is the same mixture of philosophy and empirical fact as there is to be found in Gestalt theory. It embraces above all a certain philosophical position on the nature of perception.

Piaget begins his exposition and argument by considering what he calls primary perceptual illusions. Although this is not Piaget's way of putting it, these are illusions like the Müller–Lyer illusion which seem to depend entirely on features of the perceptual object, and not upon the subject who experiences them. This is not to say that the subject cannot come to be less affected by them than he was originally. Indeed it is crucial to Piaget's point of view that these illusions are liable to development so that they can be treated genetically. His main thesis is that the overestimation of some feature of an object like its length is due primarily to centration or fixation of the object, and that the reverse effect which takes place when an illusion decreases with age or practice is due to coordination of centrations. This works in a complex way, especially when, as in the Müller–Lyer illusion, there is overestimation of the length of one line relative to another. The whole thing is explained on a model which presupposes "encounters" between elements of the perceived figures and elements of the sensory receptors together with "couplings" or correspondences between such encounters. The details of this theory are not easy to follow, but fortunately they need not be our concern at present. It is the general character of the account which is important, for the explanation of illusions of this kind is entirely in terms of what happens physiologically at the level of the retina. Or if it goes beyond this (and Piaget is not anxious to commit himself as to the actual embodiment of his model), it nevertheless remains true that the explanation is entirely causal, without any reference to beliefs or anything of that kind on the part of the perceiver. I do not say this in any spirit of criticism, since what is clear about these illusions is that they are *not* a function of any beliefs on the part of the perceiver.

What is important for present purposes is that Piaget in effect restricts perception to the functioning of such purely sensory systems. The diminution of an illusion in time, which Piaget puts down to what he calls "decentration" may on that account be due to, among other things, the fact that our movements put the objects in question out of fixation. Thus, what we see and how we see it is very much determined by what Piaget calls sensory motor activity, and even more by further activities on our part that arise from this. Thus, while perception is initially a function of sensory stimulation and subsequent mechanisms, it becomes in turn influenced by activity on our part. Moreover, it is this activity on our part which serves as a correcting influence upon the tendencies to distortion inherent in the purely sensory, as is evident in the primary illusions. It is for this reason that he says that "objectivity is constructed on the basis of, and in proportion to, the activities of the subject." Activities on our part, including exploration, lead to the correction of the sensory mechanisms. Yet, how this takes place remains fundamentally unclear. It is clear enough how the movements that we make may lead to the breakdown of the distortion due to constant centration of something, given the point that centration is itself a distorting factor. Decentration is in that sense a frustration or blocking of the naturally distorting mechanisms which the sense organs by themselves involve. But much perception is dependent on our concepts and beliefs. Visual perception of this latter kind is what Dretske (1969) has called "epistemic seeing," and his book, *Seeing and knowing*, is in large part a persuasive advocacy of the thesis that the range of epistemic seeing is very wide indeed. How do these concepts and beliefs latch on to the purely sensory?

Piaget is opposed to the empiricist thesis that our concepts are derived from the senses. Apart from the fact that the "structures of perception" differ fundamentally from "structures of intellect" despite some similarities (perception, for example, is always perspectival, while intellectual understanding is not), the most that perception can do is to provide the conditions for the application of the concepts formed through operations of intelligence. "Perception is of the *here and now* and serves the function of fitting each object or particular event into its available assimilative frameworks" (Piaget, 1969, p. 359). Thus the structures of perception may prefigure those of the intellect, so as to provide a ground for the application of intellectual structures, but they do not provide a source for those intellectual structures; the latter are derived from our own activity in the operations that we perform. The prefiguring of the intellect by perception is due to the fact that "they share sensory–motor roots" (Piaget, 1969, p. 362). This then is an aspect of what Piaget elsewhere calls "vertical displacement of structures." In our activity towards the world of perceptual objects we operate according to the same or similar rules, so to speak, as in our activity in formal operations. As experience develops and grows there is an interaction between subject and object which is "due to an endless construction of new schemes by the subject during his development, schemes to which he assimilates the perceived objects and in which there are no definable boundaries between the properties of the assimilated object and the structures of the assimilating subject" (Piaget, 1969, p. 364).

I cannot pretend that my summary of Piaget's thought is clear; it is difficult to clarify something that is far from clear in itself. Yet it appears that Piaget's central concern in all this is to give a philosophical account of the growth of experience in the individual. I would like to refer once again to the positions to which Piaget is on his own account opposed, and then try to see what his theory amounts to. First there is empiricism, which is the thesis that we are "given" items of information in experience, in sense data, and that we abstract concepts from what is given in this way. (Nowadays it seems difficult even to state the thesis without its appearing incoherent, since how can what is "given" constitute information if it does not already presuppose concepts?) Piaget calls this "geneticism without structure," since although empiricism can provide a theory of the development of experience, through the summations and associations of what is initially given, such development must on its account be independent of any necessary order. Experience develops simply as it happens to arise; any relationship between the elements of experience must be merely contingent. The opposing theory, rationalism, apriorism, call it what you will, presupposes that experience must from the very beginning conform to the structure that thought determines. There is nothing given in experience; the problem is rather how experience is to be fitted into what is given in thought. Piaget associates this point of view with Gestalt theory, since he holds that on that theory sense perception and thought conform to and are explicable in terms of the same structural laws. There is no real development allowed for in that theory; hence it is "structuralism without genesis." Gestaltism favors "nativism" as opposed to empiricism. Piaget's task is to afford a reconciliation between the two opposing views, just as it was Kant's task to afford a reconciliation between rationalism and empiricism on a more straightforward epistemological plane. That is why it is right to see Piaget as an essentially Kantian thinker. Just as Kant's reconciliation between empiricism and rationalism came through the idea that experience is determined by categories which are a function of the human mind, so Piaget's reconciliation between empiricism and nativism comes through the idea that experience develops according to structures which are, likewise, a function of the human mind in its relationship to the world. In his introduction to *The mechanisms of perception* (1969), Piaget puts the idea in terms of what he calls "the relational method." What he seems to have in mind is the idea that at any stage, experience is determined by what and how the mind relates. (There are Hegelian undertones in this; one might compare some of the argument in the opening chapters of Hegel's *Phenomenology of mind*, 1910.)

One might even compare this with the line of thought to be found in Wittgenstein. He too is very much of an antiempiricist thinker, and is opposed to the idea that there is anything "given" in sensation—something which I take to be implicit if not explicit in his argument in *Philosophical investigations* (Wittgenstein, 1953, Part I, p. 242) about the impossibility of intrinsically private languages and of the idea that words for sensations could be given a meaning in terms of those sensations alone without reference to a common language of which they must inevitably form a part. He is equally opposed to the idea that there is a rigid form to thought that can be abstracted from the language that we use. It is this, as I take it, that is a large point of his reference to alternative language games, which imply alternative ways of construing the world. Yet this does not mean that there is an absolutely free house, that there are no limits to the organization of experience other than the relative ones which a given society imposes—important as these particular limitations are. For our thought and experience are determined by "forms of life." Indeed, in one place in the *Philosophical investigations* (p. 226) Wittgenstein speaks of these forms of life as the "given." They are the one thing that we cannot get round the back of, so that they cannot be construed as merely conventional or in some sense relative. How we see colors, for example, and what relations we take as holding necessarily between them is a function of what Kant called our form of sensibility; it is a function of what discriminations our sense organs enable us to make in relation to the world as it affects those sense organs (see again Hamlyn, 1971, and compare Aune, 1967). There are analogous limits on the possibility of experience imposed by the nature of thought in general (though I feel far less certain about the direction of Wittgenstein's thought on this issue). These are limits in forms of life, in the sense that we cannot think of perception, thought, or any of the other faculties which human beings (and to some extent animals) are capable of except as functions of the life that they lead in the world in which they find themselves. The important point that Wittgenstein is trying to make is that our experience and what we can be said to know must be seen in this light and against this background. The limits which circumscribe what we *can* know and experience are neither conventional nor simply contingent in the sense that we can conceive what it would be like for things to be otherwise. If other forms of life are possible, we can have no real conception of what it would be like to experience them.

One clear implication of all this is that although what we *can* experience has its limits, all experience which, as perception does, gives rise to knowledge must be concept-dependent, conceptually mediated. To perceive the world at all one must have some understanding, if only of a rudimentary kind, of what one is perceiving. William James said that the first object of acquaintance in the individual is the universe; and there is something in this, in that we must, if we are to attribute perception to a child at all, attribute to it the awareness of an object as opposed to merely passive sensations. At first there can be no distinction of one object from another; hence the first object of awareness is indeed everything. The distinguishing of one object from another and the general elaboration of awareness of the world is thereafter a product of the individual's interaction with his environment, including his social environment, and is therefore conditioned in part by what he is, by his form of life, and in part by what there is to interact with. But understanding and experience must develop hand in hand. To have a concept of X we must have not only a formal understanding of what X is, something that could be given in formal definitions, but also a knowledge of what X is to be applied to, of what sort of things count as being X; and the latter demands experience. This point is the other side of that quotation from Wittgenstein that I have referred to before—that "if language is to be a means of communication there must be agreement . . .

in judgments." The agreement in judgments referred to is agreement about what counts as falling under the descriptions that language makes possible. It is not, then, that we have experiences from which we abstract our concepts, nor the reverse, that by some mysterious means we develop concepts which we apply to experiences. Both of these views take too limited a view of the concept of "experience." We have sensations of course, but these provide merely the conditions for the application of concepts in experience. In the sense of "experience" in question, sensations provide none in themselves. Experience involves knowledge, and for this concepts and understanding are necessary.

In this light let us now go back to Piaget, for in many ways, but not all, Piaget's line of thought fits in with what I have said. In the first place, although he restricts perception, at least some of the time, to the purely sensory, he seems to think of it merely as providing the conditions for the application of concepts in experience. That is the implication of the remark that I quoted earlier—"Perception is of the *here and now* and serves the function of fitting each object or particular event into its available assimilative frameworks" (Piaget, 1969, p. 359). It also provides one way of taking his view that the intellect is prefigured by perception. I am not sure, however, that that is all there is to it. For he sometimes includes under the heading of "perception" the sensory motor system, and in that case it would be the movements that we make at that level that would prefigure the operations performed at a higher and more cognitive level. This view is reinforced by the fact that he tries to subsume the corrective process that takes place as we build up experience of the world under the single concept of "decentration." The use of this concept implies, at the sensory motor level, that the movements that we make bring about causally a multiplicity of fixations which serve to counteract the distorting effect of any one centration. Correction is in this case a purely mechanical process which is a statistical effect of the plurality of points of view produced by, for example, movement. But the corrections that we make in our view of the world as a result of fresh experience and new understandings are not of this kind at all. That is why I said earlier that it remains fundamentally unclear how correction of sensory mechanisms takes place once concepts are involved; such correction can take place only with regard to what is already conceptually mediated. I think, therefore, that Piaget uses the notion of "decentration" quite equivocally.

It may be that Piaget would not be upset by this criticism. He speaks frequently of the "filiation" between perception and intelligence. He also maintains, in the introduction to *The mechanisms of perception* (Piaget, 1969, p. xxiii), that while "neurophysiology is exclusively *causal*" and "psychology is based on implication" (a remark to which, perhaps, some contemporary philosophers in the Anglo-Saxon tradition might be sympathetic), "there need be no conflict between physicochemical causality and psychological implication any more than between physical or material experience and the logico–mathematical deductions used to explain it; there is an isomorphism between causality and implication (which is the source of psycho–physiological parallelism), and the future harmony between causal physiology and analyses based on implication should be sought on the basis of the relations now existing between experimental or causal, and mathematical or implicative, physics." There is much in that remark which requires examination, though I have no space to do so here. It is, however, clear that it will not do to explain the relationship between neurophysiological mechanisms and "psychological" operations of a corrective sort on the analogy of the relationship between experimental and theoretical physics. It seems to me that if it is in this sense that perception prefigures intelligence, the prefiguration rests on an analogy only—an analogy between the sense in which a mechanism of the kind envisaged by Piaget for perceptual decentration can be corrective, and that in which the process by which we develop our experience and knowledge of the world is corrective. It is, I suggest, no more than an analogy, and we should not think of decentration in the strict sense as corrective at all if it were not for the fact that we have a prior conception of how a thing should look, and that decentration is supposed to be a counteracting influence against a tendency which is by the same standard deforming. In fact the story about centration and decentration is about the mechanisms (much more complicated than is ordinarily supposed, if Piaget is right) which make perception possible. They are, strictly speaking, neither corrective nor noncorrective; they merely make correction possible. Why there should be mechanisms of such complexity and cumbrousness that fixation leads naturally to distortion, so that counteracting mechanisms are necessary, is another matter.

If we waive all these (perhaps rather crucial) objections, there is still one further question to ask. If Piaget is right in thinking of perception as supplying the conditions for the development of concepts in experience, what are the grounds for thinking that development must have a determined order and structure? In attempting to answer this question we are confronted with the further question of the relationship of empirical findings to philosophical theory. For there is, on the one hand, the wealth of empirical observations which I have already acknowledged; and on the other hand, there is the claim for some sort of necessity in the order of development, a necessity which could not be inferred from empirical observations alone. I suspect, as I have suggested earlier, that Piaget thinks that the necessary order and structure of development has a status something like that of Kant's categories; it is a necessary feature of the human mind in its relation to the world, it is part of our form of life. It is a necessary condition of what we call experience. It is *prima facie* difficult to see why this should be so in all its details. There might nevertheless be something to be said for the position that there are necessary priorities and posteriorities in the ordering of experience, and it is to this question that we must now turn.

First, however, let me sum up in a general way what I have been saying about Piaget's position. In effect I have put Piaget in that tradition of psychology, of which the Gestalt psychologists are the most obvious example, which comprises to one extent or another a reaction against the sensationalist/associationist position. That position involved a mixture of philosophical and psychological issues, and the same must be true, in consequence, of the reactions. The only real basis for the atomism of associationism was the doctrine of atomic sensations and ideas which it inherited from the British Empiricist philosophers such as Hume. The Gestaltists put in its place another theory of the "given" derived from Husserl and ultimately Brentano. Piaget's own reaction is more in the Kantian or idealist tradition, but his theory is as much dependent on a philosophical position as were those of the others that I have mentioned. My own opinion is that the mixture of philosophical and empirical issues involves in each case a muddle, that the philosophical and psychological questions which are at stake are different from each other, and that there are no grounds for the belief that philosophical questions can be answered by appeal to empirical evidence or vice versa. On this I can at present only be dogmatic, although I can refer for the argument in the case of Gestalt theory to my *Psychology of perception* (Hamlyn, 1957). If I am right, however, my answer to the question, "What relevance has genetic epistemology in the more orthodox sense?," must be that in a certain sense genetic epistemology *presupposes* a traditional epistemological position. If it has implications for epistemology, it is in that sense and for that reason, and not because of its status as a psychological theory.

IV. Epistemological Priorities in the Growth of Understanding

I have argued elsewhere (Hamlyn, 1967, p. 32) that there are such things as epistemological priorities in the learning of a subject, and Toulmin (1969, p. 81) has argued similarly in terms of the notion of conceptual stratification. It is to these priorities that one must look in deciding how a subject is best presented to those who have to learn it; or at least they will provide one of the considerations, for it must not be forgotten that there are many other factors including motivational and emotional ones that will determinc how a subject is best learnt. Now if it is the case, as it might well be, that a person cannot understand X unless he understands Y, it is still not open to a philosopher or anyone else to say on those grounds alone that people must be gotten to understand Y first and then X afterwards. In other words, priority for understanding does not imply temporal priority. All that a philosopher can say on the basis of his analysis of epistemological priorities is "You cannot really understand X, because you clearly do not understand Y." In effect, epistemological priorities are logical priorities of a kind. It might be argued, for example, against the current of the empiricist tradition, that one cannot really understand *red* unless one already understands *color*, since "red" means "red color," and that an understanding of *red* is not complete unless one also understands the way in which red differs from other colors in general and how it is related in particular ways to certain particular colors (for example, how red is in some sense "close to" purple or orange as it is not to, say, green). Thus *red* entails *colored* and has also certain relations with other colors. But it would scarcely make sense to suggest that one should teach someone what color is and only then what red is. It would equally make no sense to suggest that one should teach someone what red is and thereby what color is, independently of other colors. A full understanding of what red is brings along with it a nexus of understanding of other things, and one cannot be said fully to understand it until one understands that whole nexus. How far the nexus extends is something that can be decided only in particular cases; there cannot be a general rule which determines the answer for all cases. It should be noted, however, that I have spoken of a full understanding. The understanding of a concept need not come all at once; there can be degrees of understanding of it, and degrees of understanding of the surrounding nexus. That is why all that can justifiably be said in accusing someone of a failure to understand is, as I have expressed it above, "You cannot really understand X, because you do not understand Y."

There is, moreover, the point that I have labored already—that a condition of fully understanding a concept is that one should be able to apply it in relevant and suitable instances. The nexus of surrounding concepts is not an abstract network only; it must touch reality at some point or points. But one cannot say in general when and to what extent the application of the concept or of one of its surrounding concepts should come under consideration. Learning and teaching must always involve a delicate balance between abstract concepts or principles and the application of these in instances. Hence, once again there can be no rules for the promotion of understanding. Yet when these caveats have been made it is obvious that there is such a thing as conceptual stratification, as Toulmin puts it, and that to suppose that one could have certain concepts without some understanding of others would be foolish. Yet what could be inferred from this about any *temporal* ordering of the understanding, about any principles for conceptual *development*, is very uncertain. Is there anything that could be safely said on this matter, even at the most general level? For the firm points in Piaget's theory *are* very general in character—the general nature of the three stages of development and perhaps some subdivisions of them. Perhaps the main point is the general precedence of the concrete over the abstract, as exemplified in the fact that according to Piaget the period of concrete operations always precedes that of abstract operations.

The suggestion that in the growth of the understanding we are initially tied to the concrete and particular, and only gradually extend our thought into the abstract and general is a very natural one. It is a suggestion to be found in Aristotle's observation that the particular is prior relative to us even if the general is prior for knowledge in itself. Our normal picture of human beings is that they gradually extend their understanding so that what is initially understood in particular and concrete instances comes eventually to be understood in a more general and abstract form. How indeed could it be otherwise? One answer to this question is that it could not be otherwise, because the development of understanding comes through learning. Learning involves the acquisition of knowledge and understanding; indeed, it involves the use of experience. Experience itself involves confrontation with particulars, even if, as Aristotle would say, the knowledge that this confrontation entails is knowledge of the particular as a such and such. It is thus inevitable and necessary that the development of understanding involves a progression from the more particular and concrete to the more general and abstract. No acquisition of understanding based on learning could be otherwise. I do not think that this is Piaget's answer, since my impression is that he thinks of the progression as a natural order of development, not based so much on what learning is as on the natural constitution of the human mind in its relation to the world.

We could *in a sense* conceive of this progression not taking place in this order. Indeed, an extreme rationalist theory of knowledge provides such a conception. We could think of the individual as being born with a set of innate ideas which only need experience to be made explicit. Or we could imagine a science fiction story about people who are provided in some nonexperiential way with a system of understanding which then requires exemplification in experiential terms. (I do not know whether this would make an interesting science fiction story if worked out, but it conforms at least to the principle to which I adhere—that the best science fiction stories turn on philosophical points!) In such cases the growth of knowledge would not depend on learning as we understand it, but that does not matter. Or at least it matters only in the sense that this fact reveals that the story in question does not fit our form of life. It is indeed important, if it is to be used as suggested, that the details of the story that I have referred to should *not* be filled in; for any attempt to fill them in would be intelligible only to the extent that it presupposes our form of life. Hence when I say that the story does not fit our form of life, I am saying that at certain points the story remains mysterious and unintelligible. Our form of life, as I said earlier, imposes limits on our understanding, and while it is in one sense possible that there might be alternative forms of life to ours, we deceive ourselves if we think that we can make any *real* sense of that idea. Our understanding is built up from and dependent upon the common experience that we have. While we should make continual attempts to enlarge that understanding, we cannot transcend the limits that make it *human* understanding. I therefore conclude that while we can give a partial sense to the supposition of a growth of understanding which is unlike ours, it is partial only, in the sense of being merely formal; any attempt to fill in that understanding would reveal how little of an understanding it really is.

There are thus very good grounds for thinking that the direction of the growth of the understanding must be in general terms as Piaget says it is. But this is not a merely contingent fact as the reliance upon empirical observations, so necessary to developmental psychology, would suggest. Nor is it *just* a consequence of a very general fact about the nature of the human mind in its relation to the world, as the philosophical position inherent in genetic epistemology would suggest. It is that given our understanding of normal human experience, learning, and knowledge, we cannot conceive of how it might be otherwise. For this is an understanding of the *norms* which provide the criteria of application for the concepts of experience, learning, and knowledge.[2] There are thus conceptual relationships between these concepts and our understanding of normal human development. Given, then, that we are operating with these concepts, we must take the development of understanding from the particular to the general as the norm. Abnormal cases need special explanation, and this may sometimes be provided. But we can have no real conception of what it would be like for the abnormal to be the norm (see Hamlyn, 1967, pp. 41–42).

What then of the details of Piaget's account of cognitive development? It seems to me that these can only be contingent, and for that reason alterable in principle. This applies to the age norms as much as to anything

[2] Since objectivity involves (though it is not entailed by) community of understanding (the interpersonal agreement to which I have referred), these norms must, in a sense, be social. Hence the development of understanding cannot be a matter merely of the relations between the individual and his world. Piaget does, to some extent, associate objectivity with the social, but on his terms it remains something of a mystery why the association should exist.

else. There are a multitude of factors that become relevant here—social influences, cultural influences, motivational factors, the role of emotion, and so on. A human being is not after all a merely cognitive being who develops and grows in isolation. Piaget's discoveries of the details of cognitive development are interesting and important, but they should be taken in that spirit. I would stress what I have said about the details being alterable in principle. Perhaps I may be forgiven if I say a few words about the moral of this. It seems to me that in practical terms the rather wholesale way that Piaget's theory has been taken up by many educationalists has its dangers. Piaget's psychology is a cognitive one and it is excusable that it leaves emotional development largely out of consideration, but this side of things must be remembered. I have spoken already about Piaget's underestimation of social and cultural factors. There is also, perhaps, the overestimation of the efficacy of *operations*, that is, activity as such on the part of the child. But it seems to me that the worst danger in the application of Piaget's theory of education is that the details may be accepted as overly rigid, and teachers may argue that there is no point in trying to teach children certain things before certain ages. Such an attitude could be educationally disastrous. John Wisdom used to speak of the necessity within philosophy of trying to say what cannot be said. There is an equal necessity within education of trying to teach people what they cannot understand. This may be a paradoxical way of stating a truth, but it is a truth nevertheless.

V. Conclusion

It seems to me that Piaget's theory is a blend not only of the empirical and the conceptual (which would be both acceptable and inevitable), but of the empirical and the philosophical. While empirical investigations may throw up suggestions for the philosopher and vice versa, and while these suggestions may well be valuable, I am still inclined to think that a theory that rests directly upon both empirical and philosophical considerations must have a degree of incoherence. This I take to be the case with Piaget's theory. If Piaget's genetic epistemology has relevance for epistemology in the more traditional sense, this is because genetic epistemology involves as at least one component a traditional philosophical position of its own. I do not think that Piaget would deny that his theory involves a philosophical position, but he might deny that there is the kind of gap between the empirical and the philosophical that I have presupposed. Nevertheless, despite argument to the contrary, I still think that the gap exists and must be reckoned with.

References

Aristotle. *Posterior analytics*. Translated by G. R. G. Mure. London and New York: Oxford Univ. Press, 1928.

Aune, B. *Knowledge, mind, and nature*. New York: Random House, 1967.

Dretske, F. *Seeing and knowing*. London: Routledge, 1969.

Geach, P. *Mental acts*. London: Routledge, 1957.

Hamlyn, D. W. *The psychology of perception*. London: Routledge, 1957.

Hamlyn, D. W. The logical and psychological aspects of learning. In R. S. Peters (Ed.), *The concept of education*. London: Routledge, 1967.

Hamlyn, D. W. Objectivity. In R. Dearden, P. Hirst, and R. S. Peters (Eds.), *Education and rationality*. London: Routledge, 1971.

Hegel, G. F. *Phenomenology of mind*. Edited by J. B. Baillie. London: Allen & Unwin, 1910.

Hume, D. *Enquiry concerning the human understanding*. Edited by L. A. Selby-Bigge. Oxford: Oxford Univ. Press (Clarendon), 1894.

James, W. *Principles of psychology*. New York: Holt, 1890. 2 vols.

Kant, I. *Critique of pure reason*. Translated by N. Kemp Smith. London: Macmillan, 1929.

Locke, J. *Essay concerning human understanding*. Edited by A. C. Fraser. Oxford: Oxford Univ. Press (Clarendon), 1894.

Mischel, T. Scientific and philosophical psychology: A historical introduction. In T. Mischel (Ed.), *Human action: Conceptual and empirical issues*. New York: Academic Press, 1969.

Piaget, J. *The child's conception of the world*. London: Routledge, 1929.

Piaget, J. *The child's conception of physical causality*. London: Routledge, 1930.

Piaget, J. *Introduction à l'épistémologie génétique*. Paris: Presses Univ. de France, 1950. 3 vols. (a)

Piaget, J. *The psychology of intelligence*. London: Routledge, 1950. (b)

Piaget, J. *The child's construction of reality*. London: Routledge, 1955.

Piaget, J. *The mechanisms of perception*. London: Routledge, 1969.

Piaget, J. Inhelder, B., & Szeminska, A. *The child's conception of geometry*. London: Routledge, 1960.

Toulmin, S. E. Concepts and the explanation of human behavior. In T. Mischel (Ed.), *Human action: Conceptual and empirical issues*. New York: Academic Press, 1969.

Wittgenstein, L. *Philosophical investigations*. Oxford: Blackwell, 1953.

THE CONCEPT OF "STAGES" IN PSYCHOLOGICAL DEVELOPMENT

Stephen Toulmin

I. Introduction

Hamlyn's concluding paragraph (*p. 23*)* provides a perfect starting point for the arguments I want to put forward here, for the differences between our two positions are of a systematic and curious kind. Wherever he criticizes Piaget's theories, as being confused or unclear about particular matters of substance, I find myself largely in agreement with his objections; yet, over general issues of intellectual strategy, my sympathies are reversed, and Piaget's program seems to me to have merits that Hamlyn overlooks, owing perhaps to the defects in its execution. To summarize my conclusions in a single sentence: While in discussions of intellectual and mental development, one can and should *distinguish* conceptual issues from empirical issues, they cannot be completely separated or dealt with entirely *independently*. On the contrary: To grasp the true nature and complexity of "cognition," "understanding," or "conceptual thought," one must be prepared both to reanalyze our ideas and terminology in the light of new empirical discoveries, and also to restate our empirical questions in the light of better conceptual analysis.

Let me quote the statement which condenses most precisely the central point over which Hamlyn and I are at odds:

> I am still inclined to think [he says] that a theory that rests directly upon both empirical and philosophical considerations must have a degree of incoherence.

I could find this statement acceptable only if, in his turn, Hamlyn agreed that some degree of "incoherence" has a necessary and creative part to play in the development of the sciences. For, looking back at the history of, say, physics, we find essential new theoretical advances in the science again and

* Page references to this volume are given in italic type throughout.

again "resting directly upon" a mixture of empirical and conceptual, or scientific and philosophical, considerations. The arguments by which Galileo, Descartes, and Newton launched the science we know as "mechanics" were certainly as much conceptual—and even philosophical—as they were empirical, or "scientific," in the narrow sense of twentieth-century positivist cant. Nor could the basic conceptions of modern dynamics—*matter, mass, force, momentum,* and the rest—ever have been established by empirical investigations alone; in actual fact, they were quite as much the outcome of careful conceptual analyses. (See the references in Toulmin & Goodfield, 1961, Chapters 8 and 9.)

Einstein's initial work on the theory of relativity rested, likewise, at least as much on a refined reanalysis of our concepts of *space, time,* and *simultaneity* as it did on empirical observations such as the Michelson–Morley anomaly. (In any case, the Michelson–Morley result appeared anomalous only in the light of those tacit presuppositions about the concept of *simultaneity* that Einstein was concerned to reject.) As Einstein emphasized himself, he was led to his ideas about relativity, not least, by philosophical considerations derived from Hume and Mach. (See, for example, his autobiographical essay in Schilpp, 1951, p. 1 ff.) Even the principle of the conservation of energy, as formulated by Helmholtz, had a similar dual origin; though Helmholtz looked back in part to the empirical studies of men like Joule and Mayer, the crucial arguments that led him to the principle involved Kantian considerations about the categories of Substance and Causality.

So, when Hamlyn argues that Piaget has not taken sufficient care to distinguish explicitly between the conceptual and empirical aspects of his work, he is probably right. But the proper remedy may not be that which he prescribes, namely, to separate the philosophical and psychological issues, and deal with them independently. Such a separation (I shall argue) would be artificial and damaging. On the contrary, we must recognize that in a young science, like developmental psychology, some initial incoherence is unavoidable, and greater coherence can be hoped for only if we allow our conceptual insights and our empirical knowledge to cross fertilize, and so work our way gradually towards a more satisfactory account of the subject.

The present article accordingly has a severely limited purpose. I shall begin by making some general points about the methodological problems of new sciences, and I shall use these to throw light on the particular difficulties of developmental psychology. Next, I shall consider some distinctions that Hamlyn made in an earlier paper, which posed certain of the key difficulties that a philosophical onlooker feels about Piaget's theories (Hamlyn, 1967). While these philosophical distinctions are valid enough (I shall argue), it could nevertheless be dangerous to press them too far, or to interpret Hamlyn's criticisms of the theory of developmental "stages" in too oversimplified a manner. Finally, in the light of this discussion, I shall ask, in general terms, what we are entitled to demand of an account of mental or intellectual development; in particular, what part the notion of "stages" can legitimately play in such an account.

In doing this, of course, I shall not pretend to answer any substantive questions in developmental psychology, or to add directly to our stock of theoretical concepts and questions in this field. But in a new science—at this initial stage of outright methodological obscurity—it can help both our empirical enquiries and our theoretical discussions if we try to see, a little more clearly, what *forms* of questions and concepts we should be considering.

II. The Methodology of New Sciences

A. Observations and Preconceptions. A new science faces problems of several different kinds, and its progress may be slow for correspondingly different reasons. Those reasons may be *observational:* The men concerned may not yet have done enough sheer looking and seeing, so that they have not amassed an adequate body of "empirical data" about the relevant "phenomena." Alternatively, the reasons may be *theoretical:* Those involved may not yet have developed an adequate repertory of concepts or categories, so that they are not yet clear just what sorts of "phenomena" to look out for as being "relevant." Typically, however, the shortcomings of a new science are more complex, and accentuate each other. So long as neither empirical data nor explanatory categories are adequate, there is no straightforward way of moving ahead. For lack of relevant observations, theoretical concepts cannot be rapidly improved; for lack of well-established concepts, it is unclear what further empirical enquiries will be relevant. In such a situation, major advances depend on dealing with both weaknesses simultaneously, so bringing empirical descriptions and explanatory categories more closely into line.

These difficulties arise equally, whether the science in question is a *mechanical* one—concerned with the material constitution of objects and systems, and with the patterns of behavior associated with particular configurations and components—or whether it is a *functional* one—concerned with the sequences or programs by which different objects and systems maintain their characteristic forms and operations, and with the changes by which those functions typically develop, in the life history of such systems or individuals. Thus, the mere collection of chemical observations did little to create a science of chemistry until Lavoisier and Dalton brought the ideas of Newtonian physics to bear on the categories of chemical explanation, and so showed what observations were worth collecting. Likewise, the science of physiology—especially, the understanding of physiological development—could make little progress until men like Berzelius and Bernard began to apply the concepts of biochemistry in a way that threw light on the nature of physiological function itself.

Even today, our understanding of embryology and morphogenesis is extremely limited. Biologists are still uncertain *both* about the phenomena on which they should be concentrating their empirical attention, *and* about the terms in which they should be explaining those phenomena once studied. Indeed, in the present state of biological understanding, we do not even know, in one sense, what a "mature" individual really is. For the time being our judgments of "maturity" are still vague and intuitive; lacking an adequate physiological account of the process of development, we also lack satisfactory criteria for recognizing the fully developed product. That being so, we must approach all the sciences of human development with a certain patience and delicacy. By analyzing the current, everyday concept of *maturity*, in advance of more knowledge about the process of *maturation*, we can go only a little way; but to accumulate sheerly empirical studies of development, uninformed by theoretical concepts or principles, might be even less help, since it would leave us with nothing better than a glut of uninterpreted observations.

If this is the situation in developmental physiology, we must not be too sanguine in our hopes for developmental psychology. For there, too, we may not yet have a sufficient grasp, *either* of the complex factors involved in the process of psychological development, *or* of the "psychological maturity" that is its presumed product, to justify any very substantial claims. If that is the case, we shall only deceive ourselves if we think that we can say any more, at the present time, than our understanding permits. Nor is it, in that case, any disrespect to Piaget to recall that, in this field, obscurities remain even at the preliminary, methodological level. Leaving aside all detailed scientific criticisms of Piaget's "stages" of psychological development, therefore, we may still find it necessary to ask the prior, philosophical question, "What is meant by talking about 'stages' of psychological development *at all*?"

Let me begin, accordingly, by defining more exactly two complementary temptations that confront us in any new science, and indicating what form these temptations take in our particular field. Having in mind the men whose arguments illustrate these temptations most clearly, at an earlier stage in science, we may refer to them as the "Baconian" and the "Cartesian" oversimplifications, respectively. (They will correspond in certain respects to the crude "empiricism" and "apriorism" that Piaget himself condemns and attempts to avoid.) The Baconian oversimplification rests on the doctrine that the activity of *collecting facts* is, if not the be-all and end-all, at any rate—in John Austin's phrase—the "begin-all" of any new science, since, until we have deliberately collected an initial body of "empirical data," there will be no "phenomena" for the science to generalize about and explain. The Cartesian oversimplification rests on the rival doctrine that, as a preface to anything else, we must begin by *formulating clear ideas* about our new subject matter, since, until we have arrived at an explicit analysis of our initial concepts and principles, we shall have no way of knowing in what terms our subject matter is to be described, what empirical observations are relevant or significant, or how we can discuss the resulting "phenomena" with any rational confidence or consistency.

Both oversimplifications involve important half truths that throw light on the problems of developmental psychology. We must concede to the Baconian that no science continues to make progress for long, unless it has a supply of "facts" that need "explaining," so that a science in which empirical observation ceased would eventually run out of soluble theoretical problems also. At the same time (we must insist) empirical facts are relevant to a science only if they have a bearing on its current problems. A "phenomenon" is not just *any* happening within the domain of a science; it is, first and foremost, a *problematic* happening. Nor, for that matter, are facts self-describing or self-characterizing; the very statements expressing the facts to be explained in a science must be framed in terms belonging to that science—and we ourselves frame those statements, using prior concepts that we bring with us to our empirical enquiries. Nor, finally, do we ever begin from a situation wholly devoid of empirical "data." The problems and concepts that provided the initial questions for Galileo's mechanical investigations arose out of careful reflection, by men like Bradwardine and Oresme, on the varieties of change and locomotion familiar in everyday experience. At that initial stage more "observation" could add nothing to our understanding of mechanics until the implications of our common experience had first been analyzed as a source of worthwhile questions. (Collecting instances is thus of use to a science only if they are instances *of* some general type of object or happening that has significance for the science—and so, as Bacon himself put it, as the preliminary to the recognition of a "form.")

Correspondingly, we must concede to the Cartesian that any science must have clear and explicit criteria, based on its theoretical categories, for recognizing empirical facts worth collecting and empirical questions worth investigating, and that a science given over entirely to naively empirical enquiries would finally sink, under the sheer weight of accumulated observations of which no new sense was being made. Yet, once again, this half truth demands its complement. Empirical facts may not be *self-*

describing, but theoretical analyses are not *self-validating*. In this methodological respect, Descartes' claim that his own basic mathematical and physical notions were uniquely "clear and distinct" was out of order—if not a downright fudge. No set of theoretical categories can prove its own relevance in advance of being used to make our actual experiences more intelligible. This remains true even at the simplest level, for example, in Aristotelian taxonomy; we can usefully define "man" as a "featherless biped," only after checking that *number of feet* is in fact useful as a generic character for classifying living creatures, and *featheredness* is useful as a specific differentia. Likewise (for instance) in Linnaean botany, no one could have told, in advance of experience, that the two basic dichotomies, "cryptogam/phanerogam" and "monocotyledon/dictyledon," would be of such fundamental importance. Fruitful botanical study may become possible only when we have an adequate hierarchy of *taxa* for classifying our objects of study; yet we cannot arrive at such an initial hierarchy by the inner light alone. Rather, we must construct it bit by bit, in the light of our growing familiarity with the *classificanda* themselves.

In the study of psychological development, corresponding traps await us. On the one hand, we may be tempted to accumulate empirical studies of child development based on the very minimum of theoretical analysis, assuming that however a child acts, and however young it is, we can recognize its actions intuitively, and describe them correctly, in terms familiar from our experience of adults. This done, we may claim to "find," as a bare fact of observation, that the child's mental life passes through a uniform succession of "stages," whose order and characteristics are matters for empirical study, and empirical study alone. All that developmental psychology will then appear to require is more, and more detailed, observations; given enough "empirical data," the stages of development will presumably identify themselves, and the laws governing development will be arrived at in a plain Baconian way.

On the other hand, we may be tempted to approach the subject of child development in a Cartesian spirit, assuming that the end point, or product of psychological development (or enculturation) is something we already understand "clearly and distinctly" from our familiarity with adult life, in advance of detailed studies of actual development-in-progress. This done, we may claim that the "stages" of psychological development are less an expression of the child's intrinsic, "law-governed" nature, than a projection onto its life history of the complex, socially enforced and rule-structured goals of enculturation. On this account, the sequence of stages simply reflects the tasks, or skills, that the child masters in the course of its "development," "enculturation," or "education"—these three terms now becoming near synonyms. Far from having to discover, empirically, what the relations between successive stages *are* in point of psychological fact, we must now look to see beforehand, analytically, what these relations *must be* as a matter of conceptual necessity. (They are what they are, because our concept of *maturity* makes them so.) The earlier stages in development will now be, not "temporal predecessors," but "necessary prerequisites" of the later stages.

Nobody (surely) would deliberately adopt either of these extreme positions in its pure form. Yet at every point in psychological development the problem remains of striking a balance between the two sorts of considerations involved: those that reflect the complexities in the cultural behavior patterns that are the public goals of development, and those that express the inner purposes and capacities, habits and inclinations, of the developing child himself. This balance is not easily struck, and we are exposed at every point to the risk of veering, either towards a pure Baconian empiricism or towards an overanalytic Cartesianism. Those who approach the study of child development from a psychological direction are (perhaps) more prone to the first risk; those who come from a philosophical direction to the second. Thus, the "conservation" studies of both Piaget and Bruner can be criticized as adopting too empiricist an attitude to the behavior under investigation (Hamlyn, 1967; Toulmin, 1969). The experimenters seemingly ignored the socially determined—not to say conventional—character of the tasks they invited the child to perform, notably, the ambiguities in their linguistic expressions. (A young child can hardly be expected to guess intuitively by what exact standards, and in terms of what particular criteria, his interrogators intend him to deal with the ambiguous question, "Is there 'more' in the one container than in the other, or the 'same' amount in both?"; and we have no right to be surprised if his resulting behavior is, by our standards, inconsistent.)

In return, there are points at which a hasty reader might take Hamlyn and myself to be making the opposite mistake; that is, implying that "stages" can be found in education, enculturation, or psychological development, only insofar as these are built into it, through the sequence of progressively more complex tasks that the child is required to master. Yet is there in fact, in any particular culture, a standard developmental, or instructional sequence which the individual is required to go through—and is, indeed—*put through*? If there were, then nothing more might remain to be said about the "stages" of child development, once we had shown the internal complexities and interrelations involved in this sequence. But neither Hamlyn nor I (surely) would go as far as that. All that we would insist on is the *complexity* of the issues involved; in particular, the need to make it clear, in any account of developmental "stages," how the patterns and structures of public socio–cultural demands at every point exploit, and interlock with, the changing personal capacities and characteristics of the developing individual.

B. Analytical and Genetic Epistemologies. We are now ready to consider the four distinctions used, or touched on, in Hamlyn's earlier paper.

1. The first of these is also the most general: We must distinguish (Hamlyn argued) between *conceptual analyses of* "learning" and *psychological generalizations about* learning.

For instance, it may prove that twelve-year-old American schoolchildren are protected against distractions, and learn algebra twice as rapidly when their classrooms are piped with low-level background music. Supposing this to be so, it will be a purely empirical discovery, which could never be arrived at by any formal analysis, either of the particular algebraical tasks, or of the nature of "learning" in general. On the contrary, we can hope to establish such a generalization only if we already know what "learning" is, and if, in consequence, we have prior criteria for telling when the required learning tasks have been successfully completed.

2. To become more specific: When we consider any particular learning task, we can distinguish, further, between the *logical prerequisites of* the task, and the *psychological conditions for* its successful completion.

Learning to sing is one thing, learning to sing in *bel canto, lieder, Bach cantata,* or *folk song* style—at choice—is a more complex task, for which already having learned to sing is a prerequisite. Singers who come from backgrounds in which a great variety of vocal music is regularly performed may, in point of fact, have an initial advantage in mastering the more complex task, but this is in no sense a formal prerequisite. Quite conceivably, some singers might catch on to the relevant stylistic differences more effectively by approaching them (so to say) with a naive ear, and from scratch.

3. Similarly: We can distinguish between "knowledge," regarded as the *product or end result* of learning, and the *processes or stages* of "coming-to-know," which lead to that end result.

To anticipate: Some people would criticize Piaget's program of "genetic epistemology" as illegitimate by arguing that it paid insufficient respect to this distinction. On the other hand, Piaget could be defended against this criticism, if the two arms of the distinction proved to be interdependent, that is, if one could show that our philosophical account of knowledge (or cognition generally) had to be formulated in the light of empirical discoveries about learning or coming-to-know.

4. Finally: Hamlyn distinguishes between the *standard* (*or familiar, sequence* of learning which any normal human being (or, say, any normal American, or Frenchman) may be expected to go through—and which is to

that extent unproblematic—and the *unusual* (*or nonstandard*) *sequences* associated, for instance, with congenital abnormalities, which are problematic just to the extent that they deviate from, and contravene, the presumptions created by our familiar standard sequence.

Having stated these four distinctions, we can at once reformulate the methodological difficulties raised by Piaget's "genetic epistemology." For that purpose, we must ask: "Granted that Hamlyn's four distinctions can be *validly stated*, how far are we entitled to *press their application*?" Supposing that the two arms of each distinction are genuinely distinct, how far can we regard them also as entirely separate? Can we hope to say what the concept of *learning* (or its end product, *knowledge*) entails, as a matter of conceptual analysis, entirely in advance of discovering what is in fact involved in the course of learning (or coming-to-know)? Or will our understanding of the product be dependent, in certain respects, on understanding the process also? Or again, is the use of the terms "process" and "product" in this context misleading and fallacious?

Once more, two extreme lines of argument are possible.

(*a*) Some analytical philosophers, impressed by the lucidity of Gilbert Ryle's *Concept of mind*, would draw Hamlyn's distinctions, and then insist on keeping the two arms of each distinction entirely separate. Before posing empirical questions, like "Does background music help children to learn?"—they would argue—we must already know, as a conceptual matter, what the term "learning" entails. So analytical questions about the nature of learning are always *logically prior to* empirical questions about the learning process; and analytical questions about the nature of knowledge (the end product of learning) are likewise *logically prior to* empirical questions about the process of coming-to-know. By analyzing the logical prerequisites of learning, we may define a standard learning sequence which, given the socially chosen destination, is not only *normal* but *necessary;* but the only empirical questions that arise about this process have to do with the psychological conditions that enhance or inhibit the learner's capacity to master each step in the learning sequence.

If this view is correct, then the very notion of a "genetic epistemology" is incoherent. For, in that case, all conceptual questions about learning and knowledge are independent of, and logically prior to, all empirical questions about the process of learning or coming-to-know, and we can, in principle, analyze the end products of learning straightaway, without having to wait for future discoveries about the learning process. Like political philosophy for Plato, epistemology will then be securely an *a priori* subject. Empirical studies may bring to light idiosyncracies, or failures of learning, in particular individuals or groups, just as historical studies can bring to light the political idiosyncracies, or failures, of particular cities or states. But the fundamental principles of knowledge (or of the *polis*) will be independent of, and prior to, all such empirical studies, since without them we have no criteria for distinguishing the "idiosyncratic" or the "failed" from the "normal" case.

Yet can this view be maintained? Only (I believe) as a first step—if persisted in, it lapses into the Cartesian oversimplification. The key point in any reply is the following: that issues of "logical priority" arise, not between the *totality* of conceptual questions about the term "learning" (say) and the *totality* of empirical questions about the process of learning, but always between *particular* conceptual questions and *particular* empirical questions. There is no simple or cut-and-dried issue of "logical priority" as between conceptual and empirical questions, considered as general classes; rather, there is a dialectical succession—with conceptual analyses giving rise to empirical questions whose answers enable us to refine our initial analyses, and so to pose new empirical questions, etc. To recall a typical Rylean example: The notion of *curing* a disease is distinct from (and logically prior to) that of *treating* it. We can embark on, carry through, and/or evaluate, different methods of treatment only if we have the prior criterion of success provided by the notion of a *cure;* any specific treatment (that is) presupposes some corresponding conception of a cure. Yet does it follow from this that we can analyze the concept *cure,* finally and definitively, in isolation from all empirical studies of treatment? Quite the reverse is in fact the case. At the outset, our understanding of a disease warrants only a first, rough criterion of what a "cure" is, and so what result a "treatment" can aim at; experience of treating the disease allows us to clarify and refine our conception by showing us more clearly the normal course of the disease, and the symptoms that the treatment can realistically aim at remedying; this clarification in turn suggests new possibilities for treatment; etc. At the initial stage, simple recognition of the disease may entail also the recognition of certain gross, unwanted symptoms that an ideal "cure" would abolish. At every subsequent stage, however, progressive refinement of our conception of a *cure* proceeds *pari passu* with the progressive deepening in our understanding of the disease and its treatment.

(*b*) The other extreme argument starts off in precisely the opposite direction. Some psychologists are so unwilling to separate conceptual or theoretical questions about the nature of learning and knowledge from empirical questions about the conditions of learning and coming-to-know, that they would gladly evade the force of Hamlyn's distinctions, treating the conceptual issues as entirely subordinate to (and dependent on) future empirical discoveries. It is our scientific duty, they would argue, to approach the growing child with a candid eye, and to study without any preconceptions the manner in which, with the passage of time, its capacities and feelings, judgments and attitudes, progressively make their appearance, refine themselves and develop new complexities; and we must—properly speaking—employ terms like "learning" and "knowledge" only in the light of these empirical studies, as straightforward names for the end results to which this developmental process leads. Similarly with the stages of learning; let the child himself teach us, in his own life, what new complexities of behavior he is ready, year by year, to display. The learning sequence has nothing *necessary* about it, nor anything *normative*. If it turns out, as a matter of observed fact, that the learning sequences of different children show certain universal features or cluster around certain average forms, so be it; but this is the kind of fact that empirical observation alone can bring to light.

If this second view is correct, it is "analytical epistemology" that will be incoherent. For, in this case, we can say nothing about the concepts of *learning* and *knowledge*, except what our detailed psychological observations warrant. Learning will now be just a phase that children go through—like teenage rebellion—and knowledge will be something they "come out in"—like acne. Rather than saying anything premature about these topics, philosophers must simply wait and see how they in fact turn out. Nor, in this case, will epistemology have any critical or normative implications. Some teenagers develop more acne spots, some none at all, some are just about average; but there is nothing "successful" or "unsuccessful" about adolescent spottiness, no "just about right," no "deficits" or "dysacnea." If epistemology is to be wholly empirical, the same must be true of learning and knowledge; if learning is studied as a simple *phenomenon*, it ceases to that extent to count as an *achievement*. That being so, the development of cognition may be expected to vary from individual to individual, like the development of the complexion, without any implications of "superiority" or "deficit," and general conclusions about the concept of *learning* can be justified only as the outcome of psychological discoveries.

Yet this view lapses equally into oversimplification. The charms of Baconian empiricism are undeniable. How convenient it is to regard the child—*qua* experimental subject—as being isolated from his socio-cultural matrix and so free to *évoluer;* that is, to manifest his own innate direction of development! Yet this convenience is bought too dearly; if divorced from his cultural matrix, what remains of the child's "learning" at all? (What child, except perhaps a Mowgli growing up in a wolf pack, has ever been free to *évoluer* according to his own innate tendencies, undistorted by the social demands of his fellow humans? And even a wolf pack has its social ecology!) Extreme empiricism drives us, accordingly, towards a naive, Rousseau-like belief, according to which psychological development proceeds always, so to say, from the inside outwards—as the progressive expression of innate tendencies and directions—and external, cultural influences only have the effect of falsifying these "true," or innate tendencies. Man is born free, and everywhere he is in chains—thanks to his enculturation.

Some of Piaget's early work, for example, his account of the transition from egocentric to social speech, again seems to have erred in this empiricist direction, and the necessary balance was redressed by those such as Vygotsky, who emphasized the primary role of social activities in the early stages of language learning. But my present aim is not to pursue the details of this controversy. Rather, I wish to throw light on the general claims, and status, of a "genetic" epistemology, and to formulate more clearly the conceptual problems it poses for us.

C. Summary. The provisional conclusions of our discussion are as follows: First, an analytical epistemology cannot be satisfactorily handled in complete abstraction from the psychology of learning. The better we understand the course taken by *learning*, the more precise an analysis we can give of the *knowledge* which is its outcome. (In this respect, "knowing" stands to learning and studying as "health" does to curing and treating.) To that extent, philosophical analyses of our epistemic concepts might well take "genetic" factors more into account than has recently been fashionable. Second, and on the other hand, a *genetic* epistemology cannot itself be founded on a naively empiricist psychology in which knowledge, learning, and the successive stages in psychological development are treated as simple "natural phenomena" to be noted and described just as we find them, without any preconceptions. In developmental psychology, as in developmental physiology, we can pose meaningful questions—whether about maturation, or about normal and abnormal development, or about stages in learning or concept formation—only if we approach our empirical studies of child development with certain initial questions and conceptions.

Analytical and genetic studies thus need each other's support. In either case, the first need is for a middle way, one which does not begin by renouncing all prior epistemic conceptions—since without these we can state no relevant empirical questions—nor insists that our initial epistemic conceptions are final—since this will condemn them to a needless vagueness—but one which pursues empirical and analytic studies, patiently and piecemeal, in the light of one another's results.

In some respects, this proposal may appear heretical to both philosophers and psychologists. Suppose that we take Piaget's characterization of conceptual development as "genetic epistemology" seriously, even with these qualifications; this will oblige us to make our psychology of learning more theoretical—and even more philosophical—than many working psychologists would like it to be. At the same time, it will offend some philosophers also, by obliging them to keep their epistemological analyses open to reconsideration in the light of new empirical results in the psychology of learning and development. In the second half of this article I shall try to illustrate the new possibilities that are open to us if we accept this middle way, and indicate what they imply for the notion of "stages" in mental or intellectual development.

III. Concepts: Their Acquisition and Employment

A. Learning and Knowing. Before we attack this task head-on, there is one last preliminary to be completed. In comparing the relation between "learning" and "knowing" to that between "treating" and "curing," and inferring that the concept of *knowledge* can be analyzed adequately only as the product of—and as correlative with—the process of *coming-to-know*, I have once again used a form of argument which Hamlyn here challenges. If I am to go any further, I must say something at this stage to defend my procedure against these objections. His objections are in fact central to the differences between us. Though Hamlyn and I agree on the need for *distinguishing* between the conceptual and empirical issues arising in any science, notably in developmental psychology, he also insists, as I would not do, on *separating* these two groups of issues. If one supposes that the answers to conceptual questions can be decided by appeal to empirical evidence, this—in Hamlyn's opinion—not only *is*, but *must be* confusing; and he implies that many of the defects in Piaget's theories could be remedied if only this confusion were avoided. (Just what the resulting purified theories would look like, he does not tell us.)

Unless such a separation were at least possible in principle, indeed, his whole attempt to pare off the philosophical from the scientific aspects of Piaget's work would be open to question. As things stand, Hamlyn calls on philosophers and psychologists to cooperate, from either side of their disciplinary boundary fence, "in a joint sorting out of the questions they are asking" (*p. 5*); but he suggests that, once this sorting out is done, each group of men can subsequently go their respective ways, and deal with the questions so allocated to them by their own professional procedures. If, however, empirical and conceptual questions cannot after all be separated, a closer cooperation will be called for: one in which, at certain points, philosophers and psychologists dismantle the boundary fence dividing them, and consider jointly what new light empirical studies of cognitive development can throw on the philosophical analysis of epistemic concepts, and better conceptual analyses on the empirical questions developmental psychologists should be asking.

For my own part, I do not see how such a separation of conceptual and empirical issues can be maintained forever. Nor, considering the whole development of human thought, do I know how conceptual issues ever have been settled, *except* in the light of empirical experience. For how do conceptual problems arise? We attempt to state what a concept entails, or to analyze its criteria of application; we then look and see how far this analysis squares with our actual practice; as a result, we recognize shortcomings, either in our verbal definitions, or in the criteria used in applying the concept to empirical situations; and, in the light of these discoveries, we refine our initial formulation and/or criteria so as to improve the match between our ideas and our experience. In cases where the concepts in question have an established, definitive use that is not at risk, we call the resulting arguments "philosophy"; in cases where conceptual changes are expected and intended, we call them "science." But both kinds of case involve both empirical and analytical considerations, and the line between the "empirical" and the "conceptual" cuts right across that between the "scientific" and the "philosophical."

On this account, of course, the scientist's business is not simply that of "making predictions" which are to be either "verified" or "falsified"—that is, inferring particular *statements* about Nature, which experience will either bear out or show to be incorrect. Rather, his goal is to arrive at a better set of *terms*, or *concepts*, in which to describe, pose questions and think about Nature. Empirical enquiry then establishes not whether his predictions are true or false, but whether his concepts are applicable or inapplicable, relevant or irrelevant, operative or beside the point. Where the concepts of a science are changing, accordingly, the crucial questions are never purely empirical ("What *is the case* about X?") nor are they ever purely analytical ("What *do we already mean* by X?"). They are always, in Hamlyn's word, a "blend" of the conceptual and the empirical ("What *is there for one to mean* by X?").

To recall, Galileo's rolling-ball experiment settled the question of what exactly there was to be meant by the term "acceleration." Even in Galileo's own early writings, it had still been quite unclear whether "acceleration" ought to be defined in terms of the change of speed with distance or with time. Likewise, Newton's *Principia* showed what exactly there was to be meant by the term "force." This was another word whose previous intuitive, everyday use involved ambiguities and vaguenesses, and these were resolved by Newton's conceptual-cum-empirical analysis. Einstein, in his turn, was to argue in a similar way. We might define "simultaneity," if we pleased, in terms that presuppose instant communication between different frames of reference; but, so long as all actual clock comparisons depend, at best, on electromagnetic signals, the resulting definition will be irrelevant to any realistic account of our knowledge of the physical world. In actual scientific practice, the only exact sense available for us to attach to the term "simultaneous" is the one that Einstein analyzes—that is, "contemporaneous, as measured with clocks synchronized by using light-signals."[1]

To come now to Hamlyn's objections, my claim that "processes" and "products" are correlative is simply a special application of this general point. The better that medical scientists understand the mode of action of a treatment, the more exactly they will see what can be meant by "curing" the disease in question. Or, more topically, the more detailed our physiological understanding of the processes by which life is maintained, the more exactly we can see what there is for us to mean by the term "death," and what criteria can be used in determining the "moment of death." Granted, the word "dead" has an ordinary, intuitive or current meaning, and philosophers may choose to analyze this alone—with all its vaguenesses and indeterminacies. But today's "ordinary meanings of words" already reflect the empirical experience of our forefathers; so why should we ignore the empirical experience of our own generation, or refuse to consider how our own concept of "death" could be made more relevant to the real world—and so what meaning will be attached to the word "dead" in the year 2000? In this task, of course, translating the term "death" as "the end of life" will be a merely lexicographical move; the real problem is to consider, in specific detail, how better knowledge about the physiology of higher organisms affects our criteria for applying such terms as "living" and "dead."

I can now formulate the crucial point at issue between Hamlyn and myself. I claim that "learning" and "knowing" are *correlative* terms, in the same general way as "treating" and "curing," or "living" and "dying"; but he denies this. One might comment, "He has to deny it." If he is to keep philosophical (conceptual) epistemology and developmental (empirical) psychology entirely separate, it is essential for him to establish that the conceptual analysis of "knowing" is logically prior, in its entirety, to all

[1] N.B. In all these examples, empirical experience is used to answer the question of *what exactly* is to be meant by some term in the science concerned; that is, how our analysis of this concept is to be *improved*. This is no accident. The positivist program, which attempted to separate the "logical structure" of a science from its "empirical content," gained plausibility because its advocates concentrated attention on theories like Newtonian mechanics, whose basic concepts were no longer problematic, and had assumed their ideal definitive forms. By contrast, the program fails wherever the theoretical concepts involved are in flux. and we need to know *more exactly* what is to be meant by the basic terms of the science.

empirical investigations of "learning." Hamlyn relies on three arguments to establish this point, all of which strike me as formalistic and unconvincing. Thus (*a*) he invokes the distinction between *means* and *ends* in an explicitly Aristotelian manner, to argue that "learning" must be defined in terms of the "knowledge" that is its *telos*, rather than *vice versa*. Yet this is just the sort of argument that our intellectual experience since Aristotle's time ought surely to have undercut. As a matter of words, of course, a medical treatment is the *means* and the cure is the *end*, so that "curing" is the *telos* of "treating"; but this no longer entails that we perfectly understand what "curing" is in advance of considering what is involved in "treating." To Hamlyn's first argument, therefore, I can only reply: *pace* Aristotle, "means" and "ends" too are *correlative*—that is, formally distinguishable as terms, but mutually interdependent in application.

Again, (*b*), Hamlyn uses a standard Rylean analogy—namely, the distinction between "journeying" and "arriving"—to argue that we may understand what it is to have grasped a concept, but without necessarily understanding what acquiring the concept involves. Yet, as a demonstration that these two things can be kept entirely *separate*, this Rylean argument is scarcely more solid than the Aristotelian one. For the very point in dispute is whether, when a man is acquiring a concept, we have the same exact, unchanging and univocal criteria for saying, "Now he's got there," that we can have when he makes a physical journey; and we can settle that question only if we put Rylean analogies and Aristotelian generalities aside, and address ourselves to the specific topic in question. This Hamlyn himself does, when (*c*) he defines "having a concept" as "having a certain *form of understanding*," and "understanding" itself as "a *form of knowledge*"; and here we come to the heart of the matter.

Suppose that, for each particular concept, there were indeed some single, distinctive and easily identifiable cognitive skill—or "form of knowledge"—which served, by itself, to distinguish the man who had acquired the concept from the one who had not yet done so, so that, the moment he began to display this specific skill, we should be entitled to say "Now he's got there; now he's grasped the concept." In that case, I would bow to Hamlyn's argument, since we could indeed specify the "destination" of learning—that is, say what exactly it was to have grasped the relevant concept—in advance of all questions about the "journey"—that is, about what exactly was involved in acquiring it. In that case, of course, Hamlyn would be right to argue that it was of no interest to us, in judging a man's conceptual grasp, to ask *how* he got it. If (for instance) he turned out to have been injected with the necessary "form of knowledge" hypodermically, that would not affect our assurance that he had in fact "grasped" the concept, for after all, in demonstrating the necessary "form of knowledge" he would have passed the only relevant test.

But the heart of our whole problem lies in the fact that there are no such simple, unambiguous and unchanging criteria for "having concepts." The definitive tests for judging whether a dog or an infant, a child or a schoolboy, a normal adult or an aphasic, knows/recognizes/has learned what *red* is (or *four* or the *self*) are not obviously unitary or univocal. In this context, defining "having a concept" verbally as "having a certain form of knowledge" merely begs the question by encouraging us to think of "conceptual grasp" as being simple and static—even algorithmic. Yet surely (as I have argued in the earlier paper) the criteria of conceptual grasp are, in practice, both complex and context-dependent. Our readiness to attribute conceptual grasp to aphasics after brain damage, for instance, despite the absence of normal linguistic skills, depends on our knowledge that they formerly had the same linguistic skills as normal adults.[2]

Once again, we can hope to keep philosophical and empirical questions about knowledge and learning entirely separate only if we can regard the *empirical application* of our cognitive concepts as something unchanging. To the extent that the criteria of application are in fact variable from stage to stage in the human life cycle—to the extent that *what we count as* "knowing," "recognizing," or "understanding" varies, as between an infant and a newly speaking child, an adolescent, and a fully mature adult—that attempt will once again fail. In the remainder of this article, I shall be attempting to prove just this: namely, that we do not have *unitary and invariant* criteria for judging the cognitive skills of human beings, regardless of age or stage, normality or deficit, but rather our criteria are determined, in any particular context, with an eye to those variables. If this is so (I shall argue), one essential task for students of cognitive development—whether they call themselves "developmental psychologists" or "genetic epistemologists"—will be to map the changing constellations of skills in terms of which we can judge cognitive abilities, and so the changing criteria by which we are to apply cognitive terms to human beings at different ages and stages of intellectual development.

B. Language and Cognition. Let me begin by recalling how the relation between linguistic and nonlinguistic behavior varies during

[2] As Wittgenstein used to insist, the tests for a man's "understanding" of terms and concepts are not concerned *only* with the bare "forms" of knowledge; we need to ask also how he applies those terms and concepts in novel situations, and to new classes of example. To demonstrate the full grasp of a concept commonly involves recognizing how novel problems and situations call for the extended application of those terms. Thus, a man will show that he "really understands" the Newtonian concept of *force*, not just by performing stereotyped sums, according to the standard algorithms of Newtonian mathematics, but by demonstrating that he recognizes how to *reapply* the term "force"—originally learned in purely mechanical cases—to other kinds of phenomena, for example, magnetic.

cognitive development. Recent philosophical discussions of cognitive concepts—"know," "recognize," "perceive," "recall," "learn," etc.—have paid particular attention to the role of language in human knowledge; and those discussions have often ended in cross-purposes that can be resolved only if we see that their role is a changing one. Here I shall take as my text a paper by Urmson on "Recognizing" (Urmson, 1956).

The argument of this paper is (in brief) that all genuine recognition, classification, or categorization—and so all genuine "perception"—involves differentiating objects in the world along arbitrary, linguistically marked lines; that the ability to perform such differentiations is developed as one aspect of language learning; and that, for this reason, language users alone can properly be said to "recognize," "classify," or "perceive." Stated this baldly, Urmson's position must appear oversimplified, and he himself hastens to qualify it. It is true (he concedes) that a rat may learn, for example, to discriminate triangles from circles—may learn to run in different directions, say, when presented with a triangle and with a circle—and that, on this account, we may be inclined to say that the rat can "recognize" the triangle. However (Urmson replies), we can describe its learning in these terms—strictly speaking—only when it is trained in a human laboratory, to perform the discriminations reflected in our language, and then the conventional patterns of human language have been imposed on its sensory responses. All qualifications aside, however, Urmson's paper raises some fundamental issues. For the heart of his position is an assumption about the role of language in cognition of any kind; namely, that all our cognitive terms are given their primary meanings and uses as applied to the skills and capacities, achievements and performances, of mature and normal adult human beings, and that they are applied in other cases—for example, to the behavior of infants or animals, morons or lumps of iron—only in a secondary or analogical manner, and in derivative or weakened senses.

In the primary, adult sense of the term "recognize" (Urmson claims) the possibilities of "recognition" are represented in the structure of our language. When we recognize a flower, we recognize it *as* "lily," "foxglove," or "rose"; when we recognize a man, we recognize him *as* "Harold Wilson," "my uncle Jack," or "the first man on the moon—you know, what's his name . . ."; and the crucial test of recognition is the linguistic ability to apply a correct personal name, class name, or uniquely identifying description. In the other secondary, weakened senses (he would then argue) we apply the terms "recognize" and "recognition" only analogically. In some of these cases, the analogy may be fairly close. A fox is attracted to a chicken rather than a skunk, and it behaves differently towards these two kinds of prey, so we are tempted to say that it (as it were) "recognizes" the chicken. In other cases, the analogy is more remote. A magnet is attracted to the North Pole rather than to the Washington Memorial, and responds differently to those respective geographical locations, so we are tempted to say, if not that the magnet "recognizes" the magnetic meridian, at any rate that it "tells us" in what direction the North Pole lies. Yet, evidently, neither the fox nor the magnet has the intellectual—more specifically, the linguistic—capacity to sort, classify, and label different kinds of prey and places. Neither of them can therefore be said, in Urmson's full sense, to "recognize" the chicken "as" a chicken, or the North Pole "as" the North Pole.

If we are content to limit our attention to normal adult humans, Urmson's claims about the crucial importance of language for cognition may come to seem quite attractive. Yet can we really justify singling out the case of normal adult humans as *the* "primary and genuine" case, and dismissing *all* other cases as "merely analogical"? Surely (one may reply) further important distinctions need drawing *within* Urmson's class of "secondary" or "analogical" meanings. Surely the cognitive capacities of the fox—to say nothing of apes and infants—differ from those of the magnet far more than from those of the normal adult human, so that to speak in the same breath of both the fox and the magnet as "recognizing" only analogically is highly misleading.

Popular science writers (it is true) do sometimes apply cognitive terms both to inanimate objects and to purely physiological systems. The core of an electromagnet, they say, "remembers" the direction of the magnetizing field, and the lymphocytes of the body "remember" a smallpox injection. We might indeed agree with Urmson that such usages as these are "weakened" or "analogical," for, in such cases, talking about *memory* points only to the fact that the reaction of the magnetized core (or the inoculated body) to future fields (or infections) is affected by the earlier magnetization or inoculation. In these cases, the context of purposive, or ostensively purposive behavior—within which we apply cognitive terms to the behavior of foxes, apes, infants, aphasics, and normal adult humans alike—is entirely absent.

That being so, the cognitive capacities and performances of animals, children, and aphasics surely need to be *contrasted with* the as-it-were cognitive capacities of magnets and lymphocytes, rather than assimilated to them. The "remembering" of the magnetic core and the remembering of an adult human have no more than one feature in common, the "remembering" of the lymphocytes and the remembering of the adult human none at all. (The tests for judging whether or not I *myself* remember my smallpox injection do not include the acquired immunity, which indicates that the injection is, so to say, "remembered" *by my lymphocytes.*) By contrast, the "remembering" or "recognizing," "learning" or "knowing," of higher animals, juveniles, and abnormal humans has a great deal in common with that of normal adult humans, and is judged in practice by many of the same tests.

In judging the cognitive behavior of animals and infants, indeed, we may have occasion to apply any or all those tests of normal adult cognitive capacity that do not specifically involve language use; conversely, the normal adult human is expected to pass the same kinds of tests for cognition as a fox or a child *in addition to* linguistic ones. When lymphocytes, so to say, "recognize" or "remember" the smallpox virus, they react—by generating antibodies—in ways that no purposive agent either does or can do. The fox that "recognizes" a chicken, the infant that "recognizes" his feeding bottle, and the aphasic who continues to sort colors correctly, even though he can no longer name them, all share such cognitive capacities as they possess with normal adult humans—for example, with the woman who recognizes a long-lost sister, or the trained botanist who recognizes a rare form of orchid. Agents of each kind (we may say) manifest the same *generic* capacities even though the *specific* ways in which their cognitive capacities are manifested will vary from case to case. In judging that the fox, the infant, or the aphasic "recognized" or "failed to recognize" an object, accordingly, we always bear in mind the particular skills that can be expected of an agent of such and such a type, at such and such a stage in his development, and choose our criteria suitably.

Urmson's analysis must therefore be amended, in a way that makes it less paradoxical and more responsive to the specific demands of different contexts. But we can make the necessary changes only at the price of paying more attention to developmental and comparative psychology. We may concede to Urmson that, in the case of normal adult humans, the crucial tests of a man's *recognizing* something are either linguistic or "linguamorphic"—that is, having a structure isomorphic with that of language. The normal adult agent's *recognition* is best evidenced (that is) by his naming, labeling, pigeonholing, or describing correctly the person or object in question, or by his treating it in a manner specifically appropriate to a thing so labeled or described. But these tests are crucial, not because recognizing is itself a linguistic or linguamorphic activity, so that "recognizing" can be *equated with* "being able to name at sight." Rather, the basic relationship goes in the other direction.

Normal adult humans share with all the higher animals a generic capacity to discriminate between different individuals, kinds and classes—whether "natural" kinds or "conventional" kinds—but in the specific case of human beings, this capacity is further refined, registered, and put to work through the use of language. In the early, prespeech infant, cognitive capacities such as recognition are exercised in ways that are not yet "language-dependent." Subsequently, as development and enculturation proceed, the child learns progressively to handle, classify, and name objects and people in accordance with linguistic or "linguamorphic" schemata; as a result, linguistic tests acquire a correspondingly greater importance. Still, this does not happen all at once. In considering whether a five-year-old recognized something we could hardly insist on his naming it correctly, as we might perhps with a twenty-five-year-old. Eventually, however, the growing youth acquires systems of words relevant to all the modes of recognition that are functional in his life, and for which he is sensorily and/or intellectually equipped. Beyond this point, we expect him to manifest his recognition both in his nonlinguistic behavior, and also in all relevant linguistic ways. (Notice that one naturally says not just—as a matter of prediction—"we expect *that he will* . . . ," but—as a normative matter—"we expect *him to* . . ."; beyond this point, linguistic skills become not just predictable, but obligatory.)

To sum up, as development and enculturation proceed, the relevant tests of recognition and other cognitive capacities change. At the outset, they have about them nothing essentially language-dependent. By the fully adult stage, they have become radically language-dependent. During the intervening stages, there is a changing balance between skills that are strictly linguistic (for example, naming, describing, and labeling), linguamorphic (for example, sorting in terms of an arbitrary classification), and language-independent. Thanks to the complex taxonomic and linguistic skills in which he is trained, the human being develops specific linguamorphic capacities of kinds that the ape and the infant necessarily lack—for example, the capacity to "recognize" a particular plant "as" a half-grown specimen of the orchidaceous species *Serapis pseudocordigera*. For all this refinement, however, "recognition" and other cognitive capacities retain a common generic core. In saying that the pheasant recognizes me as a hunter, that the house dog recognizes me as a friend of the family, that the young child recognizes me as his father, that the shop assistant recognizes me as a regular customer, and that the doctor recognizes me as an overweight depressive—using the same word "recognizes" in each case—I am not guilty of punning or gross ambiguity. The *force* of the term "recognition" is similar in each case; it is the *criteria* or *tests* that vary from pheasant to human, and from wordless infant to expert adult.

For every type of living creature, and at each stage in its development, certain types of skill or discrimination provide the relevant and significant tests of cognitive capacity. Cognitive skills and achievements are judged within contexts where living creatures, in the course of pursuing their own purposes, do what they can to discriminate such significant differences. (That is why we can speak of the fox recognizing the chicken, but of the magnet only, as it were, "recognizing" the North Pole; the magnet is serving *our* purposes, the fox is pursuing *his own.*) In considering some living creatures, at certain stages of their development, linguistic criteria may be of the first importance; for others, and at other stages, they may be totally irrelevant. This being so, the question, "Does *recognition* involve the exercise of linguistic competence?" can—with all due respect to Urmson—have no unique and universal answer. Circumstances alter cases, and cases alter criteria. During human development, from infancy to maturity, the relations between the linguistic and the nonlinguistic elements in cognition change very markedly. What precise combination, or balance, of linguistic and nonlinguistic skills we can properly demand at any particular stage of development before agreeing to say that a child "recognizes" or "knows" or "perceives" something, can be decided only when we understand better how these two allied types of cognitive skill *come to be related.*

In discussing the example of "recognizing" at such length, my motive has not (of course) been a mere desire to pick a bone with Urmson. Our discussion has, in fact, some more general consequences. To begin with, it reinforces our earlier conclusion, that analytical epistemology must be open, on one side, to reconsideration in the light of developmental and comparative psychology. The terms "recognize" and "recognition" cover not a single fixed skill, but a whole family of related skills, activities, and achievements characteristic of creatures having well-marked, highly structured sensory systems and capable of living autonomous lives. In the specific case of human beings, this capacity is progressively associated with, refined by, and expressed through the use of such linguistic instruments as names, taxa, and classificatory descriptions. A complete conceptual analysis of "recognition"—embracing criteria and tests, as well as direct implications—can thus be given only if we consider *both* how the capacity for sensory discrimination varies from species to species, and from one stage of development to another, *and also,* more particularly, how language enters into the exercise of this capacity during human development, and eventually becomes a crucial element in it. At the same time, the discussion reinforces our earlier methodological suggestion, namely, that developmental psychologists, as much as philosophers, need to bear continuously in mind the *changing* relationship between linguistic, linguamorphic, and language-independent elements in cognition. If we wish to identify definite and distinct "stages" in psychological development, that changing relationship promises to be one of the key variables.

IV. Functional Achievements and Their Description

A. Egocentrism and Socialization. At this point, accordingly, let me return to my first, methodological topic, and sharpen up the problems posed by the notion of developmental "stages." I shall concentrate on two questions: (*a*) "Do the inner complexities of language give us any reliable index to the 'stages' of cognitive development?"; and (*b*) "Does psychological development follow a single, uniform sequence of 'stages,' or should we describe it, rather, as involving a number of separate but interacting sequences?" These two questions are, of course, related. The first of them takes it for granted that cognitive development can best be divided up into successive "phases" or "stages," by considering how far the child has progressed towards the fully fledged use of language; and, if that were so, we might expect developmental psychologists with different philosophies of language to classify the "stages" of cognitive development on quite different systems and principles. If it subsequently turned out, however, that the complex tasks and skills embodied in language do not form a unique sequence of subtasks and skills—to be learned in a single compulsory order—we could not then hope to arrive, by this route, at a unique and unambiguous set of "stages" capable of serving as the theoretical framework for a general account of psychological development.

We can confirm the first of these expectations by recalling the difference of opinion between Piaget and Vygotsky (referred to earlier) about "egocentrism" and "socialization." The differences between the two men's respective philosophies of language played a leading part in this dispute. Piaget has always seen the child as an individual whose behavior is of primary interest as expressing the flowering of its inner capacity in the presence of the situations with which it has to deal. At the outset, accordingly, Piaget saw no reason to differentiate between the "socialization" of the child's linguistic behavior and that of its nonlinguistic behavior. As it moved progressively from "egocentric" playing by itself (say with a rattle) on to "socialized" playing with others (say, in team games), it also presumably moved progressively from "egocentric" vocalizing to itself, or babbling, to "socialized" vocalizing for others, using a communal language.

Vygotsky (1934), by contrast, saw an essential opposition in this respect between language and much of nonlinguistic behavior. For him, the child's linguistic behavior could not help but be "socialized" from the word Go. Language proper begins only when the child is drawn into certain communal "language games," during which the mother (or mentor) utters the appropriate, conventional words or phrases. Only subsequently does the child gradually "internalize" these words and phrases in the course of applying and repeating the "language games" by and for himself. While his *general* behavior may thus become progressively more "socialized," in the sense of "other-regarding" or "outer-directed," his *cognitive* behavior becomes progressively more "egocentric"—that is, more "autonomous" and "inner-directed."

How are we to account for this reversal of emphasis? It was not that Vygotsky had made observations, or discoveries, that contradicted Piaget's empirical results. Rather, it was that he brought to the planning of his empirical work quite a different interpretation which can be related to his own Marxian philosophical position. As in the case of Luria and Yudovich (1959), the references to Marx in Vygotsky's writings are not pure genuflexions. Their philosophy of language is, in fact, consistent with a general Marxian position, according to which all conventional, culturally conditioned patterns of behavior (language included) must be construed with an eye to their social functions, as varieties of *praxis*. This "socially oriented" view of language should not be dismissed as a mere ideological prejudice, any more than Piaget's "individually oriented" view; it is simply that Piaget and Vygotsky—coming to developmental studies with individualist and socialist preconceptions, respectively—ended by describing linguistic and cognitive development in ways that complemented rather than contradicted one another.

It already begins to appear, therefore, as though there may be several different ways—all of them legitimate—of characterizing the steps by which the child acquires a linguistic and cognitive grasp, and so several alternative ways in which linguistic criteria can be used to define a theoretical sequence of "stages" in cognitive development. From one point of view, the child's vocal utterances will be considered as so many varieties of individual self-expression; the gradual transition from babbling to communal language will then present itself to us (as to Piaget) as a form of "socialization." From another point of view, language will be regarded as a set of instruments whose uses are governed by the collective rules and conventions of a particular "linguistic community"; in that case, the transition from communal speech to inner thought will present itself to us (as to Vygotsky, and to Wittgenstein) as a move from "socialized" to "internalized" speech. Yet these represent only two of the possible lines along which the development of human cognitive behavior can legitimately be divided. Piaget and Vygotsky focus attention on only two, out of the ten or a dozen distinct variables, or design features, by which the differences between language and other modes of behavior can be characterized. (On these "design features," see Hockett, 1958.)

What is still far from clear—what cannot safely be assumed in advance—is whether, in the course of the child's development, all these distinct features become differentiated in strict parallel. If that were indeed so, we might then use their "consensus" to describe the grasp, utilization, and refinement of language in terms of a single, unambiguous sequence of "stages." But if, on the other hand, these variables change independently and provide no such obliging consensus, the task of defining "stages" of development will be that much the more intractable.

B. Functional Development in Physiology and Psychology. In the light of these difficulties, what is to be done about the notion of "stages" in developmental psychology? The way out of our quandary (I believe) is to moderate our expectations, and to recognize that the "time schedules" or subdivisions adopted in any developmental science are unadvoidably arbitrary. The notion of developmental "stages" may provide a framework for empirical description, but it is no guide to the discovery of rigorous, theoretical "laws." To use a jargon word from developmental physiology that Erikson has already borrowed for his own purposes, a theory of psychological development is inevitably an "epigenetic," rather than a "genetic" theory.

Let me explain what I mean by this. In developmental physiology, as much as in cognitive psychology, the scientist's primary interest is in the organism's *functional achievements*. He is concerned with the development of organs and bodily structures (that is to say) with an eye to the *novel functions* they enable the creature to perform. More exactly, the developmental physiologist's primary concern is with "functions" in the sense of "gross" or "vital" functions, rather than of "local" functions. (The "local" function of, for instance, the pancreas is to secrete insulin: that is, by secreting insulin, it contributes to maintaining the digestion, healthy growth, and other "gross" or "vital" functions of the entire organism. On the relevance of this pervasive ambiguity to cognitive psychology, see Luria, 1966, quoting Anokhin, 1940.) As contrasted with, say, cytochemistry, developmental physiology is therefore an *outward-looking* science; its basic preoccupation is with the changes in bodily structure through which the developing organism becomes able to deal more effectively with its environment, and its "stages" are accordingly defined in terms of the achievement of such "outer-directed" capacities. To put this point in a phrase, physiologists find the *milestones* to segment the organism's developmental history not by hunting for discontinuities in its interior physico–chemical processes (or local functions), but rather by using the *achievement* of new, externally directed gross (or vital) functions to mark its growing physiological competence. The appearance of a new vital function may thus mark a "milestone" in its physiological development, without necessarily being accompanied by specific discontinuities in the local functioning of its component parts. After a child has become capable of walking, for instance, its legs may continue growing just as they were doing before.

If I say that developmental physiology is an "epigenetic" science, I simply wish to register the implications of that fact. When subdividing the period of development into "stages," physiologists proceed neither in a purely empiricist manner—assuming that all significant functional changes will show up as observed discontinuities in the local physico-chemical functioning of organs and tissues—nor in a purely analytical manner—laying down in advance the sequence in which new vital functions must necessarily appear. Rather they proceed in an intermediate way. They use their general understanding of the organism's conditions of life to define the different functions that it must in due course achieve if it is to arrive at a normal maturity; and "maturity" is in this context a "normative" concept. But they carefully avoid prejudging the question, whether the establishment of those functions either must—or does in fact—always proceed in the same order, and involve the same internal changes in local function.

To that extent, developmental physiologists have abandoned the hope of establishing any *law* of development through "stages." (It may in fact turn out that some gross functions are always achieved before certain others, for reasons to be explained in terms of the local functioning of the organs called into play; but physiologists can hope to decide which specific functions are so related—and why—only after a great deal of careful investigation.) Instead, they aim to give an account of development in two successive installments: first, describing "epigenetically" the sequence by which the developing organism normally acquires new gross or vital functions, and investigating only secondly the "genesis" of these functions, by studying the interior changes in local functioning on different levels of its biophsics and body chemistry. In some cases, no doubt, these "genetic" studies will bring to light parallel changes on several different levels (for example, the local changes in lungs and lung tissues as the newborn infant begins to breathe for itself), but this is certainly not the universal rule. Striking changes in gross function are not in every case accompanied by equally striking discontinuities in the local functioning of all the relevant organs, organelles, cells, and cell parts.

From the theoretical point of view, then, the notion of "stages" now plays less fundamental a part than formerly in human physiology, and an acceptable sequence of developmental "stages" can be established only on certain understandings. To begin with, the very notion of "stages" is now regarded only as a descriptive convenience, not as a concept of great theoretical profundity or significance. In the nature of the case, the "milestones" by which physiologists segment the individual's life cycle into "stages"—conception, birth, walking, puberty, . . . ,—are heterogeneous, arbitrary, and frequently selected *ad hoc*. What exact unit periods it is worthwhile to distinguish as "stages" depend upon the purposes of each particular physiological enquiry. No single sequence of stages can be "acceptable" by any absolute standards; though one broad sequence may have a general utility for the purpose of physiological description at a gross level, quite other milestones may be more convenient and illuminating when it comes to understanding (say) cerebral or pulmonary, skeletal or sexual development.

The heterogeneity and arbitrariness of our "milestones," and of the "stages" they are used to define, reflect in turn the multiplicity of different levels on which physiological changes are continually taking place. From the molecular control of protein and nucleic acid synthesis in the ribosomes and chromosomes of individual cells, up through organelles, tissues, and organs of growing complexity to the gross physiological functioning of the entire bodily frame, the development of the human organism involves processes of many different kinds, on many different scales, and any particular set of developmental "milestones" will commonly involve distinctive changes on a few of these levels only. If attention is confined to any one level—subcellular processes, for instance—all students of cell biology may be able to agree on a suitable sequence of "milestones" and "stages." But, the more levels we consider at once, the vaguer and more arbitrary our "stages" will become, and for general purposes we are left with little better than the familiar prescientific divisions into "infancy" and "adolescence," "maturity" and "senescence."

To turn back now to developmental psychology, there we are faced with all the complexities of developmental physiology, and more besides. None of the levels of physiological development—even the molecular level—can safely be ignored by psychologists. (Though the first enthusiastic speculations about RNA and memory were wild and fanciful, the precision of many cognitive functions is so exact that the physiological mechanisms involved must surely be on a molecular level.) Meanwhile, emotional and moral development need to be considered with half an eye on hormonal development, while the changes in the child's perceptual, linguistic, and intellectual skills must be related to the growth in complexity and interconnectedness of the maturing brain. Two further sets of behavioral complexities are superimposed in addition on these different physiological levels: one of these is concerned with the acquisition of general skills of progressively greater elaboration and delicacy, the other with socialization, language learning, and the establishment of other culturally based patterns of behavior.

Neither of these behavioral complexities is much easier to disentangle than those of physiology. Once again, (1) these considerations have to be broken down into different levels. As time goes on, the child (*a*) learns to control certain of his bodily movements, so that they become smooth and recognizable "actions"; (*b*) learns to link individual actions into regular sequences, either in play or for serious ends, so shaping his spontaneous activity into "behavior"—in the everyday sense of "correct behavior," as contrasted with "misbehavior," not that of psychological "behaviorism"; (*c*) learns to introduce arbitrary, conventional elements into his behavioral sequences, and to interpret such "symbolic" elements in the behavior of others; (*d*) learns to apply such sequences, first overtly (publicly) and later in an internalized way (privately), as instruments and procedures for solving problems, so developing a capacity for articulate "thought"; (*e*) learns to describe his own procedures, and the considerations upon which his trust in them is based, so turning routine problem solutions into "knowledge"; etc. And on each of these levels we can make a further distinction between those general capacities that are common to all normal humans (walking, feeding, home making, *langage*, etc.) and those particular forms or features that are specific to particular cultures (goose stepping, chopstick handling, apartment living, the French *langue*, etc.).

Once again, also, (2) certain of these behavioral developments are "prerequisites" for others, not just in the formal sense of Hamlyn's example (*red* and *color*), but in the material sense in which, say, ovulation is a "prerequisite" of conception, and general manual dexterity a "prerequisite" for learning to repair watches. Yet this will again be true of only some pairs of skills; elsewhere, we must discover as we go along just how far, in point of fact, the various developmental sequences display uniformities or parallels. And only after these uniformities and parallels have been established can we seriously consider setting up a single sequence of functional achievements to serve as "milestones" defining general "stages" of psychological development. Even then, our account of psychological development will only be an *epigenetic* one. As in physiology, it will be a descriptive convenience rather than a matter of great theoretical significance; and, the more levels we embrace in a single sequence of "stages," the vaguer and the more arbitrary our subdivision will become.

There is one major difference between the physiological and psychological cases: We are tempted to see, in psychological development, an inherent order and necessity that clearly does not exist in physiological maturation, whereas the actual differences between the two kinds of development are rather ones of degree. This temptation is understandable; after all, fully fledged adult conduct does have an inner structure or complexity (associated with the distinctions between bodily movements, actions, behavioral sequences, symbols, etc.) that can easily be projected back onto the child's life history and interpreted as defining a "natural" or "necessary" sequence of stages. Yet this is a mistake, for two reasons. In the first place, we are immediately concerned here with a number of parallel sequences, rather than a single succession of "stages." The child does not learn, first, to perform all the unit actions he will ever need, next to build these into a complete repertory of standard behavioral sequences, then to treat certain actions as symbolic, etc. Rather he acquires and refines his motor, behavioral, symbolic, and other skills throughout his whole lifetime. So we must begin by considering separately the development of each distinct type of capacity. All the different elements in adult cognition are not just added to one another, in succession, during infancy and adolescence; rather, they fit together in different patterns, at different points in the child's life.

Before developmental psychologists can establish a general sequence of developmental "stages"—far less, generalize about the "laws" governing psychological development from "stage" to "stage"—they have a great deal of preliminary work to do. First, they must have mapped the sheer physiological development of the limbs, organs, bodily mechanisms, and local functions that are called into play in normal human conduct. (The fact that a human child does not walk at one week old, for instance, gives rise to no psychological questions.) They must then see whether the various physiological changes involved display sufficient uniformities and parallels to define an acceptable timetable of "physiological maturation," to serve as the background to their own psychological studies. Next they need to consider separately the steps by which each of the relevant behavioral capacities—for bodily control, sequential behavior, symbolization, internalization, problem solving, etc.—is elicited and developed in the course of a child's life, and look to see in what different patterns all those various capacities are associated at one point or another in life. Only then will it be time to select "milestones," so as to define general "stages" of psychological development, and, even then, there will be no guarantee that the "stages" relevant to one psychological enquiry will do more than rough justice to other psychological changes—still less, to the overall character of psychological development as a whole—if there is such a thing.

Even more than in physiology, again, the resulting "stages" will be, not only arbitrary, but *normative*. Whereas the physiological notions of "maturity" and "maturation" serve, in a quite innocent sense, as "norms" of physiological development—being used to define the "deficiencies" and "deficits" that mark off the color-blind, the aphasic, and the spastic as "abnormal," rather than merely "different"—the psychological notions of "maturity" and "maturation" also overlap normatively into the area of *ethics*. (For example, a certain level of mathematical competence is not just definitive of the linguistic term "normal human adult," nor is it just something frequently found in actual human adults. Rather it is something we regard as *desirable in*, and *obligatory for* adult human beings—a mark, not just of how they *tend to* develop, but how they *ought to* develop.) To this extent, any classification of psychological "stages" will represent not merely an intellectual idealization embodying the arbitrary elements typical of any abstract theory, but also an ethical ideal of human development—a conception of mental growth and cultivation that we use as a template for judging, as well as for understanding, the child's growing ability to deal with the world in an intelligent, rational and morally sensitive way.

To say all this is not to dismiss the task of defining "stages" of psychological development as impracticable. It is only to register the limits within which any such sequence must be constructed. The concepts of "stages" in developmental psychology (I have been arguing) is at best a descriptive convenience, rather than a basis for the discovery of "laws" or "mechanisms" of development. And our choice of "stages" in psychology will be at least as "value-loaded" as the same choice in developmental physiology; in the psychological case, indeed, our conception of "maturity" inevitably commits us to some general view about the capacities which it is *desirable* for adolescents to develop—and so to an *ethical* opinion about the "true nature" of Man.

V. Conclusion

In this article, I have confined myself to some very broad conclusions about the general character and methodology of *any* developmental psychology. Later contributors will help to show how far Piaget's theories meet the conditions I have here analyzed; in particular, how far they recognize the multiplicity of parallel sequences involved in the child's growth and maturation—and so guard against the criticism that they impose a scheme of "stages" on psychological development arbitrarily, from outside, rather than discovering it by careful scrutiny and comparison of the changes taking place upon all relevant levels. My own private suspicion is that, in this respect, Piaget has not been careful enough. When, for instance, he attacks the problem of perceptual development by considering only two levels—one of "physico-chemical causality," the other of "psychological implication"—he is surely using theoretical instruments whose crudity was pardonable in Kant's time (and Hamlyn is clearly right in emphasizing the importance of Piaget's Kantian training), but is far less easily justified today.

On matters of substance, therefore, I am inclined to regard Hamlyn's criticisms as important, and potentially damaging, especially his objection that Piaget underestimates the social, cultural, educational, and ethical aspects of child development. (We cannot, of course, object to a man's basing his account of intellectual and moral development on certain ethical views about the desirable goals of that development; but we are entitled to challenge him if he fails to acknowledge the social component in his theoretical analysis—as though the child's ethical judgments appeared spontaneously and autonomously from within its own untutored activities.) In this respect, it must be asked whether one can really abstract the child's development to as great a degree as Piaget implies from its social and educational context. For my part, I very much hope that Peters and Kohlberg discuss the dangers inherent in such an abstraction in their contributions to this volume.

In conclusion, then, my differences from Hamlyn are concerned with questions of method rather than of substance. They are none the less serious for that, and I would like to persuade him to soften some of his more hard-and-fast dichotomies. Like him, I believe that Piaget's account of psychological development is based quite as much on concepts derived from the Kantian philosophy in which he was first trained, as on the results of his own experiments and observations; so that it needs to be criticized as much on conceptual as on empirical grounds. Unlike Hamlyn, I believe that some such mixture of conceptual and empirical considerations was unavoidable—rather than being an unnatural "blend" or "confusion"—and that a philosophical critique of developmental psychology is a necessary preface to any more profound understanding of Piaget's empirical findings. Any philosophical defects in Piaget's theoretical concepts will (in short) be damaging to the claims of his account, even as psychology; and we shall arrive at a better "theory of cognition"—or, to use the traditional phrase, at better "principles of human understanding"—only in the light of *both* better conceptual analysis *and* better empirical information.

To return to where we began, the discussion of "human understanding" is one of those areas in which, in our own day, the line separating empirical issues from conceptual issues, or "scientific" from "philosophical," is thinnest. Granted, we can legitimately *distinguish* between these two pairs of issues, and enquire how far any particular discussion of, say, "stages" of psychological development is concerned with conceptual, and how far with empirical matters. Granted, furthermore, such an enquiry may be particularly valuable—and even urgent—when we are faced with the particular sorts of unclarity that Hamlyn points to in Piaget's theoretical discussions. Yet I must repeat, by distinguishing two groups of issues one does not automatically succeed in setting them apart from one another. While Hamlyn is clearly right in finding a "blend" of conceptual and empirical questions in Piaget's writings, he is not so clearly right in demanding that these two distinguishable components be separated, and dealt with independently. On the contrary, if my own argument is correct, the theory of "cognition," or "human understanding," will make progress only when those who contribute to it—whether under the name of "psychologists" or "epistemologists"—take proper care to consider conceptual issues *as* conceptual issues *in the light of* the best empirical information, and frame their empirical questions *as* empirical questions *in the light of* the best available conceptual refinements.

If I personally find myself learning more about mental and intellectual development from such Russian psychologists as Vygotsky and Luria than I do from Piaget, that too is because their theoretical analysis is, at certain points, *philosophically* more discriminating and acceptable than his. Their Marxian background compels them to pay explicit attention to just those social and educational factors that Hamlyn finds lacking from Piaget's theories; and their account of language learning as an instrument of socialization and enculturation is that much the more congenial to philosophers familiar with, for example, Wittgenstein's arguments about "language games."

This is not, of course, to say that Vygotsky's analysis of, for instance, the different kinds of aggregate and pseudoconcept that precede the child's abstract grasp of "concepts" proper is by any means the last word on the subject. Philosophers (Heaven knows) have not been idle since Marx, and we should be in a position by now to refine further on the theoretical questions and strategies of the Russian school of developmental psychologists. It was with just such an end in view, indeed, that I argued in my earlier paper for a collaboration between analytical philosophers—who are aware both of the delicate conceptual and linguistic issues involved, and of twentieth-century insights into the importance of "language games," "symbolic forms," etc.—and empirical psychologists, who have much to offer philosophers in the way of new and relevant observations. From such a collaboration could come a better understanding of the nature of "concepts," and the different parts that language plays in thought and action, at different stages in human life, and in different cultures.

Such a collaboration, will, however, demand a new open-mindedness on both sides. On the part of the psychologists, it will require a preparedness to acknowledge (as Einstein did) that their theoretical concepts may be inadequate for philosophical reasons. On the part of the philosophers, it will require a preparedness to admit that some of their key terms (for example, the term "concept" itself) are ill defined for lack of attention to the changing character of linguistic and cognitive activities at different stages of human development. A book such as this provides a forum—perhaps the only available kind of forum—for exploring the new questions that would face us, both as philosophers and as psychologists, if we were prepared to adopt this open-minded attitude, and move more freely across the boundaries between our respective disciplines.

Postscript

It would be a pity if secondary points, whose origins are partly terminological, were to overshadow the substantial agreement between Hamlyn, Kaplan, and myself. For that agreement—so far as it goes—provides a constructive place from which to carry the present discussion forward. We seem (for example) to agree very largely on two significant methodological issues. These are (*a*) that Piaget's account of intellectual development in the individual child leaves it quite obscure how this development is related to the collective conceptions and/or "forms of life" characteristic of the culture, or phase, into which the child grows up; and (*b*) that the internal relations and/or stratifications of our collective conceptions and intellectual procedures create certain "epistemological priorities" which must be properly allowed for in any adequate account of intellectual development.

As to (*a*), the main problem is to avoid a "stand off" between nativists and environmentalists: that is, between those who see the fully fledged conceptions of causality, morality, conservation, and the like toward which both the individual child and the culture of the human species are seemingly developing as a uniquely valid expression of the inborn species-specific capacities of every human being, and those who would interpret all such conceptions as the arbitrary products of particular cultures. In this connection there is a significant difference of emphasis between Hamlyn's treatment of Wittgenstein's term *Lebensformen* ("forms of life") and my own. I deliberately stressed the cultural aspects of this notion, even to the extreme of hinting at a kind of "cultural relativism" that Wittgenstein himself would certainly not have advocated explicitly. But this relativism was in no way central to my argument, since my aim was only to underline the extent to which intellectual development *does* involve "enculturation" to collective "forms"—whether or no those forms are cultural universals. By contrast, Hamlyn insists on the universality of Wittgenstein's *Lebensformen*, even to the extreme of attributing to him a kind of Kantian "absolutism" or nativism which (I believe) was equally foreign to his intentions. Yet, for the purpose of Hamlyn's criticisms of Piaget, we surely need not go so far as to equate these "forms of life" with Kant's "forms of sensibility"—as though they, too, were "a function of the discriminations" which our native capacities and physiological equipment "enable us to make in relation to the world as it affects" that inherited endowment. Rather, the essential task of this notion is to direct our attention back to those general patterns of human activity within which our collective intellectual conceptions come to be given their standard significance, while *leaving entirely open* the question how far, and in what respects these patterns reflect "native capacities" on the one hand, and "cultural functions" on the other.

That question is easily begged, and it was one of Wittgenstein's major virtues that he did treat it as a question about the "matural history of man" on which we must avoid taking any *a priori* stand, and which must be dealt empirically in advance of any theorizing. The question is begged, for instance, in some of Chomsky's more enthusiastic claims to have found the basis of human language in a universal and inborn "native capacity," unrelated to the general pragmatic functions of language; and Hamlyn is surely right to raise parallel doubts about Piaget's own theoretical analysis. For that analysis suggests that the child's "native capacities" are specifically preadapted to construct one and only one final conception of "reality," and to reinvent the same concepts of causality, conservation, etc., in all situations—so recapitulating the cultural experience of the species. True, this might yet prove to be the case in point of fact, though there are general reasons from genetics, evolution theory, and other branches of biology for doubting whether it will actually do so. But, in the meanwhile, we shall do better to assume that whatever general "native capacities" a child possesses are capable of realizing themselves in a wide range of different specific ways (or none) depending on the particular cultural context within which he has the opportunity to exercise them.

As to (*b*), we risk a similar "stand off" over the question whether or no "epistemological priorities" can be taken as implying anything about temporal order or sequences. Given Hamlyn's general determination to keep philosophical epistemology untainted by considerations from psychology, he is very cautious about reading any temporal implications into these priorities. But might he not, instead, have used this very connection in reverse, as a test for deciding which supposed "epistemological priorities" are—and which are not—genuine ones? If we are unhappy about saying, for example, that a grasp of the general concept *color* is "epistemologically prior to" an ability to recognize particular colors, that is surely a reflection of the fact that we would not accept a child as talking meaningfully about color in general *in advance of* recognizing and distinguishing colors in particular. Conversely, there can be no objection to invoking epistemological arguments (as Vygotsky and Luria do) to show that public language use is a "necessary procursor" of internalized speech, and reflexive self-criticism of one's own intellectual procedures a "subsequent development" out of the (epistemologically more primitive) learning and employment of those procedures. The step from epistemological priorities to temporal sequences must, no doubt, be taken with great discretion and in full awareness of what is at issue. Yet, at the same time, it provides one of the most powerful ways in which psychological theories and discoveries can react back onto epistemology itself. And it would be a major contribution to both developmental psychology and epistemology if it were possible to compile, analyze, and criticize an agreed table of such priorities and sequences.

There is only one point at which the present debate has apparently ended in cross-purposes as a result of the terms I chose to express my own position, in a way that must be corrected. For Hamlyn reads my remarks about "the process of" learning as implying that the acquisition of any particular concept necessarily involves in every case the same highly specific, unique and universal sequence of events, and that a philosophical analysis of the concept in question requires the discovery of this universal sequence. Nothing was further from my mind than this belief. Indeed, it never occurred to me that it was still necessary today, some twenty years after Ryle's *Concept of mind*, to guard oneself against such an interpretation. My actual point was less fanciful. Of course there is not *one and only one* invariable sequence of events by which, for example, a child learns a concept, a man dies, or an anticyclone forms; but in each case the range of possible sequences which are in fact capable of leading to such a general end result is not unlimited, and we can in each case refine our conceptions of "learning," "death," and/or "anticyclone," by plotting those limits and so finding our more exactly *what there is there* for us to mean by these terms.

In conclusion, whether the reexamination and refinement of our concept of "learning," in the light of better empirical knowledge about the possible ways of learning, is to be classified as philosophical analysis or as psychological theory, is a question of administrative niceties alone. This reappraisal requires the deployment of two different kinds of intellectual skills that are at present cultivated independently in university departments of philosophy and psychology, and pending the creation of departments of "epistemics"—already prefigured in existing "centers for cognitive studies"—such investigations will continue to involve an interdisciplinary collaboration.

This conclusion will not, I fear, satisfy Hamlyn. He claims that this is more than a professional demarcation dispute, and ends by restating his objection that

> Piaget's theory is a blend not only of the empirical and the conceptual (which would be both acceptable and inevitable), but of the empirical and the philosophical (Hamlyn, *p. 23*).

Yet what still has to be made clear is how, at the level of basic "cognitive theory" we are to draw a sharp line between "genuinely philosophical" and "merely conceptual" issues. Unless philosophers are to end up back in

Hume's situation—with one set of concepts for use inside the philosophical study, and a quite different set for use outside—they cannot really expect to have the last word on all occasions about the concepts and theoretical presuppositions of theoretical psychology, regardless of what new discoveries and insights the psychologists may turn up. Instead, they must be prepared to allow that any argument is liable to cut both ways, and that their own *philosophical* analyses may sometimes benefit as a result of being reconsidered in the light of better *psychological* understanding. In the epistemic field, the traditional issues of philosophical epistemology blend into the most general problems of psychological theory without any sharp dividing line, and are—in actual practice—inseparable from them.

References

Anokhin, P. K. The problem of localization from the viewpoint of ideas concerning nervous functional systems. *Nevropatologiya i Psikhiatriya*, 1940, **9**, 6. (In Russian.)

Hamlyn, D. W. The logical and psychological aspects of learning. In R. S. Peters (Ed.), *The concept of education*. London: Routledge, 1967. Pp. 24–43.

Hockett, C. F. *A course in modern linguistics*. New York: Macmillan, 1958. Pp. 137 ff.

Luria, A. R. *Higher cortical function in man*. Translated by B. Haigh. New York: Harper, 1966. Pp. 17–26.

Luria, A. R., & Yudovich, I. A. *Speech and the development of mental processes in the child*. Translated by O. Kovacs & J. Simon. London: Staples, 1959.

Schilpp, P. A. (Ed.) *Albert Einstein: Philosopher–scientist*. New York: Tudor, 1951.

Toulmin, S. E. Concepts and the explanation of human behavior. In T. Mischel (Ed.), *Human action: Conceptual and empirical issues*. New York: Academic Press, 1969.

Toulmin, S. E., & Goodfield, G. J. *The fabric of the heavens*. London: Hutchinson, and New York: Harper, 1961.

Urmson, J. O. Recognition. *Proceedings of the Aristotelian Society*, 1955–56, N.S. **56**, 259–280.

Vygotsky, L. S. *Thought and language*. Moscow–Leningrad: Soc. Econom. Izd., 1934. Translated by E. Hanfman & G. Vakar. Cambridge, Massachusetts: M.I.T. Press, 1962.

GENETIC PSYCHOLOGY, GENETIC EPISTEMOLOGY, AND THEORY OF KNOWLEDGE [1, 2]

Bernard Kaplan

I. Introduction

I have been charged with a twofold task: on one hand, my status as a commentator obliges me to direct my remarks to the articles of the principal contributors to this volume; on the other, I take it as a major responsibility to deal with the questions formulated by Mischel to circumscribe and focus the discussion in this book. This dual task would doubtless have been easier to handle had the principal contributors themselves focused on the guiding questions, distinguishing them from each other and answering each in a straightforward way. Alas, they have not done so. This neglect may be due, in some measure, to the inclination to construe a question as meaning something quite different from its obvious import because one has prejudged, without any warrant, that it must have this quite different meaning. Instead, therefore, of dealing with the two tasks together, I have chosen first to confront the principal issues, and only incidentally to comment on the articles of the principal contributors. I will subsequently touch on some of the specific issues raised by Hamlyn and Toulmin that are interesting in themselves, but appear to me to be marginal to the principal questions.

Let me recall the two major questions intended to guide our discussions: First, "Is a 'genetic epistemology' possible?" Second, "Is genetic psy-

[1] This commentary was written after the conference was over and goes considerably beyond the impromptu remarks made at the conference. It should be noted that Hamlyn and Toulmin did not have the opportunity to respond to some of the comments in this text, since they are introduced for the first time in this revamped and expanded written form.

[2] Editor's note: At Kaplan's request, I note that I have abridged and rearranged this article in order to save space.

chology relevant to epistemology?" Since these are two distinct questions, it is important to treat them separately.

II. Is a "Genetic Epistemology" Possible?

One is tempted, somewhat facetiously, to take this question as a specification of the Kantian one and respond: "Of course. Since a 'genetic epistemology' is actual, it must be possible." This, however, will not do, because we have not yet established the actuality of a "genetic epistemology." And clearly we cannot establish the actuality of a "genetic epistemology" unless we understand what is meant by the phrase. One way of proceeding to uncover this meaning is to scrutinize the physiognomy of the phrase. Hamlyn wisely eschews this path; he cogently observes that the phrase "does not entirely reveal its meaning." A second way is to guess at its meaning by combining certain connotations or associations of the component words. This would seem to be the way that Hamlyn believes might be chosen by many philosophers in the Anglo-Saxon tradition, who would experience a noxious gustatory hallucination of John Locke's undertaking on hearing the phrase. A third way, closely related to the second, is to connect the phrase with one of its users, recall what that person is best known for, and conclude that the phrase must really be a disguised synonym for that user's principal undertaking. This is the path chosen by Hamlyn explicitly and by Toulmin less openly. Both appear to assume that because Piaget has used the phrase "genetic epistemology" and is most renowned for his theory of intellectual development in the individual, "genetic epistemology" must refer to Piaget's theory of intellectual development in human ontogeny. A fourth, and more difficult route to travel, namely, to examine the explicit definition of the phrase or to analyze its use in the contexts in which it occurs in the writings of a specific thinker, was completely overlooked or bypassed by both of the principal speakers.

Now I will shortly undertake to puncture the bubble of misapprehension concerning the character of Piaget's "genetic epistemology" which has been wafted our way by Hamlyn and Toulmin. Before I do so, however, I would like to touch upon two preliminary issues. I believe that these issues must be brought to the fore if we are subsequently to concern ourselves with the question that has been posed to us, unhampered by unnecessary encumbrances. One of these issues is provoked by the tacit procedural assumption that "genetic epistemology" is, or ought to be, identified with Piaget's specific undertaking. The other is prompted by the facile presumption that I may have read into Hamlyn's remarks to the effect that the meaning of a term such as "epistemology" has been unambiguously settled once and for all, perhaps on the basis of a social contract among philosophers, or through precedent, or via some special insight granted to a small coterie of emancipated souls.

First, the synecdoche. Neither the concept nor the phrase, "genetic epistemology," are Piaget's exclusive properties. As Piaget himself observes (1950, p. 18, 1957, p. 14), some of the ideas underlying his undertaking were foreshadowed or realized in the work of earlier scholars, for example, F. Enriques. And there were not a few other scholars, near the turn of the century, who, titling their works in a variety of ways, purported to deal with the "evolution" or "development" of the claims to, and grounds for, valid knowledge by examining and analyzing the forms of thought taken to yield such knowledge throughout the history of science, in "racial history" and/or in ontogeny. One might mention, from Germany, Wundt's (1880) and Sigwart's (1894–1895) treatises on logic. Again, one might note Baldwin's massive work, *Thought and things* (1901, Vol. 1), in which, one should remark, the phrase "genetic epistemology" and its obvious synonym "genetic theory of knowledge" are used throughout. And, desirous of including some philosophers who may lay claim to belonging to at least some branch of the Anglo-Saxon tradition, one should not neglect to mention that among those who early sought to establish a discipline of "genetic epistemology"—to be sure, along lines different from those later pursued by Piaget—were Bosanquet (1888, Vol. 1, p. 2) and Hobhouse (1888, 1912). Finally, I should note that during the first decade of this century, the greatest of the "genetic epistemologists" initiated his inquiries—I refer, of course, to Cassirer (1903–1920, 1950, 1910).

The thrust of what I have just been talking about should be obvious. Even if one were correctly to construe the meaning Piaget gives to "genetic epistemology," the concept of "genetic epistemology" should be disembarrassed from the unhappy fusion it has undergone here with Piaget's specific attempt to orient that discipline along certain lines. It is clear that one may be led to question Piaget's particular version of "genetic epistemology" or challenge the adequacy of his achievement, and still conclude on the basis of an examination of other attempts at actualization that a genetic theory of knowledge is, indeed, possible.

The diversity of interpretations of "genetic epistemology" leads us to the second issue mentioned above, namely, that of the definition of "epistemology." If I am not mistaken, Hamlyn intimates that the connotations of that term, and hence the boundaries of the province of inquiry they establish, are somehow permanently fixed so as to render "incoherent" or improper—an "external aggression" to be repelled at all costs—any attempt by genetic psychologists, psychologists in general, and, seemingly, any practitioner of an empirical science, to insinuate the results of their inquiries into that province. Epistemology belongs to the realm of philosophy; psychology, sociology of knowledge, etc. belong to the domain of empirical sciences. The only way to ensure that they do not contaminate each other is to practice a rigorous "apartheid"—to draw a hard-and-fast line between them.

Now one may agree or disagree with this decision to segregate philosophy and psychology or philosophy and empirical science. But one should at least recognize that it is a decision on the part of a certain group of philosophers and has no binding force on others. We already know of at least one contemporary philosopher, Toulmin, who apparently rejects that decision. Another contemporary philosopher also argues against the diremption:

> The goal of epistemology is to provide a theory of knowledge, in whatever form it occurs. This aim has traditionally been conceived as a matter of logic rather than psychology, of abstract norms rather than concrete facts. But between the conception and the creation of such a logic falls the shadow of a presupposed psychology. Whether based upon the psychology or only commingled with it, every epistemology is shaped by underlying conceptions of the mind and conduct of which cognition is a product (A. Kaplan, 1963, p. 130).

And, if one decides to appeal to "tradition" to justify the exclusion of empirical inquiry from the realm of epistemology, one may find that epistemology has been defined not only as "the theory of the origin, nature and limits of knowledge" but also as "the systematic analysis of the conceptions employed by ordinary and scientific thought in interpreting the world, and including an investigation of the act of knowledge, or the nature of knowledge as such, with a view to determine its ontological significance" (Pringle-Pattison, 1906, p. 333).

It is not my intent here to quarrel with Hamlyn's choice—indeed, in many respects, I am inclined to sympathize with his view that epistemology be a normative discipline, regulative of inquiry, rather than a positive discipline shaped by the results of empirical investigation—but to emphasize that the demarcation of epistemology from empirical inquiry involves a decision and not a description of the "way things are." As Black has pointed out, in connection with the definition of "scientific method," such a controversial or problematic term is defined by "persuasive definitions" whose adequacy is "not regulated simply by the character of the concept to be defined," but depends also on "the soundness of the interest which it [the definition] is designed to serve," so that the "proceeding [is] partly normative in character" (Black, 1954, p. 3). The point is that before one criticizes any scholar's attempt to establish a "genetic epistemology," one should ascertain what concerns him in the enterprise he calls by that name, and not conclude that his enterprise is "confused" or "incoherent" on the supposition that he must mean by certain terms what one intuits him to mean.

Let us now return to Piaget's "genetic epistemology" and the misconstrual of his undertaking by Hamlyn and Toulmin. Hamlyn confidently asserts at the very beginning of his article, "Piaget has invoked the term 'genetic epistemology' to describe his theory of intellectual development in the individual." It would be illuminating indeed to know the basis on which he makes this assertion. *Prima facie,* it would seem unlikely that a person of Piaget's considerable historical erudition and critical acumen would conflate individual genetic psychology and epistemology, and one would therefore expect some textual reference to support the claim. If one turns to the first volume of Piaget's *Introduction a l'épistémologie génétique* (1950), one is quickly struck by a definition of "genetic epistemology" that runs counter to the one imputed to him. "Genetic epistemology," for Piaget, is "the theory of scientific knowledge founded on the development of this knowledge" (Piaget, 1950, Vol. 1, p. 7). And if one examines Piaget's introduction to the Program and Methods of Genetic Epistemology, one finds the following:

> Under its limited or special form, genetic epistemology is the study of successive states of a science as a function of its development. Thus conceived, genetic epistemology could be defined as the positive science, empirical as well as theoretical, of the becoming (devenir) of positive sciences *qua* sciences (Piaget, 1957, p. 13; my translation).

These definitions would scarcely comport with Hamlyn's (or Toulmin's) view of what Piaget is all about in his attempt to establish a "genetic epistemology." Nor would Piaget's general and broader notion of "genetic epistemology" fit the interpretation they give. Piaget defines this general genetic theory of knowledge "as the study of the mechanisms of the growth of knowledge." "The distinctive characteristic of this discipline would consist," Piaget observes, "in analyzing, in all the domains pertaining to the genesis or elaboration of scientific knowledge, the passage from states of lesser knowledge to states of more extended knowledge" (Piaget, 1957, p. 14, my translation).

I do not want to leave the impression that genetic psychology, for Piaget, is irrelevant to "genetic epistemology." Clearly it is not. It is Piaget's belief that any science is a social institution, a group of psychological behaviors and a system *sui generis* of signs and cognitive activities; a rational analysis of the development of a science, therefore, entails the consideration of all three of these aspects. To be sure, the systems of signs and cognitive activities constituting the states of the science at different times have primacy, since they constitute the phenomenon (the development of scientific knowledge) to be explained; but the other two aspects, namely, the sociological and psychological are indissociable from the epistemic aspect insofar as they are called upon to furnish the eventual explanation of the phenomenon (Piaget, 1957, p. 13). Indeed, Piaget goes so far as to maintain that a "systematic study of the development of any sector of scientific knowledge will necessarily be led, in attempting to disengage the sociogenetic and psychogenetic roots of this form of knowledge, to push the analysis of its formative mechanisms to the terrain of prescientific and infrascientific common beliefs [as revealed] in the history of societies . . ., in the development of the child and even [take one] to the frontiers of physiological processes and [to] the most elementary mechanism conditioning the acquisition of beliefs (connaissances) . . ." (Piaget, 1957, p. 13). These contentions show that Piaget does maintain that genetic psychology of intelligence is clearly relevant to epistemology—an issue to which we shall turn when we consider the second major question. But they also should reveal that "genetic epistemology," *à la* Piaget, is not reducible to, or identifiable with, the development of intelligence in the individual.

Let us return now to the question, "Is a genetic epistemology possible?" If one accepts Piaget's formulation of the discipline, it is not *prima facie* obvious why such an undertaking as he proposes is impossible in principle or intrinsically incoherent. Seemingly, the states of a progressive system of scientific knowledge and the transitions between such states can be described; and there is no transparent reason why one cannot attempt to ascertain the psychological and sociological factors conditioning what is accepted as knowledge at various phases in history, and ostensibly affecting the transitions to new "more advanced" claims to knowledge.

On the other hand, one may still question whether such inquiries have anything to do with epistemology, "properly conceived." Positive inquiries into the development of a science or into the psychological and sociological factors conditioning claims to knowledge belong to domains one usually designates as "history of ideas," "intellectual history," "history of science," perhaps "sociology of knowledge," but scarcely to a discipline centrally devoted to establishing the criteria for assessing the validity of claims to knowledge. Moreover, it may be argued that such positive inquiries into the history, sociology, and psychology of epistemic claims already presuppose, at least tacitly, incontrovertible resolutions of ontological and epistemological issues, and are, indeed, legitimatized as knowledge in their own right insofar as these presuppositions are accepted (see Ayer, 1956). Thus, to acknowledge these inquiries and their findings as *Erkenntniswert,* one must ostensibly assume that knowledge can be attained through the presuppositions, methods, procedures, and resultant findings of the historian, the sociologist, or any other empirical investigator. But if criteria for knowledge are presupposed by such inquiries, then, some will maintain, their "findings" cannot themselves provide the grounds for such criteria.

These considerations suggest that another major question that should have been posed concerns the relevance of "genetic epistemology," rather than "genetic psychology," to epistemology. Specifically: "Is the historico-critical examination and analysis of the grounds for, and claims to, knowledge advanced in the various sciences during the course of their development relevant to the theory of knowledge?" It may, of course, be said that this question did not have to be posed in order to be answered. Indeed, a good case can be made for asserting that this unstated question was the focal one in the controversy between Hamlyn and Toulmin. If I am not mistaken, Hamlyn's strictures against drawing any epistemological conclusions from the inquiries of genetic psychologists would apply *mutatis mutandis* to the drawing of epistemological conclusions from the development of knowledge claims in the various sciences. In other words, even if he had correctly construed the character of Piaget's "genetic epistemology," Hamlyn would have challenged the relevance of such a discipline to epistemology proper. Toulmin, on the other hand, opts for what Dewey (1938) referred to as "the principle of the continuum of inquiry." Like Dewey, Toulmin rejects any radical separation between criteriology and inquiry, and seems to insist that a theory of knowledge must grow out of reflection on the processes of knowledge acquisition in the history of the sciences. Thus, Toulmin, it seems to me, argues that both the development of the sciences and genetic psychology are relevant to epistemology.

In any case, whether I am correct or not in my inferences and extrapolations from their papers, I believe that this question is one that deserves our closest scrutiny.

III. Is Genetic Psychology Relevant to Epistemology?

Just as there are different conceptions of epistemology, so there are diverse views of the objectives, scope, and methods of genetic psychology. Even if one disregards those developmental psychologists *eo nomine* who formulate their problems in terms of atomistic and associationistic conceptions, and concerns oneself solely with the family of "genetic–structural" approaches, one observes considerable differences among the members of that family—Piaget, Wallon, Vygotsky–Luria, the Leipzig school of Gestalt psychology (Ganzheitspsychologie), Werner and others. This diversity should be noted because there are many developmental psychologists who would never think of considering their findings as having any bearing on epistemology, however conceived; moreover, they would also reject any suggestion that epistemological presuppositions may have something to do with the character of their inquiries and the nature of their findings. There are other developmental psychologists who would humbly disclaim any belief that their findings could contribute to theory of knowledge, but would accept the thesis that certain epistemological assumptions undergird their investigations and interpretations. Finally, there are those genetic psychologists—Piaget the most renowned among them—who would claim that if both disciplines are "properly conceived," there is the clear possibility of bilateral, mutually beneficial, trade relations between genetic psychology and epistemology.

If we are to deal with our second principal question fruitfully, we must expand it so as to render clear which conceptions of genetic psychology and of theory of knowledge we have in mind. Since it is beyond the scope of this commentary (and this commentator) to examine the relations of all genetic psychologies to all conceptions of epistemology, I shall here limit myself to two specifications of the question at hand: (*a*) Is the genetic psychology of intelligence (Piaget) relevant to epistemology in the usual philosophic acceptation? (*b*) Is the genetic psychology of intelligence (Piaget) relevant to epistemology in Piaget's sense?

First, I will discuss (*a*). It should be quickly acknowledged that it is only from a bird's eye view that one can speak of "epistemology in the usual philosophic acceptation." At closer range, one notices that there is no single conception of the province or problems of the theory of knowledge that evokes consensus from all schools of philosophic thought, and even within a particular school there is often considerable divergence (Wood, 1950, p. 615). One may, nevertheless, note one point of agreement: the tacit or explicit view that "the theory of knowledge" is a philosophical discipline, independent of, and immune to, the results of empirical investigations (for example, Ayer, 1956, p. 7).

Now, Piaget not only abstains from making any claims for the relevance of his genetic psychology of intelligence to *such* construals of epistemology; he positively disclaims any pertinence:

> Genetic psychology is a science whose methods are more and more closely related to those of biology. Epistemology, on the contrary is usually regarded as a philosophical subject, necessarily connected with all the other aspects of philosophy and justifying, accordingly, a metaphysical position. *In these circumstances, the link between the two subjects would have to be considered either as illegitimate or, on the contrary, as no less natural than the transition from any scientific study to whatever form of philosophical thought, less by way of inference than by inspiration and involving, moreover, the addition to the latter subject of considerations beyond its scope* (Piaget, 1952, p. 51; italics mine).

One need not possess a subtle sensibility to recognize that this disclaimer is not a devaluation of genetic psychology, but is, rather, a depreciation of the epistemological forays of philosophers. Lucubrations on theory of knowledge by those who have not directly and deeply immersed themselves in some domain of empirical or logico–mathematical inquiry are, as far as Piaget is concerned, of little epistemic worth. Such speculations may provide wit, wisdom, or solace, but, in the absence of canonical methods, controls, and intersubjective techniques of verification, they yield no knowledge (Piaget, 1957, p. 2).

Of course, Piaget's disclaimer may be disregarded by those who believe that his work does have some relevance to the epistemological theses advanced by philosophers aspiring to a systematic world view. I note his position in this matter only to undercut charges of inconsistency or incoherence based on the supposition that Piaget claims that his psychological investigations will resolve the kinds of issues in epistemology with which philosophers preoccupy themselves.

Now I will concern myself with question (*b*). Although Piaget disclaims any relevance of his studies to epistemological issues as elaborated by various philosophic schools, there is no question that he does regard his investigations as having pertinence to "epistemology" in some sense. The following quotation makes this quite clear:

> Specialists in genetic psychology, and especially in child psychology, do not always suspect what diverse and fruitful relationships are possible between their own subject and other more general kinds of research, such as the theory of knowledge or epistemology (Piaget, 1952, p. 49).

As has already been suggested, these diverse and fruitful relationships will ostensibly become manifest only when epistemology is persuasively defined in a special way that is alien to traditional philosophy.

For Piaget, a central task for the student of theory of knowledge is the analysis of the stages of scientific thought and the explanation of the intellectual "mechanisms" used by scientists of different disciplines in their struggles to grasp the nature of their particular provinces of reality. It is not the prerogative of the epistemologist to prescribe, *ab extra*, the standards which inquiry must meet in order to pass as knowledge, or to arrive at criteria of what it is to know, independent of the rules and methods instituted by inquirers in the course of establishing particular scientific disciplines. (See Dewey, 1938, p. 4.) To be sure, Piaget recognizes as an important aspect of epistemology the attempts by scientists within a discipline to articulate the fundamental categories of the discipline and to formalize the discipline as far as possible—Piaget refers to this undertaking as "normative epistemology"—but his major focus is on epistemology as a positive, genetic science, whose primary object is the sciences themselves in the processes of their formation and their progressive development. The scientific or genetic epistemologist—Piaget seems to use the adjectives interchangeably—shuns global questions concerning knowledge in general or even scientific knowledge as a whole, and concerns himself with such more limited questions as: "How [do] different forms of knowledge, rather than knowledge itself, develop?" "By what process does a science pass from one determinate form subsequently held to be inadequate to another determinate form afterwards held to be superior by the common agreement of the experts on this subject?" (Piaget, 1952, p. 51). These are clearly soluble questions, requiring the refined use of historico–critical methodology for their solution. However, one does not, as yet, see clearly how genetic psychology of intelligence can contribute to such a discipline.

Let us try, schematically, to establish this connection. To do so, we will have to continue a little longer with historians and sociologists of knowledge. It is an obvious truth for Piaget, and presumably for anyone concerned with the actual processes of knowledge formation, that the constitution of reality, as currently accepted in scientific disciplines, has emerged from earlier construals of reality, which have themselves evolved[3] from still earlier, "prescientific" conceptions of the world (see Dewey, 1938; Wartofsky, 1968). No matter how far back one goes in history (or prehistory), one never finds "point zero"—a point when there is no conception of reality, no construal of "what there is" (see Cornford, 1952; Snell, 1953; Guthrie, 1957). In general, those scholars who have reflected on the history of specific sciences and who have sought to delineate the changing conceptions of reality (physical, biological, social, etc.) have concerned themselves with "social facts" (collective representations) or have focused on the conceptions of "those subjects of superior levels who are the creators and animators of particular sciences" (Piaget, 1962, p. 170).

Assuming that the different "ontologies" accepted by a social group or propounded by specific advanced thinkers presuppose the immanent operation of correlative "forms of understanding" ("modes of thought,"

[3] Some will, perhaps, maintain that there has been no evolution of knowledge, no advances, but only a variety of specializations, each equally warranted. This would seem to have been the contention of the historicists (B. Kaplan, unpublished) and is a viewpoint urgently insisted upon today by many who seek to reject the pre-eminence of science as a way of knowing and to restore archaic and mythopoetic modes of knowing and being-in-the-world to a more central position (see Eliade, 1963; Reid, 1961; and others). I will not discuss these views here. For Piaget's opinion concerning some of the attacks on scientific inquiry, see Piaget (1962, 1965). See also Horowitz (1961).

"systems of concepts," "mentalities"), historians of science, sociologists of knowledge (compare Gurvitch, 1966), and others have sought to characterize these different organizations of thought, and to determine the conditions promoting transformations from one "social construction of reality" (Berger and Luckmann, 1966) to another. Recognizing that "the attempt to study apprehension apart from the objects of that apprehension is at every cognitive level a pursuit of shadows, and [that] the only possible way to study the organization of thought is to study the organization it finds or introduces among its objects" (Blanshard, 1939, Vol. 1, p. 81), such scholars have reconstructed the systems of concepts in operation from the records of ontologies maintained, and technical activities pursued, by the members of the different social groups or by individual investigators of a certain historic period. In effect, they have tried to answer the question: "How was it possible for members of a collectivity, or particular "scientists," to have the construal of reality which they did, in fact, have?" Or, "What forms of understanding, what concepts, what standards of knowledge must have been in play, for such a construction of reality to have obtained?"

In characterizing the forms of understanding in operation in various social groups or in individual scientists, historians of science, sociologists of knowledge, etc. have obviously maintained (or tried to maintain) an important safeguard. In their inquiries, they use the conceptual schemes and norms for knowledge acquisition governing their discipline at the time, but they refrain from imputing their forms of understanding, or their standards, to the objects of their investigations. In other words, they *use* the contemporary norms of their discipline but only *mention* the norms used by the groups or individuals they study. Tacitly or explicitly, they naturally accept their disciplinary norms as valid, but the norms and conceptual schemes of the objects of their investigations are taken as "normative facts," and no claim is made for their validity. Doubtless, some of these scholars take their own conceptual schemes and norms to be deathless and unchanging, but the wiser among them are aware of the likelihood that the standards and forms of understanding they now use may become "normative facts," to be mentioned but no longer used by a subsequent generation of investigators who have advanced beyond them.

The kinds of inquiries to which I have just alluded, carried out by historians of science, sociologists of knowledge, and others, clearly fall within the purview of Piaget's "genetic epistemology." They may also be taken to belong to a discipline of comparative psychology of intelligence—a discipline devoted to describing and explaining the different modes of adaptation of organisms ("minds") to reality, the different forms of understanding manifested under different conditions in the transactions of organisms (here, human beings) with their environments. Such inquiries, however, take us only so far. Whence these different realities of common sense or science and their correlative forms of understanding, conceptual schemes, standards, that constitute the "intellectual" modes of adaptation of adult minds to reality? One surely cannot accept the preposterous proposition that one leaps from birth into the everyday adult (preliterate, Eastern or Western) construal of the world or into the status of an innovative and creative scientist in a particular discipline. If we are to complete our genetic epistemology, we must understand the ontologies and forms of understanding of the infant and child in the process of becoming a member of a social order.

Mark well: Just as there is no place for "slick reconstructions" concerning the ontologies and forms of understanding of peoples of other places and other times, no room for merely speculative and uncontrolled stipulations of what must have been the case, so there is no place for positing the realities and forms of understanding of the child, without actual investigation of the child's relation to his world and the correlative mentality thus revealed. Mark well, again: Just as one is little concerned with the particular content of a world view but is oriented to the principles or organization informing that world view—the intellectual methods and procedures employed in the establishment of that ontology so too is one little concerned with the particular contents of the child's world of objects but is oriented to the forms of understanding, the organization of thought, reflected in such contents and their arrangement.

Beyond the importance of a "genetic psychology of intelligence" for completing the picture of the human mind's adaptation to reality, there is a further reason why an examination of the ontologies of children and their forms of understanding is important for genetic epistemology:

> Child psychology constitutes a kind of mental embryology in that it describes the stages of the individual development, and particularly in that it studies the mechanism itself of this development. Psychogenesis represents, moreover, an integral part of embryogenesis (which does not end with birth but rather with the final stage of equilibrium which is the adult status). The intervention of social factors and elements of individual experience in no way detracts from the accuracy of this statement, for organic embryogenesis is itself also partly a function of the environment . . . Once we admit comparisons of this kind, the history of the relations between embryology and other biological studies throws considerable light on the possible and, to a certain extent, the actual relationship between child psychology and [scientific] epistemology (Piaget, 1952, pp. 50–51).

As Oppenheimer (1963, p. 11) points out, "Modern embryology, based as it is on epigenetic convictions, stands on the concept that development proceeds from the general to the special [Von Baer's principle], or it falls." Piaget, in following his embryological analogy, sees the later forms of understanding as specializations of more generic, species-wide, modes of thought revealed in every child's successive construals of the world before he is capable of assimilating and accommodating to the specialized adult reality into which he must enter. Whether or not Piaget is justified by the empirical evidence in asserting a fixed sequence (albeit variable in rate) in the forms of understanding manifested by the growing child, in different societies, this embryological analogy should make it obvious why the study of the forms of intelligence in the child is so important in the genetic epistemology Piaget seeks to establish as a new discipline.

Although I have not said quite enough with regard to the question "Is genetic psychology of intelligence relevant to epistemology?" I hope I have given a sufficient indication of how, where, and why Piaget believes it to be relevant.[4] Within his construal of the discipline of a "scientific or genetic epistemology," it is difficult to show that he is mistaken.

IV. Special Questions

I now want to turn to some of the issues treated by Hamlyn and Toulmin which are of considerable interest in their own right, although somewhat marginal to the guiding questions proposed by Mischel.

A. Must a Psychological Theory Have Philosophical Presuppositions and Implications? Hamlyn makes much of the fact that Piaget's genetic psychology of intelligence has philosophical presuppositions and implications. The manner in which he develops this point suggests that he has, through this revelation, uncovered some kind of fatal flaw in Piaget's enterprise. As one can see, I have, in posing the issue, gone beyond Hamlyn's specific concern with Piaget, formulating the question in more general terms and in a different modality. It seems to me obvious that Piaget's psychological investigations (as well as his genetic epistemological inquiries) rest on philosophical presuppositions which have implications for the manner in which Piaget's undertakings are carried

[4] For examples in English of Piaget's application of genetic psychology of intelligence to epistemology, see Piaget (1952); for a related view of the connections between genetic psychology and scientific knowledge, see Brunswik (1959). For an illuminating attempt to show how the actual study of child thought may be linked with contemporary work in modal logic, see Apostel (1966).

out; this would be obvious even if Piaget had not remarked on the philosophical presuppositions of stimulus–response behaviorism and Gestalt theory, and indicated that his own work was somehow a reconciliation between empiricism and rationalism. What I find curious is why Hamlyn stresses this point. Are not all psychological theories riven with philosophical presuppositions? Do they not all, *au fond*, assume an ontology and an epistemology? (See Lovejoy, 1930.) Indeed, it is difficult for me to see how such presuppositions are escapable.

It may, of course, be the case that I have failed to grasp the real thrust of Hamlyn's strictures. His emphasis may be not that Piaget has made certain assumptions of a philosophic ("conceptual") nature but rather that Piaget has been insufficiently aware of the relation of his presuppositions to the direction of his inquiry, the nature of his methodology, the results he has obtained and the conclusions he has drawn. There may be some truth to this contention; Piaget, in not a few places, does seem to assume that he is observing things as they are, that the findings he obtains and the conclusions he reaches are independent of philosophical assumptions and are simply forced upon him by uncontaminated observation. To the extent that Piaget does operate this way, I would concur that he is mistaken.

However, this does not seem to me to be what Hamlyn inveighs against. His animus appears to be directed toward a confusion which he attributes to Piaget between issues that can only be decided through conceptual analysis and issues that can only be decided through empirical study. As an example of Piaget's ostensible confusion ("incoherence") he refers to a presumed conflation between the origins of "causality" and the scientist's or philosopher's criterion for causal attribution—that is, between "the ways in which an individual may come to an understanding of a certain notion" and "criteria for being properly said to have the concept in question" (Hamlyn, *p. 4*). Now, if this is a paradigm of Hamlyn's charge that Piaget's undertaking suffers from "incoherence," I am really at a loss as to what to say about it. It seems to me to betoken a total incomprehension of what Piaget is about. Even the slightest reading of Piaget's works would show that he takes great pains to distinguish the scientist's and philosopher's form of understanding and the forms of understanding of the child subjects whom he investigates. Even the most cursory reading would reveal that Piaget studies children's forms of understanding (conceptual systems) to arrive at the different *criteria* in play at different stages of development, not to examine the vicissitudes of the life careers of different individuals in arriving at adult notions or to gather material for the empirical adjudication of philosophical controversies concerning criteria advanced thinkers employ or should employ in their use of certain terms.[5] I do not have the space to document this point; for those who are interested in the documentation, I would refer especially to Piaget's *Défense de l'épistémologie génétique* (Piaget, 1962, p. 166), specifically to the sections dealing with the different kinds of norms, namely, philosophical, disciplinary (for example, those of psychologists), and those operative in the subjects of psychological inquiry.

Finally, it may be that Hamlyn believes that Piaget fails to abide with sufficient rigor to the distinction between "analytic" and "synthetic" truths (see Gewirth, 1953). Piaget clearly has some doubts about the warrant of any radical diremption with regard to these two species of truths—one ostensibly concerned solely with issues of meaning, the other with issues of empirical fact—but he is here in good company even in philosophical circles (Quine, 1951; White, 1950; Rudner, 1949; Waismann, 1949–1951); a sharp segregation has been recognized as difficult to maintain even by some of those who are quite sympathetic to retaining it as far as possible (see Scriven, 1960).

B. Can the Criteria of Knowledge Be Established Definitively, As a Matter of Conceptual Analysis, Entirely in Advance of Discovering What Is, in Fact, Involved in the Course of "Learning" or "Coming-to-Know"? It will not escape notice that the issue here has some kinship with the topic just discussed. In stating the question, I have tried to remain faithful to Toulmin's wording (*p. 33*), although I personally find his presumption of the affinity between "learning" and "coming-to-know" dubious. With regard to the issue as he has posed it, Toulmin attributes an affirmative answer to Hamlyn, a negative response to Piaget, and marshals his forces against the former and on behalf of the

[5] As a genetic psychologist who rejects the assumption that the forms of understanding (concepts, conceptual systems) of advanced adults spring fully formed from Zeus' brow, Piaget is concerned with the transformations of later conceptual systems from earlier ones. Thus, without reducing "causality" and the valid criteria for the correct application of causal attribution to earlier forms of thought, Piaget still insists that it is of some importance to see the structures of understanding from which "causality" in its advanced form emerges, and to account for such transformations. It may, of course, be argued that "causality" is either in operation or it is not: there is (in Eliade's phrase) no "solution of continuity." If the child does not employ the valid criteria for causal attribution, it is only a *façon de parler* to say that he is manifesting a more primitive form of causality; he is not manifesting causal reasoning at all. From this point of view, all of developmental psychology of cognition would be dissolved. Remarks suggestive of this viewpoint are presented in Lewis (1929), where it is maintained that concepts do not develop; one just leaps from one form of understanding to another. Is this the viewpoint that Hamlyn holds?

latter. Although one cannot gainsay Toulmin aligning himself where he will, I am quite convinced that Piaget would find Toulmin's characterization of his position aberrant. Of course, Piaget would reject the view that the criteria of knowledge can be established definitively by "conceptual analysis," entirely in advance of an examination and understanding of the accepted forms of knowledge in the different sciences. Even with regard to those philosophers—logicians and "normaticians"—whose work he tends to look on with some favor, Piaget would surely hold that their attempts to formalize the structure of knowledge-seeking inquiry should be founded on the activities of the scientists who pursue such inquiry, and not articulated *ab extra* as prescriptive for such inquiry. If Hamlyn would argue otherwise—as Toulmin suggests he would—then there would indeed be a conflict between Piaget and him on this issue. I find it hard to believe, however, that Hamlyn would seriously so argue.

But it is another question entirely whether Piaget would maintain that the criteria of knowledge, let us say, in physics, biology, or sociology, depend, for their definitive establishment, on discovering what is, in fact, involved in the course of "learning" or "coming-to-know," *tout court* (that is, as studied by psychologists of learning), or in learning or coming-to-know about physics, biology, and psychology during ontogenesis or cultural history. He may do so, but I doubt it; and if he does, I would think he is surely mistaken. Such an assumption would collapse the distinction between investigator's (psychologists') norms and subject norms which Piaget takes such pains to assert, and indeed make it impossible to arrive at criteria of valid psychological knowledge without first studying in some undisciplined and unregulated way the child's learning or coming-to-know about psychology.

It is yet a different question whether *a general theory of cognition* can be established solely by considering the mentation of adult scientists, and disregarding as irrelevant to such a theory all other forms of understanding—including here, not only infantile and child modes of thought, but also the modes of thought of schizophrenics, individuals in oneiric or hypnagogic states, persons who suffer from brain injury, archaic or preliterate modes of thought, and so on. (See Werner, 1957; Werner & Kaplan, 1956; 1963; B. Kaplan, 1966; 1967; Wallon, 1942; Cassirer, 1953–1957.) Piaget would surely argue against the legitimacy of such an exclusivist theory, and so would Toulmin. But who advocates such a general theory, limited to advanced thought? Does Hamlyn maintain that a general theory of cognition can ignore modes of thought or forms of understanding other than those manifested by the scientist *qua* scientist, or, in the extreme case, by the logician *qua* logician?

C. How Does One Arrive at a Description of the Development of Some Form of Understanding? On this major issue my sympathies are far more with Hamlyn than with Toulmin. I, too, find it difficult to know what to make of Toulmin's claim that one cannot analyze the criteria for recognizing when a process is completed, in a final and definitive form, until the actual course of the process has been studied. If the concept of "development" is to be given a meaning other than simply whatever takes place in the course of time, then it seems obvious to me that to study the "process" of development requires that one accept or posit a *telos*. Without such a *telos* in mind, one would not know what to look for in ontogenesis or culture history. This is not to say that the *telos* is a kind of end state acting as a "cause" (see Taylor, 1964, p. 3), or that the *telos* need be conscious, or even actually operative, in the subject, or an historical process. Rather, at the very least, a *telos* must be posited by the investigator—and it is this *telos* that governs the reconstruction of the "process of development." From this, it follows, of course, that an investigator who adopts a different *telos* as operative in the subject under consideration will arrive at a different "process of development." One further point, perhaps on the side of Toulmin: There is little doubt that an investigator who posits a *telos* to guide his inquiries and his analysis may be led, in his reconstruction of the "process of development," to refine or more fully articulate the *telos* that, at the outset, may have been tacit or relatively unarticulated. For example, this appears to have taken place with regard to Freud's criterion of "genitality" as the ideal terminus of psychosexual development.

In connection with this reconstruction of a developmental sequence, Hamlyn has, it seems to me, done a service by calling attention to the possibility, and indeed the likelihood, that an investigator may be tempted to look at ontogenetically, or historically, earlier phenomena as if they were destined to the end to which they finally come; at least he will analyze them with respect to this end. In other words, a developmental perspective conduces to a consideration of earlier phases or stages in terms of the accepted or posited *telos*, rather than as "immediate to God," and worthy of consideration and analysis without regard for a later adult, or subsequent, state of affairs.

D. Can Forms of Understanding (Conceptual Systems) in Children Be Fruitfully Investigated in Analytic Isolation from the Ambient Social Milieux? Both Hamlyn and Toulmin chastise Piaget for hoping adequately to determine the "mechanisms" of intellectual adaptation in the child without proper regard for the diversity of physical and social environments in which different children grow up. Such a criticism of Piaget is, of course, not new. More than thirty years ago, English psychologists (for example, S. Isaacs, V. Hazlitt) leveled the same kind of attack on Piaget's early work. Surely, such objections have some merit, insofar as Piaget has occasionally suggested that certain forms of understanding emerge at particular ages, and not before or after. Indeed, under the impact of Isaacs' criticism, Piaget was prompted to make it clear that the particular age of acquisition of a specific form of understanding was of only secondary interest to him, and might well vary as a function of a host of conditions, including affective and social ones; his primary focus was on the determination and explanation of the *sequence* of forms of understanding. As is well known, in both his earlier and later work, Piaget has presented pictures of the child's construction of reality which take such sequences to be invariant "stages."

The emphasis on invariant sequences rather than particular ages in the acquisition of forms of understanding does not change the issue. The question still remains whether assertions about invariant sequences are compromised or vitiated by Piaget's manifest unconcern for the specificities of the social-affective contexts in which his subjects dwell. How is it possible for Piaget, or anyone else, to maintain that there are invariant sequences in the child's conception of reality, space, time, number, causality, morality, etc., without examining representative samples of children of different ages from a representative sampling of social environments?

Clearly, if it were maintained that one arrives at a thesis about invariant sequences of forms of understanding in ontogenesis through inductive procedures, then a failure to study children from diverse environments would constitute a methodological oversight of considerable proportions. Moreover, even if one undertook the variety of cross-cultural and cross-subcultural studies needed to provide a firmer underpinning for inductive generalizations concerning invariant sequences, any such generalizations—as Hamlyn rightly points out—would be contingent and provisional, subject to change, alteration, or rejection given further empirical study on children growing up under different environmental circumstances.

That invariant sequences in the ontogenesis of forms of understanding are proposed in the absence of studies sampling the widest variety of environments, already suggests that the proposal does not rest on inductive grounds; that such invariant sequences are taken somehow to be necessary, further indicates that the thesis—whatever claims are made for it—cannot be supported by mere empirical generalizations. Without arguing the case in detail, it seems to me that any claim for an invariant sequence—a necessary order of emergence—must rest either on a genetic (nativistic) argument concerning a hierarchy of dispositions (that is, evidence showing that putative later forms in the sequence cannot be manifested in the absence or suppression of earlier forms); or, on evidence of a logical order showing that the putative later forms presuppose the "earlier" forms. In the last instance, one would, in effect, be stating what is meant by the development of intelligence—the development of forms of understanding—empirical phenomena being used merely to illustrate that theoretical possibilities are in fact actualized. Whatever may be overtly stated in this matter, I believe that anyone who asserts necessary invariant sequences is ultimately resting his case on one or another of these grounds. It is for this reason that there is no need to sample diverse and heterogeneous social environments in order to arrive at the thesis of an invariant sequence. Whether any of these grounds can themselves be grounded is another matter.

V. Conclusion

There are many more issues raised by Hamlyn and Toulmin that are worthy of serious discussion, but this commentary has long exceeded its bounds. Let me bring it to a close with a final observation—at least a self-admonition and perhaps an admonition to others. If we are to talk intelligently about knowledge and its acquisition, it may be useful to remind ourselves of T. H. Huxley's remark: "If a little knowledge is dangerous, where is the man who has so much as to be out of danger."

References

Apostel, L. Psychogenése et logiques non classique. In F. Bresson (Ed.), *Psychologie et épistémologie génétiques: Thèmes Piagetiens.* Dunod, Paris: 1966.

Ayer, A. J. *The problem of knowledge.* Baltimore: Penguin, 1956.

Baldwin, J. M. *Thought and things.* Vol. 1. London: Macmillan, 1901.

Berger, P. & Luckmann, T. *The social construction of reality* New York: Doubleday (Anchor), 1966.

Black, M. *Problems of analysis.* Ithaca, New York: Cornell Univ. Press, 1954.

Blanshard, B. *The nature of thought.* Vol. 1. New York: Macmillan, 1939.

Bosanquet, B. *Logic: Or the morphology of knowledge.* London and New York: Oxford Univ. Press, 1888. 2 vols.

Brunswik, E. Ontogenetic and other developmental parallels to the history of science. In H. M. Evans (Ed.), *Men and moments in the history of science.* Seattle: Univ. of Washington Press, 1959. Pp. 3–21.

Cassirer, E. *Substanzbegriff und Funktionsbegriff.* Berlin: B. Cassirer, 1910.

Cassirer, E. *Das Erkenntnisproblem.* Berlin: B. Cassirer, 1903–1920. 3 vols.

Cassirer, E. *The problem of knowledge.* Vol. IV. Translated by W. Woglum & C. Hendel. New Haven, Connecticut: Yale Univ. Press, 1950.

Cassirer, E. *The philosophy of symbolic forms.* Translated by R. Manheim. New Haven, Connecticut: Yale Univ. Press, 1953–1957. 3 vols.

Cornford, F. M. *Principium sapientiae.* Cambridge: Cambridge Univ. Press, 1952.

Dewey, J. *Logic: The theory of inquiry.* New York: Holt, 1938.

Eliade, M. *Myth and reality*. New York: Harper (Torchbooks), 1963.

Gewirth, A. The distinction between analytic and synthetic truths. *Journal of Philosophy*, 1953, **55,** 397–425.

Gurvitch, G. *Les cadres sociaux de la connaissance*. Paris: Presses Univ. de France, 1966.

Guthrie, W. K. C. *In the beginning*. Ithaca, New York: Cornell Univ. Press, 1957.

Hobhouse, L. T. *Theory of knowledge*. London: Macmillan, 1888.

Hobhouse, L. T. *Mind in evolution*. London: Macmillan, 1912.

Horowitz, I. L. *Philosophy, science and sociology of knowledge*. Springfield, Illinois: Thomas, 1961.

Kaplan, A. Freud and modern philosophy. In *The new world of philosophy*. New York: Vintage, 1963.

Kaplan, B. The comparative developmental approach and its application to symbolization and language in psychopathology. In S. Arieti (Ed.), *American handbook of psychiatry*. Vol. III. New York: Basic Books, 1966. Pp. 659–688.

Kaplan, B. Meditations on genesis. *Human Development*, 1967, **10,** 65–87.

Kaplan, B. Strife of systems: The tension between organismic and developmental points of view. Unpublished manuscript. (Submitted on invitation in 1967 for publication in a volume of essays in honor of L. von Bertalanffy.)

Lewis, C. I. *Mind and the world order*. New York: Scribners, 1929.

Lovejoy, A. O. *Revolt against dualism*. Lasalle, Ill.: Open Court, 1930.

Oppenheimer, J. K. E. von Baer's beginning insights into causal-analytical relationships during development. *Developmental Biology*, 1963, **7,** 11–21.

Piaget, J. *Introduction a l'épistémologie génétique*. Paris: Presses Univ. de France, 1950. 3 vols.

Piaget, J. Genetic psychology and epistemology. *Diogenes*, 1952, **1,** 49–63.

Piaget, J. Programme et methodes de l'épistémologie génétique. In E. W. Beth, W. Mays, & J. Piaget (Eds.), *Épistémologie génétique et recherche psychologique*. Études d'épistémologie génétique, 1. Paris: Presses Univ. de France, 1957. Pp. 2–84.

Piaget, J. Défense de l'épistémologie génétique. In E. W. Beth, J. B. Grize, *et al.* (Eds.), *Implication, formalisation et logique naturelle*. Études d'épistémologie génétique, 16. Paris: Presses Univ. de France, 1962. Pp. 165–191.

Piaget, J. *Sagesse et illusions de la philosophie*. Paris: Presses Univ. de France, 1965.

Pringle-Pattison, A. S. Epistemology. In J. M. Baldwin (Ed.), *Dictionary of philosophy and psychology*. Vol. 1. London: Macmillan, 1906. Pp. 333–336.

Quine, W. Two dogmas of empiricism. *Philosophical Review*, 1951, **55,** 20–41.

Reid, L. A. *Ways of knowledge and experience*. London: Allen & Unwin, 1961.

Rudner, R. Formal and non-formal. *Philosophy of Science*, 1949, **16,** 41–48.

Scriven, M. The logic of criteria. *Journal of Philosophy*, 1960, **58,** 857–868.

Sigwart, C. *Logic*. New York: Macmillan, 1894–1895. 2 vols.

Snell, B. *The discovery of mind*. Cambridge, Massachusetts: Harvard Univ. Press, 1953.

Taylor, C. *The explanation of behaviour*. New York: Humanities Press, 1964.

Waismann, F. Analytic-synthetic. *Analysis*, 1949–1951, **10–11.**

Wallon, H. *De l'acte a la pensée*. Paris: Flammarion, 1942.

Wartofsky, M. *Conceptual foundations of scientific thought*. New York: Macmillan, 1968.

Werner, H. *Comparative psychology of mental development*. New York: International Univ. Press, 1957.

Werner, H., & Kaplan, B. The development approach to cognition: its relevance to the psychological interpretation of anthropological and ethnolinguistic data. *American Anthropologist*, 1956, **58,** 866–880.

Werner, H., & Kaplan, B. *Symbol formation*. New York: Wiley, 1963.

White, M. G. The analytic and synthetic—an untenable dualism. In S. Hook (Ed.), *John Dewey: Philosopher of science and freedom*, New York: Dial Press, 1950. Pp. 316–330.

Wood, L. Recent epistemological schools. In V. Ferm (Ed.), *A history of philosophical systems*. New York: Philosophical Library, 1950. Pp. 516–538.

Wundt, W. *Logik*. Stuttgart: Enke, 1880.

Part II

Basic Issues in the Psychology of Cognitive Development

A. The Development of Physical Concepts

THE DEVELOPMENT OF PHYSICAL CONCEPTS [1]

Harry Beilin

Long after their formal academic divorce, philosophy and psychology still maintain a close if difficult relationship. Although psychology forced itself away from philosophy, some influential philosophers have been quite skeptical of psychology as a source for adding either knowledge or truth to philosophical inquiry (for example, Broad, 1925). Similarly, most psychologists consider philosophy of little use in their activities. The most radical position is represented by antitheoretical behaviorists who reject any theorizing, not because theory is impossible in psychology, but in the belief that it is premature considering the state of the science. Other psychologists, less radical on the issue, engage in a good deal of philosophizing in the guise of psychological theorizing. The distinction between psychology and philosophy in these instances is difficult to make. An example of this is to be seen in the recent discussion in a psychological journal of "the proper meaning of the term stimulus" (Hocutt, 1967; Gibson, 1967). Nevertheless, it is the rare psychologist who feels that his primary activity as a psychologist has any direct consequence for problems in philosophy. The exception is Piaget, who in fact prefers to be characterized more as an epistemologist than as a psychologist. The basis for this preference rests on the claim that the nature of knowledge is related to how knowledge is acquired. He uses the term genetic epistemology,[2] an old one to philosophy, to characterize his position. Certain features of this claim will be examined in this paper

[1] The author's experiments referred to in this paper were, except for one study, supported by grants from The National Institute of Child Health and Human Development, HD-00925-01-08.

[2] The term "genetic" is ambiguous as understood in English and as used in this context. The sense in which it is used by psychologists is closer in meaning to "ontogenetic" or "developmental" than to genetic inheritance or gene function as such. "Developmental" has superseded "genetic" in general use, at least among American psychologists. In philosophy, "genetic" often refers to the origins of knowledge whether developmental or otherwise.

through an examination of Piaget's account of how the child develops a conception of physical reality.

A distinction should be made first between Piaget's general theory and the subtheories which account for specific categories of development, such as moral development, the development of concepts of physical space, and others.

I. Aspects of General Theory

The study of cognitive development usually takes the form of investigations into conceptual development, conceptual behavior, concept formation, and concept attainment. Common interest is in the concept. The concept has become the epistemological "unit" of analysis in psychology as it is in analytic philosophy. Piaget's interest in concept formation and concept development, however, is subsidiary to an interest in the mechanisms whose operations result in concepts as end products. Two consequences result from this emphasis. First, it places Piaget squarely among the mentalists in that these mechanisms and processes are inferred entities created to explain observed behavior. Second, the emphasis upon covert mechanisms and processes has led to the characterization of an active process organism, although this is not a necessary consequence of taking a mentalist position.[3]

These days, the mentalism of Piagetian theory is not unique among psychological theories. The rebirth of interest in cognitive psychology reflects a renaissance of mentalist philosophizing within psychology. The contemporary concern with cognition[4] has directly subverted traditional behavioristic psychology through the updating introduction of notions such as "mediating responses" and "verbal mediation" into stimulus–response theories. Even though such covert mediation is usually couched in

[3] Piaget is apparently not too concerned about being found in the "mentalist" camp. He says, in characterizing a group of developmental theorists with whom he ostensibly associates himself, "Not being afraid of a certain 'mentalism' which the aforementioned theorists proscribe [he refers here to behavioristic learning theorists] they substitute for a single behavioral action the idea of 'conduct' which they define, in common with Janet and many others, as behavior plus the internalized activity which accompanies various forms of 'being conscious' " (Piaget, 1968b, p. 176).

Fodor (1968) argues also that the mentalist position is not inconsistent with materialism in that mentalist terms created to account for behavior may in turn find an adequate explanation in neurological structures and events.

[4] One must distinguish between cognitive theory and cognitive process. Many behaviorists recognize the existence of cognition (which they express as cognitive behavior), but use noncognitive theories to explain them.

response language, its very covertness adds mentalist baggage to the usual behaviorism. As Chomsky's analysis of Skinner's work on language also shows (Chomsky, 1959), mentalism has entered into the behaviorists' thinking in even more subtle and uninvited ways.

Mentalist concepts in Piaget's theory enter as terms of great generality (for example, assimilation), and also as terms of more limited applicability (for example, conservation). Those of more limited applicability have been more readily acceptable to psychologists. The notion of "conservation" is widely discussed, while the more general and more theoretically important concept of "equilibration" is less noted and presumably less readily accepted. It is not entirely clear whether this is because the more general type of concept is theoretically unacceptable, whether its presentation by Piaget is too difficult to understand, or because the possibilities for empirical tests are so much more remote. In the "conservation" case, the term is readily tied to very specific experimental manipulations and observable behavior,[5] whereas with "equilibration," and like terms, a connection to empirical data is much more difficult to demonstrate convincingly. At the same time, many complain of the difficulty of Piaget's exposition, while not a few openly reject the theory.

Whether mentalistic concepts aid in explaining behavior, that is, in providing adequate understanding of the regularities in intellectual functioning, is still a very lively philosophic issue. For many psychologists the question is academic, since this type of explanation is stimulating an enormous amount of broad-ranging research. The more specific question of whether Piagetian explanation is the most appropriate or adequate to given aspects of behavior, also produces spirited discussion and is being dealt with issue by issue. With conservation, for example (wherein a quantitative concept such as length is conceived as invariant in the face of perceived alterations in the position or form of an object of a particular length), some behavioristically oriented investigators argue that "learning sets" or "attentional learning" mechanisms (Gelman, 1969; Kingsley & Hall, 1967) more adequately explain the conservation phenomenon than the Piagetian "operations" or "reversibility by compensation" and "reversibility by inversion." Although alternative behavioristic explanations are tied to particular experimental procedures and results, they can still be characterized as instances of mentalistic concepts, since the explanations refer equally to inferred entities or processes beyond the scope of direct observation, and are not at the same time theories of neurological process.

The mechanisms of thought, then, are the central concern of Piaget's

[5] This has not prevented some gross confusions from appearing in the experimental literature, however. For the discussion of one such example, see Beilin (1968).

psychological system.[6] For both his psychology and his theory of knowledge, however, these mechanisms have to be seen in the perspective of a constructivist epistemology. Piaget consistently makes a point of rejecting aprioristic theories of knowledge (and nativist theories in psychology), as well as radical empiricist theories of knowledge (and behaviorist theories in psychology). One might suppose that logical empiricism or the oft-cited ascription of Kantianism would satisfactorily describe the Piagetian position. Although elements of both logical empiricism and Kantianism are to be found in his theories, Piaget himself finds the essential tenets of these positions unsatisfactory.

For him, "that which is knowable and that which changes during the genesis of knowledge is the relation between the knowing subject and the object known" (Inhelder, 1962). Knowledge is constructed out of the intrinsically (natively) given structures of the organism (or intrinsically given laws) which interact with the products of experience. The construction (knowledge) is not defined wholly by the innately given structures, since knowledge is changed and affected by experience. Nor is knowledge solely a product of experience with an objectively given reality, since the utilization of data of the world is determined in part by the nature and status of the organism at the time he contacts reality. In this interaction the subject is active. His action is not a reflexive (that is, passive) response to the environment by virtue of the operation of some instinctual program, nor does he respond to his experience simply by registering and representing that experience through some form of sensationally based mental imagery. Piaget is sometimes accused of idealism, particularly by Russian psychologists, because his constructions are more than a copy of reality, that is, they are a product of a subjective component determined by the particular maturational and genetic status of the organism. Piaget's constructivism, as he sees it, is neither idealist nor realist, since the construction of knowledge relies on two sources of data, the available structures of mind and the products of experience.

The construction of knowledge, more specifically, takes place through the operation of two general processes under the control of an internal self-

[6] Piaget's intent, at least in the ultimate case, is to refer to the "real substrate" of behavior or physiological function. Even the abstract models he constructs, which are probabilistic, algebraic, or logical, he conceives as an attempt to explain "real" operations or causal relations. "If (the) model is itself 'abstract,' the term abstract means simply 'common' to the different conceivable 'real' models" (Piaget, 1968b, p. 179). Piaget differentiates his abstract models from the type used by Hull and others, which he characterizes as the application of an existing logical system in the process of formalizing a theory. He feels the developmental type of explanation with which he is concerned lends itself to a particular form of abstract model and does not require the application of an existing but external abstract system.

regulating mechanism (*equilibration*). The first of these is the *assimilation* process. It involves the incorporation of environmental data (through physical or mental activity) into existing cognitive structures. The products of new experience are incorporated into mind only to the extent that they are consistent with existing structure.[7] Since the infant is born with an existing repertoire of innate reflexive mechanisms, these provide the original base to which experience is assimilated. The other process under the control of the equilibrating mechanism is *accommodation*. This represents the subject's response to external stimulation by which existing cognitive structures are effectively utilized for adaptive purposes by becoming integrated with other internal structures or by differentiating as they are applied to new experience. "It is the process by which the individual adapts, modifies or applies its inner organization to the particular environmental reality . . ." (Furth, 1969, p. 245). In most situations in which the organism functions, both assimilative and accommodative aspects of development take part, although one process dominates, depending upon the demands of reality. Play activity, particularly symbolic play, for example, is interpreted as an assimilative activity. Memory, in the sense of evoking a past event, on the other hand, is accommodative in that only existing structures are brought to bear upon a particular event. Furth (1969), a leading interpreter of Piagetian theory, attributes to assimilation the active constructive role by which the data from experience are transformed and integrated with already generalized cognitive structures. He associates accommodative activity with the application of available structures to individual events that results in the differentiation of these structures. Parenthetically, in emphasizing the differentiating features of accommodative activity, Furth tends to overlook the role of accommodative processes in problem solving wherein the coordination and integration of existing structures plays a significant role. It is probably the case that many types of deductive reasoning involve this integrating type of accommodative activity. Additionally, in the kind of propositional thinking that occurs in mathematics, accommodative activity can occur quite independently of the demands of external reality. That is, it can occur in response to data generated by the thought process itself. While Piaget recognizes the existence of such abstract thought, he gives little direct attention to it and deals instead with thinking that is generated in response to external demands. This may account, in part, for his insistence upon recourse to the data of experience, a point that many of his early critics were inclined to ignore.

[7] Generalized dimensions of action or objects are assimilated, not specific acts or objects (Furth, 1969).

Interestingly enough, Piaget has been rarely criticized for the environmentalist aspects of his theory. He is more often characterized (and usually for the wrong reasons) as a nativist. I will argue, however, that Piaget is *at least by implication* a preformationist, and more specifically, a maturationist. If he is not so by his own description, his data suggest that he should be (Beilin, 1969b). The reason for this is that the course of cognitive development delineated by Piaget and his co-workers, and confirmed in a variety of independent studies, is that of a fixed sequence of stages. Each stage is represented as a qualitatively different organization of cognitive functions that emerges out of the amalgamation of past structures and contemporary experience. The invariant sequence of stages is immune to environmental influence, although the onset of a stage varies with social and cultural conditions. A fixed developmental sequence which is impervious to environmental influence must be in large measure under the control of some type of species-specific genetic programming, since the alternative probability of consistent cultural experience in a wide variety of social environments is small. The transaction with the environment that Piaget emphasizes so strongly is, then, only facilitative. It provides the data from which knowledge is constructed, but the structuring is in accord with rules specified in the genetic program that controls intellectual functioning, in a manner probably analogous to the way genetic programming controls the development of morphological and physiological properties of the species. Piaget argues that such notions do not account for the origin of new knowledge or for novelty, which his theory is specifically designed to do (Piaget, 1969). In regard to this, it is necessary to distinguish between two types of novelty—species novelty and individual novelty. In the development of intelligence or cognition, novelty, in the sense of developing new processes or mechanisms of thought (for example, induction), is likely to be a very rare event in the history of the species. Such novelty is to be accounted for by the same propositions that explain the evolution of the species and the emergence of novel species qualities, namely, theories of genetic coding, natural selection, mutation, and so on. Novelty in individual cognition can be thought of in two senses. When novelty occurs as the rare event in which a process change occurs, then it is explicable in the same evolutionary terms as indicated above. The more usual individual novelty, however, is in the content of ideas, not in the processes of thought. Whereas the processes of thought are under rather strict genetic control, particular concepts (including class concepts) are generated, at least in part, in response to environmental events. The possibilities for creating new concepts are practically unlimited. These concepts, however, are the products of thought and although novel categories of such concepts are constantly constructed, they still function in relation to "biological" controls that govern the function of the pure fundamental thought processes. Thus, it is quite reasonable to accept that the self-regulating mechanism basic to intellectual development, posited by Piaget, requires the nutriments of experience for the realization of the possibilities that inhere in genetic structure.

Since specific knowledge of physical reality requires data from the external world, it is trivial to assert that experience is necessary to the acquisition of knowledge. The more fundamental question is in what way, if any, experience affects or influences the natively given processes that control the processes of thought. The question becomes one of whether experience acts as the stimulus for the evocation of innate ideas, or provides the material out of which innate dispositions or faculties construct ideas.

It was Locke's attack upon innate ideas that set the stage for modern arguments, and inasmuch as his views involve developmental issues they are of particular interest here (Fraser, 1894). First, Locke challenged those who held to the innate idea thesis to name any idea that might not be referred to the data of experience. Then, since some ideas characterized as innate (for example, identity, substance, God) never become conscious to *some* men, and *no* men are conscious of these ideas at birth, it followed for Locke that there are no innate ideas. (The latter is predicated on the supposition that an idea cannot be in the mind without the mind being conscious of it, a notion attacked by Leibniz but still far from dead.)

Fraser (1894) comments that it is difficult to find anyone who would have denied these two points. Maybe, he says, Locke had Descartes in mind, but by an innate idea Descartes means something antecedent to all experience, potential in the constitution of the understanding and not necessarily in consciousness. This means only that the mind has an innate faculty for universal ideas. Though this is one of the things Descartes means by innate ideas, Keeling (1968) shows that, while Descartes is not fully clear on the issue, he does include in discussing what is innate about ideas the notion that it is ideas themselves which may be innate. "Primitive" geometrical ideas which involve no affirmation or denial for their verification (Keeling, 1968, p. 182) are in this category. In addition to certain specific ideas being innate, Descartes considers our thinking about ideas as innate. The difficulty in Descartes' theory of innateness arises, not from postulating a tendency that is innate, but from postulating a special class of ideas "which is the proper business of this capacity to reinstate in mind from time to time" (Keeling, 1968, p. 184). At the same time, Descartes is explicit that he does not mean that the child is born consciously thinking about certain ideas (for example, equality).

The fundamental question is whether the rationalist position requires that specific ideas be innate. While Piaget implies that it does, it is not at all clear why this should be so. It is perfectly reasonable to accept as innate only the faculty or disposition to have certain ideas, and to hold that experience furnishes suitable occasions for arousing the innate capacity or provides the occasion and material for the construction of ideas. It is this view that Chomsky expresses: "There is nothing incomprehensible in the view that stimulation provides the occasion for the mind to apply certain innate interpretive principles, certain concepts that proceed from the 'power of understanding' itself, from the faculty of thinking rather than from external objects directly" (Chomsky, 1968, p. 72). Chomsky is incorrect, however, in characterizing Locke's position as a caricature of rationalism since, as already indicated, Descartes does specify some classes of ideas as innate.[8]

The constructionist position of Piaget can be incorporated into a rationalist epistemology. Piaget himself accepts that the child is born with innately given precognitive structures that dominate his early functions. He also holds that biological adaptive processes never cease to function in the human repertoire and implies that the process of *equilibration* itself is biologically determined. One may assume, then, that the mechanisms of cognitive construction are under similar control and that innate systems of rules regulate the manner in which ideas are generated by the mind. Progressive cognitive construction in an order, suggested by Piaget, is consistent with such a formulation. It is a hypothesis that Chomsky apparently accepts too, for he defines as a research goal for psycholinguists the revelation of "a succession of maturational stages leading finally to a full generative grammar" (Chomsky, 1968, p. 76), and the development of hypotheses "about initial (linguistic) structure rich enough to account for the fact that a specific grammar is constructed by the child. . ." These selected quotations may not be sufficient to make a constructivist out of Chomsky, any more than my arguments may be successful in making a nativist out of Piaget—but what I am proposing is a view that might be called "constructive rationalism," a view that better defines the acquisition of knowledge in the child than does interactionism or transactionalism, with its apparent contradictions.[9]

[8] Keeling quotes from Descartes' letter to Mersenne: "I hold that all those (primitive geometrical ideas) which involve no affirmation or denial are innate in us, for the organs of sense bring us nothing like the idea that arises in us on the occasion (of their instantiation) and so these ideas must have been in us beforehand" (Adam & Tannery, Vol. III, p. 418, quoted in Keeling, 1968, p. 182). Also, see Fraser (1959, Footnote, p. 39) on innateness in Locke's argument.

[9] Piaget holds, as did Locke, that any recourse to nativism is a "lazy" way out of solving important problems (Piaget, 1968a). It is quite clear, however, that the task of providing adequate nativist models is anything but easy. The efforts of molecular

II. Perception and Cognition

Even for the rationalist, then, it is an important question how the data of experience enter into the construction of knowledge. There are many possible explanations, assuming that consensus is possible on what is meant by knowledge. [The recent controversy between Chomsky and Putnam, Goodman and Ryle (Chomsky, 1968, 1969) adds a contemporary note to the latter perennial issue.]

The most common approach to explaining how experience eventuates in thought, at least common to such empiricists as Locke and Hume, is to start with the registration of sensation from external and internal stimulation. Sensation is translated either directly or indirectly into perceptual data. Perceptual data, considered often as representations of reality, are then acted upon to create concepts. Knowledge may thus be differentiated into perceptual knowledge and conceptual knowledge, although in some instances they are considered as two aspects of the same kind of knowledge. As a rule, sensation in itself is not considered to provide direct knowledge.

At least two issues are involved here. One concerns sensation and perception as sources of knowledge; the other, the nature and role of representation. As to the first issue, Piaget denies the differentiation between perceptual and conceptual knowledge by, in effect, introducing cognition into perceptual activity. Without denying the significance of "perceptual activity," he does deny that such activity leads to knowledge without the intervention of "operativity" (Furth, 1969). Since perceptual activity is inconceivable without operativity, perception becomes one aspect of the process by which (cognitive) knowledge develops. Operativity refers to the active aspects of cognition. It denotes those cognitive structures and functions that yield generalized forms of intellectual action such as are involved in constructing (for example, classes and relations), transforming (for example, transitivity relations), and incorporating the elements of thought (for example, whole–part relations and numerical operations). A critical feature of intellectual operations is their reversible nature, that is, an operation once carried out can be negated by an inverse action. For example, the displacement of an object in a particular direction for a measurable distance can be reversed by an inverse displacement that returns the object to its original position. Operative knowledge is constructed, however, from "figurative" elements, that is, from organizations

---

biologists, ethologists, and generative linguists attest to this fact. One might just as easily say that recourse to experience is the coward's way out, since it avoids facing up to the delineation of the biological mechanisms by which intellectual development occurs.

of sensory data. "Perceptual activity" is considered distinct because data so obtained are not transformed directly into knowledge. Only by being acted upon in an operation do perceptual data become objects of knowing, and become part of the operation itself by being assimilated to it. In figurative perception, however, the organism registers sensory input and responds to it by applying existing structures (that is, accommodates to it), but it does not incorporate the sensory data into the existing system of structures and so does not in any way generalize the experience, as when it is assimilated. Even in these instances, perception is not a passive encounter with external stimulation. Instead, perceptual experience is "constructive" in the sense that existing schemata undergo change, usually as a differentiation of the schema and the response. New, more differentiated, schemata emerge even though sensory data add nothing of a generalizable nature to existing structures.

As evidence for this view, Piaget cites observations which show that only after an infant develops eye–hand coordination, which is a sign of the development of sensory–motor schemata, is he capable of choosing the larger of two objects in conditions where the apparent size of the larger object is smaller to the child. In such instances, perceptual data themselves provide no adequate "knowledge" of reality unless the data are integrated into an operational or preoperational system. Studies of optical illusions and the perceptual constancies provide, although not unequivocally, further evidence for Piaget that perceptual activity does not of necessity lead to veridical responding without the intervention of operational thinking.

The source of knowledge, then, is not sensation or perception as such, but action in the form of implicit or internal mental activity. While the schemata of thought have their origin in sensory–motor coordinations that involve physical action upon objects, as in grasping, pulling, and pushing, these actions later are carried out covertly. An example of such mental action is covert grouping, not of actual objects, but of their attributes. While perceptual activity comes increasingly under the control of logical and prelogical operations, perceptual activity remains in the individual a probabilistically functioning process. Operative knowledge, on the other hand, is absolutistic, being closer to logical "certainty" and universal generalizability.

While perception and, in addition, imagery and imitation, play significant roles in the development of true knowledge, that is, operative knowledge, they nevertheless represent a distinctly different class as instruments of figurative knowing. While these functions are important in the activities of the very young child, it is not until they become associated with the development of reversible operations, which occurs about the ninth month, that they can be identified as part of what is human intelligence and knowledge.

Distinctions between sensation, perception, and thought have a long history. So has the identification of knowledge with cognition and the denial of it to sensation. Perception is often considered in a unique and difficult intermediate position. Thus Locke saw "sensitive knowledge"—that is, sense perception which witnesses to the real existence of something outside sensation—as less certain than either "intuitive knowledge" (for example, our immediate intuition that "a circle is not a triangle") or "demonstrative knowledge" (for example, of geometrical theorems by deduction from intuitively certain axioms). In his view, knowledge comes not from sensation itself, but from relations among ideas that associate the elements of sensation. Further, certain knowledge is associated with the intuition, not of external reality, but of relations among ideas in the mind, and the unit of knowledge is the mental proposition (that which relates ideas).

These conceptions have been elaborated or argued in many different ways by philosophers since Locke. But, in spite of the diversity of viewpoints that can be found in modern philosophy, there seems to be some agreement among both empiricists and rationalists that while sensation provides the ultimate data of reality, these data do not in themselves constitute knowledge. Reason and thought are seen, by both rationalists and empiricists, as independent capacities largely autonomous from sensation. Reason makes contact with the world through sense impressions or images and is responsible for producing both knowledge and error.

The Piagetian position, like most others, takes sensation to be distinct, although to Piaget, no system, not even that of sensation, functions independently of existing structure. Even if Piaget does not agree with the Kantian *a priori* organization of sense impression, he does hold that the data of sensation have to be assimilated to existing organization to become knowledge. Perceptual activity, through which sensation functions, does not contribute to knowledge unless some kind of cognition enters into the operation. In this sense, Piaget is in accord with those philosophers who interpret perception as an activity that produces knowledge only when reason, thought, or understanding enters into it. Where he differs from them is in the assertion that perceptual knowledge, like any other operative knowledge, becomes knowledge only by being assimilated to existing structure. Again, Piaget is in agreement with those who hold that cognitive activity leads to certain knowledge, while perceptual activity as such is probabalistic.

III. Representation and Knowledge

The cognitive representation of experience plays an important role in theories of knowledge.[10] In Piaget's theory, it takes the form of motoric and kinesthetic representation, as visual or auditory imagery, and as linguistic and other types of symbolization. In most epistemologies, representation, if not actually knowledge itself, is the intermediate source of knowledge. It is the "object" which is stored and acted upon to become knowledge. In an even broader sense, ideas and knowledge itself may be conceived as representations of reality. In Piaget's system, representation is the end product of a process of knowledge acquisition, and not the origin of knowledge. As already indicated, the central process in thinking is the "operative function," by virtue of which sensory data become assimilated to existing structure. Existing structures, the most primitive of which are the organism's original mental equipment, are not themselves representations. When the individual, by virtue of an assimilative experience, makes a response to the environment, some representation of the total event occurs in the form of a symbol. The symbol has two aspects: the figurative (that is, involving some sensory or motor event), and the operative (referring to meaning, that is, to its significate). Both make it possible for the person to represent to himself events and actions not directly in his sensory or perceptual experience. Piaget considers that in a broad sense all operative thought may be considered "representational" in not being based upon direct perception or movement but on "a system of concepts or mental schemes" (Furth, 1969). In a more restricted sense, representation is associated with sensory, imaginal, and abstract symbols. Piaget considers these representations or systems of representation as instruments in the service of thought and not as thought itself. Language as one such system of representation is not the object of thought or the process by which thought takes place, but the outcome of the symbolic (thought) process. If a child is provided through instruction with the linguistic representation of a logical rule, this may sometimes enable him, as with an arithmetic algorithm, to solve a specific problem; but it will not necessarily generate a logical operation that is endowed with the intellectual flexibility to generalize to other problems of the same general form. Nor will it provide the reversible flexibility necessary to alter the form of the logical equation (Beilin, 1969a). Providing information to children in linguistic form thus leads to no necessary increase in understanding or knowledge. To take a specific example, explaining the concepts involved in the qualitative

[10] A discussion of various theories of representation as well as Piaget's conception of it is to be found in Furth (1968, 1969).

measurement of area to five-year-old children, through a variety of instructional methods, will lead to little success in the task as compared with doing the same with eight-year-old children who already have an operational system to which the verbal data can be assimilated (Beilin & Franklin, 1962). Only operativity in interaction with such symbolic representation will facilitate thought. There have been a great many experimental attempts in recent years to train very young children in a variety of logical operations (Sigel & Hooper, 1968). While these attempts are sometimes interpreted as efforts at comparing or testing training procedures, or as attempts to push down the age at which the child can begin to learn from instruction, their more important function is to test the imperviousness of mental development to environmental influence. The general inability of a variety of methods, including verbal ones, to do more than provide limited algorithms for the solution of specific problems attests to the powerful autonomy of the developing mental system. The inability of linguistic methods to do more than this provides evidence for the dependence of linguistic symbol systems on the development of a more fundamental cognitive structure (Beilin & Kagan, 1969).

Operational thinking is also critical for visual imagery. When, for example, the attention of a young child is directed to the level of water in a rectangular jar, or the same information is presented pictorially, continuous visual experience, or the experimenter's verbal specification of the rule that the water line remains horizontal irrespective of jar rotation, has practically no effect upon the child's knowledge of this phenomenon when he is less than five years of age. The ability to deal with pictorial representation, or with images when objects are not present, is not enhanced by such visual or verbal experience (Beilin, Kagan, & Rabinowitz, 1966). How children acquire the operative schemata relevant to this task is another question, of course; but when children lack the appropriate logical or prelogical operations, experience with objects and imagery itself is insufficient for knowledge of the physical phenomenon.

A persisting issue in the discussion of representation by epistemologists is whether representation is of the particular or the general. Thus, Locke held all ideas to be particular, but particular ideas could become general by being taken "representationally" as generic images. Descartes, on the other hand, held that one could "imagine" the particular, but not have a generic image. One could imagine (have the image of) a particular triangle of three sides, but one could only reason about a figure of 1000 sides. Kant dealt with this problem through his concept of the schema. Given the concept of a triangle of any number of sides, one could construct a schema which would show what the triangle looks like, and with that schema one could tell whether a given figure were a triangle by simply comparing it with the schema.

"Template matching" theories obviously have their origins in these ideas, as do some of Piaget's notions about schemata.

For Hume, all ideas were copies of impressions, and most empiricist theories after Hume adopt the copy feature of representation as a fundamental aspect of the development of ideas. Thus, Russell held that the constituents of thought, which correspond to the words of language, that is, of propositions, are images; Wittgenstein, on the other hand, was not willing to commit himself to what they are (Pears, 1967). Analytic philosophers who follow Wittgenstein think that Russell's recourse to images leads to unnecessary mentalism (Mischel, 1969), but Wittgenstein's unwillingness to specify the constituents of thought has only left an unsolved problem. The entire emphasis, in the analytic tradition, on language, leaves the relation between language and mind that much more of a puzzle.

Piaget's position differs from that of those philosophers who hold that thinking is with images or other representations (tokens) of the external world. Rather, the assimilative process directly involving operational activity yields images and symbols (including concepts) as the products of thought. The significate of the symbol is a concept, and it is only through concepts that symbolic thought can be said to represent external reality. The concept itself, then, is not thought but the product of a symbolic thought process. The concept in this sense makes it possible to have "representation" of both the particular and the general. Images may in a narrow sense "represent" a particular object, but they too are only a product of the symbolic function and not merely a trace of perception. Thus, representation is the product of an active process of mind, and not the imprint of a passive reception of sensory input. While images and motoric and kinesthetic products may represent particulars, linguistic and other symbols may represent concepts which are of the general. Piaget's conception may come closest to the Kantian notion of the schema, but in a strict sense a schema is not a representation.

In sum, the Piagetian conception of knowledge is based upon the following propositions:

1. Knowledge is constructed. It is not a copy of reality nor an interpretation of reality. It is constructed both from the data of experience and from data provided by the biological characteristics of the organism.

2. Knowledge is constructed in the mind of the individual by means of a self-regulating mental mechanism. This mechanism controls the functions of two processes. Assimilation involves the incorporation of the regularities (or general rules) of active experience into already existing mental structures. Experience is not sufficient for creating knowledge of the real world if the relevant structures are not available to incorporate the results of that

experience. The other process, accommodation, is one of applying or integrating already available structures or operations to new experience. Knowledge in this case is constructed out of the products of prior constructions.

3. The origin of thought is not to be found in the data of sensation or perception but in action, that is, in mental activity involving functions associated with prelogical and logical operations. Operativity, which may involve the use of sensory and perceptual data, leads to the construction of knowledge, while perceptual and sensory data *per se* do not.

4. The constructive nature of knowledge implies that the child or adult plays an active rather than passive role in creating knowledge. He is neither passive in his reasoning nor is he a passive recipient of stimulation from the physical world. The data of experience received through sensation and perception are not merely "representations" of reality. Rather, they are incorporated into and integrated with existing structures in the mind through the action of intellectual operations. These symbolic representations, whether sensory (kinesthetic, visual, auditory, etc.) or conceptual, are the products of, rather than the sources of, thought.

5. Development of the capacity to construct knowledge is a long process. It proceeds by stages in the development of the individual. Although experience with the real world is necessary for constructing knowledge, mental mechanisms and processes which become functional only with the maturation of the organism are equally necessary. This suggests that the mechanism by which thought processes develop is under the control of species-specific genetic programming, and while experience may have the effect of accelerating or delaying mental development, it will not alter its essential character.

With these considerations of Piaget's general theory as background, we can consider some of the details of the development of the child's conception of the physical world.

IV. Development of the Child's Concept of an Object

The child responds to the world of objects long before he develops a concept of objects. Yet the manner in which he deals with objects from the time of birth has a bearing upon his ultimate knowledge of the world. One of the principal features of the Piagetian contribution is the evidence that the origins of thought are to be seen in the child's behavior from birth to the time when the first evidence of intelligent action appears, dated somewhat arbitrarily at about the ninth or tenth month. While there is little intelligent behavior as such during the child's first months, the sensory–motor coordinations that are acquired during this period progressively elaborate into the elements of cognition. The concept of the object is among the first of these developments. The technique Piaget employs to determine whether a child has the concept of an object is deceptively simple. It is based upon the contrast of the child's behavior directed to objects that are present with his behavior toward objects that vanish. This approach is typical of his experimental method—he discovers or develops a task that elicits differential responding among children of different ages. These behaviors are analyzed from the age when children fail the tasks, through intermediate stages, to the age when the tasks are fully mastered. Piaget's emphasis is more on the qualitative nature of the response (physical as well as verbal) and what this implies about the child's thought, than upon success or failure in the task *per se*.

The general significance of the object concept is that a true conception of physical reality, of space, of substance, and of causal relations is dependent upon such a conception. Piaget starts by asking whether the infant's conception of the world is like the adult's with objects that have substance, permanence, and constant dimension. If the infant does not, and Piaget is convinced the evidence confirms they do not, then it is necessary to explain how such conceptions are acquired (Piaget, 1954).

The earliest relevant behavior appears within the first two weeks of life, when the infant shows that he is capable of finding the nipple and differentiating it from the surrounding integument. By the fifth or sixth week he smiles for familiar faces and acts with surprise or discomfort to strange sounds and images. These acts of differentiation and recognition, however, are not evidence that the world is segmented into objects, that is, have the properties of being "permanent, substantial, external to the self and firm in existence" (Piaget, 1954, p. 5). If object recognition were sufficient to a concept of the object, then such responsiveness, says Piaget, should be manifest also in a belief in the permanence of the object. What he observes, though, is that in the early months of life no manifestation of such a belief in object permanence is evident. While it is true that the elements of such a belief develop early, as in the coordination of sight and hearing (for example, the child tries to look at objects he hears), localization in space is not sufficient to confer objectivity on the thing that is both seen and heard. Although the child may pursue objects that he senses, these differ from a "true search" for the object, in that true search is active, while the infant's early looking patterns manifest only simple (passive) expectation, or the extention of interrupted action. In true search, the child introduces his own movements that go beyond those of the actions of the object.

The developmental progression of the object concept is such that in the earliest stages, the infant will pursue an object to the place where it disappears, and if the object does not reappear, he will soon give up looking. Later, when there is "search," but not "true search," the child reactivates earlier response patterns such as reflex sucking or staring at the place where his mother's image disappeared. In what Piaget characterizes as the third stage in object concept development, which appears between the third and sixth month, the child begins to grasp what he sees, and brings before his eyes objects he touches. These actions reflect a more progressive coordination between his visual and tactile competencies. It is not until the ninth or tenth month, however, that the child actively searches for vanished objects in conditions where he is able to remove solid materials that cover, obscure, or obstruct his path to the object.

Piaget draws an analogy, and a particularly purposeful one, between scientific methods of gaining knowledge and the methods used by the child in his efforts to form an objective conception of the world. In the realm of scientific activity, he observes, every *objective* phenomenon permits correct prediction, yet some *subjective* phenomena also yield correct prediction. In addition, some fortuitous events can lead to predictive success. We therefore require another condition for objectivity, namely, that the phenomenon has to lend itself to distinct experiments whose results are in accord with predictions. However, since some subjective qualities may be linked to constant physical properties (as is subjective color with the wavelengths of light), only a third condition can succeed in dissociating what is really objective from what is subjective. That condition is the deduction of the phenomenon from a total causal system. The child, says Piaget, achieves a conception of the objective world in analogous fashion. At first the object is only the extension of anticipation or prediction (through accommodative movements). Then at the point of intersection of various schemata, in which the object is assimilated to various courses of action (such as the search for the whole when only a part of it has been seen, and suppression of obstacles that prevent perception of the object), the child, in effect, tests his anticipations and predictions. These behavior patterns still do not connote true search or true objectivity, since in these instances the child still does not attribute independent existence or independent trajectories to the object, but acts as though they were only extensions of his own behavior. When the child is able to organize simultaneously a spatio–temporal network in which objects appear in a succession of events with a notion of cause and effect, then true search begins and objectivity is achieved. So, "only that phenomenon constitutes a real object which is connected in an intelligible way with the totality of a spatio–temporal and causal system. . ." (Piaget, 1954, p. 87). The evidence for this is seen when the child no longer grasps for objects where he first saw them, nor even where he last saw them before they disappeared, but can search for the object through a series of physical displacements. If the object is placed in a box which is then emptied under a cover, it will be searched for under the cover rather than in the box. The achievement of this level of competence in the object concept, in addition to reflecting true objectivity, represents the development of the first conceptual invariance and the foundation for the construction of reality.

This exposition of object concept development is designed to expose some of the difficulties as well as the strengths of Piaget's system.

First, the identification of the object concept as necessary to all conceptualization of the physical world is an important insight comparable to the philosophers' identification of substance as a basic unit in the analysis of physical reality. Without a concept of the permanent object there can be no invariance of other physical concepts, no conception of an objective world, and no conception of causality. While philosophers have traditionally concentrated on the achievement of ideas of space or substance as totalities, or on the differentiation of the particular from the universal, Piaget shifts the emphasis to the object concept as the more fundamental unit. He substantiates the necessity of this concept on both logical and empirical grounds.

Piaget then asks whether the child's conceptualization of the physical world is qualitatively the same as that of the adult. He makes the claim that it is not. Even actions that appear the same for both have to be interpreted differently because their significance changes with the context of actions that surround them. (This question is different from the traditional question as to whether the child is born with thoughts. What Piaget implies is that even if the child were born with thoughts, they would be different in kind from those of the adult.) Piaget thus delineates the defining attributes of the object concept that explain the differences between "advanced" and "primitive" behavior. The adultlike concept is evident in the behavior of "true search." In behavioral terms, true search is defined as action that continues when the object disappears, when the action proceeds through displacements, etc. With these behavioral criteria it is possible to eliminate false-positive instances, that is, instances that might be (legitimately) mistaken for the true concept. Movements, for example, that involve searching but lack initiated action, and are not continued independently of the movement of the object are rejected as instances of true search.

After the behavior patterns of children at primitive, intermediate, and advanced levels have been analyzed in terms of the defined attributes of the concept, their developmental patterns are interpreted in relation to concomitant behavioral developments (in the case of the object concept, causality and the ideas of substance and space are the concomitant developments). Finally, Piaget incorporates and interprets these developments into his more comprehensive theory involving the abstract functions of accommodation and assimilation.

One difficulty with this particular methodological approach is that it seems circular. The differences between behaviors at different ages are used as the basis for defining the concept. The object concept is thus defined as requiring "true search" which is typical only of the older child and adult. Once the concept is so defined, it is used to show that only the adult or older child has the concept. It is doubtful, however, whether this represents a real embarrassment to the theory or the method.

A more serious difficulty may be that it uses adult behavior as the criterion of reality. Acceptance of the adult view predicates that the child lacks conceptual knowledge of the object. The fact, for example, that the infant continues his quest for the nipple when it eludes him is not taken as evidence of an object concept because the movement is accommodative, that is, it represents the continued use of an existing action or schema in respect to the object and is not a new assimilative act. Some psychologists would question whether the actions of the infant are not "true search," even if they accept Piaget's characterization of the term's defining attributes.

A third difficulty is over the definition of the term. Some psychologists would maintain that the aforementioned simple perceptual action is sufficient evidence for the object concept. A variant of this argument is that the perception of the object at birth is directly translated into a "concept" of the object. The phenomenon involving true search would then be a more sophisticated type of cognition that should be identified by another name.

Whatever the merits of these alternative possibilities, the phenomenon Piaget attempts to characterize involves both the data of observation and an interpretive theory designed to explain the data. The notion of "true search" is part of a theoretical explanation created to account for the observed data. It is not necessary to ask whether the data sought out the theory or the theory sought out the data; together they constitute the method by which Piaget attempts to illuminate the issue. The data of observation cannot stand by themselves in this system any more than the theory. On this score, it is quite incorrect for some psychologists to characterize Piaget as a descriptive psychologist. His descriptions are too infused with explanation to be pure description. More often than not, psychologists who are of this opinion are simply willing to accept the "facts" but not the interpretations.

V. The Construction of Space

The child's construction of space does not rest exclusively upon the development of the object concept. The objectification of substance is only a part of a broader development in which the elaboration and construction of space itself is only a part. The totality of this development is associated with the acquisition of intellectual functions. It is also interpreted in relation to the controversy over innate and environmental influence.

> In wishing to reduce to the minimum the innate realities which serve as the point of departure for the construction of space, one cannot deny the existence of two fundamental facts: first, the very functioning of biological and psychological assimilation entails a priori an organization by groups; and second from the beginning of their activity the organs of perception apply this organization to the displacements they perceive (Piaget, 1954, p. 209).

The "group" referred to here is a "self-enclosed system of operations" so that within the system it is possible to return to the point of departure by some inverse operation. Every kind of psychological organization embodies these group operations, which constitute a totality of interdependent processes. The group embodies the main logical principle of these psychological organizations.

Piaget's general theory states, first, that all human intellectual and perceptual development is organized under the control of some form of innate and experientially developed structural and/or functional organization. This organization is inferred from the observed regularities of behavior. In Piaget's delineation of intellectual development, it plays a considerable role, a role which increases with age. Second, the "groups," as indicated, are mental organizations which function in accord with logical rules. In the periods of prelogical operations (2–7 years), and of concrete operations (7–11 years) that follow the stage of sensory motor intelligence (0–2 years), these logical groups are organized as two major logical systems: the logic of classification and the logic of relations. Later, in the period of formal operations (11 years on), a level of intellectual functioning is achieved which makes it possible to think (to solve problems, etc.) according to propositional logic, in which the thought correlates of propositional statements can be operated upon by identity, negation, reciprocal, and correlative transformations. These four transformations constitute a group through operations of combination and multiplication.

Piaget aims to demonstrate continuity in the logical properties of action and thought from birth on. Logical thinking is not simply a type of thought that is acquired through learning and instruction. Rather, the processes of thought are acquired through the development of structures and operations that operate themselves in accord with an abstract set of logical rules. Development during the first years of life, in which the child constructs his conception of space, is indicative of prelogically organized processes that eventuate in adult logical thought.

The development of a logical "group" is illustrated in the six-month-old child's rotation of objects. The child, when given a rattle with the handle away from himself, will never turn the object over right away. Each time he comes to perceive the handle, which may take some time, he will turn it over to put it into an orientation with which he is familiar and then take the handle to his mouth to suck (Piaget, 1954, p. 125). Such movements of rotation represent a primitive group, or the elements that go into a group, in that the movement of the object is negated by another movement of rotation. The displacement and the negation of the displacement constitute the (prelogical) group.

The progressive construction of space requires two distinguishable mechanisms, which are nevertheless related. One involves the progressive structuring of the spatial field; the other, the desubjectification of its elements. The first behaviors, reflexive in nature, are structured according to hereditarily given coordinations that control sucking, sight, etc., and are followed by further coordinations of sight and prehension which are increasingly influenced by the child's own actions. With more advanced prehension, the child displaces objects and puts them into recurring trajectories. It is after this that the child is able to search (not true search) for vanished objects, although he is not able to concern himself, as he will later, with the free movement of bodies in motion or treat his own body as an object. With directed searching, which follows in the order of development, structuring extends to the aggregate of physical displacements of an object which the child is able to perceive sequentially. As a consequence, the child deductively reconstitutes the moved objects, even though they are not visible. It is evident from this that the structuring of space parallels in many respects the development of the object concept.

Accompanying the structuring of space is the desubjectification of space, which Piaget says is related to the development of consciousness. Again, inferences concerning the development of consciousness derive from observations of the child's behavior. Increased consciousness is accompanied by a progressive reduction and elimination of initial unconscious egocentrism. When egocentrism is lost, the child is able to place himself in space and is capable of behaving toward himself as an object that is part of space.

While arguing for an interactionist interpretation of the origin of group structure, Piaget observes, or is willing to concede, that one must distinguish between group organization in general, and particular "spatial intuitions of the organs of perception." The hereditary element in development, he says, impresses upon every spatial construction a shape that permits the formation of groups, although specific spatial constructions are not predetermined as completed structures. While these statements are made within the context of an assertion that space is the product of an interaction between the organism and the environment, he seems at this point almost willing to say that the structures that construct space are formed according to a genetically determined blueprint (Piaget, 1954, p. 317). But if group structure is genetically determined, then it is questionable whether the structuring of space can be altered in any significant way by experience, except in specific content. Piaget may mean only that the imprint of heredity is so marked at birth, and that experience increasingly determines the character of group organization; but Piaget's description of the nature of logical thought processes and of the logic implicit in thought would not particularly suggest this, except in regard to the content of the organization.

The idea that space is not constructed solely from the experience of things outside us is one that is shared by Kant, although his position is more radical. We discover empirically, Kant says, that an object is to the left or right of another, but that objects in general are in a spatial relation of some kind is not an empirical generalization from specific spatial statements because the very discovery that X is to the left of Y presupposes that we have some idea of space in general. Yet, it is not conceptual either, but based upon *a priori* intuition (not even empirical intuition) (Kemp, 1968, p. 17). Piaget specifically argues against this kind of apriorism. He continually asserts that the construction of space results from an interaction of heredity and experiential factors. Nevertheless, Piaget's ideas have a similarity here to the ideas of Kant. In spite of the attempt by Piaget to dissociate himself from Kantian views, the biologically deterministic nature of general group structure sounds in the end remarkably like him.

In sum then, Piaget sees in the construction of space the beginning of a logic of relations, of group logical structures that provide organization to the movements of the child as he acts in accord with a progressive construction of space. This is a construction that has increasing structure, and is increasingly released from subjective notions of reality. The end of the development is a capacity to elaborate a highly differentiated space in which the child is an object among other objects that have substance and permanence.

VI. Development of Causality

To illustrate Piaget's description and interpretation of the construction of physical reality I have concentrated on the first two years of life, in the stage of sensory–motor intelligence. It is during this era of the child's life that one also discovers the origins of the conception of causality. This development, again, is associated with the development of space, objects, and temporal order.

The first instance of a causal event in the life of the child is when he fortuitiously sets in motion some interesting phenomenon, as occurs when he accidently hits a suspended rattle in his bassinet and immediately tries to reproduce the event. These actions, which usually eventuate in a habit, constitute the most elementary causal relation, although a qualitative change occurs when these actions become dissociated from fortuitous events and become associated with intentionality. When this change occurs, it becomes possible to distinguish means from ends, and causality becomes separate from the child's personal activity. The child who, instead of just grabbing a ball, carefully and deliberately pushes it along the top of a table till it goes over the edge, and then, when the ball is returned to the starting point, repeats the action with great glee, illustrates this differentiation of means from ends.

This is also a period in which the child begins to see objects as having negative and positive action independent of himself. If an object is an obstacle in his path to a goal, he begins to treat it as negating his intentions. Other objects are treated as intermediaries or means of positive action if they aid or can be used in pursuit of objects (Piaget, 1954, p. 317). The adjustment of objects to other objects suggests a progressive accommodation of means to ends, as well as the "spatialization of causality" and its "objectification." This development is enhanced when the child acquires the ability to use and create new means, through experimentation with the objects available to him, in order to achieve some objective. This occurs when he discovers that a stick can be used to push a ball or a doll even when the object is beyond his reach.

Piaget sees two processes in these developments: one is "efficacy"; the other "phenomenalism." Efficacy refers to the assimilation of events to personal activity; phenomenalism is accommodation to the empirical data associated with that activity (Piaget, 1954, p. 316). In the beginning of development, causality is an indistinguishable mixture of these two processes, so that there is no differentiation between the self and objects. It is only with experience in the world that personal activity becomes progressively differentiated from objects. That is, objects begin to be seen as different from the self, and as having independent existence, and ultimately, the self is seen as an object that stands in a particular relation to other objects.

What Piaget is willing to concede to Hume is the notion that causality springs from reflex activity and that the earliest habits derive from experience. Piaget denies, however, that the idea of causality can be achieved only through such habits. Thus, in the early days, the infant is able to associate a sound with an image. He turns his head in the direction of a sound to find an associated visual image, but this relation remains phenomenalistic. It represents a response (made possible by available schemata) to an external stimulus, but it is not much more than that. It is certainly causal in a very primitive sense, but even so it is not merely a habit, since the activity takes place within an organization of behavior, even at this primitive level. The habits constructed by association are not autonomous, since they are always supported by complex structures which make them possible. Again, the mechanisms that support these are inferred by Piaget. They are the general mechanisms of intellectual development—the primary, secondary, and tertiary circular reactions that Piaget posits as the functional regularities in early behavior common to the development of the object concept, the construction of space, and the development of causality. The inference from such regularities to a primary organization is related to the idea that the functioning of the schema, as in a gesture that reproduces an interesting event, presupposes that the subject establishes a (mental) connection between the perceived result and a particular aspect of his activity. This implies that at least some primitive "understanding" is achieved that goes beyond mere association. In the early stages, the causal relation between subject and object represented in these schemata is not a rational one, since it relies too exclusively on personal activity; but with progressive structuring and desubjectification of space, the child is led to rational activity.

The thesis which Piaget here asks us to accept is that an organizational structure or a set of functional relations creates understanding in the child, while the associations of habit do not constitute understanding.

Piaget is aware of the philosophic history of the issue and takes his own stand in relation to it. He objects first to the radical empiricism of Hume, which he attacks largely because of the reductionist thesis that causality is nothing more than a habit built on associations. As already said, Piaget accepts the fact that habit plays a role, particularly during very early development, when associations are made between objects seen and movements carried out by the child. He objects, though, to the omission of the context of existing organization to which the habit has to be assimilated. He also objects to the purely external empirical connections that Hume posits as the basis for causality, although Hume, of course, was concerned with the associations of ideas rather than the events which they copied. The notion of empirical connection ignores the empirical fact, says Piaget, that the first causal relations occur on the occasion of personal activity and never solely on the basis of an external relation among objects. Hume, he says further, holds the child to develop causal knowledge through progressive awareness of his own activity, at first through diffuse sensations of effort and desire, and then through more and more precise awareness of his movements and intentions. Piaget questions whether this is possible by noting that the cause and the effect cannot be placed on the same plane at the outset of the child's experience; for such "homogeneity" between subject and object is acquired only through the increasingly complex elaboration of schemata, and not by experience and association alone. While Piaget rejects the Humean associationist thesis, he does implicitly accept that causality evolves out of the contiguity in experience between cause and effect, in the sense that it develops out of the transaction between subject and object.

Piaget takes exception to another view of causality expressed by M. de Biran, which he characterizes as an example of vitalism. In this view, action by the self gives rise to a direct intuition of causality, "awareness of voluntary activity (is) conceived as a primary datum" (Piaget, 1954, p. 309). While Piaget himself emphasizes that personal activity is the origin of causality, he does not see such activity as providing a direct intuition of causality; rather, as in all aspects of development, the notion of causality is a construction to which the early activity of the child contributes. He cites the work of J. M. Balwin, in addition to his own observations, to make evident how difficult it is to attribute direct intuition of self to the infant, and for that matter to attribute differentiation of self and object to the very young child. While he agrees with de Biran that consciousness arises from contact with things, he points out that the action of the subject is already engaged in a construction, which consciousness only extends. Just as Hume does not persuade Piaget to reduce causality to pure phenomenalism, so de Biran does not persuade him to identify causality with "efficacy."

The third position he rejects is apriorism, the view that causality is a category of mind with a permanent and necessary structure. It is the structural invariance of intelligence necessitated by this view that is objectionable to Piaget. A corollary of the aprioristic conception of causality is that, the mind comes to apprehend the relation of causality bit by bit, but with no fundamental qualitative change. It follows too, says Piaget, that inasmuch as the structure basic to causality is imposed by the mind, it should present a permanent content. Whether the latter point is necessary to an *a priori* (that is, nativist) position is questionable. Nevertheless, Piaget argues that empirical studies of intellectual development establish that structural transformations occur in a stagewise fashion, which disconfirms the ideas of invariance of structure and content. Piaget acknowledges the possibility that the cause–effect relation remains invariant in the course of these developmental transformations, while at the same time he questions whether it is possible to conceive of a relation independently of the factors it unites. He adds: "to be sure, there exists one invariant whose manifestations are visible throughout the history of causality. But that invariant is functional and not structural in nature . . .

it is the functional permanence of assimilation which is the source of causality . . ." (Piaget, 1954, p. 314).

Since functional relations occur because of some implicit (even if not specifiable) structure, it is difficult to see what the primary source of such functional invariance can be if it is not some internal program that controls both the functions and the structural transformations. Such an *a priori* "structure" may account for the invariant transformations and still be compatible with the possibility of differing contents.

Another view of causality interprets its construction as a practical adaptation of the organism, having only provisional value and rooted neither in internal necessity nor in the nature of the external world. Piaget ascribes this view to "conventionalism," which refers to the creation of methods of adaptation developed from among many possibilities having only an arbitrary relation to external reality. He thinks that this view is also contradicted by the data, because the development of causality leads to schemata that reflect an increasingly close union between the nature of the deductive processes and experience. While he concedes that the early phases of development might be seen according to the conventionalist view, in later development the spatial schemata that result from the activity of the subject come closer to the characteristics of physical reality. The structures thus developed are not arbitrary and could not be easily substituted for by others.

In true Cartesian fashion, the only position left to Piaget after denying these alternatives is that "causality is an organization of the universe caused by the totality of relations established by action and then by representation between objects as well as between object and subject" (Piaget, 1954, p. 315).

Piaget's theory of the construction of causality leaves unclear, however, in spite of his rejection of apriorism, whether he believes that the cause–effect relation is a necessary one (albeit a functional necessity), or results from the nature of reality itself. If we look to philosophical accounts of this matter, we find that Locke, the empiricist, differentiates causality in the abstract—that is, any change must, as a necessity of reason, have a cause—from causality as the particular cause of a specific change which is found from experience. He also uses the "universal" principle of causality that "whatever has a beginning must have a cause" as a true principle of reason (Fraser, 1894). Descartes shares this view to some extent, asserting as intuitively certain a principle similar to the popular "from nothing comes nothing" (Keeling, 1968). While Kant holds that experience is necessary for knowing what caused any change, his basic point is that particular causal laws are valid of experience only because of the *a priori* validity of the causal principle itself (Kemp, 1968). Kant thus perpetuates the distinction between particular causal connections known through experience and the general principle known independent of experience. The point to be borne in mind here is the distinction between logical necessity and psychological necessity (the necessity of constructing the casual relation). To the extent that Piaget is a realist, one would expect that if logical necessity characterized reality, then psychological necessity would follow. In claiming that causality becomes known through the interaction of an innate system with the world through experience, Piaget fails to specify the ultimate source of causality. One can hardly deny the broad assertion that both hereditary structure and experience are necessary to the development of causality, but this is of little help. The fixed progression in which causal relations become known suggests again that the structures extracted from experience, as well as the structures that permit the extraction of experience, are under the control of an innate mechanism that makes only one kind of causal development possible. But these structural developments result not only in the conception of causal relations as such, but also in the apparently anomalous conceptions of a time-reversed universe, past/future asymmetry, and antimatter—features which suggest that the attempt to specify a particular type of logical property as necessary is a questionable undertaking.

Piaget's achievement in regard to the concept of causality, then, is in the clarification of the course of development and the specification of some of its mechanisms.

VII. Time

The development of a primitive and "practical" notion of time occurs within the first two years of life. The general development is from a knowledge of "subjective series" to "objective series." By a subjective series Piaget means a chain of events caused by the subject's own actions as illustrated in the infant's ability to shake his legs in order to make the crib shake. There is a definite time series in that the infant shakes first and then awaits the result in movements of the crib. Later, when the child is able to systematically search for a vanished object, he can take into account a series of object displacements made by another person. A child who has shown that he can find an object that was hidden in A, and now sees it disappear in B, will be able to go directly to B (whereas previously he would look to A). The events constitute an objective series because the child arranges external events in temporal order, not just his personal activities and their extensions.

Again, the development of time in the period of sensory–motor development is intimately associated with the development of space, causality, and objectification. From the parallel development and common patterns of these functions, it is possible to infer that a common structural or functional organization either accounts for the development or results from it.

VIII. Practical Intelligence and Conceptual Thought

The first two years of life, although they establish the basic patterns of development, only embody what Piaget characterizes as "practical" intelligence. It is practical in the sense that it leads to practical adaptation, the goal of which is success in particular activities or in the utilization of particular personal or environmental resources. It does not result in knowledge as such or in "norms of truth," which are possible only for conceptual thought. An important achievement of the Piagetian system is its demonstration of the continuity in development between practical intelligence and true intelligence, and the identification of the structural similarity between these stages.

There is an additional difference between sensory–motor intelligence and conceptual thought, and this is the role played by social experience. Sensory–motor intelligence is an adaptation of the individual to the world of things without "socialization of the intellect" as such, whereas conceptual thought is "collective thought obeying common laws." It is through "cooperation with other persons that the mind arrives at verifying judgments." "Whether conceptual thought is rational because it is social or vice versa, the interdependence of the search for truth and of socialization seems to us undeniable" (Piaget, 1954, p. 360). In an almost surprising way, Piaget is generalizing to conceptual thought his approach to the development of moral thinking. What is common to both developments is an evolution out of the social experience of having to come to terms with the "generalized other," that is, coming to see the world from the vantage point of the "other." This is illustrated in the three-mountain experiment which demonstrates how the child, between 4 and 6 years of age, begins to conceptualize space as a problem of seeing the world from the position of another. In the experiment, the child is asked to select a picture from a series placed before him that shows what a doll sees as it is moved in a circle (up to 360°) around the three mountains fixed on the table, with the child himself remaining in a fixed position relative to the mountains. Two generalizations emerge from the experiment. First, the child goes through a progression that parallels what occurred in the sensory–motor period (a transition from subjectivization to objectification), although now at a conceptual level. Second, appropriate conceptualization of spatial relations is associated with the ability to depersonalize the conception of space so that the field can be viewed as the doll sees it, rather than as the child himself views it. This development from egocentricity to objectivity encompasses his relations with both the physical world and the social community. While Piaget is not willing to accept the Russian psychologists' position that the origins of thought are social, he does provide a major role for the social process in the development of conceptual thought, at least to the extent that the social context provides the source and motivation for verification.

Another feature of the relation between stages of thought is the phenomenon of "temporal displacement," by which Piaget means that in another period in the child's life he appears to repeat in general form a pattern of development that occurred at a prior level. This takes two forms. One appears as a type of regression; the other involves a parallel development that occurs with more advanced structures and functions. The latter is of greater interest and is evident in the period of preoperational thought which intervenes between the sensory–motor period and the period of concrete operations. The conservation capacities associated with the concepts of number, weight, volume, length, and area, for example, repeat on the level of conceptual thought a series of stages analogous to those experienced on the sensory–motor level. "Just as the baby begins by believing that objects return to the void when they are no longer perceived and emerge from it when they reenter the perceptual field, so also the six-year-old child still thinks the quantity of matter augments and diminishes according to the form the object takes, and that a substance which dissolves is completely annihilated" (Piaget, 1954, p. 371).

When the simple practical schemata are replaced by systems of classes and "thoughtful" relations, the child becomes capable of dealing with the world independently of immediate perception. The deductive constructions that the child achieves through the development of the schemata of conservation, as well as the more abstract classification and relational logics, provide the child with the capacity to arrive at deductions which his experience alone will not suffice to explain.

In detailing the construction of space, Piaget attempts to show that mathematicians who use the term "geometrical intuition" to describe knowledge of space intend more by this than a direct "reading" or apprehension of the properties of objects. Piaget believes that these "intuitions" can be accounted for in terms of their development from the actions of the child. "It is precisely because it enriches and develops physical reality instead of merely extracting from it a set of ready-made structures, that action is eventually able to transcend physical limitations and create operational schemata which can be formalized and made to function in a purely abstract deductive fashion" (Piaget, 1956, p. 449). As already indicated, action is first manifest in the form of sensory–motor activity regulating perception. In the following stage of "nascent mental imagery," actions play a formative role. The image is at first no more than an internal imitation of actually performed actions, but later becomes an imitation of actions only potentially capable of being performed. Finally, action at the level of concrete operations and then of abstract operations, becomes apparent in the purer and richer forms of the operations themselves. (Purer, because they go beyond the physical objects with which they are concerned; richer, because in operational form, actions are reversible and may be combined indefinitely.)

The operations on which the conception of space depends are important in three ways. First, the order of their psychological development is in broad outline the same as that of formal geometrical construction. In both cases topological relations (involving, for example, proximity, order, and enclosure) precede projective relations (for example, points, lines, and horizontality), as well as Euclidean relations (such as triangulation and proportions). Both in psychological operations and formal geometrical constructions, projections and Euclidean relations are equivalent in the complexity of the basic notions from which they derive.

Second, the developmental data introduce a new element into the classical discussion opposing intuition and logic: "to the extent that actions are internalized as operations, the initial perceptual and empirical intuitions become rational and coherent even before having been formalized as propositions. Thus the rigour of the system of concrete operations exceeds that of elementary intuition without reaching that of abstract operations, the basis of hypothetico–deductive propositions" (Piaget, 1956, p. 450).

The third and most important consideration is that "concrete operations of a logico–arithmetical character deal solely with similarities (classes and symmetrical relations) and differences (asymmetrical relations) or both together (numbers), between discrete objects in discontinuous whole independent of their spatio–temporal location. Exactly parallel with these operations there exist operations of a spatio–temporal or sub-logical character, and it is precisely those which constitute the idea of space" (Piaget, 1956, p. 450). By being sublogical they are no less rigorous logically, for if they were expressed in propositional form, they would be indistinguishable from logical–arithmetic operations. These sublogical operations emphasize continuity rather than discontinuity; they deal, for example, not with class inclusion but part–whole inclusions for single objects. The concept of proximity is substituted for that of resemblance, difference in order for difference in general, and the concept of qualitative measurement for that of number. Since these constitute objects of various kinds, they are accompanied by symbolic images (mental images or pictorial representations) rather than the images that accompany class or number concepts.

The importance of these sublogical operations is that they explain why "the persistence of a core of intuition is often admitted, even in the most abstract form of axiomatic geometry." This core is only the proof, however, "that the basic concepts of spatial proximity and succession are sublogical in origin" (Piaget, 1954, p. 450) and not intuitive. These sublogical operations are associated with elementary topological relationships which involve, as already indicated, proximities, order, and so on. They also involve constituting projective relationships like the addition and subtraction of (neighboring) parts of an object, as well as rectilinear order, and so on.

Once they have evolved fully, all operations, whether sublogical (spatio–temporal) or logico–arithmetic (independent of proximity), can be performed abstractly. They can be carried out by a formal deduction and can be expressed in propositional language. This does not take them out of the realm of operations or actions, however, since in Piaget's view, propositions always describe operations, or the results of operations, and their implications and incompatibilities are still operations even if they are one step removed.

The sublogical and logical operations of time conceptualization show a parallel progression. Time as a logical concept involves the order of the succession of events and the duration of intervals separating events. In the preoperative and concrete operational stages of intellectual development, these aspects of the concept are elaborated very simply, that is, qualitatively without any operations of measurement. In the later portions of the period, measurement operations become a part of the child's notions of time.

What one discovers in the progressive structurization of the time concept is that the conception of simultaneity and succession, as well as duration, are related to the child's conception of speed. While in the preoperative stage the succession of events is grasped independently of the operations of duration, these two types of operation become coordinated in the period of concrete operations. A true concept of time, however, is not achieved until the child has a systematic concept of speed which incorporates the operations of both duration and succession. Psychologically speaking, time is defined by the coordination of speeds, just as space is defined by the coordination of displacements, that is, movements, irrespective of the attribute of speed (Piaget, 1955).

Although time is usually identified by philosophers with the idea of duration and the relation between durations (for example, Descartes), it is practically never identified with the idea of speed, which is a relation between velocity and distance. For Descartes, duration is a real characteristic of bodies, an ultimate property of space, but the conception of time depends upon the mind that compares durations. In a similar vein, Leibniz attributes the concept of time to changes in perception which awaken in us the idea of duration, but this perception only enables mind to think of time. According to Kant, time is an *a priori* intuition, the form of inner sense, in contrast to the intuition of space, the form of outer sense; in his view, the capacity for receiving sensations is so constructed that whatever material is received is inevitably arranged in a temporal order, while objects are inevitably arranged in a spatial order.

Again, Piaget in taking a constructivist position denies that innate systems of organization give rise to the conception of time. Piaget introduces the psychological requirement that a conception of speed is associated with the construction of time, but from a logical point of view the concepts of time and speed are not independent. One can, therefore, argue in Kantian fashion that the concept of speed has implicit in it the concept of time. Piaget probably would not dispute the point, but would rather direct attention to the way in which all of the elements that enter into the construction of time develop: at first they are parallel, then they converge and are coordinated into a single set of operations that make time and all its related concepts possible.

IX. Conclusion

Inherent in Piaget's general system is the view that the logical structure of mathematical and physical systems is paralleled by the order of psychological (logical thought) development. When the logical relations described by philosophers or logicians differ from psycho–developmental order, Piaget argues that the philosophers are mistaken in their characterizations. This is instanced by what Piaget says of Russell's definition of number:

> . . . Russell's solution to this problem is too simple. For him and his followers, two classes have the same number when there is a one-one correspondence between their elements . . . Russell [tries] to reduce cardinal number to the notion of "class of classes" and ordinal number, dissociated from cardinal number, to the notion of "class of relationships" . . . (Piaget, 1952, p. 182).

> Our hypothesis [is that number] is at the same time both class and asymmetrical relation, it does not derive from one or the other of the logical operations, but from their union, continuity thus being reconciled with irreducibility. . . Number is at the same time a class and an asymmetrical relation, the units of which it is composed being simultaneously added because they are equivalent, and seriated because they are different from one another (Piaget, 1952, p. ix).

Piaget holds that number, as a fusion of class and asymmetrical relations into a single operational whole, has a logical explanation which he attempts to provide (since he believes that Poincaré's and Brunschvicg's conception of whole number as "essentially synthetic and irreducible" is not adequate either); but this does not seem nearly as important to Piaget as the psychological explanation. The psychological explanation based upon developmental data indicates that each number is a whole, born of the union of equivalent and distinct terms, which is constituted through the cognitive processes of inclusion and seriation.

The logical and mathematical consequences of this interpretation, however, are not explored by Piaget. While it may be significant to an explanation of how the child comes to understand number that seriation and asymmetrical relations have to be simultaneously known, it is not clear that logic and mathematics require these assumptions in order to elaborate a coherent and useful theory. Piaget's view may be a function of his belief that mathematics relates to a "real" world and is not simply a system of heuristics. Piaget also probably thinks that if mathematical deductive systems are to be applicable (as explanatory systems) to empirical data, they need to emerge out of such data. This philosophy of science position blurs the distinction between analytic and synthetic knowledge which represents the keystone of the logical empiricist position, but then Piaget explicitly argues against that position.

In sum, Piaget is asserting that the basis for a valid epistemology is to be found in a "genetic epistemology"; that understanding the nature of mind and its products is the same as understanding how the mind and its products develop. Is this a claim that can be tested? The situation at the moment is such that epistemological analysis as developed by philosophers does not seem to stand up very well against experimental data in psychology, at least developmental data. Of course, few psychologists have tried to encompass both bodies of knowledge. Looked at the other way around, it is not clear that the data of psychological research, to the extent that they have a bearing on epistemological issues, have been of any significant use to philosophers. But it also could be argued that few philosophers know anything of the results of such developmental studies of cognition; certainly they know much less than philosophers of science know of research in physics. At the moment, then, Piaget's claims are very much a challenge to both philosophers and psychologists.

In addition to his general epistemological claim, Piaget makes a number of assertions of varying specificity that bear on epistemological issues. The most important of these is the interpretation of mind that holds that nothing enters mind which is not assimilable to already existing structures, and the complement, that when no new capacities are acquired, response to reality is made only to the extent that existing structures are brought to bear upon it.

Further, the mechanisms by which the mind develops (assimilation and accommodation) are held to be under the control of a self-regulatory system (equilibration) that is organized and progresses only through the interaction of hereditary and experiential elements. It is through these interactions that knowledge is constructed.

What I propose, in addition, is that Piaget's data reveal that the processes by which knowledge is acquired are under the control of natively given genetic processes which determine both the form that behavior takes and the structures formed out of experience.

References

Beilin, H. Cognitive capacities of young children: A replication. *Science*, 1968, **162,** 920–921.

Beilin, H. Stimulus and cognitive transformation in conservation. In D. Elkind & J. H. Flavell (Eds.), *Studies in cognitive development: Essays in honor of Jean Piaget.* London and New York: Oxford Univ. Press, 1969. (a)

Beilin, H. Developmental stages and developmental processes. Paper presented at the Invitational Conference on Ordinal Scales of Cognitive Development, California Test Bureau, Monterey, California, 1969. (b)

Beilin, H., & Franklin, I. C. Logical operations in area and length measurement. *Child Development,* 1962, **33,** 607–618.

Beilin, H., & Kagan, J. Pluralization rules and the conceptualization of number. *Developmental Psychology,* 1969, **1,** 697–706.

Beilin, H., Kagan, J., & Rabinowitz, R. Effects of verbal and perceptual training in water level representation. *Child Development,* 1966, **37,** 317–329.

Broad, C. D. *The mind and its place in nature.* London: Kegan Paul, 1925. (Quoted in S. V. Keeling, 1968, p. 295.)

Chomsky, N. Review of Skinner's "Verbal behavior." *Language,* 1959, **35,** 26–58.

Chomsky, N. *Language and mind.* New York: Harcourt, 1968.

Chomsky, N. Knowledge of language. *Times Literary Supplement,* 1969, No. 3507, 523–525.

Fodor, J. A. *Psychological explanation: An introduction to the philosophy of psychology.* New York: Random House, 1968.

Fraser, A. C. (Ed.) Introduction to *An essay concerning human understanding,* by J. Locke. Vol. 1. London and New York: Oxford Univ. Press (Clarendon), 1894. (Dover edition, 1959.)

Furth, H. G. Piaget's theory of knowledge: The nature of representation and interiorization. *Psychological Review.* 1968, **75,** 143–154.

Furth, H. G. *Piaget and knowledge: Theoretical foundations.* Englewood Cliffs, New Jersey: Prentice-Hall, 1969.

Gelman, R. Conservation acquisition: A problem of learning to attend to relevant attributes. *Journal of Experimental Child Psychology,* 1969, **7,** 167–187.

Gibson, J. J. On the proper meaning of the term stimulus. *Psychological Review,* 1967, **74,** 533–534.

Hocutt, M. On the alleged circularity of Skinner's concept of stimulus. *Psychological Review,* 1967, **74,** 530–532.

Inhelder, B. Some aspects of Piaget's genetic approach to cognition. In W. Kessen & C. Kuhlman (Eds.), Thought in the young child. *Monographs of the Society for Research in Child Development*, 1962, **27**, 19–34.

Keeling, S. V. *Descartes.* (2nd ed.) London and New York: Oxford Univ. Press, 1968.

Kemp, J. *The philosophy of Kant.* London and New York: Oxford Univ. Press, 1968.

Kingsley, R. C., & Hall, V. C. Training conservation through the use of learning sets. *Child Development*, 1967, **38**, 1111–1126.

Mischel, T. Scientific and philosophical psychology: A historical introduction. In T. Mischel (Ed.), *Human action: Conceptual and empirical issues.* New York: Academic Press, 1969.

Pears, D. F. *Bertrand Russell and the British tradition in philosophy.* London: Collins, 1967.

Piaget, J. *The child's conception of number.* London: Routledge, 1952.

Piaget, J. *The construction of reality in the child.* New York: Basic Books, 1954.

Piaget, J. The development of time concepts in the child. In P. H. Hoch & J. Zubin (Eds.), *Psychopathology of childhood.* New York: Grune & Stratton, 1955.

Piaget, J. Quantification, conservation and nativism. *Science*, 1968, **162**, 976–981. (a)

Piaget, J. Explanation in psychology and psychophysiological parallelism. In P. Fraisse & J. Piaget (Eds.), *Experimental psychology: Its scope and method.* Vol. 1. J. Piaget, P. Fraisse, & M. Reuchlin, History and method. New York: Basic Books, 1968. (b)

Piaget, J. Response to Beilin's "Developmental stages and developmental processes." Paper presented at the Invitational Conference on Ordinal Scales of Cognitive Development, California Test Bureau, Monterey, California, 1969.

Piaget, J., & Inhelder, B. *The child's concept of space.* London: Routledge, 1956.

Sigel, I. E., & Hooper, F. H. *Logical thinking in children: Research based on Piaget's theory.* New York: Holt, 1968.

Wiener, P. P. (Ed.) *Leibniz: Selections.* New York: Scribner, 1951.

Windelband, W. *A history of philosophy.* Vol. 2. New York: Macmillan, 1901. (Harper Torchbook edition, 1958.)

COMMENTS ON BEILIN'S "THE DEVELOPMENT OF PHYSICAL CONCEPTS"

John H. Flavell

Unlike most of the other articles in this volume, Beilin's is primarily expository in orientation. That is, it attempts mainly to inform the reader of certain aspects of Piaget's theory which he may not be familiar with, aspects which bear on the topic of this volume. Accordingly, the article begins with an extended summary of Piaget's theory of knowledge and knowledge acquisition, taken in relation to classical philosophical positions on these topics, and concludes with a description of his theory and findings regarding such physical concepts as those of object, space, causality, and time. Since I found Beilin's exposition of Piaget to be largely accurate, and since I also found the relatively few interpretative additions to Piaget he makes mostly congenial to my own biases, there would be little substance to any sort of conventional critique of Beilin's paper that I might attempt. What I would like to do instead is simply to discuss certain problematic topics which Beilin touches upon, particularly those which find echoes in some of the other articles in this book. I believe that these particular topics are vitally important ones for developmental psychologists to be thinking about, and I also believe that developmental psychologists have to date not paid sufficient attention to them. Thus I have come to free associate to Harry Beilin, not to criticize him.

I. Determinants and Outcomes of Cognitive Development

Beilin argues that Piaget's view of cognitive development is actually more maturationistic and preformationistic than Piaget himself admits it to be. I believe that Beilin is correct in so arguing. I further believe, with Beilin, Lenneberg, Chomsky, Wohlwill, and others, that increasing attention will have to be paid in the future to the possible biological-organismic as contrasted with environmental contributions to, and constraints on, human cognitive development. It is obvious, however, that consideration of environmental effects must continue to figure very prominently in any such genetically determined, maturationistic conception of how development proceeds, if that view is to be taken seriously, and I would submit that there is at present no good theory about these environmental effects.

Consider the following assertion which Beilin, or Lenneberg, or anyone of that persuasion might make: A given genetically programmed thought form gradually emerges in the course of development, assuming that the organism is a neurologically intact human being *and assuming a normal human environment.* I suspect that there are indeed such thought forms —more on this below—but I have trouble thinking clearly about the "normal human environment" part of the statement. It seems to imply that there must be invariant features common to a wide range of perhaps quite diverse and different looking environmental objects and events, such that no specific event or group of events are necessary to the development of that thought form, but that these higher-order, invariant features which any and all possess constitute necessary nutriments or "aliments" for that development. However, the identification of likely invariants of this sort amid the great variety of environmental inputs will be no easy task. Let me put the issue in a more general context. I personally take as a major objective for our field the search for possible *universal* outcomes of human cognitive development, that is, properties of adult cognition which are common to all normal people in all societies, and which are the result of ontogenetic change rather than being present at birth. If such properties exist, it seems reasonable to expect that the environmental contributions to their genesis must consist of the aforementioned invariants of human experience, and I for one would like to find some way to identify and describe these invariants. The point I am making is that the role of the environment within a more maturationistically oriented view of development is subtle and hard to conceptualize, but its conceptualization is a necessary task.

Since language is commonly identified as an environmental input of relevance to cognitive development, let me add a few comments. Beilin speaks for Piaget in arguing that language and other representational devices are the products of thought and its development, not its source or essence. Most psychologists, and most of the philosophers who have contributed to this volume, judging by their articles, impute to language a much more essential and important role in thinking than Piaget does. My own suspicion is that the role of language in thinking is in fact generally overestimated—I wonder, for example, how many philosophers know of the work of Furth (1966) and others, which shows that deaf children possessing only very minimal language are nonetheless quite capable of solving Piagetian concrete operational problems. At the same time, it has yet to be demonstrated that anything resembling formal operational, reflective, and speculative thinking can occur in the absence of a rich linguistic system, of either the natural language or the sign language variety. Such a system might well be regarded as indispensable for complex and extended trains of thought even if one did not—as I do not—regard language as anything like the essence of thinking. Linguistic symbols are in some ways akin to percepts, in that they provide meaningful inputs to a thinking process—they provide it with things to think *of* and *about,* without themselves constituting the thinking process itself. As I see it, linguistic processes serve fundamentally as cognitive subsidiaries, in rather the same way that perceptual and memory processes do. However, I suspect that this subsidiary role assumes a crucial importance for at least the higher forms of human thinking. I might also mention a possibility that is a kind of corollary to this view; namely, that language inputs (for example, verbal teaching) may also play a more important part in the *acquisition* of formal operations than in the *acquisition* of lower-order skills.

II. Developmental Sequences

Beilin also talks about the problem of the sequencing of cognitive-developmental acquisitions, as do Peters, Hamlyn, Toulmin, and others. Developmental psychologists are, or certainly should be, interested in looking at the degree to which sets of developmental attainments are acquired in an invariant order, invariant across children and across environments, and more importantly, in looking at possible explanations for the degree of invariance found. I am coming to believe that some putative invariant sequences will require quite different explanations than others. A quote from Beilin will introduce the problem. He says: "A fixed developmental sequence which is impervious to environmental influence must be in large measure under the control of some type of species-specific genetic programming . . ." (*p. 90*). Let me propose three sample developmental sequences: the first one is a clear case of what Beilin has in mind; the second and third, I submit, do not really fit Beilin's model at all. The first is the developmental sequence: seeing–walking. There is no logical reason why human beings should not be able to walk before they can see—the actual sequence is simply a biological, maturational one for our species, and surely uninfluenced by any modifications of the environment which do not actually damage the child. The second sequence is first animistic, then veridical classifications of living versus nonliving things. Given the nature of the perceptual system and the cue structure of the domain to be classified (particularly, salience of noncriterial cues like movement), it is highly plausible that an animistic conception of life should prevail initially. Notice, however, that the structure of the environment is definitely contributing to the obtained developmental sequence here, not the case in the first example. It is presumably the homogeneity of this environmental structure for all developing humans that guarantees the invariance of this particular sequence. The third sequence is that of concrete operations—formal operations. While I would certainly agree that the developmental attainment of formal operations could well be "under the control of some type of species-specific genetic programming," I would argue that the *sequence*, first concrete operations then formal operations, is the result neither of genetic programming nor of the structure and sequencing of environmental inputs. Rather, the order is a *logically* necessary one, arising from the very nature of formal operations (that is, operations performed upon the results of well-established and readily serviceable concrete operations). One can then, perhaps, classify sequences into at least these three types: (*a*) strictly maturational sequences, arising from the evolutionary history of the species and modifiable only through future evolutionary change; (*b*) sequences largely determined by the structure of the natural environment, assuming the operation of certain types of natively given cognitive tendencies, and conceivably modifiable by drastic, highly "unnatural" restructurings of the environment; and (*c*) logically necessary sequences, arising out of the intrinsic properties of the cognitive acts which form the sequence (one act analytically rather than empirically requisite for the other), and thus completely unalterable *qua* sequence. I should add that this kind of analysis of developmental sequences is both highly tentative and incomplete, lest anyone be tempted to take it too seriously.

One final comment is in order, to reinforce the view that developmental sequences are a very complicated business. I have the feeling—and I gather that Toulmin (*p. 53*) does too—that development may turn out to be more of a parallel and cyclical affair than a straightforward linear one. Consider again the example of the concrete operations–formal operations sequence. It seems highly implausible to me that formal operations do not begin to appear until the subject's ability to deploy concrete operations has reached its maximum. More likely, there is considerable overlap and parallelism in these two developments. It may even be that the advent of formal operations works backward, as it were, to contribute to the further solidification and stabilization of these developmentally and logically prior concrete operations. I think that cycles of mutual, reciprocal facilitation between emerging cognitive skills may actually be the rule rather than the exception in cognitive development, however much such a state of affairs may blur and complicate our ideas about developmental sequences.

III. Equilibration

Beilin also alludes to what is becoming a vexing problem for developmentalists when he states that "the mechanisms by which the mind develops (assimilation and accommodation) are held to be under the control of a self-regulatory system (equilibration). . ." (*p. 118*). It may come as a surprise to some of the philosophers here that there exist in the psychological literature no really good, critical treatments of Piaget's equilibration concept, despite the fact that it may be the only serious candidate we presently have for a true "mechanism of development." In fact, one of the happiest fringe benefits of contributing to this volume has been, for me, the opportunity to read Mischel's really admirable analysis of this concept. Like Mischel, I also have some questions about its utility as an explanatory concept, although these questions do not wholly coincide with his. More than Mischel, perhaps, I am even unclear as to *exactly* what psychological phenomena "equilibration" is and is not supposed to denote. For instance, I am not certain that all instances of "equilibration" have to do with processes one would comfortably label as "cognitive conflict," although the two terms are usually regarded as interchangeable by developmental psychologists. However, suppose that one were for argument's sake to take equilibration to mean cognitive-conflict resolution, how adequately and completely would such a process "explain" cognitive development? Leaving aside Mischel's cogent criticisms on this point, let me argue first of all that conflict resolution could not, in itself, be *the* single, necessary and sufficient vehicle of cognitive change. In order for cognitive conflict to occur and give rise to progressive cognitive changes, there have to be some ancillary developments that themselves cannot readily be explained by a process of conflict resolution. First, the two potentially conflicting cognitive items must become available to the child, that is, he must develop the ability to know or perceive them. Second, he must apprehend the items *as* conflicting or incompatible, and the capacity for this kind of apprehension may well have its own genesis also. Most of us child watchers have had the experience of seeing children wholly fail to sense patent incongruities between contiguous assertions; most adult watchers have also had the same experience, no doubt. Third, the subject must be impelled to resolve the sensed conflict in a cognitively progressive fashion, rather than for instance, as one of a number of possible options, clinging even more rigidly and defensively to his prior interpretation of things. There are other possible prerequisites one might add, for example, possessing the necessary conceptual wherewithal to discover a satisfactory higher-order explanation, assuming the child has opted for cognitive progress. What I am saying is that the experience of cognitive conflict, when examined carefully, seems to require the construction of some cognitive bridges which lead up to it and lead out from it, and it is difficult to see how the construction of these bridges could be explained in cognitive conflict terms. It may even be—although I am not yet wholly sure I believe this—that cognitive conflicts are not all that commonly implicated in major, Piagetian-type cognitive acquistions anyhow, even in the modest, insufficient-condition role that I have just assigned to them. For some acquisitions, such as the formal operational ability to find all possible pairwise combinations of a set of elements, precursive conflict-resolution conditions are rather hard to imagine, even in the abstract. For others, such as the conservations, they are easier to imagine in contrived, training-study settings than in real-life, spontaneous development (I might add that the induction of a state of genuine cognitive conflict in children is surprisingly difficult, even in the laboratory). As they develop, children obviously come to "know" that a given quantity of water remains the same when simply poured from one vessel to another, but it seems unlikely that they acquire this knowledge by anything resembling Piaget's four-step equilibration process, which inexplicably assumes prolonged confrontation with the actual conservation problem itself. Mischel argues that Piaget's equilibration model is not an empirical theory of the developmental process, but rather a "conceptual framework" (*p. 348*) within which to order and analyze empirical data on cognitive development. I think it is currently an open question whether it will even prove to be a useful framework, especially if construed exclusively in cognitive conflict terms—and particularly if conceived as *the* vehicle for developmental change. Although I am not yet sure exactly what the term "mechanism of developmental change" ought to imply, I feel pretty sure that there must be a number of them operative, rather than a single one.

IV. Philosophy and Developmental Psychology

Let me conclude with some brief comments about what I assume to be the central topic of this volume, namely, the contributions of developmental psychology and philosophy to an understanding of conceptual thinking and its development. I find especially interesting here the question of what each of these two disciplines might contribute to the solution of the other's problems. Not having a very good feel for philosophical problems, I hesitate to enter the debate between Hamlyn and Toulmin concerning the relevance or nonrelevance of cognitive-developmental research to epistemological problems; however, I find myself more in agreement with Toulmin than with Hamlyn. If an abundance of varied evidence suggests, for example, that children do in fact behave and develop as if the relation of mind to external reality were of a particular sort, how could such evidence possibly be irrelevant to one's choice of epistemological position? I suspect that philosophical thinking about the mind which proceeds too long without contact with real, flesh-and-bone examples of minds in action could readily go astray, even when the problems thought about are so-called analytic ones. I think I have occasionally sensed the effects of such insulation, especially from live child thought, in reading the philosophers' contributions to this volume; I certainly know I have sensed it in myself when I have gone too long without actually observing or testing real children.

It is the possible contributions that might flow from philosophy to developmental psychology, however, that I personally find most interesting. A good case would be made that we cognitive-developmental types are prone to ignore bodies of theory and evidence from other disciplines that might be of real use to us. As I see it, our fundamental job is to describe and theorize about the ontogenetic history of the adult human mind. However, this undertaking requires a detailed image of what conceptual processes and products finally get developed—an image of the cognitive-developmental "target," or as Taylor put it, the "*terminus ad quem*" (*p. 415*). Now the study of adult cognitive processes, for example, is currently an exciting and fast-moving field; I am referring to the sorts of studies of memory, perception, and attention that Neisser (1967), Norman (1969), and others have summarized. It is my distinct impression that most developmentalists have not paid close attention to this body of work, despite the fact that new discoveries about adult cognition may mean new or more refined developmental "targets" for us to investigate. In the same way, philosophical analyses of mature, "normative" thought may also enrich our image of, to paraphrase Toulmin (p. *38*), "what there is to mean" by cognitive development. There is yet another kind of contribution that philosophers could make to our field, however, and one quite different from that which the adult-cognition people could provide. I am referring to conceptual analyses of the processes and forms of development itself, as contrasted with the outputs or products of that development. The penetrating discussions of equilibration, sequences, stages, and the like by Mischel, Toulmin, and others at this conference are ample proof that philosophers can make unique contributions to our thinking about these troublesome topics—unique in the sense that their background and training leads them to formulate and analyze these issues in ways that would not likely occur to us. The plain fact is that developmental psychologists can use all the help they can get in defining and analyzing their problems, and it was a pleasant surprise for me, at least, to discover that philosophers may actually be able to help us.

References

Furth, H. G. *Thinking without language: Psychological implications of deafness*. New York: Free Press, 1966.

Neisser, U. *Cognitive psychology*. New York: Appelton, 1967.

Norman, D. A. *Memory and attention: An introduction to human information processing*. New York: Wiley, 1969.

FROM PRAXIS TO LOGOS: Genetic Epistemology and Physics [1]

Marx W. Wartofsky

I. Genetic Epistemology and Physical Science

Let me begin with a claim: Genetic epistemology is exactly what it claims to be. It is *not* developmental psychology. Genetic epistemology is a theory (or the domain of theories) about the growth of knowledge. Its theoretical claim is that developmental psychology is relevant to the study of the growth of knowledge, and in this respect, it is a radical theory. It is a standard view in the history and philosophy of science that the psychology of concept formation, or of theory formation, in the sciences is to be sharply distinguished from the epistemological analysis of theory and theory change; that, whereas the psychological study of the genesis of concepts and theories may give us insight into the mind or the behavior of scientists, it is ultimately irrelevant to the objective question of the epistemological status of such concepts and theories as knowledge or truth claims about the physical world. At one time, the distinction was sharply made between "contexts of discovery" and "contexts of justification," and epistemology proper was seen to be concerned only with the latter. (Here lies one source of the division between "philosophy" and "psychology," which Beilin talks about.) But the claim of genetic epistemology is radical on precisely this count; it asserts that the growth of knowledge may be studied in the psychology of concept and theory formation, and moreover, that scientific thought has its genetic origins in the typical structures and stages of cognitive growth in childhood.

Let me make a stronger claim: for Genetic epistemology, there is no distinction in principle between the history of physics and developmental psychology. Rather there is a division of labor between those who study the growth of knowledge phylogenetically, in the context of the history of

[1] Discussion of the article by Beilin, "The Development of Physical Concepts," *p. 85.*

the species (that is, its *cognitive* history, as against, say, its biological or social or economic history), and those who study the ontogenesis of cognitive growth in typical individuals. Piaget's enterprise, seen in this light, is only incidentally "psychology," in the normal acceptance of this term (if there is a "normal" acceptance). It is rather part of a much bolder theoretical enterprise, more akin to Giambattista Vico's historicism, or to Hegel's *Phänomenologie des Geistes,* or to Marx's historical materialism, or to Spencer's evolutionism, than it is to the small-bore experimentalism of "child psychology," in any of its typical disciplinary cubbyholes. Piaget's treatment of the development of physical concepts acquires its intellectual force and dramatic quality from his overriding developmental theory. The drama comes from a powerful tension between a neo-Kantian emphasis on species structures, as universal genetic patterns or forms of cognition, recapitulated by each individual of the species in each generation, and a neo-Hegelian emphasis on the unfolding (literally, "de-velopment") or maturation of species knowledge in the history of science. The tension is there despite the fact that the latter is a tacit framework, whereas the former is the explicit context of Piaget's experimental work. But the *telos* of Piaget's developmental psychology is scientific truth; the child's stages are, recursively viewed, steps towards a "correct" world view of physical reality, such as is achieved in adult scientific thought. This places Piaget squarely in the tradition of developmental historians of science of the French school (Meyerson, Lalande, and Brunschvicg), as well as in the tradition of that Mach for whom scientific thought was a biologically adaptive instrument of human action, and who saw the history of physics as a systematic development of the methodological principle of the "economy of thought."

Let me repeat the claim made here in another way: *The history of the development of physical concepts and theories is the history of physics; and genetic epistemology deals with the recurrent and underlying human conditions for the development of physics.* Is the claim, then, that the child's conception of objects, of causality, of space and time, of number, is part of the history of physics; that the developmental psychology of concept formation is to be woven into the "prehistory," or the "prescientific period," of the development of physical thought?

Perhaps the difficulty lies in the understanding of the term "history." If "history" is understood as a reconstruction of the past of the human species, and if "physics" is understood as systematic theory construction, observation, and experiment, dealing with matter (its constitution, structure, laws of motion, and change), then the developmental psychology of physical concept formation is an ontogenetic concern, with phylogenetic overtones only in the thinnest sense: namely, that the individual is an ideal type of the species and therefore simply exemplifies species characteristics. That is, such an ontogenetically oriented developmental psychology has to do with the species as species—with its biological and psychological structures and functions, once they are already evolved. *History*, on the other hand, presumably begins where speciation ends. Biological evolution having achieved a certain adaptive structure, ends (or at least our concern with it ends). To the extent that ontogeny recapitulates phylogeny, the individual simply realizes its species character in its development. On such a view, it would seem proper to distinguish *history* from *genesis*; and the history of physics from the genesis of physical concepts in the individual, or in the species. The latter is therefore a *species* study (akin to anatomy and physiology), and is, in a certain sense, part of biology—albeit of a ramified biology which deals with cognitive structure and function of the species. (The legitimation of such an approach in biology is already contained in the characterization of the species as *Homo sapiens.*) The genesis of physical concepts, on such a view, is not an historical study. Thc history of physical concept and theory formation presupposes the species already formed, the species structures of cognition already at hand, and simply goes on to recount or reconstruct the temporal adventures of the species in developing physical theory. Thus, the history of physics and the developmental psychology (or biology) of cognitive growth are seen as utterly distinct.

Beilin begins his account by reporting that Piaget prefers to be characterized as an epistemologist rather than as a psychologist. Let me take this seriously, as Beilin intends, and then argue that if it is true, the foregoing dichotomy between *history* and *genesis* will not hold up. If, as Beilin points out, Piaget's claim to be an epistemologist rests on his view that the nature of knowledge is related to how knowledge is acquired, then the history of physics and the genesis of physical concepts in the child are part of one and the same enterprise. But this is an exceptionally strong claim: namely, that physics and the genesis of physical concepts in the child are part of one and the genesis of physical concepts in the child are part of one and the same enterprise. But this is an exceptionally strong claim: namely, that *history* is *phylogeny*; that stages of historical development of physical theory are, in effect, stages of phylogenetic knowledge acquisition by the species, and in this sense are to be counted as part of its natural history, or at least, as an extension of its natural history, as a cognitive species. But then, the curious result is that *ontogeny recapitulates history*, that the ontogenesis of physical concepts and theories recapitulates the cognitive history of the species acquisition of physical knowledge. More specifically, the claim is that the ontogenesis of physical concepts is a part, and the recurrent and underlying part, of the history of physics; that it is the common starting point, the eternal womb of physical theory; and that the very condition for understanding physics and for its continued growth is the common species character of its fundamental concepts of space, time, and object, and the concomitant concepts of number and causality.[2]

This is a heady thesis, both for its speculative breadth and for its integrative potentialities. It is not simply that the child develops into the man, but that the child develops into Man, that is, into a species individual; and that an understanding of the history of science bears on (and is borne upon by) an understanding of concept development in the child.

The talk about ontogenesis and phylogenesis masks a more fundamental point: What is arrived at, both by the developing individual, and by the species, in its cognitive growth is knowledge of the external world. Therefore, what is involved here is not simply the genesis of concepts taken as a descriptive, empirical study. Rather, the study is normative, and teleological. For the claim is that the development of physical concepts is a progressive and adaptive one—that it eventuates in *knowledge*; that the conceptual network and the theories thus evolved approximate more adequately to truth. Thus, the study is not simply one which concerns the history or genesis of physical concepts, but their adequacy as well. This is the force of the epistemological emphasis in Piaget, and in this sense, he is the heir and executor of the tradition which includes the historian–epistemologists of science like Mach, Meyerson, Lalande, and others. But Piaget turns the enterprise to distinctive considerations: How is the genesis of physical concepts, as an epistemological concern, to be studied not alone in the framework of the history of physics, but in the living recreation of its foundations in every generation—that is, in the child's achievement of a conception of the physical world? In short, Piaget's genetic epistemology asks for an account of the mechanisms, structures, and functions of human thought which make physics possible, but distinctively asks for an account of their origins and early development in childhood.

In a sense, Piaget is asking Kant's question in the First Critique: "How is Science Possible?" But where Kant's epistemology gives a transcendental deduction of what structures of mind would be necessary for science to be possible, Piaget's genetic epistemology gives a developmental account of such structures.

The developmental account, however, differs widely from Kant's in one crucial respect. Though it is bound to something like conditional or biologically evolved *a priori* conditions for knowledge and for concept forma-

[2] This would presumably hold as well for other contexts. The ontogeny of social development or of socialization would be seen to recapitulate the phylogeny (the species history) of socialization or social formation, of property right, of communality, of rules and laws, etc.

tion, Piaget's developmental account takes its departure from the phenomenology of *praxis*, from the concrete circumstances and experiences of action. Like Kant, Piaget knows where he has to get to; the articulated concepts of *space, time, object, causality, number*. The forms of perception, the concepts of the understanding, stand for Piaget, as for Kant, as the *telos* of the theory. There it must attain. But Piaget's methodology is, ultimately, not Kant's transcendental deduction, legislated by what a rigorous and sustained rationality finds necessary, *a priori*, for the possibility of science—that is, what reason reconstructs as the necessary conditions for rational comprehension of the physical world. Piaget's methodology is closer to Aristotle's functionalism, asking rather: What would an organism, so constructed and in such a world, require for its preservation and for its growth? What instrumentalities of action, habit, thought, would equip it to fulfill its "nature"?—its "nature" being nothing more mysterious than its typical patterns of maturation, its well-being, its sociality (vague but plausibly definable characteristics of the species). Piaget's notion of "stages" is anything but a simple, empirically derived description of the move from action to concept. Rather, it is a teleologically conceived theory of maturation, of typical growth of the individual, from neonate organism to species being, that is, to cognitive adult member of a scientific community. The *telos* is quite clear: it is *truth*. Its mechanism is equally clear—it is what Piaget calls "true search," but might just as well have called the search for truth, since what characterizes "true search" is its methodology, and the norm for this methodology is one or another version of scientific, or prescientific inquiry. Without this *telos*, one could reduce Piaget's genetic epistemology to descriptive developmental psychology. But *knowledge* is a normative term; its acquisition is not simply a natural process (though it is certainly also that), but an achievement. The stages of cognitive growth are thereby not simply sequential, but developmental, cumulative, and adaptively successful. Cognitive development is not simply a *fact* of ontogenesis, but a *norm* of ontogenesis. But the norm is not simply ontogenetic, not simply set by the biologically *a priori* structures of the organism, as biological individual. Rather, the norm is set by the cognitive development of the species, in the history of science. A Newton, a Planck, an Einstein simply represent what the capacities of the species are, in attaining knowledge of the physical world. The account of the child's development of physical concepts is an account of the early and typical development of these capacities.

That is how I understand Piaget's enterprise. These prefatory remarks therefore set the context for the discussion of Beilin's thoughtful and well-elaborated reconstruction and critique of Piaget's views on the development of physical concepts. At the same time, these remarks address themselves right off to Beilin's conclusion that "it is not clear that the data of psychological research . . . have been of any significant use to philosophers" (*p. 117*). I have already suggested what the relation is between philosophy and developmental psychology—or more accurately, developmental psychology in the context of genetic epistemology. Put this way, Beilin's question about the testability of the claim that understanding the nature of mind "is the same" as understanding how it develops (*p. 117*) almost answers itself. Developmental psychology is the applied, experimental inquiry into the conditions and typical structures and sequences of cognitive growth; it is, in effect, applied or experimental epistemology, as distinct from the related scientific enterprise, analytic epistemology. Its theoretical context is genetic—that is, it is epistemology viewed in the contexts of the origins of knowledge, and of the evolution or growth of knowledge; further, it is essentially a naturalistic epistemology with a strong instrumentalist bias, in that the attainment of knowledge is seen as an adaptive utility in normal maturation of the individual, and in the history of cognitive development of the species. The origins of our concepts and theories in action, in the *praxis* necessary for human life, and the redirection of our concepts and theories to the rationalization of *praxis*, both attest to the functional character of theory in the life of the species. In such a context, philosophy and developmental psychology can hardly be seen as exclusive, but are rather different emphases within the same enterprise.

This is a roughly reconstructed Piagetism, and it may strike psychologists as odd, even if they are aware of Piaget's own insistence on the term "epistemology," and his philosophical biases. (It often strikes competent and hard-working physicists as odd that such otherwise sober scientists as Einstein, Poincaré, or Bohr should have permitted themselves to waste so much useful professional time on matters "philosophical," when they might have been doing *real* work.) But without Piaget's notions of *genesis* and *structure*, without the framework of epistemology proper (as against "psychology"—a distinction which Piaget makes and violates constantly), his notion of *physical concept* cannot be realized.

A physical concept is one whose appropriate or fully developed instance is to be found in physics, that is, in the most current physical science. The evolution of that concept is to be traced in the history of physical thought, that is, in the history of physics proper. And the origins of that concept are to be found, presumably, in the prehistory of physics, that is, in the history of primitive thought, at some "beginning" which arises out of human action, or practice, and out of the human capacities or structures with which such practice is undertaken. But since we have little access to prehistoric man, we study this genesis analogically in children, *who may be said to recapitulate the stages of this prehistoric conceptual development.* This is, in effect, what Piaget (1970) calls "the fundamental hypothesis of genetic epistemology."

Now what is normative and what is not, in the study of the growth of knowledge? One may say that any study of "growth" is already imbued with a teleological spirit, at least in that qualified sense of teleology which views growth as a normal pattern, with an ordered sequence of stages, in which the earlier stages are preconditions for the later ones. Such a "law of development" is not teleological in the sense that it is foreordained with respect to some conscious end in view; nor does it require conscious goal-seeking at any stage. The organism need not be said to "know" its end in view, any more than one would ascribe such a knowledge, say, to the foetus in its stages of development and growth. But such a pattern of growth is ordered with respect to a "normal" sequence, and as such, it is lawlike. This sort of developmental pattern, or law of development, has been characterized as "teleonomic" rather than "teleological," by Pittendrigh, to distinguish such developmental patterns in biology from conscious goal-seeking with an end in view; and it seems clear that this is the kind of "teleology" which Aristotle has in mind in his naturalistic and nonmental account of organic development (see Wartofsky, 1968, p. 261). Piaget may be said to have a similar notion of growth, normative in this qualified sense, when he distinguishes "psychological" from "epistemological" questions. That is, apart from the normative question of *truth*, or of *truth seeking*, one may deal with normal cognitive sequence as an "empirical" question. One need not, therefore, ascribe greater approximation to truth in the later stages, or, to put it differently, the pattern of cognitive growth may not be, and need not be, interpreted as a pattern of epistemological growth. The latter would require a criterion of growth of knowledge such that one could determine a passage from ignorance to knowledge. In short, the latter would require a definition of truth and a criterion of truth, and the ordering of stages of growth would be determined by this criterion, rather than by any temporal or maturational sequence. Now the two alternative sequences may be identified, or they may be confused. A psychological sequence of perceptual and conceptual maturation may be taken to be identical with, or at least isomorphic with, a sequence of epistemological attainment, on some explicit theory of their correlation. But it is more likely that the two will simply be confused one with the other. Piaget tries very hard to keep them apart, and therefore to distinguish genetic psychology from genetic epistemology. He separates the question of epistemological achievement from the question of psychological development, by being explicit about the criterion of conceptual success; he takes it to be, in effect, the successful socialization of the child with respect to the norms of the adult community. In cognitive terms, this means the conceptual socialization of the child with regard to the norms of adult common sense and adult natural science, mathematics, and logic. But he leaves the epistemological status of these adult norms open. For example, in *The child's conception of physical causality* (1960), he poses the question of the relation of child thought to reality (or external reality) as a "psychological" rather than an "epistemological" problem, on the grounds that he is adopting as a norm the view of world reality of contemporary science and contemporary common sense, but is not intruding upon the epistemological question of the status of this scientific world view. Piaget writes, "For our part, we shall confine ourselves to psychology, to the search, that is, for the relation between child-thought and reality as the scientific thought of our time conceives it. And this view, narrow and question-begging though it appear, will enable us to formulate very clearly several outstanding problems" (1960, p. 238). But he adds, shortly thereafter, the following, on the relation which this "restricted method" may have to a wider theoretical program:

> It may very well be that the psychological laws arrived at by our restricted method can be extended into epistemological laws arrived at by analysis of the history of the sciences: the elimination of realism, of substantialism, of dynamism, the growth of relativism, etc., all these are evolutionary laws which appear to be common both to the development of the child and to that of scientific thought.
>
> We are in no way suggesting, it need hardly be said, that our psychological results will admit straight away of being generalized into epistemological laws. All that we expect is that, with the cooperation of methods more powerful than our own (historical, sociological methods, etc.), it will be possible to establish between our conclusions and those of epistemological analysis a relation of particular case to general law, or rather of infinitesimal variation to the whole of a curve (Piaget, 1960, p. 240).

However one takes Piaget's methodological qualifications, or his separation of psychological from epistemological considerations, the wider theoretical program sets the framework for the narrower methodology nevertheless. Piaget eschews dogmatism in avoiding a simplistic claim for the "truth" of the adult world view, or of contemporary science. Yet, it *is* his norm, and it is his norm on genetic grounds. Science is the outcome of species adaptation; it is, so to speak, an organic development, deriving from the interplay of *praxis* and the structures which the human organism brings to its experience. Therefore, Piaget has put the epistemological question into a developmental framework as well. What criteria of rationality, of criticism, of analysis, of practical test *can* there be for epistemic claims, which are not themselves the products of human action and reflection? If the epistemological status of the contemporary scientific world view is itself to come under critical scrutiny, it can only be by a cognitive apparatus evolved under the very conditions studied in genetic psychology. And insofar as such a reflective conceptual criticism is part of the enterprise of the history of science, of historical sociology, of sociology of knowledge, of analytic epistemology—that is, of critical reflective disciplines whose subject matter *is* this very domain of adult thought itself—to that extent too is Piaget's *own* study a contribution to epistemology; and where this is explicit, it is the content of his genetic epistemology. In fact, Piaget's explicit hope is that the psychological studies of child thought may themselves contribute to the clarification of *scientific* questions. Thus, he recounts the effect of Einstein's question to him on the primitivity of time or speed, in the child's conception of the relative motions of objects: Einstein's question, in 1928, set off a whole series of psychological studies by Piaget and his collaborators; these psychological findings were later utilized in the work of the French relativistic physicists, Abelé and Malvaux (1954). Piaget uses this example to make a point concerning the relation of child psychology and genetic epistemology:

> In certain instances, the genetic study of the construction of concepts and operations provides a response to questions posed by the sciences with respect to their methods of knowledge. When this is the case, child psychology becomes extended into a "genetic epistemology" (Piaget, 1967, pp. 83–84).

Strictly speaking, one may question this "extension," on the grounds that even here, the wider epistemological question as to the validity of the scientific world view, or its "truth," is not touched on, but only the correlation of child thought with the articulated and systematic thought of the adult world as expressed in science. One may argue that the contribution which genetic *psychology* makes to science is simply one of suggesting fresh conceptual standpoints, derived from the child's thought, as interesting starting points for theoretical construction in physics. In this sense, the reconstruction of the child's world view, in a systematic fashion, is analogous to the interpretation of classical metaphysical constructs in the history of philosophy, as themselves a heuristic for scientific thought and theory construction (see Wartofsky, 1967). But I would argue in defense of the *epistemological* content of such reconstructions and interpretations—they are part of the ongoing analysis and critique of concepts, which is linked to the formulation of testable hypotheses, and this *is* an epistemological enterprise which concerns epistemological issues in the philosophy of science.

In this sense, the relation of *Praxis*, of concrete practice and action in the world, to *Logos*, to the construction of conceptual systems or theories which serve both as rational explanations and as guides to action, is similar in the genesis of the child's thought and in the genesis of scientific thought. Piaget has already suggested analogies between child thought and, for example, the genesis of the physical world view of the pre-Socratics (Thales, Anaximander, Anaximenes, and others; see Piaget, 1931). But these thinkers were the generators and founders of physical science, and not simply "childish philosophers." If an antigenetic view would argue that one should separate the genesis and history of science from science "proper" and from the epistemological questions in science, it would also argue that genetic psychology and genetic epistemology are separate. The same questions arise in both cases, indicating that the general issue is the same, and that the relation of genetic psychology to genetic epistemology bears on the relation of the history of science to the epistemology of science, or more broadly, to the philosophy of science (an issue which has finally reared its head among philosophers of science). I would go further and suggest that Piaget's model of the reciprocity between genesis and structure, and his account of the activity[3] of the subject in constructing such logical, mathematical, and physical structures, is as viable for the "genetic epistemology" (or historical epistemology) of science, as it is for the genetic epistemology of child thought.

To sum up: The relation of genetic epistemology to the development of physical concepts needs to be seen not simply in the context of the development of the child's conception of physical causality, or of number, or of space and time, but in the context of contemporary physical science, mathematics, and logic, *and* in the context of the history of science. At the minimum, this is required because the stages of cognitive development are seen by Piaget within the framework of socialization of the child—that is, of the achievement by the child of the world view of adult common sense and contemporary science. (Where these latter two are in conflict, more interesting problems and opportunities arise.) But beyond this, if Piaget's work is seen as having epistemological import, then the development of child thought becomes an aspect of the development of species knowledge, and as such it is part of either the prehistory of physics, or of the ongoing cognitive ground for the cultural continuity of physical science; that is, the child's development of such concepts becomes the cultural or social "apprenticeship" without which the cultural transmission of scientific

[3] On the activity of the subject as "practical activity," Piaget notes that the spirit of Kant's proposal that perception is "organized" by the subject should be taken not in a "transcendental" way, as Kant took it, but in terms of the "real constructions" which arise in actual perceptual activity. He sees in this the content of Marx's *Theses on Feuerbach* (see, especially, Thesis V), in which "practical, human-sensuous activity" is counterposed to "sensuous contemplation" (Piaget, 1969, p. 362, footnote 1). By extension, given Piaget's account of the relation of perception to conceptual thought, this same "practical activity" is the matrix and genesis of conceptual–theoretical structures, as these are, in turn, the organizing modes of practical activity, in that reciprocity of genesis and structure which Piaget sees as his distinctive view. The relation of this view to Hegelian and Marxist notions of dialectic interaction of subject and object seems *prima facie* clear, but needs to be examined further.

thought, and the provision of intellectual cadres for the continuation of scientific thought, could not take place. This may be seen as having only descriptive import, as a matter of the sociology of science or of knowledge; but in fact, the attainment of knowledge, as a quest for truths about the world, is the content of scientific inquiry. And insofar as the child, in its cognitive development, is made a participant in this quest, the epistemological import of its development is clear, though the epistemological questions concerning this development still remain to be studied. Piaget liberates analytic epistemology from the narrower constraints of formalism, and from the dogmas of analytic self-sufficiency, by bridging the gap between child psychology and genetic epistemology. That the bridge remains problematic attests to the difficulty of the question, but not to its irrelevance.

II. On Piaget's "Mentalism"

There is a fast and loose characterization of "mentalism" abroad in the land, both in philosophical and psychological discussion. Beilin is correct in talking about a "renaissance of mentalist philosophizing in psychology," if we accept his very broad characterization of "mentalism"— namely, the ascription of "cognitive mechanisms" to the organism, or the introduction of "terms of great generality," like *equilibration*, or of more limited applicability, like *conservation*. On these grounds, anything beyond functional correlation of data statements is "mentalist," and even the hardiest behaviorist is tainted with mentalist heresy, once he strays from measurement statements and their correlation. The confusion here seems to be between "mentalist" and "inferred-entity theorist." The latter is a mentalist only if the "inferred entities" (mechanisms, operations, capacities, etc.) are "mentalistic." But this depends on some specified demarcation of "mental" from "physical" (or, at the very least, "nonmental"), and the issue remains unjoined if the demarcation is not specified. For example, *drive* is not a "mental" term, but an *abstract* term, presumably a functional term, characterizing a disposition, or a set of dispositions. But unless "disposition" in turn is characterized as "mental," there is no ground for characterizing a drive theorist as a mentalist.

There is a more restricted sense of "mental" which Beilin adduces, however, which derives from "inferred entity" talk, but which specifically avers "covert" or "internal" cognitive operations, and these, presumably, are operations of the mind. Now there is a certain liberation from the self-conscious constraints of philosophical behaviorism, in freely talking, once again, of the "mental." But the strength of the claim which such usage makes, or the characterization of the operations or structures which it suggests, has to be carefully assessed. This has to do with general problems of theory construction or model building. If Piaget talks about *equilibration, conservation, reversibility, assimilation,* or *accommodation, these* are clearly theoretical terms of wide import and of great abstraction. But they are just as clearly functional terms, that is, general terms for specifiable operations, introduced both to order and to explain a large variety of particular operations. All instances of a certain operation can be characterized as instances of reversibility, whatever the specific contexts, because of formal similarities in the operation. So too with the other terms. What tempts us to characterize these terms as mentalistic is that these operations are ostensibly covert, internalized, and take place "in the mind" at a certain stage of development, though at an earlier stage, as action concepts, they are exemplified in outward behavior, in the manipulation of objects, in body, hand, or eye movements. So too with the notion of *structures* of the mind: functions presumably bespeak structures, as the abiding or developed forms which account for the functions. Structures of the mind are reducible therefore to dispositions, faculties, or capacities, evoked appropriately in interaction with an environment, and attested to by the regularity or universality of their evocation under similar environmental conditions. But what makes such structures "mental"? In a trivial sense, they are "mental" just because that is what we mean by "mental," and nothing more. But then, "mentalism" is a fake issue, since even the most physicalistic antimentalist will find no great discomfort in talking about "structures" as typical values of a set of response variables under typical stimulus conditions. If what makes such general terms for operations or structures "mentalistic" is something more than this, we have to know *what* more. If it is the speculative or constructive latitude which Piaget permits himself, in his introduction of such general and abstract terms, then "mentalism" is no more than an index of theoretical imaginativeness. The *S* matrix in quantum mechanics is, on this account, just as "mental" as equilibration in Piaget's genetic epistemology. If the objection is that, in the one case, we are talking about physical entities *tout court,* and in the other, about cognitive ones, then the distinction is simply a handy one, and "mentalist" comes to no more than "cognitivist." So what? That Piaget is a cognitivist is no great discovery. And to permit the perversities of an old-fashioned and ill-advised behaviorist reductionism to dictate that all who refuse to be held within its injunctions are hereafter to be labeled "mentalists" is simply to substitute one perversity for another. Perhaps "mentalist" should be used thus: physicist, biologist, mentalist—that is, as a synonym for psychologist. Since even Skinner eschews the "empty organism" view, what is left?

So much for Piaget's "mentalism." It ascribes to him only the methodological freedom to construct *theories,* rather than to simply "report the facts." But since this has been the prerogative of every other science, and moreover, is a condition for its even claiming to *be* a science, what is all the fuss and bother about in psychology? I would venture to guess that the issue *does* concern theory construction, about which psychologists have been self-conscious and shamefaced for two generations, simply because they have had to reject *some* classical theories as less than fruitful, if not downright misleading. So what? Piaget's theoretical constructs may prove to be false, misleading, fruitless over the long run. But he is a scientist and so he theorizes. He is a psychologist, and so the theoretical constructs he proposes are "mental." And so he is a "mentalist." But then, so is every psychological theorist, in this vacuous sense of "mental." Nor do we need the Fodorian apologies, that, in fact, there may be neurophysiological structures to "explain" the mental structures or operations, so that one may be a "mentalist" and a "materialist" all at once. Since when is it the case that methodological diversity entails metaphysical dualism? Now, that there are deep issues here, I will not deny. But they are not the ones raised in the contemporary hoopla over "mentalism." Chomsky introduces "mind" by methodological fiat, as a theoretical framework for the theory of language acquisition (and also as a rhetorical ploy within an uptight discipline, in order to *épater les bourgeois*). Piaget proposes theoretical terms for "mental" operations, because he is dealing with knowledge and its growth, and "knowing" may harmlessly be described as "mental," in a grand old tradition. The fetishism of "mentality," which Ryle takes as the object of his special critique, and which has become a local industry (small manufacturing) in Anglo-American philosophy, should not blind us to the vacuousness of the charge of "mentalism" in Piaget's case. Being "squarely among the mentalists in that these mechanisms and processes are inferred entities created to explain observed behavior" (Beilin, *p. 86*) is no more than being "squarely among the scientists who create theories to explain the way the world is."

III. From "Mentalism" to "Innatism"

More crucial than confusions made or distinctions drawn concerning "mentalism" is the real issue involved in *nativism* or *innatism*. There is a weak sense of *innatism*, which surely characterizes Piaget's view. If the terms *assimilation* and *accommodation* are to make any sense at all, then there must be some structure or character *to which* the child assimilates or accommodates his new experience. The logic of the process requires, therefore, a structure prior to experience, to which it is assimilated or accommodated. But this is a weak sense indeed, since one can argue that such structures are not native but are the acquisition of earliest experience; in effect, the imprinting, on some almost totally plastic organism by its original, neonate experience. Now this obviously goes too far, for we are not born genetically innocent, but are indeed the heirs to our species evolution. The question, therefore, is how to interpret claims about *cognitive* structures. Perceptual mechanisms and structures, according to Piaget, have their roots in organic processes, but are developed in interaction with an external environment. Cognitive structures are developed in this interaction, not apart from perception, but as an aspect of the development of perception. As Beilin makes clear, Piaget clearly distinguishes his own position, on the genesis and status of such cognitive structures, from that of the empiricists (associationists or inductivists, like G. E. Müller) and from innatists or apriorists (even among the Gestaltists—Piaget specifically mentions W. Metzger—who disclaimed this characterization). Piaget writes, "it is necessary to oppose the geneticism without structure of empiricism and the structuralism without genesis of Gestalt phenomenology with a genetic structuralism in which each structure is the product of a genesis and each genesis merely the passage from a less evolved structure to a more complex one. It is in this context of an active structuring that the exchange between subject and object take place" (Piaget, 1969, p. 364).

Beilin correctly criticizes the views which ascribe innatism to Piaget. But he puts the burden of *apriorism* on Piaget's notion of fixed developmental stages, and characterizes him therefore as a "preformationist" or a "maturationist." If there is, in fact, a "fixed" and "built-in" developmental sequence, "impervious to environmental influence" with respect to its sequence structure, though facilitated by transactions with an environment, this is innatism enough. Indeed, Beilin ascribes such a sequence (if it were to exist) to a species-specific genetic programming; such a notion of a genetic program impervious to environmental influence (except perhaps in the facilitation of these built-in stages) is as innatist as one can reasonably get, without going all the way, to a notion of "innate ideas" which includes specific "content of idea" as well as "form." But Beilin dismisses, as untenable, the alternative possibility of "consistent cultural experience in a wide variety of social environments." Here, perhaps, Piaget needs defense. For, after correctly characterizing Piget's view as neither innatist nor empiricist, and after correctly assessing Piaget's emphasis on the activity of the subject, and on interactionism, Beilin still ascribes a strong *apriorism* and innatism to Piaget, by way of his maturationism. But Piaget is quite explicit in rejecting such a view, which he characterizes as "structuralism without genesis." He sees the strongest influence of such a view in Gestalt psychology, and he sees it as stemming from the work of Husserl (specifically, the influence of Husserl, 1913). Piaget describes Koffka as holding such a view, namely, that "development is determined entirely by maturation, i.e. by a preformation which itself obeys Gestalt laws. Genesis remains secondary to the fundamental preformist perspective" (Piaget, 1967, p. 146). In contrast, Piaget characterizes his own view as decidedly different in that it requires "true reciprocity of structure and genesis," and therefore no preformation. His thesis is that "genesis emanates from a structure and culminates in a structure." Thus, there is no fully plastic organism, as a radical associationist–empiricist might claim; at every stage there is *some* structure, but a structure plastic enough to develop, that is, to be modified or reconstructed in the interaction with an environment. Conversely, therefore, "every structure has a genesis," says Piaget; and, "there are no innate structures: every structure presupposes a construction." This seems clear and explicit enough as a rejection of innatism in the sense of preformationism. But the question may still be asked, as Beilin asks it: granting that there are no preformed structures of perception or of cognition, is there a preformed maturational sequence which is itself a *second-order* structure that is innate? Or does Piaget's anti-innatism hold also for the maturational sequence? Can the sequence be *changed*—that is, not merely slowed down, speeded up, or repressed? Can there be jumps in the sequence? Are there alternative sequences? In the criticism of Koffka, cited above, Piaget seems straightforward in his rejection of a fixed and preformed maturational sequence. Yet it seems clear that the scientific aim of Piaget's work is to establish certain laws of maturational development, certain "fixed" sequences of perceptual and cognitive attainment.

Here the issues and confusions on the question of innatism all rise to the surface (as they have in the discussion of Chomsky's "innatism" in linguistics), and it is worth sorting out just what the claim (or the charge) of innatism contains. The strongest claim for innatism is that our "ideas" are innate, or that "language" is innate. But of course, the strength of the claim depends entirely on what one means by "idea" or "language." The strongest innatism might claim (as in Plato's case) that the "idea" of *circle* is innate, as a precondition for the experience of something as a circle; and that such "ideas" are universals of which the particular experiences are instances or exemplars. In the linguistic cases, the strongest claim would be that *a* language is innate, that is, some natural language, say English or Chinese. But this is patently absurd. The modified innatist claim is that universal formal structures of language are innate (as "species-specific genetic programs," perhaps?), in the sense that, as Chomsky might put it, grammatical competence is a necessary condition for language acquisition, and that such grammatical competence bespeaks a grammar, as the universal formal structure which is mapped onto the surface structure of speech (thus, mapped differently onto various phonetic, syntactic, and semantic "surfaces" in different natural languages, but, at the level of its deep structure, universal for all languages). There is a reading of this view that makes it a plausible hypothesis: namely, that there is a biological component of the evolved organism which may be characterized as structural, and which is genetically determined, or at least, genetically cued or specified. Thus, it is biologically *a priori*, and in this sense, innate. Thus far, Piaget would agree, I think. But what exactly is such a species-specific structure? It is plain enough, if we take various organs of the body as our examples. The lungs, for example, have the "competence" to effect a transfer of oxygen and carbon dioxide simply as a function of their physiological chemical structure (that is, in conjunction with the heart, circulatory system, the structure of blood cells, the characteristics of gas diffusion through a membrane, etc.). But there does not seem to be a *development* of lung function in maturation (except in the fetal stage, and in the transition to air breathing at birth), though there is growth. However, in language acquisition, as in perceptual and conceptual growth, there is a pattern of development which may be characterized as a sequence of stages, in which elements of the later stage are not present in the earlier ones. What is "innate" in such a case cannot be the acquired language, or perceptual skill, or the acquired concepts. We are forced back, therefore, either to (*a*) an underlying formal structure which perdures through such acquisition, and provides the permanent framework through all the developmental stages (for example, universal grammar, in its "deep structure" or Kantian *a priori* forms of perception or of the understanding); or (*b*) an underlying pattern of the development of structures, that is, a second-order structure which remains permanent or constant (or fixed) as the *form* of first-order structural change, that is, as the specification of the sequence stages of structural change. Such a second-order structure is, in effect, a law of evolution or of development. But what sort of "structure" is this? It is clearly not to be understood as an organ, or as a physiological structure in the ordinary sense. To call it "genetic preprogramming" makes use of a metaphor whose import is not clear in the case of cognitive or conceptual growth, though it does make sense to talk of genetic control or specification of a sequence of maturation in biological terms—for example, stages of myelination of neurons, of the development of the musculature of focus and accommodation in the eye, or of hormonal regulation of physical growth patterns or of sexual maturation. These latter may be characterized as "preformed" in terms of "genetic preprogramming." But does Piaget allege that this sort of developmental sequence is characteristic of perceptual or cognitive growth? Is preprogramming or preformation requisite for all developmental or evolutionary laws? Apparently not, for he specifically inveighs against such a view (for example, in Koffka, as we have seen, but also in his rejection of Kantian *apriorism* in its transcendental, or "necessary" form). Piaget holds, rather, that the reciprocity of structure and genesis has to be a "genuine" reciprocity, that is, such that the genesis actually generates new structures by modification of older ones. On such an interactionist view, the only thing that can "fix" a developmental sequence is the joint operation of structure and environment, in the crucible of practical and critical activity by a subject. Since genesis is a necessary condition for the emergence of structure, and since genesis and prior structure (or equivalently, structure and subsequent genesis) are the necessary and jointly sufficient conditions for any new structure, as Piaget urges that they are, then "imperviousness to environmental influence" cannot make sense, and we are driven to seek our universals of developmental sequence elsewhere than in "genetic preprogramming."

Piaget holds a more dialectical and less mechanistic view than the one Beilin ascribes to him, I think. The fixity of developmental sequence does not require preformation, but does require universals of *both* structure and environment; and both of these may plausibly be held to be provided in any normal human context. What such a fixed developmental sequence may be said to be impervious to are *accidents* of environmental influence—by definition, therefore, those environmental variations do not, or cannot affect the sequence, in its ordinal structure, but can only cause variations *within* the maturational order—that is, speed it up, slow it down, repress some elements of it, elicit others, etc.

I see a difficulty with this formulation too, however. It introduces, in effect, a *caeteris paribus* clause into the account of development, which simply underwrites "normal" developmental patterns (that is, those which have a high distribution in the experimenter's sample, or worse yet, those which he chooses to take as "fair sample" or paradigm cases) as the *universal* cases, or patterns of development.

There is still another conceptual difficulty with the notion of maturational sequence as a universal and "fixed" sequence of stages, if the fixity is taken as a product of the joint operation of structural and genetic universals: Given some sequence, ABCDF, which is reconstructed as the "normal" case, and given some alternative sequence ABDEF, in which the element C does not appear, and in which a new element E appears, do we then say that we have two "incomplete" mappings of some prefigured structure, ABCDEF, one of which is "normal" simply on grounds of distribution? Or do we have two alternative sequences, with only certain similarities, and no prefigured or preformed "deep structure" of which they may be said to be "incomplete" mappings? Which of the two sequences represents a law of development? Piaget, I suspect, would answer with Leibniz, *Natura non facit saltum*, and that "skipped" stages simply do not occur, because (in our example) D in the second sequence just could not be the same stage as D in the first sequence, since it was not generated out of the same previous structure. (The D which is a modification of C is not the same as the D which is a modification of B.) We may compensate, in experience, for missing structures, as, for example, the blind do. But the result is a different structure from that acquired by the sighted. Still, where the compensation has to do with *cognitive* structures, there may be equivalences, so that the same set of formal properties of a group of operations (for example, in logical or mathematical concepts, or in the basic formal concepts of reversibility) may be achieved. But the physical intuitions in that modality (for example, sight) will simply be missing, and will be substituted for, to the extent that there is an isomorphism at the perceptual level, by physical intuitions (and operations) in another sense modality (for example touch).

In short, it seems to me that Piaget need not be characterized as a preformationist, even in the qualified way which Beilin suggests, but should be given his due as an interactionist. The "fixed" maturational sequence requires fixity in both the native structures which the organism brings to its experience, and in the structures of that experience itself, as they are features of the objective world of the subject's activity: of his physical and his cultural and human world. Socialization (conceptual socialization included here) is not merely a matter of imposing some *a priori* sociality of man's innate nature upon his experience; nor is it merely a matter of fully plastic adaptation to the demands of an objectively sundered world which imprints its "own" patterns on us. And it is too much to assume that the pattern of socialization—for that is what cognitive growth is, in its deepest implications—is genetically preprogrammed. But, it therefore seems to me too much to assume that Piaget assumes it, for the logic of his argument provides for formation without preformation, for sequence and law without design, and for the development of concepts without innate determination of their form or content or sequence. What remains, as the most general thesis concerning the emergence of physical concepts, is a meta-theory of development, which guides Piaget's work, and which is so easily accepted and so easily acceptable to common sense that its audacity and its heuristic power are too often overlooked: namely, the thesis that *praxis* and *logos* are indissoluble, and that in the genetic sequence of human development, the separation of *logos* from *praxis* is impossible.

References

Abelé, J., & Malvaux, C. *Vitesse et univers relativiste.* Paris: Sedez, 1954.

Husserl, E. Ideen zu einer reinen Phänomenologie und phänomenologische Philosophie. In *Jahrbuch für Philosophie und phänomenologische Forschung.* Vol. 1. Halle: Niemeyer, 1913.

Piaget, J. Children's philosophies. In C. Murchison (Ed.), *Handbook of child psychology.* Worcester, Massachusetts: Clark Univ. Press, 1931.

Piaget, J. *The child's conception of physical causality.* Paterson, New Jersey: Littlefield, 1960 (reprint).

Piaget, J. *Six psychological studies.* Edited by D. Elkind. New York: Random House (Vintage), 1967.

Piaget, J. *The mechanisms of perception.* Translated by G. N. Seagrim. London: Routledge, 1969.

Piaget, J. *Genetic epistemology.* Translated by E. Duckworth. New York: Columbia Univ. Press, 1970.

Wartofsky, M. Metaphysics as heuristic for science. In R. S. Cohen & M. Wartofsky (Eds.), *Boston studies in the philosophy of science.* Vol. 3. New York: Humanities Press, 1967. Pp. 123–172.

Wartofsky, M. *Conceptual foundations of scientific thought.* New York: Macmillan, 1968.

Part II

Basic Issues in the Psychology of Cognitive Development

B. The Development of Moral Concepts

FROM IS TO OUGHT: How to Commit the Naturalistic Fallacy and Get Away with It in the Study of Moral Development [1]

Lawrence Kohlberg

I. Genetic Epistemology and Moral Psychology

The general questions discussed in this book are (*a*) "What can the psychological study of the development of concepts tell us about their epistemological status?" or, "Can developmental psychology help solve philosophical problems?" and (*b*) "What does the psychological study of concept development require in the way of epistemological assumptions about knowing?" or, "Can philosophers help psychologists solve developmental problems?"

I think psychologists are clear as to why child psychology needs epistemology. Many of us feel that the study of cognition by American child psychology failed to progress for two generations because of an inadequate epistemology, sometimes called logical positivism or behaviorism. The critical defect of this epistemology for child psychology was that it did not allow the psychologist to think about cognitive processes as involving knowledge. The critical category of the Stimulus–response approach was "learning," not "knowing," where the concept of "learning" did not imply "knowing." Accordingly, S–R theory assumes that the

[1] In revising this article, I have attempted to deal with some of the issues raised by Peters' and Alston's comments. While I cannot thank them for accepting my presumptuous contentions, I can thank them for taking my contentions seriously enough to make sympathetic, penetrating, and helpful comments. It should also be noted that Alston's comments are based on an earlier version of my article, prepared prior to the Binghamton conference; what appears here is a thorough revision of that article which incorporates, in places, attempts to answer some of Alston's criticisms of the earlier version. The empirical psychological side of the work discussed here is more fully documented in Kohlberg (1969), and Kohlberg and Turiel (1971). The philosophic contentions in their application to education have been discussed in Kohlberg (1970a, b). The research discussed has been supported by NICHD Grant 0246903.

process of learning truths is the same as the processes of learning lies or illusions. It explains the learning of logical operations or "truths" in terms of the same processes as those involved in learning a social dance step (which is cognitively neutral), or those involved in "learning" a psychosis or a pattern of maze errors (which are cognitively erroneous).

To study cognition, one must have some sort of concept of knowledge in terms of which children's development is observed. Piaget's fundamental contribution to developmental psychology has been to observe children's development in terms of the categories (space, time, causality, etc.) which philosophers have deemed central to knowing. The fact that the cognitive categories of the philosopher are central for understanding the behavior development of the child is so apparent, once pointed out, that one recognizes that it is only the peculiar epistemology of the positivistic behaviorist which could have obscured it.

In my own area, moral development, the epistemological blinders psychologists have worn have hidden from them the fact that the concept of morality is itself a philosophical (ethical) rather than a behavioral concept. When I started my research on the psychology of moral development, I was aware of the necessity for orienting to philosophic concepts of morality (Kohlberg, 1958), and I believe it is mainly for that reason that I have uncovered some quite important facts not previously noted. I was not aware, however, that empirical developmental study might contribute to the solution of distinctively philosophic problems in both normative ethics and metaethics. The focus of this article is upon the implications I now believe my genetic studies have for philosophic ethics; hence the title "from is [the facts of moral development] to Ought [the ideal content and epistemological status of moral ideas]." My assumption that one needs to orient developmental research to philosophic concepts of morality will not be very controversial to this group. One can be pluralistic as to philosophic concepts and arrive at the same research conclusions: Piaget need not have an ultimately correct concept of causality, as a philosophic category, to conduct valid research on the empirical development of causal concepts. Similarly, whether one starts from Kant, Mill, Hare, Ross, or Rawls in defining morality, one gets similar research results. While philosophic concepts of morality differ from one another, their differences are minor compared with the differences between almost any philosophic concept of morality and such psychological concepts of morality as "conscience is a conditioned avoidance reaction to certain classes of acts or situations" (Eysenck, 1961) or "moral values are evaluations of action believed by members of a given society to be 'right' " (Berkowitz, 1964).

However, when one turns from using philosophy to orient empirical research to claiming that empirical research results help clarify and define an ultimately adequate, universal, and mature conception of morality, one enters much more controversial ground. As Alston puts it,

> . . . unless Kohlberg can do more than he has done to show that his choice of a definition of "moral" is based on something more than a personal preference among the variety of definitions that have been proposed, the fact that his later stages conform more exactly to his conception of moral judgment has no objective significance. . . . If Kohlberg wants to investigate the development of moral reasoning according to some arbitrarily selected criterion of "moral," well and good; he may come up with something interesting. But if he wants to use the developmental approximations to the purely moral in his sense as a basis for pronouncements as to how people *ought* to reason in their action-guiding deliberations, that is another matter. If these pronouncements are to carry any weight, he will have to show that this sense of "moral" which is functioning as his standard has itself some recommendation other than congeniality to his predilections (*pp. 276–277*).

Now, obviously a developmental psychologist must be a fool to enter the den of philosophical wolves (even if they were all as tolerant and gentlemanly as Alston and Peters) with a set of "Is to Ought" claims unless he has to. It is my belief that the developmental psychologist must eventually do so for two reasons. First, it is necessary for any ethically justifiable educational or other practical application of his research findings. It is almost self-evident that no psychologist would engage in moral research with the notion that the use of such research is the creation of instrumentalities of manipulation and control to be made available to adult "socializing agents." By any philosophic definition, it is not moral to subject a child to such manipulation. It was because of this practical concern, the concern to develop my research implications into an active program of moral education (Kohlberg 1970a, b; Blatt & Kohlberg, 1971), that I first began to worry seriously about the implication of my moral research for a definite ethical position. Earlier, my major philosophic claim was that the stimulation of development is the only ethically acceptable form of moral education. I believe this claim can be upheld regardless of my more controversial claim (in this article) that I have successfully defined the ethically optimal end point of moral development. Ultimately, however, a complete approach to moral education requires consideration of this more controversial claim.

The second reason I have entered the philosophic arena is more theoretical and more specifically relevant to the theme of this book. My article may be read as a partial answer to the issue raised by Peters when he says

> . . . [Kohlberg's] findings are of unquestionable importance, but there is a grave danger that they may become exalted into a general theory of moral development. Any such general theory presupposes a general ethical theory, and Kohlberg himself surely would be the first to admit that he had done little to develop the details of such a general ethical theory (*p. 264*).

I agree with the position implied by Peters' comment, the position *that a psychological theory of ethics (or of cognition) is incomplete, even as a psychological theory, if its philosophic implications are not spelled out.* I claim, persuaded by some of my philosopher friends, that an ultimately adequate *psychological* theory as to why a child does move from stage to stage, and an ultimately adequate *philosophical* explanation as to why a higher stage is more adequate than a lower stage are one and the same theory extended in different directions.[2]

As I understand Piaget, he takes the same position, that is, he takes his theory of cognitive stages to be a *theory of genetic epistemology,* rather than to be a purely psychological theory. Put in other terms, an adequate psychological explanation of cognition or of morality must include an explanation of the universality of these concepts throughout humanity, an explanation which cannot be purely psychological in the usual sense. Hence, I would claim not only that the cognitive psychologist needs the epistemologist, but also that part of the measure of the psychologist's success is his contribution to a solution of epistemological problems.

The psychologist cannot study cognition or morality in an epistemologically neutral way, and I shall argue that it is not epistemologically (metaethically) *neutral* to say, as Berkowitz has, that, "moral values are evaluations of action believed by members of a given society to be 'right' " —it is metaethically *wrong.* If the psychological study of concepts presupposes an epistemological position, must not the results of psychological inquiry lead to both partial validation and partial correction of its initial epistemology? B. Kaplan and I argue that this must be the case. That insight into the "is" (the development of knowledge and morality), and insight into the "ought" (epistemological and moral norms and criteria) must have some relationship seemed obvious to philosophers and psychologists of fifty years ago such as Dewey, Mead, and Baldwin. One wonders whether it was anything but the desperate desire of behaviorists, logical positivists, and analytic philosophers to set up "independent disciplines" (or "games") of psychology and philosophy which made them think the psychologist–philosophers of fifty years ago were wrong.

In ethics, the start of the fifty-year separation was Moore's attack on the "naturalistic fallacy," the fallacy of deriving ought statements from is statements. My article weaves uneasily through many forms of the "naturalistic fallacy," treating some as genuine fallacies, others as not. The one form of the "naturalistic fallacy" which this book presupposes, however, is the "fallacy" that the "ought" statements of philosophers of knowledge and morality, and the "is" statements of psychologists of

[2] In particular, I want to thank Dwight Boyd for first pointing out this congruence and for numerous fruitful discussions on this and related topics.

knowledge and morality should be based on mutual awareness. I hope the readers of this volume will give us all A for effort if they recognize that our task involves closing a fifty-year gap between two professions.

II. Universals and Relativity in Moral Development

It has already been noted that we started our studies of moral development fifteen years ago with the notion (*a*) that there were universal ontogenetic trends toward the development of morality as it has been conceived by Western moral philosophers, and (*b*) that the development of such "rational" or "mature morality" is a process different from the learning of various "irrational" or "arbitrary" cultural rules and values. While these notions were mere assumptions fifteen years ago, we believe our longitudinal and cross-cultural research has now turned these assumptions into well-verified factual conclusions. Our first step in this article is to show that the common assumption of the cultural relativity of ethics, on which almost all contemporary social scientific theorizing about morality is based, is in error. While there are major theoretical differences among sociological-role theorists, psychoanalytic theorists, and learning theorists, they all view moral development and other forms of socialization as "the process by which an individual, born with behavior potentialities of an enormously wide range, is led to develop actual behavior confined within the much narrower range of what is customary and acceptable for him according to the standards of his group" (Child, 1954). Thus, moral and social development is defined as the direct internalization of external norms of a given culture.

A second process assumption, closely linked to the assumption of ethical relativity, is that morality and moral learning are fundamentally emotional and irrational *processes* based on mechanisms of habit, reward and punishment, identification, and defense. If common social-science theories are in error in assuming value relativity, then their further notions as to the processes of moral development and functioning are also likely to be in error, or at least to yield only partial insights into morality.

In the next section we shall go on to consider the evidence for a non-relativist "cognitive-developmental" theory of the developmental *process*. Our account will be based on a rejection of the relativity assumption and an acceptance of the contrasting view that "ethical principles" are the end point of sequential "natural" development in social functioning and thinking; correspondingly, the stimulation of their development is a different matter from the inculcation of arbitrary cultural beliefs. Before considering our theory of process, however, we must consider relativism as a doctrine that can be evaluated regardless of preference for one psychological process theory or another. Here, then, we consider whether the empirical propositions derivable from the relativity postulation are factually correct statements about variations in human moral behavior and judgment.

While our discussion focuses upon relativism as a doctrine about "is," about the facts of individual and cultural variability of morals, we need also to come to grips with relativism as a doctrine of "ought," that is, of the possibility of rational ethics, of men coming to agreement about issues of right or wrong through guidance by rational standards.

A. Relativism, Tolerance, and Scientific Neutrality: Some Confusions of Social Science. Brandt (1961, p. 433) has pointed out that ethical relativism, as understood by contemporary social scientists, usually consists of three beliefs: (*a*) that moral principles are culturally variable in a fundamental way; (*b*) that such divergence is logically unavoidable, that is, that there are no rational principles and methods which could reconcile observed divergencies of moral beliefs; and (*c*) that people ought to live according to the moral principles they themselves hold. Brandt adds:

> It is important to see that the first two principles are distinct. Failure to see this distinction has been one of the confusions which have beset discussions of the subject. . . . We shall call a person who accepts the first principle a *cultural relativist.* In contrast, we shall reserve the term *ethical relativism* for the view that *both* the first and second principles are true. According to our terminology, then, a man is not an ethical relativist unless he is also a cultural relativist; but he may well be a cultural relativist without being an ethical relativist (Brandt, 1961, p. 433).

As held by many social scientists, however, value relativism is often a confusion between the idea that "everyone has their own values," and the idea that "everyone ought to have their own values." In other words, the value-relativity position often rests on logical confusion between matters of fact (there are no standards accepted by all men), and matters of value (there are no standards which all men ought to accept), that is, it represents the "naturalistic fallacy."

To illustrate, I shall quote a typical response of one of my psychology graduate students to the following moral dilemma:

> In Europe, a woman was near death from a very bad disease, a special kind of cancer. There was one drug that the doctors thought might save her. It was a form of radium for which a druggist was charging ten times what the drug cost him to make. The sick woman's husband, Heinz, went to everyone he knew to borrow the money, but he could only get together about half of what it cost. He told the druggist that his wife was dying, and asked him to sell it cheaper or let him pay later. But the druggist said, "No, I discovered the drug and I'm going to make money from it." So Heinz got desperate and broke into the man's store to steal the drug for his wife.
>
> Should the husband have done that? Why?

Part of her reply was as follows: "I think he should steal it because if there is any such thing as a universal human value, it is the value of life, and that would justify stealing it." I then asked her, "Is there any such thing as a universal human value?" and she answered, "No, all values are relative to your culture." This response illustrates a typical confusion of the relativist. She starts out by claiming that one ought to act in terms of the universal value of human life, that it is logical and desirable for all men to respect all human life; but she fails to see that this does not conflict with the *fact* that all men do not always act in terms of this value, and so ends up denying the possibility of making a value judgment going beyond herself.

The girl's confusion is only one of a number of "fallacies" frequently found in social scientific arguments for relativism. Philosophers who are aware of these logical confusions do not generally accept ethical relativity and assume that there is a rational enterprise termed "normative ethics." But ethical and cultural relativism has a very powerful hold on social scientists which is not expilcable in terms of the facts of cultural relativity. In essence, this is because social scientists think relativism is required by attitudes of (*a*) questioning the arbitrary or conventional nature of the morality of their own culture, (*b*) fairness to other cultures and to minority groups, and (*c*) scientific value neutrality or objectivity in studying values. Accordingly, I shall briefly try to show [making use of some of Brandt's, 1959, logical distinctions] that *cultural relativism* neither gives nor receives logical support from these *ethical relativist* postulates, which most of us think of as central to a social-scientific orientation.

We have already mentioned the first, most general, fallacy behind relativism, namely, the confusion between ethical relativity and cultural relativity. This "naturalistic fallacy" is exemplified by the following argument in Feuer's *Psychoanalysis and ethics:*

> Statements as to "ultimate values" are, testable. . . Nietzsche's "ultimate value," the satisfaction of the will to power, presupposes a testable theory of human nature. Nietzsche assumes that the drive for power is basic and ineradicable in every human being. If this theory of human nature is confuted, the ethical doctrine, which is its expression, collapses with it. For statements about "ultimate values" are psychological assertions, and all the methods which are employed in psychological science can be used for their verification.
>
> An assertion that a value is ultimate is, in effect, an affirmation that there is a corresponding unconditioned and irreducible drive in the human organism. . . Rational values are those which diminish frustration and repression. . .
>
> When Nietzsche says that "power" is an ultimate value, his assertion is not validated by the psychological facts of man. Power-seeking is not a primitive motivation. . . [but the result of] gnawing anxieties far within one's unconscious. . . The distinction between authentic values and inauthentic ones is one between values which are expressive of the primal drives of the organism and those which are anxiety-induced (Feuer, 1955, pp. 5–11).

Feuer's argument is that ethical statements about the "rationality" or "authenticity" of values (for example, of sex as opposed to power) can be directly derived from establishing empirical truths about their origins. This commits the naturalistic fallacy by identifying a value judgment with a factual judgment. We may accept the factual truth of the statements "sexuality is an unconditioned drive" and "expressing sexuality diminishes frustration and repression," and still question the ethical statement "sexual expressions are authentic values," or "sexual expression is right and good." To ignore this "open question" is to commit the naturalistic fallacy. As Frankena puts it,

> The 'open question' argument is that we may agress that something has P, and yet ask significantly, "But is it good?" or "Is it right?" That is, we can sensibly say, "This has P, but is it good (or right)?. . . Likewise, one can say, "This has P but it is not good (or right)", without contradicting oneself (Frankena, 1963, p. 82).

Feuer, like Flugel (1955), and many other psychoanalytic ethicists, denies that it is really possible to ask the open question when he says

> We cannot say that we can define or analyze the meaning of "good." For in a strict sense, we might say that ethical terms cannot be logically analyzed, they can only be psychoanalyzed. Ethical language differs, in this respect, from scientific language. . . (Feuer, 1955, p. 23).

Let us imagine Feuer to be an actual analyst talking to a patient. Feuer tells the patient, "Your striving for power is irrational and inauthentic and bad." The patient asks the questions, "But why is it bad? Why should I give it up?" Feuer replies, "Because it is based on anxiety." The patient then asks "the open question," that is, "But why does that make it bad?" And Feuer says "That is a meaningless question, words like good and bad have no true meaning, only scientific description has true meaning." The patient at this time either replies plaintively "What did you mean then, telling me my power striving was bad?" or else starts climbing the walls. The patient is left climbing the walls because Feuer is taking a position similar to that of the graduate student cited earlier. He starts out by absolutistically defining "authentic," "rational" values, and ends up with the relativistic statement, "ethical terms cannot be logically analyzed, they can only be psychoanalyzed."

A negative rather than assertive form of the same confusion is the move from "There are no universal human values" to "There ought not to be any universal human values; every person or culture ought to do its thing." An extreme relativist might say, "Some people strive for power, some do not, therefore one cannot say 'One ought not to strive for power.' " Brandt gives examples of such "official" social scientific confusions:

> An executive committee of the American Anthropological Association, in a pub-

lished statement on human rights, included the remark that '*respect* for differences between cultures is *validated* by the scientific fact that no technique of qualitatively evaluating cultures has been discovered.' (Brandt, 1959, p. 288).

> Melville Herskovitz writes . . . 'The relativist point of view brings into relief the *validity* of every set of norms *for* the people whose lives are guided by them' (Brandt, 1959, p. 288).

But this is a fallacy since:

> It is one thing for a person to have a certain ethical opinion or ethical conviction, and another thing for that ethical opinion to be correct. . . It does not follow directly from the fact that the Romans approved of infanticide and we do not, that infanticide was really right for them and really wrong for us or that it is neither right nor wrong for everybody (Brandt, 1959, p. 84).

Very often the confusion of "is" and "ought" also operates in the reverse direction. Instead of the facts of cultural diversity leading to confusion about ideal morality, relativistic ideas of tolerance (ethical relativism) lead to confusions about the facts (cultural relativism). Confusions about (*a*) the facts of cultural relativism, in turn rest on confusion between (*b*) "ethical relativity," and (*c*) "ethical tolerance" as moral doctrines. An illustration of this confusion of (*b*) and (*c*), as well as of (*a*) and (*b*), is provided by the statement of the American Anthropological Association. American anthropology developed a passionate moral conviction that the nineteenth-century assumption of the cultural superiority of "white civilization" was both intellectually blind and socially destructive to people in other cultures. Quite correctly, the anthropologists felt that these "white cultural supremacy" doctrines violated fundamental moral principles of justice, respect for human personality, and tolerance for diversity of belief and values. Instead of recognizing that their concern for tolerance was based on "white civilization's" universalizable principles of justice, anthropologists attempted to support their pleas for tolerance on the grounds that no principles were universalizable.

The second basic fallacy, then, is the confusion between (*b*), the relativistic ethical proposition "no moral beliefs or principles are absolutely valid," and (*c*), the nonrelativistic liberal's proposition, "It is a valid moral principle to grant liberty and respect to any human being regardless of his moral beliefs or principles." We shall argue that (*c*) is valid but does not depend for support on (*b*). Indeed, if the principle of tolerance, (*c*), is ethically valid, the principle of ethical relativity, (*b*), cannot be, since the principle of tolerance, if valid, is not itself "relative," "arbitrary," etc.

Stated in a different way, the confusion is between (*b*), the relativity of moral principles, and (*c*), the relativity of blaming or punishing persons or groups who do not act in accordance with those principles. We shall argue later that valid (stage 6) universal moral principles of obligation do not directly generate any obligation to blame, or punish people who deviate from those principles. One may question the justice of punishing or even blaming a ghetto adolescent who steals without questioning principles of justice which make it an obligation for that adolescent not to steal. *One may then deny that there are any precise justifiable rules for blame and punishment without being a relativist in the sense of denying that there are basic moral principles.* A related confusion of the relativist is the notion that the function of moral principles is to judge cultures or societies as wholes, and because one cannot legitimately make absolute moral evaluations of one culture as worth more or less than another, there are no nonrelative moral principles. Moral principles, however, prescribe universal human obligations; they are not scales for evaluating collective entities.

The import of these confusions for the handling of facts may be illustrated by social-scientific opinion about "class differences in moral values." Reviews of the many studies of class differences in Piaget or Kohlberg measures of moral judgment in many cultures (Kohlberg, 1963a; Kohlberg & Turiel, 1971) all show the same thing: that the direction of age change is the same for lower-class and middle-class children in all cultures on all measures, showing regular age trends in either class group, but that middle class children advance faster and further on these measures in all cultures. It is a simple matter of fact that middle-class children are advanced on measures of moral age development. The fact, however, has been interpreted by relativistic social scientists (for example, Bronfenbrenner, 1962) as indicating that "Piaget's (or Kohlberg's) measures of moral development are based on culturally biased "middle-class standards." The facts are denied on the (confused) ground that the developmental measure is "unjust to," "biased against," lower-class children, and that it is "relative to middle-class standards."

A related example comes from repeated research results indicating that lower-class and ghetto children cheat and steal more than middle-class white children. Fearing prejudice, social scientists have argued that honesty is a "middle-class value" in terms of which lower-class children should not be judged. In fact, however, the research studies repeatedly indicate that honesty is verbally ranked just as high (or higher) by lower-class black children and adults as by middle-class whites (studies summarized in Kohlberg, 1963a). While it is much more difficult for a ghetto child or parent to act "honestly" than for a middle-class child (because of differences in social perspective and situational opportunities), it is just as much of a value to the ghetto child.

The ethically "rational" position for the social scientist to take is that awarding blame to groups with higher crime or dishonesty rates is itself morally ungrounded, since moral principles require treating each child as an individual of equal fundamental moral worth. Anyone would recognize that rounding up a group of ghetto dwellers and imprisoning them all because some are criminals would be unjust collective punishment. Collective blame of groups with a high crime rate is equally unjust. To combat this injustice does not require an effort to prove that there is no valid conception of justice, for example, that acts of injustice (including theft) are all "culturally relative."

We have cited examples in which social scientists reject both fact and the natural intuition that there is something universally "rational," "ethical," or "mature" in principles of justice which prohibit stealing. We have suggested that this is because a belief in ethical relativity (*b*) is illogically derived from a concern for ethical tolerance (*c*) toward minority groups or cultures, and then confused with facts about cultural relativism (*a*).

A third related fallacy behind much social-scientific thinking is *the confusion of ethical relativism* (*b*) *with "value neutrality" or "scientific impartiality."* We have already noted that Berkowitz thinks it "neutral" to define moral values as "evaluations of actions generally believed by the members of a given society to be either 'right' or 'wrong' " (Berkowitz, 1964, p. 44). In fact, this doctrine is not scientifically neutral or impartial, because it prejudges the facts. It assumes that there are *no* culturally universal criteria which might aid in defining the field of the moral, and that variations in cultural evaluations may not themselves be assessed as more or less adequate or moral in terms of some universal criterion. We may gather the import of the definition by imagining a similar strategy for defining scientific beliefs, for example, that they are "beliefs about the world generally believed by members of a given society to be true or false." This implies that there are no universal characteristics which distinguish scientific beliefs from other beliefs, that is, that arrival at beliefs through some culturally universal conception of scientific method or reasoning is irrelevant to their definition as "scientific," and that the adequacy of the belief may not be judged independent of its conformity to group opinion. As social scientists, we reject such a definition of science. Recognizing it as epistemologically faulty, we also recognize that it cannot be a useful basis for social-scientific explanation. A psychologist or social historian who explained the development of Darwin's belief in evolution in the same terms as he explained the development of an Anglican Bishop's belief in Divine Creation would simply be a poor social scientist. We must at least consider that the same possibility exists in the moral sphere.

Berkowitz's definition of moral values reflects a special form of the relativist's third confusion, that is, the confusion between an *a priori* definition of morality in terms of cultural relativity, and the conclusion that morality is culturally relative. Since most people or cultures do not agree that morality is defined by the values of the majority, why is Berkowitz's definition less arbitrary than that of a Catholic priest who defines morality as belief in the catechisms? Concealed behind Berkowitz's definition of morality there lies a normative ethical theory and a social-science theory. The ethical theory is that morality derives from social contract and is justified by its contribution to the welfare of society (our stage 5). The social-science theory is the Durkheim theory that the social psychological origins of morality are to be found in the collective beliefs of the group, as these form a system above the beliefs of individuals. These theories might be acceptable, but this requires justification and cannot be assumed to be antecedent to inquiry.

The confusion of "scientific neutrality" with relativism involved in Berkowitz's definition does not derive from a confusion of "is" and "ought," but from the view of men like Weber, who distinguish between a rational sphere of social-science methods and findings ("is"), and a sphere of values ("ought"), toward which a rational man or a scientist must take a stance of "value neutrality," that is, recognize that his position is personal, arbitrary, and historically conditioned.

This brings us to the fourth confusion, *the confusion between the "rational" as "the scientific or factual" and the "rational" as the "value neutral."* The concept of the "value neutrality" (*d*) of the social scientist assumes ethical relativity rather than justifies it. To assume ethical relativity is to rule out the possibility of rational methods of coming to ethical agreement without considering the validity of such methods in actual detail. Weber himself argues that one moral idea cannot be siad to be more adequate than another, and that there is no moral progress. But his argument is legislative, not based on careful analysis of empirical trends. He says:

> The use of the term 'progress' is legitimate in our disciplines when it refers to 'technical' problems, i.e. to the 'means' of attaining an unambiguously given end. It can never elevate itself into the sphere of 'ultimate' evaluations (Weber, 1949, p. 38).

But Weber cannot legislate that "moral progress" is an illegitimate concept for a social scientist, nor can he legislate that rational agreement is impossible for philosophers; these issues are subjects for inquiry.

The point is that when Weber takes a value stand (including the stand of value neutrality), he attempts to support it by a very careful rational argument. Moreover, as Brandt (1959, p. 272) points out, moral philosophers can define methodological criteria of moral judgment and argument with about as much agreement and clarity as philosophers of science can define methodological criteria of scientific judgment and argument. Thus, although Weber denies the possibility of a "neutral" attitude to matters of ethical adequacy, philosophers engage in discussions of the adequacy of moral principles with a set of methodological rules for impartial argument analogous to those of scientists discussing matters of fact. Indeed, Weber's own arguments about value neutrality seek to conform to roughly those criteria of value discussions.

Weber properly postulates the need for scientific neutrality in inquiry, that is, the need to examine factual–causal connections in behavior regardless of the desirability of these connections. In this he is quite correct. However, he then confuses the scientists' use of some criterion of adequacy of the value systems studied with "bias." But factual investigation need not, and cannot, be based on ignoring the criteria of adequacy of the behavior investigated. To establish "objective" scientific–historical connections in the growth of Darwin's beliefs about evolution presupposes some justifiable standpoint about the cognitive–scientific adequacy of these beliefs. The same is true with regard to the growth of moral beliefs.

In summary, we have listed a number of confusions and *a priori* assumptions which have severely biased social scientists in favor of both cultural relativity and ethical relativity in advance of considering the facts about cultural variability and the philosophic arguments about the possibilities of rational moral agreement. These confusions have led social scientists to argue that the scientist cannot find moral development or evolution, and that moral philosophers cannot come to agreement. We have tried to demonstrate a truism: It is illogical to claim that something is impossible in advance of inquiry. We may now go on to the results of our empirical inquiry.

B. Empirical Studies of Moral Development and Their Implications. For fifteen years, I have been studying the development of moral judgment and character, primarily by following the same group of 75 boys at three-year intervals from early adolescence (at the beginning, the boys were aged 10–16) through young manhood (they are now aged 22–28), supplemented by a series of studies of development in other cultures.

These studies have led us to define the stages described in Table I. The methods by which we have defined these stages are responses to hypothetical moral dilemmas, deliberately "philosophical," some found in medieval works of casuistry. (A complete treatment of the dilemmas and their scoring can be found in Kohlberg & Turiel, 1971.) When I first decided to explore development in other cultures by this method, some of my anthropologist friends predicted that I would have to throw away my culture-bound moral concepts and stories, and start from scratch learning the values of that culture. In fact, something quite different happened. My first try was a study of two villages—one Atayal (Malaysian aboriginal), one Taiwanese. When my guide, a young Chinese ethnographer, started to

TABLE I

DEFINITION OF MORAL STAGES

I. Preconventional level

At this level the child is responsive to cultural rules and labels of good and bad, right or wrong, but interprets these labels in terms of either the physical or the hedonistic consequences of action (punishment, reward, exchange of favors), or in terms of the physical power of those who enunciate the rules and labels. The level is divided into the following two stages:

Stage 1: *The punishment and obedience orientation.* The physical consequences of action determine its goodness or badness regardless of the human meaning or value of these consequences. Avoidance of punishment and unquestioning deference to power are valued in their own right, not in terms of respect for an underlying moral order supported by punishment and authority (the latter being stage 4).

Stage 2: *The instrumental relativist orientation.* Right action consists of that which instrumentally satisfies one's own needs and occasionally the needs of others. Human relations are viewed in terms like those of the market place. Elements of fairness, of reciprocity, and of equal sharing are present, but they are always interpreted in a physical pragmatic way. Reciprocity is a matter of "you scratch my back and I'll scratch yours," not of loyalty, gratitude, or justice.

II. Conventional level

At this level, maintaining the expectations of the individual's family, group, or nation is perceived as valuable in its own right, regardless of immediate and obvious consequences. The attitude is not only one of *conformity* to personal expectations and social order, but of loyalty to it, of actively *maintaining*, supporting, and justifying the order, and of identifying with the persons or group involved in it. At this level, there are the following two stages:

Stage 3: *The interpersonal concordance or "good boy—nice girl" orientation.* Good behavior is that which pleases or helps others and is approved by them. There is much conformity to stereotypical images of what is majority or "natural" behavior. Behavior is frequently judged by intention—"he means well" becomes important for the first time. One earns approval by being "nice."

Stage 4: *The "law and order" orientation.* There is orientation toward authority, fixed rules, and the maintenance of the social order. Right behavior consists of doing one's duty, showing respect for authority, and maintaining the given social order for it's own sake.

III. Postconventional, autonomous, or principled level

At this level, there is a clear effort to define moral values and principles which have validity and application apart from the authority of the groups or persons holding these principles, and apart from the individual's own identification with these groups. This level again has two stages:

TABLE I (*continued*)

Stage 5: *The social-contract legalistic orientation*, generally with utilitarian overtones. Right action tends to be defined in terms of general individual rights, and standards which have been critically examined and agreed upon by the whole society. There is a clear awareness of the relativism of personal values and opinions and a corresponding emphasis upon procedural rules for reaching consensus. Aside from what is constitutionally and democratically agreed upon, the right is a matter of personal "values" and "opinion." The result is an emphasis upon the "legal point of view," but with an emphasis upon the possibility of changing law in terms of rational considerations of social utility (rather than freezing it in terms of stage 4 "law and order"). Outside the legal realm, free agreement and contract is the binding element of obligation. This is the "official" morality of the American government and constitution.

Stage 6: *The universal ethical principle orientation.* Right is defined by the decision of conscience in accord with self-chosen *ethical principles* appealing to logical comprehensiveness, universality, and consistency. These principles are abstract and ethical (the Golden Rule, the categorical imperative); they are not concrete moral rules like the Ten Commandments. At heart, these are universal principles of *justice*, of the *reciprocity* and *equality* of human *rights*, and of respect for the dignity of human beings as *individual persons*.

translate the children's responses, he would start to laugh at something at which I would giggle when I first heard it from American children. There are cultural differences, but they are not what made him laugh. To illustrate, let me quote for you a dilemma, similar to the Heintz dilemma on stealing, adapted for the villages investigated:

> A man and wife had just migrated from the high mountains. They started to farm, but there was no rain, and no crops grew. No one had enough food. The wife go sick, and finally she was close to dying from having no food. There was only one grocery store in the village, and the storekeeper charged a very high price for the food. The husband asked the storekeeper for some food for his wife, and said he would pay for it later. The storekeeper said, "No, I won't give you any food unless you pay first." The husband went to all the people in the village to ask for food, but no one had food to spare. So he got desperate, and broke into the store to steal food for his wife.
>
> Should the husband have done that? Why?

Our stage 2 types in the Taiwanese village would reply to the above story as follows: "He should steal the food for his wife, because if she dies he'll have to pay for her funeral and that costs a lot." In the Atayal village, funerals were not such a big thing, and the stage 2 boys would say, "He should steal the drug, because he needs his wife to cook for him." In other words, we have to consult our ethnographer to know what content a stage 2 child will include in his instrumental exchange calculations, but what made our anthropologist laugh was the difference in form between the

TABLE II

ASPECTS OF MORAL JUDGMENT

I. The modes of judgment of obligation and value

A. Judgment of right
B. Judgment of having a right
C. Judgment of duty and obligation
D. Judgments of responsibility—conceptions of consequences of action or of the demands or opinions of others one should consider over and above strict duties or strict regard for the rights of others
E. Judgment of praise or blame
F. Judgments of punishability and reward
G. Justification and explanation
H. Judgments of nonmoral value or goodness

II. The elements of obligation and value

A. Prudence—consequences desirable or undesirable to the *self*
B. Social welfare—consequences desirable to *others*
C. Love
D. Respect
E. Justice as liberty
F. Justice as equality
G. Justice as reciprocity and contract

III. The issues or institutions

A. Social norms
B. Personal conscience
C. Roles and issues of affection
D. Roles and issues of authority and democracy, of division of labor between roles relative to social control
E. Civil liberties—rights to liberty and equality to persons as human beings, as citizens, or as members of groups
F. Justice of actions apart from fixed rights—reciprocity, contract, trust, and equity in the actions or reactions of one person
G. Punitive justice
H. Life
I. Property
J. Truth
K. Sex

child's thought and his own, a difference definable independently of the particular culture.

It is this emphasis on the distinctive form (as opposed to the content) of the child's moral thought which allows us to call moral development universal. In all cultures, we find the same aspects or categories of moral judgment and valuing; these aspects are listed in Table II.

Our notions of moral categories come from both the Piagetian psychological tradition and from traditional ethical analysis. Piaget's structural analysis of cognitive development is based on dividing cognition into basic categories such as logic, space, time, causality, number. These categories define basic kinds of judgments, or relationships, in terms of which any physical experience must be construed—that is, it must be located in spatial and temporal coordinates, considered as the effect of a cause, etc. Piaget's cognitive categories derive from Kant's analysis of the categories of pure reason, and for Kant there is an analogous set of categories of pure practical reason, or of action under the mode of freedom.

Kant's categories of moral judgment are not as useful for our purposes as is Dewey's treatment of moral categories, which echoes Kant's distinctions in a way closer to our own use. Says Dewey:

> The distinctively intellectual judgment construes one object in terms of other similar objects and has necessarily its own inherent structure which supplies the ultimate categories of all physical science. Units of space, time, mass, energy define to us the limiting conditions under which judgments of this type do their work. The limiting terms of moral judgment (of the judgment construing an activity and content in terms of each other) constitute the characteristic features, or *categories*, of the object of ethical science, just as the limiting terms of the judgment which construes one object in terms of another object constitute the categories of physical science. A discussion of moral judgment from this point of view may be termed the "Logic of Conduct." Ethical discussion is full of such terms; the sensuous and the ideal, the *standard* and the right, *obligation* and duty, freedom and *responsibility* are samples (Dewey, 1903, p. 22).

The particular terms listed by Dewey we term *Modes*, that is, terms defining *functional kinds* of moral judgment. Equally basic are *Elements* or Principles of judgment such as Welfare, Respect, and Justice. As Table II indicates, we also find universal moral *issues*, or values (the application of the categories to content area or institutions), ranging from law to authority to life. Any given moral judgment may be simultaneously assigned to a mode, to an element, and to an issue in our scheme. Each mode, element, and issue is defined at each of the stages of development. As an example, Table III defines the orientation of each stage to the Issue "Value of Human Life," and gives concrete examples of the way this value is defined at each of the stages.

The concept of stages just described implies something more than age trends. First, stages imply invariant sequence. Each child must go step by step through each of the kinds of moral judgment outlined. It is, of course, possible for a child to move at varying speeds and to stop (become "fixated") at any level of development; but if he continues to move upward, he must move in accord with these steps. The longitudinal study of American boys at ages 10, 13, 16, 19, and 23 suggests that this is the case.

TABLE III

SIX STAGES IN CONCEPTIONS OF THE MORAL WORTH OF HUMAN LIFE

Stage 1: No differentiation between moral value of life and its physical or social-status value.

Tommy, age ten (III. Why should the druggist give the drug to the dying woman when her husband couldn't pay for it?): "If someone important is in a plane and is allergic to heights and the stewardess won't give him medicine because she's only got enough for one and she's got a sick one, a friend, in back, they'd probably put the stewardess in a lady's jail because she didn't help the important one."

(Is it better to save the life of one important person or a lot of unimportant people?): "All the people that aren't important because one man just has one house, maybe a lot of furniture, but a whole bunch of people have an awful lot of furniture and some of these poor people might have a lot of money and it doesn't look it."

Stage 2: The value of a human life is seen as instrumental to the satisfaction of the needs of its possessor or of other persons. Decision to save life is relative to, or to be made by, its possessor. (Differentiation of physical and interest value of life, differentiation of its value to self and to other.)

Tommy, age thirteen (IV. Should the doctor "mercy kill" a fatally ill woman requesting death because of her pain?): "Maybe it would be good to put her out of her pain, she'd be better off that way. But the husband wouldn't want it, it's not like an animal. If a pet dies you can get along without it—it isn't something you really need. Well, you can get a new wife, but it's not really the same."

Jim, age thirteen (same question): "If she requests it, it's really up to her. She is in such terrible pain, just the same as people are always putting animals out of their pain."

Stage 3: The value of a human life is based on the empathy and affection of family members and others toward its possessor. (The value of human life, as based on social sharing, community, and love is differentiated from the instrumental and hedonistic value of life applicable also to animals.)

Tommy, age sixteen (same question): "It might be best for her, but her husband—it's a human life—not like an animal, it just doesn't have the same relationship that a human being does to a family. You can become attached to a dog, but nothing like a human you know."

Stage 4: Life is conceived as sacred in terms of its place in a categorical moral or religious order of rights and duties. (The value of human life, as a categorical member of a moral order, is differentiated from its value to specific other people in the family, etc. Value of life is still partly dependent upon serving the group, the state, God, however.)

Jim, age sixteen (same question): "I don't know. In one way, it's murder, it's not a right or privilege of man to decide who shall live and who should die. God put life into everybody on earth and you're taking away something from that person that came directly from God, and you're destroying something that is very sacred, it's in a way part of God and it's almost destroying a part of God when you kill a person. There's something of God in everyone."

TABLE III (*continued*)

Stage 5: Life is valued both in terms of its relation to community welfare and in terms of being a universal human right. (Obligation to respect the basic right to life is differentiated from generalized respect for the socio–moral order. The general value of the independent human life is a primary autonomous value not dependent upon other values.)

Jim, age twenty (same question): "Given the ethics of the doctor who has taken on responsibility to save human life—from that point of view he probably shouldn't but there is another side, there are more and more people in the medical profession who are thinking it is a hardship on everyone, the person, the family, when you know they are going to die. When a person is kept alive by an artificial lung or kidney it's more like being a vegetable than being a human who is alive. If it's her own choice I think there are certain rights and privileges that go along with being a human being. I am a human being and have certain desires for life and I think everybody else does, too. You have a world of which you are the center, and everybody else does, too, and in that sense we're all equal."

Stage 6: Belief in the sacredness of human life as representing a universal human value of respect for the individual. (The moral value of a human being, as an object of moral principle, is differentiated from a formal recognition of his rights.)

Jim, age twenty-four (III. Should the husband steal the drug to save his wife? How about for someone he just knows?): "Yes. A human life takes precedence over any other moral or legal value, whoever it is. A human life has inherent value whether or not it is valued by a particular individual."
(Why is that?): "The inherent worth of the individual human being is the central value in a set of values where the principles of justice and love are normative for all human relationships."

An example of such stepwise movement is provided in Table III. Tommy is stage 1 at age 10, stage 2 at age 13, and stage 3 at age 16. Jim is stage 4 at age 16, stage 5 at age 20, and stage 6 at age 24. (See Kohlberg, 1963, 1969, for a more detailed discussion of empirical findings.)

Second, stages define "structured wholes," total ways of thinking, not attitudes toward particular situations. As can be seen in Table IV, which illustrates prepared arguments ("motives") for and against stealing the drug, a stage is a way of thinking which may be used to support either side of an action choice, that is, it illustrates the distinction between moral form and moral content (action choice). Our correlational studies indicate a general factor of moral level which cross-cuts aspect. An individual at stage 6 on a "cognitive" aspect (universalized value of life) is also likely to be stage 6 on a "motive" aspect (motive for difficult moral action in terms of internal self-condemnations). An individual at stage 6 on a situation of stealing a drug for a wife is likely to be at stage 6 on a story involving civil

TABLE IV

MOTIVES FOR ENGAGING IN MORAL ACTION (ASPECTS 10 AND 13)[a]

Stage 1: Action is motivated by avoidance of punishment, and "conscience" is irrational fear of punishment.

Pro—If you let your wife die, you will get in trouble. You'll be blamed for not spending the money to save her, and there'll be an investigation of you and the druggist for your wife's death.

Con—You shouldn't steal the drug because you'll be caught and sent to jail if you do. If you do get away, your conscience would bother you thinking how the police would catch up with you at any minute.

Stage 2: Action motivated by desire for reward or benefit. Possible guilt reactions are ignored and punishment viewed in a pragmatic manner. (Differentiates own fear, pleasure, or pain from punishment consequences.)

Pro—If you do happen to get caught, you could give the drug back and you wouldn't get much of a sentence. It wouldn't bother you much to serve a little jail term, if you have your wife when you get out.

Con—He may not get much of a jail term if he steals the drug, but his wife will probably die before he gets out, so it won't do him much good. If his wife dies, he shouldn't blame himself, it wasn't his fault she has cancer.

Stage 3: Action motivated by anticipation of disapproval of others, actual or imagined hypothetical (for example, guilt). (Differentiation of disapproval from punishment, fear, and pain.)

Pro—No one will think you're bad if you steal the drug, but your family will think you're an inhuman husband if you don't. If you let your wife die, you'll never be able to look anybody in the face again.

Con—It isn't just the druggist who will think you're a criminal, everyone else will too. After you steal it, you'll feel bad thinking how you've brought dishonor on your family and yourself; you won't be able to face anyone again.

Stage 4: Action motivated by anticipation of dishonor, that is, institutionalized blame for failure of duty, and by guilt over concrete harm done to others. (Differentiates formal dishonor from informal disapproval. Differentiates guilt for bad consequences from disapproval.)

Pro—If you have any sense of honor, you won't let your wife die because you're afraid to do the only thing that will save her. You'll always feel guilty that you caused her death if you don't do your duty to her.

Con—You're desperate and you may not know you're doing wrong when you steal the drug. But you'll know you did wrong after you're punished and sent to jail. You'll always feel guilty for your dishonesty and lawbreaking.

TABLE IV (*continued*)

Stage 5: Concern about maintaining respect of equals and of the community (assumng their respect is based on reason rather than emotions). Concern about own self-respect, that is, to avoid judging self as irrational, inconsistent, nonpurposive. (Discriminates between institutionalized blame and community disrespect or self-disrespect.)

Pro—You'd lose other people's respect, not gain it, if you don't steal. If you let your wife die, it would be out of fear, not out of reasoning it out. So you'd just lose self-respect and probably the respect of others too.

Con—You would lose your standing and respect in the community and violate the law. You'd lose respect for yourself if you're carried away by emotion and forget the long-range point of view.

Stage 6: Concern about self-condemnation for violating one's own principles. (Differentiates between community respect and self-respect. Differentiates between self-respect for general achieving rationality and self-respect for maintaining moral principles.)

Pro—If you don't steal the drug and let your wife die, you'd always condemn yourself for it afterward. You wouldn't be blamed and you would have lived up to the outside rule of the law but you wouldn't have lived up to your own standards of conscience.

Con—If you stole the drug, you wouldn't be blamed by other people but you'd condemn yourself because you wouldn't have lived up to your own conscience and standards of honesty.

[a] Source: Rest, 1968.

disobedience (helping slaves escape before the Civil War). It should be noted that any individual is usually not entirely at one stage. Typically, as children develop they are partly in their major stage (about 50% of their ideas), partly in the stage into which they are moving, and partly in the stage they have just left behind. Seldom, however, do they use stages at developmental removes from one another.

Third, a stage concept implies universality of sequence under varying cultural conditions. It implies that moral development is not merely a matter of learning the verbal values or rules of the child's culture, but reflects something more universal in development, something which would occur in any culture.

Figures 1 and 2 indicate the cultural universality of the sequence of stages which we have found. Figure 1 presents the age trends for middle-class urban boys in the United States, Taiwan, and Mexico. At age 10 in

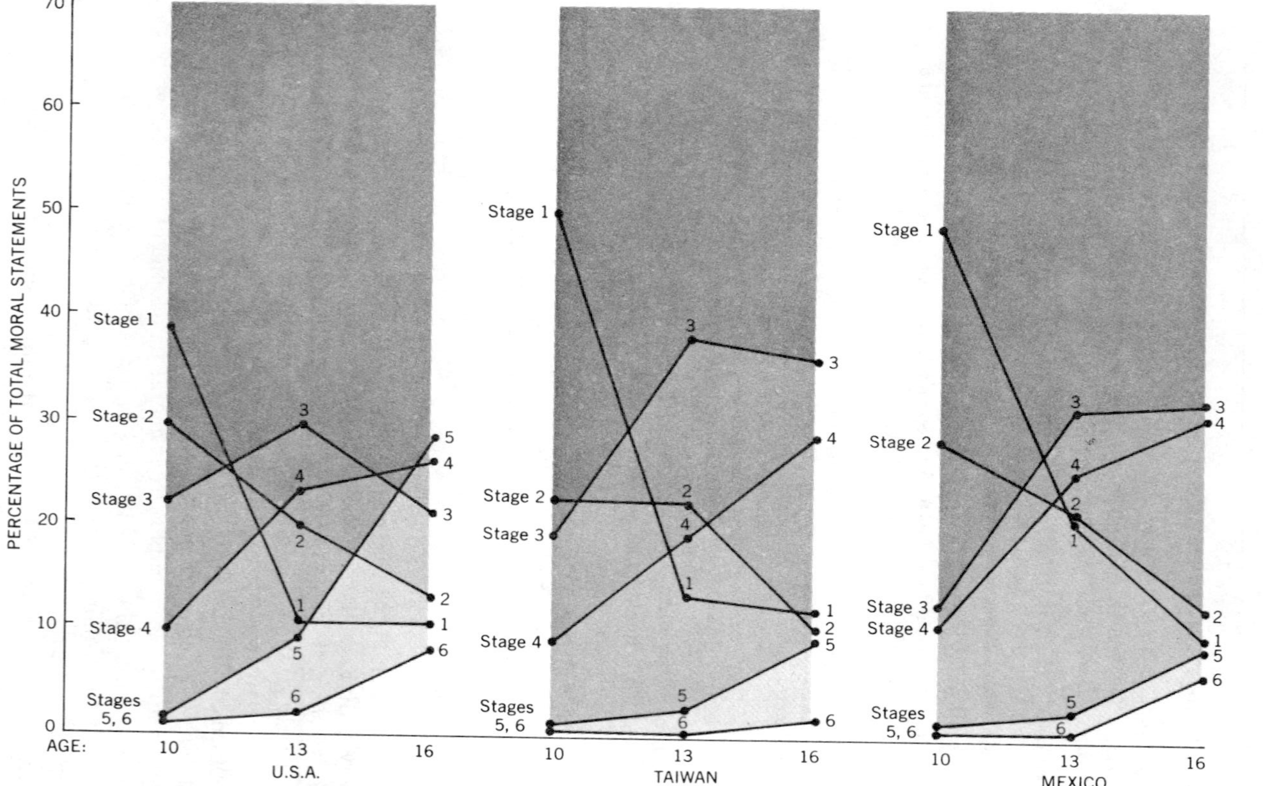

FIG. 1. Middle-class urban boys in the United States, Taiwan, and Mexico. At age 10, the stages are used according to difficulty. At age 13, state 3 is most used by all three groups. At age 16, U.S. boys have reversed the order of age 10 stages (with the exception of 6). In Taiwan and Mexico, conventional (3–4) stages prevail at age 16, with stage 5 also little used (Kohlberg, 1968b).

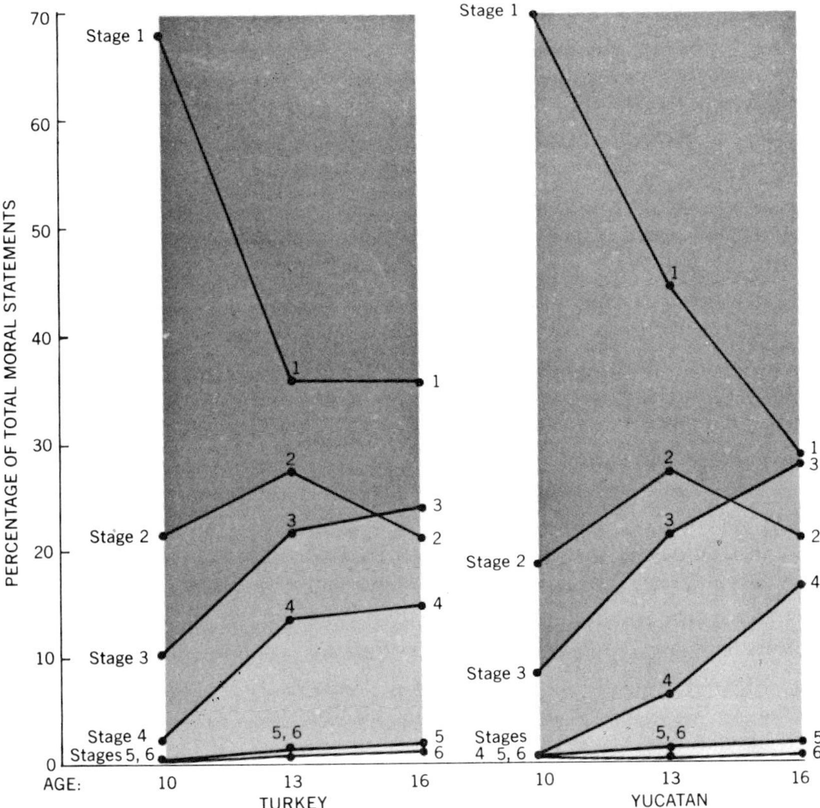

FIG. 2. Two isolated villages, one in Turkey, the other in Yucatan, show similar patterns in moral thinking. There is no reversal of order, and preconventional (1–2) thought does not gain a clear ascendency over conventional stages at age 16 (Kohlberg, 1968b).

each country, the greater number of moral statements are scored at the lower stages. In the United States, by age 16, the order is reversed, so that the greater proportion use higher stages, with the exception of stage 6 which is rarely used. The results in Mexico and Taiwan are the same, except that development is a little slower. The most conspicuous feature is that stage 5 thinking is much more salient in the United States than in Mexico or Taiwan at age 16. Nevertheless, it is present in the other countries, so we know that it is not purely an American democratic construct. Figure 2 indicates results from two isolated villages, one in Yucatan, one in Turkey. The similarity of the pattern in the two villages is striking. While conventional moral thought (stages 3 and 4) increases steadily from age 10 to 16, at 16 it still has not achieved a clear ascendency over premoral thought (stages 1 and 2). Stages 5 and 6 are totally absent in this group. Trends for lower-class urban groups are intermediate in rate of development between those for the middle-class and the village boys. Our studies then suggest that the same basic ways of moral valuing are found in every culture, and develop in the same order.

It should also be noted that we have found no important differences in development of moral thinking between Catholics, Protestants, Jews, Buddhists, Moslems, and atheists. Children's moral values in the religious area seem to go through the same stages as their general moral values, so that a stage 2 child is likely to say "Be good to God and he'll be good to you." Both cultural values and religion are important factors in selectively elaborating certain themes in the moral life, but they are not unique causes of the development of basic moral values.

If basic moral values or principles are universal, the relativist's next defense is to say that the ordering or hierarchy of these values is idiosyncratic and relative. For instance, one might agree that everyone would value both life and property rights, but that which is valued most depends upon a culturally relative hierarchy of values. In fact, however, basic hierarchies of moral values are primarily reflections of developmental stages in moral thought. Anyone who understands the values of life and property will recognize that life is morally more valuable than property. Even at stage 2, boys know that the druggist in the story would rather save his own life than his property, so that the druggist's property is less valuable than the woman's life. Table III, defining the six stages in the development of the basic moral category, the value of life, suggests these are steps not only in conceptions of life's value, but also in the differentiation of life from other values and in the hierarchial dominance of life over such values as that of property. (Another example of such hierarchies of value is the current problem of law and order versus justice, see Kohlberg, 1970b).

Let us make explicit the implications of our studies for doctrines of *cultural relativity.* Extreme relativism denies that there is a culturally universal meaning to moral terms and implies that (*a*) differences in value standards between individuals or groups cannot be legitimately *evaluated* as more or less moral or adequate, and (*b*) that value differences cannot be *explained* by a theory of morality, but must be explained by a theory of psychological need, or of culture and subculture. Thus, sociologists have pointed out that delinquent actions may be motivated by the need to "do right" or conform to standards, both the standards of the delinquent gang and the great American standard of fast success. A psychiatrist has suggested that, "While from the standpoint of society, behavior is either 'good' or 'bad,' from the standpoint of the individual it always has some positive value. It represents the best solution for his conflicting drives that he has been able to formulate" (Josselyn, 1948). From either view, moral character terms are external value judgments useless for understanding the child. Extreme relativists would thus deny the the usefulness of defining individual differences in moral terms at all, holding that to label individual differences as more or less moral is simply judging them by arbitrary standards which have no scientific value or meaning.

A more popular view among social scientists is moderate, sociological relativism. Moderate relativism starts with the notion that while the content of moral rules and beliefs varies from group to group, all groups have something called morality which has common formal and functional properties. As stated by Brandt,

> Anthropologists tell us that everywhere language enables one to distinguish between the desired and the desirable, the wanted and the good or right. So we can infer first that everywhere there is some sort of distinction between momentary impulse or personal desire, and what is good, desirable, right, or justifiable in some sense or other. Second, the great utility of rules regulating what is to be done in types of recurrent situation is obvious. The importance of such rules for social living will lead us to expect that surviving societies will have some kind of authoritative rules of this sort, and hence some concept like "it is legally obligatory to" or, for more informal rules, "it is morally obligatory to," or both (Brandt, 1959, p. 87).

Brandt is saying that there are culturally universal meanings to moral terms. All cultures use moral terms, all have those categories we called the modes of moral judgment ("obligation," "moral evaluation," "punishment and reward"). But while all cultures use the moral modes, the content that is judged moral, or to which the modes apply, varies from culture to culture.

We call this moderate relativism "sociological" because this doctrine has been used to justify the notion that morality is a socio–cultural product, that it originates at the social-system level, not the individual level. While all groups or societies require rules (ethical form), the content of these rules is determined by the requirements of the particular society. The implication of the sociological doctrine is that both the culturally universal and the culturally arbitrary components of morality develop in the individual through internalization of the external culture, that is, the "universal functional requirements of society" are learned by the individual in the same way as are the arbitrary standards of a particular culture.

Examples of such sociologistic theories are those of Sumner (1906) and Durkheim (1925), which make a sharp distinction between a culturally universal moral form and culturally variable moral content. Durkheim admits that, in spite of the culturally variable content of rules and principles, there is a culturally universal moral attitude of obligation

(Kant), but he argues that it arises from the culturally universal sense of the group's authority rather than from the validity of any moral principles as such. Sumner's (1906) variation of the argument is that all societies have moral terms, but these terms refer to the standards of the specific society, that is, "X is right" basically means "X is in accord with the mores of my society."

Sociological relativists treat variations in moral beliefs and actions within a culture as radically distinct from moral variations between culture. Durkheim holds that an individual's attitude to the norms of his group is more or less moral depending upon the extent to which he displays respect for, and attachment to, cultural moral content. One cannot, however, characterize the differences in norms from one society to another as being more or less moral, since the essence of morality is the form of respect for the norms of the group; differences in the content of these norms is irrelevant to the fact that they involve the moral form (respect). As a doctrine about the empirical nature of morality, Durkheim's doctrine assumes that theories explaining differences in norms from culture to culture are not theories as to why some individuals are more or less moral (feel more or less respect) than others. As a normative doctrine, it holds that children within a culture may be judged as more or less moral, and that the less moral child should be made more moral, but that cultural differences cannot as such be morally evaluated, and that moral education should be one thing in one culture, another in another.

In contrast to both extreme and sociological relativism, we have first pointed out that there are universal moral concepts, values, or principles, that there is less variation between individuals and cultures than has been usually maintained in the sense that (*a*) almost all individuals in all cultures use the same thirty basic moral categories, concepts, or principles; and (*b*) all individuals in all cultures go through the same order or sequences of gross stages of development, though varying in rate and terminal point of development.

Second, we have pointed out that the marked differences between individuals and cultures which exist are differences in stage or developmental status. There are marked individual and cultural differences in the definition, use, and hierarchical ordering of these universal value concepts, but the major source of this variation, both within and between cultures, is developmental. Insofar as these individual differences are developmental, they are not morally neutral or arbitrary. This means empirically that the theory which explains cultural and individual differences in values is also the same general theory as to why children become capable of moral judgment and action at all. It means normatively that there is a sense in which we can characterize moral differences between groups and individuals as being more or less adequate morally. We are arguing then that even moderate or sociological relativism is misleading in its interpretation of the facts: not only is there a universal moral form, but the basic content principles of morality are universal.

We do not quite mean by this that moral principles are shared by all men. This has been suggested, for example, by Asch (1952) when he says that differences in values "are frequently not the consequence of diversity in ethical principles but of differences in the comprehension of a situation." But while this is true, the vast differences which Asch interprets as due to "differences in level of knowledge" are something more; they are fundamental differences in principles or modes of moral evaluation. Our positive definition of a "moral principle" is a moral mode, element, or value defined at a certain developmental level. Moral stages constitute "principles" in the sense that they represent the major consistencies of moral evaluation within the individual not directly due to factual beliefs. (Our evidence for this is that factor analysis indicates a single "stage" factor cutting across all moral situations, and all aspects of morality on which the individual is assessed.) In this perspective, our findings lead us to conclude that there are differences in fundamental moral principles between individuals or between groups, differences in stage. However, these stages or "fundamental ethical principles" on which people differ (*a*) are culturally universal, (*b*) occur in an invariant order of development, and (*c*) are interpretations of categories which are universal.

These findings are not compatible with moderate or sociological relativism. This view has some plausibility at the conventional level, where there is some truth to the Durkheim–Sumner argument that the basic meaning of "X is wrong" is "X violates the rules of my group." But this is not true for moral judgment at either the preconventional or the postconventional levels. It is also true that the conventional level has a vast amount of "stretch" to absorb arbitrary but socially authoritative content. However, this does not indicate the absence of universal content to conventional morality. A stage 3 Southern conservative racist may "stretch" what is "nice" or "loving" to absorb a great deal of racist behavior, as he may stretch "maintaining social order" or "giving people their just due." Nevertheless, the basic content of the "principles" appealed to by the conventional person is not arbitrary.

As an example, we say that killing innocent civilians in war is considered morally right in some cultures (Japanese, Vietnamese, Nazi), but not in others (American). What the Song My massacre and the public opinion polls about it prove, however, is that American conventional morality finds such a massacre right under many circumstances just as does the Vietnamese. We have found that the one enlisted man who clearly resisted engaging in the massacre was at the principled level, rather than adhering strongly to conventional American values. The somewhat greater stretch of conventional Vietnamese morality does not indicate a cultural difference in moral principle. This is an accommodation to cultural givens, or to what "most people do," and does not mean that the core moral concepts of the conventional morality are merely culturally variable internalizations.

In sum, our evidence supports the following conclusions: There is a universal set of moral principles held by men in various cultures, our stage 6. (These principles, we shall argue, could logically and consistently be held by all men in all societies; they would in fact be universal to all mankind if the conditions for socio–moral development were optimal for all individuals in all cultures.) At lower levels than stages 5 or 6, morality is not held in a fully principled form. Accordingly, it is more subject to specific content influence by group definition of the situation than is principled morality. Nevertheless, the more generalized and consistently held content "principles" of conventional morality are also universal. Even stage 6 principles are somewhat accommodated to cultural content, for example, Lincoln and Jefferson were able to partially accommodate their principles to slavery in response to social pressure. Accommodations at the conventional stage are much more marked, but this does not mean that conventional principles, any more than stage 6 principles, are direct reflections of cultural content.

Our finding that our two highest stages are absent in preliterate or semiliterate village culture, and other evidence, also suggests to us a mild doctrine of social evolutionism, such as was elaborated in the classic work of Hobhouse (1906). He worked out the stages of moral evolution of cultures given in Table V, which parallel our own stages in many ways.[2]

Our data indicate that while cultures differ in most frequent or modal stage, a culture cannot be located at a single stage, and the individual's moral stage cannot be derived directly from his culture's stage. There are, however, differences in the frequencies of the higher stages in various cultural groups, related to the cognitive and social complexity of the group. It is easier to develop to stage 6 in modern America than in fifth-century Athens or first-century Jerusalem, even though Americans like Lincoln and King still get killed for being stage 6. Furthermore, there is historical "horizontal decalage" or an easier extension of principles of stage 6 thought; Socrates was more accepting of slavery than was Lincoln, who was more accepting of it than King.

[2] It will be noted that Hobhouse does not distinguish between our stages 1 and 2, and inverts the order of our stages 3 and 4. The reasons for this descrepancy are briefly discussed elsewhere (Kohlberg & Turiel, 1971).

TABLE V

COMPARISON OF KOHLBERG AND HOBHOUSE SYSTEMS

Kohlberg		Hobhouse	
Stage 1	Obedience and punishment orientation	Stage 1	Taboo and private or group vengeance
Stage 2	Instrumental hedonism and exchange		
Stage 3	Orientation to approval and stereotypes of virtue	Stage 3	Ideals of character
Stage 4	Law and order orientation	Stage 2	Social rules and maintenance of a social order of unequal statuses
Stages 5–6	Orientation to principles of justice and welfare	Stage 4	General ethical principles of justice based on equal rights

It is very interesting to note that cultural relativists have never attempted to refute the basic facts convincingly organized by Hobhouse. Indeed Westermarck, a leading critic of moral evolutionism, essentially concedes the facts in *Ethical relativity* when, after noting the fundamental similarity of the content of values or moral rules in savage and civilized societies, he recognizes certain major differences in form between the meaning of these rules. He says:

> When we pass from the lower races to peoples more advanced in civilization we find that the social unit has grown larger, that the nation has taken the place of the tribe, and that the circle within which the infliction of injuries is prohibited has been extended accordingly. And if we pass to the rules laid down by moralists and professedly accepted by a large portion of civilized humanity, the change from the savage attitude has been enormous (Westermarck, 1960, p. 203).

Westermarck, then, accepts what other writers have claimed were trends toward moral evolution, but argues against calling those trends "evolution," not on scientific grounds, but because he believes that what is meant by a "higher" or more "developed consciousness" can be "nothing else than agreement with the speaker's own moral convictions." While Westermarck assumed that one cannot define the more advanced without an arbitrary value standard, Hobhouse or our own group define a "developed consciousness" by objective measures of ontogenetic or historical sequence, measures quite independent of "agreement with the speaker's conviction."

Our developmental research also suggests that the confusion of ethical and cultural relativity is part of *an extreme ethical relativism* characteristic of a transitional phase in the movement from conventional to principled morality (Kohlberg & Kramer, 1969). In about 20% of college youths, the transition from conventional to principled thought is marked by extreme relativism accompanied by an apparent retrogression to stage 2 instrumental hedonism. As examples of such adolescent relativism, in response to our Heinz dilemma, a college student, age 20, said:

> He was a victim of circumstances and can only be judged by other men whose varying value and interest frameworks produce subjective decisions which are neither permanent nor absolute. The same is true of the druggist. I'd do it. A husband's duty is up to the husband to decide. If he values her life over the consequences of theft, he should do it.

A high school student, age 18 said:

> There's a million ways to look at it. Heinz had a moral decision to make. Was it worse to steal or to let his wife die? In my mind I can either condemn him or condone him. In this case I think it was fine. But possibly the druggist was working on a capitalist morality of supply and demand.

But our longitudinal study shows that *all* our extreme relativists eventually moved on to principled stages (Kohlberg & Kramer, 1969). Usually they moved to stage 5, and became methodological nonrelativists, representatives of the view that there is a rational way of coming to moral agreement though the content of moral principles may be arbitrary. Occasionally, however, they moved on to stage 6, to the recognition of universal substantive principles behind the moral point of view.

This suggests that relativism, like much philosophy, is the disease of which it is the cure; the very questioning of the arbitrariness of conventional morality presupposes a dim intuition of non arbitrary moral principles. A purely conventional person can accept the relativity of the rules of his group because he seeks nothing more. Intense awareness of relativity, however, implies a search for, or a dim awareness of, universal principles in terms of which conventional morality seems arbitrary. Royce pointed this out long ago, and termed "the moral insight" the recognition that the sense of relativity itself presupposes an implicit valid universal principle (Royce, 1885, pp. 132–141).

III. The Cognitive-Developmental Theory of Moralization

In the previous sction we presented evidence *that* there is a culturally universal invariant sequence of stages in moral judgment. In this section we shall present a psychological theory explaining (*a*) why there are culturally universal elements to morality at every stage, and (*b*) *why* movement is always upward and occurs in an invariant sequence. Our psychological theory as to why moral development is upward and sequential is broadly the same as our *philosophical* justification for claiming that a higher stage is more adequate or more moral than a lower stage.

We shall argue that we are not committing the naturalistic fallacy by simply postulating that the later in time is the better. Rather, we are proposing a psychological theory to explain why the moral ideas which are later in time come later and supplant earlier ideas, based on the thesis that the cognitively and ethically higher or more adequate must come later than the less adequate and supplant the earlier because it is more adequate. In other words, we are explaining the ontogenesis, or time order, of idea systems in terms of their philosophic adequacy rather than inferring from order in time to philosophic adequacy. As Alston correctly says, there is nothing surprising about our claim that the scientific theory as to why people move upward from stage to stage coincides with a moral theory as to why they *should* prefer a higher stage to a lower "just because the 'scientific' theory has built into it claims about the relative worth of the various stages" (*p. 274*).

A. Evidence for an Order of Psychological Adequacy in Our Stages. Insofar as assumptions about philosophical adequacy function as explanatory constructs in our psychological theory, they have been empirically tested. The most direct test of these assumptions are the studies of Rest (Rest, Turiel, & Kohlberg, 1969; Rest, 1971), studies which form the core data which link our psychological explanations to issues of philosophic adequacy. In these studies, adolescents were first pretested with standard moral dilemmas, then asked to put in their own words prepared arguments at each stage pro and con a choice for each of two newly presented dilemmas (for example, stealing the drug in the Heinz dilemma). An example of these arguments was presented in Table IV. (Similar statements were also used for the aspects of law, life, and rights.) Typically, adolescents distorted arguments higher than their own moral stage into ideas at their own stage or one below. An extreme example is a bright 17-year-old, stage 2 boy, interrupting the stage 6 conscience statement (that is, not to steal and let your wife die is not living up to your own standards of conscience, see Table IV) as:

> Yes, that's right, its a matter of personal conscience, if he cares enough for her to steal for her, he should steal it. If not he should let her die. It's up to him.

Here the boy translates the stage 6 conception of conscience into a stage 2 conception that "everyone has his bag, he should do what is instrumental to his desires."

In contrast to such distortion downward of stages *above* their own, adolescents had no difficulty comprehending arguments *below* their own modal stage. All subjects understood all arguments at or below their own level. Some subjects understood thinking one and occasionally two stages above their dominant or modal stage. In such cases, however, they showed some (20%) use of the higher stages which they comprehended. In other words, where subjects comprehended stages higher than their own major stage, (*a*) it was usually only the next stage above their own, and (*b*) they were already in transition to the higher stage. One major implication of these findings is that our stages constitute a hierarchy of cognitive difficulty with lower stages available to, but not used by those at higher stages. (The detailed nature of this cognitive hierarchy is discussed in the next section.)

The fact that our stages constitute an order of *cognitive difficulty* and *inclusiveness*, however, does not indicate that the stages constitute an order of *moral adequacy*. The fact that Kant's moral theory is more difficult to understand than that of Mill does not mean that it is a more adequate theory. Rest, however, also found that his adolescent subjects did perceive the statements for each stage as representing a hierarchical order of *perceived moral adequacy*. This was most clearly the case for the stages which they comprehended. The order of perceived "goodness of thinking" corresponds to the order of stages comprehended by the subjects. There was also a tendency to rank stage 5 and 6 statements high, even when they were not comprehended, but it was much less clear-cut.[3] From this, one would predict that, eliminating the stage at which he is, the subject should most assimilate moral judgments one stage above his own, and assimilate much less those which are two or more stages above, or one or more stages below, his own. These predictions have been clearly and consistently verified in four different experimental studies (Turiel, 1966; Rest, 1971; Rest, Turiel, & Kohlberg, 1969; Blatt & Kohlberg, 1971).

In this sense, a psychological theory which has "built-in claims about the relative worth of the various stages" receives strong empirical support. But this empirical support does not philosophically prove the greater moral adequacy of the higher stages. A distinguished moral philosopher who took the moral judgment questionnaire wrote an accompanying note saying "I am not sure whether you will score my responses as stage 5 or stage 6. They may sound stage 5 in content, but I believe they have an underlying stage 6 rationale. However, if I am mistaken, will you please follow the Rest and Turiel procedures and send me some stage 6 responses so that I may

[3] One interpretation of the preference for higher stages which are not comprehended is a Platonic intuition of a higher form of the good, an interpretation elaborated in Kohlberg (1970b) and in Rest, Turiel, and Kohlberg (1969). This interpretation, however, is purely speculative at this point.

move one stage up and be saved." Indeed by our scoring manual, the philosopher was judged as a mixture of stages 5 and 6, so we sent him some pure stage 6 responses. Needless to say, this philosopher was not "saved" as easily as were Rest's subjects, and continues to elaborate his mixture of stage 5 and 6 ethics.

A Freudian psychologist faced with such resistance would dismiss it as defensive, saying that one cannot expect a man who has invested years in publishing stage 5 philosophy to abandon it, as do Rest's uncommitted adolescents. It is possible, however, that Rest's adolescents are philosophically wrong in judging stage 6 as better than stage 5, perhaps responding merely to its nobler ring. Still, it is clear that there are some ways in which stage 6 is more adequate, and these determine the nonphilosopher's preference. Whether they should determine an ultimate philosophic judgment of (moral) adequacy, we shall discuss in later sections.

B. Stage Order and Stage Movement in a Cognitive-Developmental Theory. We must now clarify the sense in which a logical normative analysis of the adequacy of moral ideas can lay claim to being a psychological theory or explanation of their development. Such analysis explains within the total context of a general theory or approach termed "cognitive-developmental" (Kohlberg, 1969). A cognitive-developmental theory of moralization holds that there is a sequence of moral stages for the same basic reasons that there are cognitive or logico–mathematical stages, that is, because cognitive-structural reorganizations toward the more equilibrated occur in the course of interaction between the organism and the environment. In the area of logic, Piaget holds that a psychological theory of development is closely linked to a theory of normative logic. Following Piaget, we claim the same is true in the area of moral judgment.

A "cognitive-developmental" theory of moralization is broader than Piaget's own theory, however. By cognitive-developmental I refer to a set of assumptions common to the moral theories of Dewey and Tufts (1932), Mead (1934), Baldwin (1906), Piaget (1932), and myself. All have postulated (*a*) *stages* of moral development representing (*b*) *cognitive-structural transformations* in conception of self and society. All have assumed (*c*) that these stages represent successive modes of *"taking the role of others"* in social situations, and hence that (*d*) the social-environmental determinants of development are *its opportunities for role-taking.* More generally, all have assumed (*e*) an *active* child who structures his perceived environment, and hence, have assumed (*f*) that moral stages and their development represent the *interac ion* of the child's structuring tendencies and the structural features of the environment, leading to (*g*) successive forms of equilibrium in interaction. This equilibrium is conceived as (*h*) a level of *justice,* with (*i*) change being caused by disequilibrium, where (*j*) some optimal level of match or discrepancy is necessary for change between the child and the environment.

These assumptions of our *psychological* theory correspond to parallel metaethical assumptions of a *moral theory*, that is, to assumptions as to the basic nature and validity of moral judgment. Surely, metaethical assumptions must be compatible with, if not derived from, acceptable psychological theory and findings on moral judgment. If there is irrefutable evidence that forms of moral judgment clearly reflect forms of cognitive-logical capacity, the emotivist notion that moral judgments are the expressions of sentiments is wrong. Again, the existence of six qualitatively different systems of moral apprehension and judgment arising in invariant order is clear evidence that moral principles are not the intuitions of an inborn consicence or faculty of reason of the sort conceived by Butler or Kant. And if stages of moral judgment develop through conflict and reorganization, this is incompatible with the notion that moral judgment is a direct apprehension of natural or nonnatural facts. Our interactional theory claims that moral judgments and norms are to be ultimately understood as universal constructions of human actors which regulate their social interaction, rather than as passive reflections of either external facts (including psychological states of other humans), or of internal emotions.

Both psychological and philosophical analyses suggest that the more mature stage of moral thought is the more structurally adequate. This greater adequacy of more mature moral judgment rests on structural criteria more general than those of truth value or efficiency. These general criteria are the *formal* criteria which developmental theory holds as defining all mature structures, the criteria of increased differentiation and integration. Now, these formal criteria (differentiation and integration) of development map into the formal criteria which philosophers of the formalist school have held to characterize genuine or adequate moral judgments.

From Kant to Hare, formalists have stressed the distinctively *universal* and *prescriptive* nature of adequate moral judgments. The increasingly prescriptive nature of more mature moral judgments is reflected in the series of differentiations we have described, which is a series of increased differentiations of "is" and "ought" (or of morality as internal principles from external events and expectations). As we shall elaborate later, this series of differentiations of the morally autonomous or categorical "ought" from the morally heteronomous "is" also represents a differentiation of the moral from the general sphere of value judgments.

Corresponding to the criterion of integration is the moral criterion of universality, which is closely linked to the criterion of consistency, as formalists since Kant have stressed. The claim of principled morality is that it defines the right for anyone in any situation. In contrast, conventional morality defines good behavior for a Democrat but not for a Republican, for an American but not for a Vietnamese, for a father but not for a son.

The way in which these criteria are embodied in our stages is indicated by Table III, the moral worth of human life. The series is a series toward increased prescriptivity, because the moral imperative to value life becomes increasingly independent of the factual properties of the life in question. First, the person's furniture becomes irrelevant to his value, next, whether he has a loving family, and so on. (It is correspondingly a series of differentiation of moral considerations from other value considerations.) In parallel fashion, it is movement toward increased universality of moral valuing of human life. At stage 1, only important persons' lives are valued, at stage 3 only family members, at stage 6 all life is to be morally valued equally.

These combined criteria, differentiation and integration, are considered by developmental theory to entail a better equilibrium of the structure in question. A more differentiated and integrated moral structure handles more moral problems, conflicts, or points of view in a more stable or self-consistent way. Because conventional morality is not fully universal and prescriptive, it leads to continual self-contradictions, to definitions of right which are different for Republicans and Democrats, for Americans and Vietnamese, for fathers and sons. In contrast, principled morality is directed to resolving these conflicts in a stable self-consistent fashion. (In response to Alston's criticisms (*p. 274*), we will try to clarify and elaborate these points in subsequent sections, where we will try to show how stage 6 can be justified as an adequate or rational ethic.)

C. The Cognitive Components and Antecedents of Moral Development. The psychological assumption that moral judgment development centrally involves cognitive development is not the assumption that this is an increased "knowledge" of rules found outside the child, in his culture and its socialization agents. Studies of "moral knowledge" and belief (Hartshorne & May, 1930) at younger ages indicate that most children know the basic moral rules and conventions of our society by the first grade. Studies and tests of moral knowledge at older ages have not been especially enlightening. By insisting on the cognitive core of moral development, we mean rather that the distinctive characteristic of the moral is that it involves active *judgment*, as Alston (1968) seems to me to have clearly demonstrated from a philosophic point of view. Judgment is neither the expression of, nor the description of, emotional or volitional states, it is a different kind of function with a definite cognitive structure.

We have studied this structure of judgment as the child's use and interpretation of rules in conflict situations, and his reasons for moral action, rather than as correct knowledge of rules or conventional belief in them.

Our cognitive hypothesis is, basically, that moral judgment has a characteristic form at a given stage, and that this form is parallel to the form of intellectual judgment at a corresponding stage. This implies a *parallelism* or *isomorphism* between the development of the forms of logical and ethical judgment. By this we mean that each new stage of moral judgment entails a new set of logical operations not present at the prior stage. The sequence of logical operations involved is defined by Piaget's stages of logico–mathematical thinking.

We said in the last section that our empirical data were consistent with the hypothesis that our moral stages are "true stages" meeting the following criteria:

1. Stages imply invariant order or sequence under varying environmental conditions.
2. Stages imply a "structured whole," a deep structure or organization uniting a variety of superficially different types of response; they imply qualitative differences in mode of response rather than quantitative increase in information or in strength of response.
3. Another criterion is that stages are *hierarchical integrations.* This implies that higher stages include lower stages as components reintegrated at a higher level. Lower stages, then, are in a sense available to, or comprehended by, persons at a higher stage. There is, however, a hierarchical order of preference for higher over lower stages. This condition is also met by our stages, as we discussed in considering the Rest studies (Rest, 1968; Rest, Turiel, & Kohlberg, 1969).

Since Piaget's logical or cognitive stages also meet these criteria (Kohlberg, 1966a, 1968), it is logically necessary that the two sets of stages be isomorphic. Moral stages must have a logical organization or explication if they are "true" stages. In a given stage, each aspect of the stage *must logically imply* each other aspect, so that there is a logical structure underlying each moral stage. Further, an invariant sequence of stages implies a *logical order* among the stages. Stage 3 must imply stage 2 and must not imply stage 4, etc. Such a logical order within a stage and between stages implies that the stages themselves involve logical operations or relations. In other words, a higher moral stage entails a lower moral stage, at least partly, because it involves a higher logical structure entailing a lower logical structure.

This provides an explanation for the fact that movement in moral thought is usually irreversibly forward in direction, an explanation which does not require the assumption that moral progression is wired into the nervous system or is directly caused by physical natural forces. It also helps explain why the step-by-step sequence of stages is invariant. The sequence represents a universal inner logical order of moral concepts, not a universal order found in the educational practices of all cultures, or an order wired into the nervous system. This inner logical order is suggested by the statements in parentheses in our tables. These indicate that each new basic differentiation made by each stage logically depends upon the differentiation before it; the order of differentiations could not logically be other than it is.

But the isomorphism of cognitive and moral stages does not mean that moral judgment is simply the *application* of a level of intelligence to moral problems. We believe moral development is its own sequential process rather than the reflection of cognitive development in a slightly different content area. A child deprived of all moral social stimulation until adolescence might perhaps develop "principled" or formal operational, logical thought in adolescence, but would still have to go through all the stages of morality before developing moral principles rather than automatically reflecting his cognitive principles in a morally principled form of thought. While moral stages are not simply special applications of logical stages, logical stages must be *prior* to moral stages, because they are more general. In other words, one can be at a given logical stage and not at the parallel moral stage, but the reverse is not possible.

To summarize, there is a one-to-one *parallelism* or *isomorphism* between cognitive and moral stages, but this correspondence does not mean high or perfect empirical correlation between the two. This is because a person at a given cognitive stage may be one or more stages lower in morality. Our theory predicts that all children at a given moral stage will pass the equivalent-stage cognitive task, but not all children at the given cognitive stage will pass the equivalent moral task. The results of three relevant studies conform to the prediction. It was found that

1. Almost all (93%) children aged 5–7 who passed a moral reasoning task at stage 2 passed a corresponding task of logical reciprocity or reversibility. However, many (52%) children who passed the logical task did not pass the moral task (Kohlberg & De Vries, 1969).

2. Few (16%) children aged 9–11 at the conventional stages (stages 3 and 4) of morality failed a corresponding task involving the inversion of reciprocity in a cognitive role-taking task. Some (25%) children who passed the role-taking task did not achieve conventional moral judgment (Selman, 1971).

3. All adolescents and adults using stage 5 or 6 reasoning are capable of

formal reasoning on the Inhelder and Piaget pendulum and correlation problems. Many adolescents and adults capable of the latter show no stage 5 or 6 moral reasoning (Kuhn, Langer, & Kohlberg, 1971).

These findings support what we all know, you have to be cognitively mature to reason morally, but you can be smart and never reason morally. The findings are also supported by findings relating moral judgment to IQ or mental age. While mental age on standard intelligence tests is not a direct indication of Piaget cognitive stage, the two kinds of tests correlate quite well (r = 70–80, Kohlberg & De Vries, 1969). Accordingly, IQ tests correlate with moral maturity, but not as well as Piaget tests (Kohlberg & De Vries, 1969).

D. The Affective-Volitional Components and Antecedents of Moral Judgment Development. One reason for the assymetry between cognitive level and level of moral judgment might be that cognitive potential is not actualized in moral judgment because of a will, or desire, factor. It is obviously to one's self-interest to reason at one's highest level in the cognitive realm, less clearly so in the moral realm. Stage 6 may be the cognitively most advanced morality, but perhaps those *capable* of reasoning that way do not wish to be martyrs like Socrates, Lincoln, or King, and *prefer* to reason at a lower level.

Put in a slightly different way, we all know it is easier to think reasonably about physical matters than about moral matters, and this may be due to disruption by will, desire, and emotion in the moral realm. This is an extension of the issue raised by Alston when he distinguishes between having and using a concept, and points out that a person "might conceivably possess the concepts of stage 4, 5, or 6, even though he does not habitually employ them in his moral thinking" (*p. 270*). But this explanation of the discrepancy between logical–intellectual level and moral level is not adequate, since there is not that much discrepancy between comprehension and usage of moral thought. The Rest studies indicate that subjects very seldom understand higher modes of thinking which they do not use spontaneously. While the explanation is not adequate, it does explain some of the slippage involved in the relatively low correlation between intelligence and moral judgment measures (see Rest, 1971).

Discussions of cognition and affect usually founder under the assumption that cognitions and affects are different mental states leading to the question "Which is quantitatively more influential in moral judgment, states of cognition or states of affect?" In contrast to irrational emotive theories of moral development such as those of Durkheim and Freud, the cognitive-developmental view holds that "cognition" and "affect" are different aspects, or perspectives, on the same mental events, that all mental events have both cognitive and affective aspects, and that the development of mental dispositions reflects structural changes recognizable in both cognitive and affective perspectives. It is evident that moral judgments often involve strong emotional components, but this in no way reduces the cognitive component of moral judgment, though it may imply a somewhat different functioning of the cognitive component than is implied in more neutral areas. An astronomer's calculation that a comet will hit the earth will be accompanied by strong emotion, but this does not make his calculation less cognitive than the calculation of a comet's orbit which had no earthly consequences. Just as the quantitative strength of the emotional component is irrelevant to the theoretical importance of cognitive structure for understanding the development of scientific judgment, so the quantitative role of affect is relatively irrelevant for understanding the structure and development of moral judgment.

The astronomer example is misleading, however, in that affective aspects of mental functioning enter into moral judgment in a different way than in scientific judgments. Moral judgments are largely about sentiments and intuitions of persons, and to a large extent they express and are justified by reference to the judger's sentiments. The development of sentiment, as it enters into moral judgment is, however, a development of structures with a heavy cognitive component. As an example, we presented in Table IV six stages in the development of sentiments of fear, shame, and guilt as they enter into moral judgment. The emergence of self-condemnation as a distinctive sentiment in moral judgment is the final step in a series of differentiations, which, like all differentiations in development, are cognitive in nature. This series of differentiations is related to those (presented in Table III) involved in the development of human life, on the face of it not an "affective" concept. Both spring from the central differentiations involved in the stages as a whole (see Table I). This is shown by the fact that there is a good empirical correlation between a child's stage on the life concept and on the guilt concept. Further, the slip between logical and moral development is not particularly large in the area involving concepts of sentiments. Thus, a child's stage on the aspect "concepts of moral sentiments" correlates well with his stage on nonaffective concepts, and correlates about as well with IQ as do the nonaffective concepts.

In general, then, the quality (as opposed to the quantity) of affects involved in moral judgment is determined by its cognitive-structural development, and is part and parcel of the general development of the child's conceptions of a moral order. Two adolescents, thinking of stealing, may have the same feeling of anxiety in the pit of their stomachs. One adolescent (stage 2) interprets the feeling as "being chicken" and ignores it.

The other (stage 4) interprets the feeling as "the warning of my conscience" and decides accordingly. The difference in reaction is one in cognitive-structural aspects of moral judgment, not in emotional "dynamics" as such.

E. Social Role-Taking Component and Antecedent of Moral Judgment Development. A more adequate explanation of the slip between intelligence and moral judgment contrasts the physical–intellectual not with the affective, but with the social. As we shall document, moral concepts are essentially concepts of social relationships as manifested in social institutions. Common to all social institutions or interations are conceptions of complementary roles defined by rules or shared expectations. Ever since the brilliant analyses of Mead (1934) and Baldwin (1906), sociologists and social psychologists have clearly recognized that social cognition and judgment differs from cognition of physical objects because it involves "role taking." The primary meaning of the word "social" is the distinctively human structuring of action and thought by role taking, by the tendency to react to others as like the self, and to react to the self's behavior from the other's point of view. The centrality of role taking for moral judgment is recognized in the notion that moral judgment is based on sympathy for others, as well as in the notion that the moral judge must adopt the perspective of the "impartial spectator" or the "generalized other," a notion central to moral philosophy from Adam Smith to Roderick Firth.

A great deal of variance in level of moral judgment remaining after the intellectual variance is removed is accounted for by social environmental factors which may be called "amount of opportunities for role taking." Piaget's theory (1932) has stressed peer-group participation as a source of moral role taking, while other theories (Mead, 1934) stress participation in the larger secondary institutions, or participation in the family itself (Baldwin, 1897). Research results suggest that all these opportunities for role taking are important, and that all operate in a similar direction by stimulating moral development rather than producing a particular value system. In four different cultures, middle-class children were found to be more advanced in moral judgment than matched lower-class children. This was not because the middle-class children heavily favored a certain type of thought which corresponded to the prevailing middle-class pattern. Instead, middle-class and working-class children seemed to move through the same sequences, but the middle-class children seemed to move faster and farther. Similar but even more striking differences were found between peer-group participators (popular children) and nonparticipators (unchosen children) in the American sample. Studies underway suggest that these peer-group differences partly arise from, and partly add on to, prior differences in opportunities for role taking in the child's family (family participation, communication, emotional warmth, sharing in decisions, awarding responsibility to the child, pointing out consequences of action to others). In particular, Holstein (1971) found that amount of parental encouragement of the child's participation in discussion (in a taped "revealed differences" mother–father–child discussion of moral conflict situations) was a powerful correlate of moral advance in the child.

An explanation of differential moral advance in terms of role taking is an explanation in terms of social cognition which differs from an emotional interpretation of differential moral advance. The environment which provides role-taking opportunities is not necessarily a warm, loving, identification-inducing environment, and an environment deprived in role-taking opportunities is not necessarily cold or rejecting. A certain minimum amount of warmth in face-to-face groups or institutions is required if a child or adolescent is to feel a sense of participation and membership in the group. However, the conditions for a child's maximal participation and role taking in a group is not that he receive maximal affection from the group, or that the group be organized on communal affiliation lines. At the extreme negative end, impersonal cold environments are also deficient in role-taking opportunities. In traditional orphanages, a large majority of children are still at the preconventional level (stages 1 and 2) at age 16 (Thrower, 1971). At the more positive end (as environments promoting moral development), are both certain types of middle-class families and the kibbutz, not an especially warm or emotionally responsive or personal environment (Bar-Yam & Kohlberg, 1971).

F. Justice Components and Antecedents of Moral Judgment Development. One obvious implication of claiming that moral judgment rests on role-taking is that moral judgment entails a concern for welfare consequences. This is true even at stage 1. At every stage, children perceive basic values like the value of human life, and are able to empathize and take the roles of other persons, other living things. An example of such spontaneous sympathetic valuing was my son's first moral action which occurred at age four. At that time, he joined the pacifist and vegetarian movement, and refused to eat meat, because as he said, "it's bad to kill animals." In spite of lengthy Hawk argumentation by his parents about the difference between justified and unjustified killing, he remained a vegetarian for six months.

The example also indicates that our moral stages are not a simple extension of sympathetic or altruistic feelings toward a wider and wider class of sentient beings. If this were the case, my son's concern for killing animals would be scored as stage 6 instead of a stage 1 conception of human life (see Table III). To understand the cognitive-structural components of role taking beyond sympathetic tendencies, we may complete my son's story. Like most Doves, my son's principles recognized occasions of just or legitimate killing. One night I read to him a book of Eskimo life involving a seal-killing expedition. He got angry during the story and said, "You know, there is one kind of meat I would eat, Eskimo meat. It's bad to kill animals, so it's all right to eat them." We can easily recognize that my son not only had a sense of empathy, but a sense of justice, though a stage 1 "eye for an eye, tooth for a tooth" sense of justice. Justice, or reciprocity and equality, then, is also part of the primary experience of role taking in social interaction (Erikson, 1950; Mead, 1934; Homans, 1950; Malinowski, 1929; Piaget, 1932), and we believe it is this component of justice which is central to the cognitive-structural transformation of role taking involved in movement from stage to stage.

The psychological unity of role taking and justice at mature stages of moral consciousness is easily recognized. For example, Tillich (1966) says that "the idea of justice, the various forms of equality and liberty, are applications of the imperative to acknowledge every potential person as a person." But this psychological unity of empathy and justice in moral role taking is also apparent at the very start of moral experience in my son's stage 1 response. My son "took the role of the seal" in the sense of empathically experiencing its predicament. This in turn implied a stage 1 sense of justice as equality, as the equal treatment of men and seals, and a stage 1 sense of justice or reciprocity in the demand for an eye-for-an-eye retribution on its Eskimo hunter. Such stage 1 concepts of justice become differentiated, integrated, and universalized with development until they eventually become Tillich's stage 6 moral sense.

When we move from role taking to the resolution of conflicting roles, we arrive at the "principle" of justice. A moral conflict is a conflict between competing claims of men; you versus me; you versus a third person. The precondition for a moral conflict is man's capacity for role taking. Most social situations are not moral, because there is no conflict between the role-taking expectations of one person and another. Where such conflicts arise, the principles we use to resolve them are principles of justice. Usually expectations or claims are integrated by customary rules and roles. The principles for making rules and distributing roles (rights and duties) in any institution, from the family to the government, are principles of justiceor of fairness.At advanced stages, the most basic principle of justice is equality; treat every man's claim equally, regardless of the man. Equality is the principle of distributive justice; but there is another form of justice, commutative justice or reciprocity. Punishment for something bad, reward for something good, and contractual exchange, are all forms of reciprocity, which is equality in exchange. Arguments about what is just are either arguments about the relative claims of equality (everyone deserves a decent minimum income) versus reciprocity (only those who work hard should get the rewards of hard work), or arguments about equal liberty or opportunity versus equal benefit.

We have claimed that "role-taking tendencies" and the "sense of justice" are interlocked. While role taking in the form of sympathy often extends more broadly than the sense of justice, organized or "principled" forms of role taking are defined by justice structures. In order for roles and rules to represent a socio–moral order, they must be experienced as representing *shared expectations* or *shared values*, and the general *shareability* of rules and role expectations in an institution rests centrally upon a *justice structure* underlying specific rule and role definitions. As stated by Rawls,

> The primary subject of the principles of social justice is the basic structure of society, the arrangement of major institutions into one scheme of cooperation. These principles govern the assignment of rights and duties and they determine the appropriate benefits and burdens of social life (Rawls, 1971).

Because the central mechanisms of role taking are justice structures of reciprocity and equality, institutions better organized in terms of justice provide greater opportunities for role taking and a sense of sharedness than do unjust institutions.

Social environments or institutions not only facilitate moral development through providing role-taking opportunities, but their justice structure is also an important determinant of role-taking opportunities and consequent moral development. The formation of a mature sense of justice requires participation in just institutions. We are currently engaged in analyzing the perceived justice level of certain institutions for adolescents, for example, high school and reform school, as these influence the moral development of their inmates. Impressionistic observation suggests that many reform schools have an official level of justice which is a stage 1 obedience and punishment orientation, while the inmate peer culture has a stage 2 instrumental exchange orientation. An inmate high in participation in either of these structures is not likely to advance in moral judgment, even though in another sense he may be provided with "role-taking opportunities."

G. Cognitive Conflict, Equilibrium, and Match in the Development of Moral Judgment. We have said that moral principles are cognitive structural forms of role taking, centrally organized around justice as equality and reciprocity. The concepts of role taking and justice, then, provide concrete meaning to the cognitive-developmental assumption that moral principles are neither external rules taken inward, nor natural ego tendencies of a biological organism, but rather the interactional emergents of social interaction. As expressed by Piaget,

> In contrast to a given rule, which from the first has been imposed upon the child from outside . . . the rule of justice is a sort of imminent condition of social relationships or a law governing their equilibrium (Piaget, 1948, p. 196).

Piaget argues that just as logic represents an ideal equilibrium of thought operations, justice represents an ideal equilibrium of social interaction, with reciprocity or reversibility being core conditions for both logical and moral equilibrium. While the sense of justice would not develop without the experience of social interaction, it is not simply an inward mirror of sociologically prescribed forms of these relations, any more than logic is an internalization of the linguistic forms of the culture.

In Piaget's theory, which we follow, the notion that logical and moral stages are interactional is united to the notion that they are forms of equilibrium, forms of integrating discrepancies or conflicts between the child's schemata of action and the actions of others. Opportunities to role take are opportunities to experience conflict or discrepancy between one's own actions and evaluations and the action and evaluations of others. To role take in a moral situation is to experience moral conflict, for example, the conflict of my wishes and claims and yours, or yours and a third party's. The integration is provided by the basic principles of justice of a stage. Social environment, then, stimulates development by providing opportunities for role taking or for experiences of socio–moral conflict which may be integrated by justice forms at or above the child's own level.

In contrast to this, exposure to higher stages of thinking presented to the child by significant figures in his environment is probably neither a necessary nor a sufficient condition for upward movement. The amount of change occurring in the Turiel (1966, 1969) and Rest (1971) studies of passive exposure was extremely slight. One reason for this is that a child at a given stage does not necessarily comprehend messages at the next stage up. Rest (1971) found that the only children who comprehended messages one stage above their own already showed substantial (20%) spontaneous usage of that stage of thought, and it was these children who accounted for all of the learning or assimilation of models at one stage up. Presumably, then, movement to the next stage involves internal cognitive reorganization rather than the mere addition of more difficult content from the outside. Following cognitive-developmental theory, Turiel (1969) postulates that cognitive conflict is the central "motor" for such reorganization or upward movement. To test this postulate, Turiel is now conducting a series of experiments presenting children with varying combinations of contradictory arguments flowing from the same stage structure, as illustrated by the examples in Table IV. Without going into the details, the studies should provide concrete evidence for the general notion that stage change depends upon conflict-induced reorganization. What Turiel hopes to show is that exposure to the next stage up effects change not through the assimilation of specific messages, but by providing awareness that there are other, better or more consistent solutions than the child's own, forcing him to rethink his own solution.

If Turiel's analysis turns out to be correct, exposure to the next higher stage will prove to be only the first of a variety of environmental events promoting cognitive conflict. Others are exposures to real or verbal moral conflict situations not readily resolvable at the child's own stage, and disagreement with and among significant others about such situations. All of these sources of conflict have been combined in the moral discussion classes conducted by Blatt (Blatt, 1969; Blatt & Kohlberg, 1971). In some of these classes, the teacher would present dilemmas and focus arguments between adjacent stages (that is, stage 2 versus stage 3, etc.), and this led most of the children to move up one stage, an advance retained over the control groups one year later. In other classes, children simply discussed moral dilemmas without teacher direction. Arguments between adjacent stages often developed naturally, and there was considerable change, varying with the class ability and interest in free discussion. (In the leaderless groups with high interest in discussion, upward change was about as great as it was in the teacher-led groups.)

These findings of Blatt suggest that the effects of naturally occurring moral discussions upon moral judgment be understood in the theoretical terms we have outlined, those of inducing cognitive conflict in the child, and subsequent reorganization at the next level of thinking.

IV. Moral Stages as a Hierarchy of Forms of Moral Integration

We may summarize our cognitive-developmental theory as claiming that (*a*) moral judgment is a role-taking process, which (*b*) has a new logical structure at each stage, paralleling Piaget's logical stages; this structure is best formulated as (*c*) a justice structure, which (*d*) is progressively more comprehensive, differentiated, and equilibrated than the prior structure. To concretize these claims, we may trace the progression of the role-taking or justice structure through the stages. This will show how each stage is able to do things that prior stages could not, how it is a more differentiated, comprehensive, and integrated (equilibrated) structure than its predecessor.

While psychological study of the greater equilibration of successive stages cannot be used to directly construct criteria of ethical adequacy, it can help isolate these criteria, which then require philosophical defense. Normative ethical debate generally centers around evaluating normative theories which constitute various forms of our stages 5 and 6. However, it is fairly evident that stage 4 is more adequate than stage 3, and stage 3 than stage 2, etc. Our analysis of the exact sense in which this is the case gives us some criteria for more controversial evaluations. If stage 6 can be shown to have the same properties relative to stage 5 that stage 5 has to stage 4, and if these properties are recognized as making stage 5 better than stage 4, then we have constructed an argument as to why stage 6 is better than stage 5. Our procedure will be to show (*a*) the new logical operation present at each stage, (*b*) the way in which this operation creates a new and more integrative or equilibrated form of justice as (*c*) this notion of justice forms the core of a socio–moral order.

A. Stages 1 and 2. We reported earlier that all children at stage 2 or higher were able to pass Piaget tests of logical reciprocity or reversibility. They knew that they were their brother's brother, or that a person facing them would have a right hand counterposed to their own left hand. Stage 1 children who fail these tasks of logical reciprocity think that bad acts or persons will and should be followed by bad events (punishment), but they do not define "justice" as reciprocal equal exchanges between distinct individual persons. Stage 1 thus defines the "socio–moral order" in terms of differentials of power status and possessions, rather than in terms of equality or reciprocity. The "principles" maintaining the social order are obedience to the strong by the weak, and punishment by the strong of those who deviate. As examples, a son should give his father money that he has been promised and earned, because "it's his father, he owns him; he has to do what he says;" or a "troublemaker" should be the one to be sent on a suicide mission in the army "because he's bad and he has to do what the captain says."

In contrast, stage 2 has a clear sense of fairness as quantitative equality in exchange and distribution between individuals. Positively, it prescribes acts of reciprocity conceived as the equal exchanges of favors or blows, or acts of cooperation in terms of a goal of which each person gets an equal share; negatively, it deems right noninterference in the sphere of another, for example, "You shouldn't hurt or interfere with me, and I shouldn't hurt or interfere with you." Where social or moral action requires more than this, it becomes, for stage 2, either a matter of selfish whim ("what he feels like doing"), or else an "inappropriate" extension of individual exchange and equality concepts (for examples, stage 2 subjects frequently say one should steal a drug to save a friend's life "because you may need him to do the same for you someday").

B. Stage 3. The limits of stage 2 are revealed by its response to role-taking tasks at which stage 3 succeeds. Selman (1971) used two role-taking tasks which distinguish children at (or above) stage 3 from those below stage 3. The first was a guessing game requiring the child to conceal a coin which another child would then pick. Passing the task entailed recognizing that the other child would anticipate that the finder would try to anticipate him. An immature response would be to hide the dime "because the other boy would want the dime." A mature response would be "He might think that I'll try to fool him by hiding the dime so he may not pick the dime." Eighty-four percent of children at stage 3 or above passed this task, that is, the cognitive prerequisite of stage 3 is recognizing a simultaneous or mutually reciprocal orientation. This reversal or inversion of an originally reciprocal orientation is the logical operation central to moral role taking. This is illustrated by Selman's second task; comprehension of the Golden Rule. Almost all the children in the study were able to state the formula "do unto others as you would have them do unto you." They were then asked "Why is it a good rule?" and "What would it tell you to do if someone just came up and hit you on the street?" To the latter question, most of the ten-year-olds said "Hit him back, do unto others as they do unto you." They interpreted the Golden Rule as stage 2 reciprocity of actual exchange or revenge, instead of in terms of stage 3 *ideal* reciprocity involving considering what you would wish if you were in the other's place. Their justification of the Golden Rule was also stage 2; "If you follow the Golden Rule, other people will be nice back to you." Where children were able to correctly interpret the Golden Rule, they were at stage 3 or above on the moral judgment scale. The intellectual effort required for understanding the formula is indicated by a ten-year-old stage 3 boy: "Well the Golden Rule is the best rule, because like if you were rich, you might dream like that you were poor and how it felt, and then the dream would go back in your own head and you would remember and you would help make the laws that way." The difficulty in comprehending the Golden Rule is that of imagining oneself simultaneously in two different roles oriented to one another.

The stage 3 sense of justice centers on the Golden Rule ideal of imaginative reciprocity, rather than exchange. Related to this is stage 3's conception of equity, that is, it is fair to give more to a more helpless person, because you can take his role and make up for his helplessness. Both ideal reciprocity and equity orient obligation to initial unilateral helping followed by gratitude, rather than to strict equal exchange. They disallow vengeance, because it is neither Golden Rule reciprocity nor does it restore the relationship. As Piaget points out, what the child comes to regard as just is "primarily behavior that admits of indefinitely sustained reciprocity . . . The child sets forgiveness above revenge, not out of weakness, but because 'there is no end to revenge' (quote by a boy of ten)" (Piaget, 1948, p. 323). Characteristically, then, a stage 3 conception of justice is integrated with a conception of a good (positive and stable) interpersonal relationship. The socio–moral order is conceived of as primarily composed of dyadic relations of mutual role taking, mutual affection, gratitude, and concern for one another's approval.

But the ideal role taking of stage 3 is limited because it is indeterminate. The person engaged in practicing the Golden Rule is not requiring the person whose role he is taking to himself abide by it. The Golden Rule, as ideal dyadic role taking, does not arrive at a determinate, equilibrated, or just solution to moral conflicts, because it does not tell us whose role to take. Should the husband put himself in the druggist's or his wife's place in deciding whether to steal the drug? Customarily, stage 3 decides by taking the roles of those with whom he has ties; he also has a stock of stereotypes of "nice" or "mean" people which tend towards the same decision. One would personally take the role of one's wife, not the druggist, and this is consistent with community approval. The "impartial spectator" would "put himself in Heinz's place and see how desperate he was and how he would need the medicine too" says a stage 3 boy. At stage 3, role taking is both guided by, and congealed in, a bag of virtues and role stereotypes. Indeed, as Adam Smith in his excellent exposition of the stage 3 elements of moral psychology (*Theory of moral sentiments*, 1759) shows, there is a fit between our notions of the virtues and their natural meaning as facilitating role taking or sympathy with the individual agent and motive of an act.

In sum, stage 3 notions fit best the institutions of family and friendship which can be grounded on concrete, positive interpersonal relationship. But its limits are clearly seen in the idealized Christian ethic which says "Act as if all men loved one another, and if you meet a man who does not respond with love to love, then turn the other cheek." In practice, most of those who think and live this ethic also render unto Caesar that which is Caesar's. What is Caesar's is the stage 4 morality of law, order, and government.

C. **Stage 4.** We saw that a stage 3 conception of role taking and justice could not easily be extended outside of concrete dyadic interpersonal relationships. Stage 4 solves these problems by defining justice in terms of a system, a social *order* of roles and rules which are shared and accepted by the entire community, and which constitute the community. In terms of role taking, this means that each actor must orient to the other's orientation as part of a larger shared system to which they both belong, and to which all are oriented.

Accordingly, justice is no longer a matter of real or ideal reciprocity or equality between individuals, as dyads, but a matter of the relations between each individual and the system. Questions of positive reciprocity are questions of the relation of individual work and merit to the rewards of the system, "a good day's work for a good day's pay"; merit should be rewarded by the system and every individual must contribute to society. Accordingly, stage 4 positive reciprocity is exchange of reward for effort or merit, not interpersonal exchange of goods or service. Negative reciprocity is even more clearly centered on the social system: vengeance is the right of society and is conceived not as vengeance but as "paying your debt to society." The equality element of justice appears primarily in terms of the uniform and regular administration of the law, and as equity in an order of merit. Social inequality is allowed where it is reciprocal to effort, moral conformity, and talent, but unequal favoring of the "idle" and "immoral," poor, students, etc., is strongly rejected.

It is apparent, then, that stage 4 justice is primarily a principle for societal order rather than for personal moral choice. Furthermore, it is not an ideal principle for arranging the social order, but is the pattern of maintaining the distribution of reward and punishment in an already existing system. For stage 4, justice and maintenance of the basic rules and structure of society are much the same.

We have stressed as our key definition of stage 4 that it is a Law (or rule) -and-Order-Maintaining perspective. Other moral psychologists (Freud, Piaget) have failed to distinguish between the stage 4 *rules-and-authority* maintaining perspective and the Stage 1 rules and authority *obeying* perspective. Because of this confusion, Piaget and Freud have treated a stage 4 orientation as a primitive stage of direct internalization of external commands. Sociologists of morality, like Durkheim, more adequately describe the rule-maintaining side of stage 4 morality, and are correct in seeing it as the "normal" adult morality of any society. In every society studied, stage 4 is the most frequent mode of moral judgment in adults. But our data, indicating that it is an advanced sequential emergent from prior stages quite unlike it, suggest that it is neither a direct internalization of current adult collective rules and beliefs (Durkheim), nor a primitive internalization of parental taboos and authority (Freud, Piaget). Because stage 4 reflects a late step in role taking, it has a more "rational" core than most social scientists have believed.

D. Stage 5. Some moral philosophers and social scientists have argued that we must be satisfied with stage 4 normative ethics because (*a*) all norms and values are relative, so that there is no ground for morality better than our culture's, and (*b*) moral norms ungrounded in collective belief are unsatisfying to their propounders as well as others. In the view of sociologists like Durkheim (1924) and Sumner (1906), or of organicist philosophers like Hegel and Bradley (1962), a more ideal and abstract morality is a fictional construction, detached from social reality and incapable of securing social agreement or emotional support. Our research "disproves" these contentions by showing that, independent of the intellectual constructions of moral philosophers and intellectuals, there arise moralities beyond stage 4 which represent a substantial body (25%) of society, and which more adequately handle moral problems than does stage 4.

The obvious limits of the stage 4 perspective, oriented to *maintaining* rules and social order are (*a*) it defines no clear obligations to persons outside the order (for example, the nation–state) or to persons who do not recognize the rules of one's own order; and (*b*) it provides no rational guides to social change, to the creation of new norms or laws. The core development of stage 5 is the elaboration of a "rational" approach for *making laws or rules*, a law-making perspective which is clearly distinguished from the law-maintaining perspective.

Stage 1 completely confuses these two perspectives, for example, a ten-year-old boy tells us "We should have a law that children under ten have to be in bed by eight. Then kids wouldn't get into trouble." Stage 3, at its best, advises the lawmaker to take the perspective of the obeyer of the law, without a specification of what the lawmaker's perspective requires in addition to sympathy with the obeyer. At stage 4, the lawmaker's perspective is confused with the law-maintainer's perspective; it is not the perspective of a rational individual, it is the perspective of "society" which, if democratic, is the perspective of the "general will." This is expressed as:

> I don't think anyone should disobey any law. Most people must have thought it was good to pass it, a minority bad. . . . It's still the will of the people.

Primarily, stage 4 is law-maintaining, and the legislator, like the citizen, has a perspective primarily determined by the given rules and values of society, which he must maintain.

In contrast, stage 5 clearly has a perspective necessary for rationally creating laws *ex nihilo*, rather than maintaining and solidifying rules. One element of this perspective is rule utilitarianism. Now, even stage 4 justifies rule obedience on the ground that "if one person starts breaking the law, everyone will, and chaos will result." But this form of "rule utilitarianism" justifies any rule once made; it does not help specify what rules are to be made. Thus, at stage 4, "rule utilitarianism" is defined in terms of consequences for maintaining a given society, whose value is taken for granted. In contrast, at stage 5, consequences are defined in terms of criteria for a blueprint of society, criteria by which one law or society may be said to be better than another. The stage 4 confusion between a law-maintaining and a lawmaking perspective is the confusion between what Rawls (1968) terms "justifying an action falling under a practice" and "justifying the practice." The focus of stage 4 is upon "justifying an action falling under a practice"; the answer to "Why should the judge punish the criminal?" is "Because he broke the law and was found guilty." Stage 4 will also go on to "justify the practice" by reference to welfare consequences. The answer to "Why should we have trials and punishments?" is "To stop people from committing crimes and hurting good citizens." But this is only a justification of the institution to other citizens; it is not a justification of the particular form of the practice, nor a criterion for improving the practice.

The distinction between the *law-maintaining* and the *law-creating* perspective is also expressed in two different attitudes of respect for law and society. At stage 4, it is a matter of defending the order against its enemies. Hostility and punitiveness toward criminals, dissidents, and enemies abroad both feeds upon, and feeds, a respect for law, nation, and God, attacked by these enemies. The purpose of law and order is to defend the individual citizen ("Good American") against the common enemy, and the enemy is defined as someone disrespecting law and order. The law-maintaining attitude confuses the individual self-interest and welfare of the law defender with the maintenance of the collective structure. It also confuses the core of the collective structure with that which enemies attack (for example, private property is conceived as the core of our society, rather than as an institutional arrangement for maximizing the welfare of the individuals composing society).

When attention shifts from the defense of law and order to the legislation necessary to maximize the welfare of individuals, an entirely different attitude of respect for law is involved. The law's function then is seen as adjudicating between the property rights and interests of one group of individuals as opposed to another, rather than as protecting the property rights of all decent citizens. Such adjudication requires conceptions of justice or liberty and equality prior to property rights, as well as a rational mode of calculating economic welfare. And it must be based upon procedural rules which are formally just or impartial. Of these procedural rules, constitutional democracy is paramount. While stage 4 elevates majority rule or the general will into a sacred entity, the stage 5 notion of democracy is one of procedural mechanisms ensuring representation of individuals or pluralistic minorities, and making law or society attractive to all of its members.

The procedural arrangements called Constitutional Democracy can make law and society attractive to a rational member because they rest on his consent, provide equal representation for his self-interest, and include a Bill of Rights protecting his individual liberties (natural rights prior to law and society). It is clear that these procedural arrangements are prior to, and more "sacred" than (*a*) the concrete rules they generate, and (*b*) the actual enforement of these rules in particular cases. For stage 5, it is more important to maintain procedures of due process for criminals, for stage 4 to secure the conviction of a particular criminal.

When we turn to the stage 5 procedural rules for lawmaking, we find that they all invoke one or another element of the contract notion. This social-contract notion is a procedural legislative principle which presupposes that both the obeyer of the law and the lawmaker have the proper orientation, and that the lawmaker has received the rational consent of the individuals composing society. In general, all sacrifices of rational self-interest to maintain the expectation of others are contractually defined for stage 5, for example, marriage and family obligations, work obligations. Further, the stage 5 conception of contract as a procedure for generating rules, contracts with a stage 4 conception of contrast as committment to preexisting rules and expectations. While stage 4 recognizes the importance of keeping your word, such a keeping your word is maintaining your committment to role obligations defined by society (for example, keeping your marriage vows), not a definition of obligation by mutual agreement.

The social contract which is the basis of the stage 5 socio–moral order is a justice conception which presupposes reciprocity of the partners to the agreement and equality between them prior to the agreement, though the form of agreement takes priority over substantive justice, once agreement has been reached. Contract and due process are fundamental, and since contracts cannot be binding without the liberty of the contractees, liberty typically takes priority over the other elements of justice (reciprocity and equality) in the stage 5 view. Accordingly, the typical stage 5 conception of distributive justice is one of equality of opportunity, that is, equality of formal liberty to attain substantive equality. For stage 4, social injustice is failing to reward work and to punish demerit; for stage 5, it is failing to give equal opportunity to talent and interest.

We have stressed stage 5 as a lawmaking perspective, rather than as a moral perspective, because in ontogenetic development the formation of a stage 5 lawmaking perspective occurs before the formation of a stage 5 moral rule-making perspective. Rule utilitarianism was first historically developed as a principle of legislation or legislative reform, designed to validate and qualify the claims of the law and the state, rather than to validate moral rules as such. But it is important to recognize that critical moral philosophy and constitutional democracy arose together in the Western World, first in Athens, then in Reformation European thought.

To see why this might be the case, consider our finding that stage 5 presupposes what Piaget terms formal operational thought. Formal operations are logical operations upon operations, combining all possibilities and giving rise to hypothetico–deductive thinking. Regularities or "laws" are no longer simple inductions or empirical correlations, but are seen as exemplifications of universal logical possibilities. One implication of the recognition of possibilities is a sense of the arbitrariness of the individual's own role and rule system, and with it the dawn of critical or metaethical thinking. The formal operational capacity to think about thought is, in the moral realm, the capacity to think about moral judgment, rather than to think about persons, events, and institutions. The development of formal operations, then, allows the child a new level of reflectivity, in which he can view idea systems as self-contained arbitrary systems, and can consider the critical "meta" questions distinctive of moral philosophy. Just as the adolescent asks "What is it to be logical or scientific?" "What is a valid basis of logic or science?" etc., so he asks "What is it to be moral?" "What is a valid basis for ethics?" Unlike stage 2 egotistic relativists, who equate "should" with their interests and wishes, adolescent relativists discard the category of "should" on metaethical grounds of relativity.

Further, the question "Why should I be moral?" is raised for the first time at the formal operational level. A stage 2 instrumental egoistic child could never raise the question, since "to be moral" means nothing more than to serve the self in a context of social exchange. Stage 3 and 4 children do not raise the question, because for them it would mean "Why should I be the kind of self I am?" or "Why should I be part of society?"; "Why be moral?" for the conventional means "Why not be a criminal, inhuman being?" But adolescents in a skeptical metaethical phase can imagine themselves "outside society," or stripped of their stage 3 and 4 ideas and attitudes, as stage 2 instrumentally egoistic men. Accordingly, an increased orientation to instrumental egoistic consideration is found even in those adolescents who move from stage 4 to stage 5 without disruptive ethical relativism. It is understandable, then, that many of the classical arguments for stage 5 moralities are social contract arguments designed to show that commitment to social law is the best strategy for the stage 2 instrumentally egoistic man.

The metaethical questioning which appears typically as a transitional phase in the movement from stage 4 to stage 5 does not always lead directly to stage 5 thinking. Instead, it may generate a number of ideologies whose common feature is an exaltation of the self or of an ideological group as the supreme end from which all "moral" directives should be derived. While our work suggests that such college student ideologies are usually short-lived transitional phases (Kohlberg & Kramer, 1969), there is no doubt that under some social conditions such ideologies become stabilized orientations. At their moral worst, these ideologies declare themselves "beyond good and evil," and the examples of Hitler and Stalin force us to take this amorality seriously; at their best, they celebrate a moral conscience little distinguishable in its principles from the stage 3 or 4 moral sense, but held as the sacred possession of an inner self whose moral integrity comes before both community welfare and rational discussion. We do not consider such ideologies as independent moral stages, however, because they come in many forms, are usually unstable and transitional, but most importantly because they do not represent new modes of normative ethical reasoning. They employ stage 2, 3, or 4 modes of ethical judgment, though they may give them unconventional content.

In summary, we are claiming that stage 5 is the first of two and only two possible novel, consistent, systematic, and stable modes of moral judgment which provide answers to the skeptical and relativistic questioning which constitutes the dawn of moral philosophy (the other mode being stage 6); regardless of the diversities of metaethical positions of moral philosophers, there are only two broad structures of normative ethics (together with their mixtures) open to philosophical elaboration. To indicate why this is so, we have tried to show that social contract, rule utilitarianism, and the conception of law as the protection of individual interests and liberties are a set of interlocked conceptions "answering" the problems raised by a critical or skeptical orientation to morality and society. The social-contract doctrine not only answers the critical awareness of the conflict between rational self-interest and social law, it also answers the problem of the relativity of laws and mores. Law is nonarbitrary when it accords with constitutional procedures which a rational man could accept without prior cultural values or conditioning. Particular laws are arbitrary, but still binding to a rational man in this context. But, as we shall see, there are a set of unsolved problems left by stage 5, and these require a different conception of moral rationality, a conception we term stage 6.

E. Stage 6. For stage 5, laws should be made by constitutional contractual procedures in order to maximize the welfare of all, and laws should be obeyed as part of the contract of a citizen with society. But what should the actor do in situations where legal definitions do not exist or are questionable? Some situations are covered by stage 5's sense of contract, or the requirement that one not violate the rights of others even where not legally protected, or by rational considerations of self-interest. For most stage 5 subjects, however, there is a vast field of relativity or arbitrariness in individual moral choice outside the sphere of law, social contract, and agreement. Among the most compelling of such situations are those demanding civil disobedience of constitutionally legitimate laws because they prescribe unjust behavior. Here is Jaye, a predominantly stage 5 medical student, attempting to cope with the dilemma of whether it was right to break the law and aid slaves to escape before the Civil War:

> We have a law that says something must be done and so in disobeying this law they are doing wrong. However, it would seem that the basic law itself is morally wrong and so *from a moral point of view*, the right thing to do is to disobey the law.
>
> (Why is the law morally wrong?)
>
> Because it is treating human beings as animals.
>
> (Are you saying slavery is wrong or that in your opinion it is morally wrong?)
>
> All I can say is that it is my opinion. I can't speak for anyone else. I think it was wrong, but I think you would have to take it back to the framework of the people of that time. Many people sincerely felt they were not dealing with human beings, maybe in that framework it was morally right from their point of view.
>
> (Then is it genuinely morally right to help the slave escape?)
>
> Here we have a situation of an individual-reaching in his mind the decision that something determined by the state is wrong. Now I think it is perfectly valid that an individual can have his own feeling and opinions. However, if he makes the decision that this law is wrong and decides to disobey it, he must do so with the full realization that it is the state's prerogative to do whatever it can to uphold this law. In breaking the laws the people were acting in a way they thought was morally right and what I would say is morally right, but nevertheless, the action was outside the bounds of society.

Clearly, this stage 5 subject is in a bind, he is not in a stable state of equilibrium, he does not have an adequate ethic. He is not satisfied with viewing civil disobedience as morally relative, and yet he has no firm principles for defining something morally nonrelative or universal.

The first question we must ask is whether an extension of the stage 5 legislative perspective to the making of moral rules and role norms outside the sphere of law can provide a systematic "moral point of view" that will solve such problems. The view that this can be done is, in one form, the notion that morality is embodied in "moral language," and that moral philosophy is an analysis of "ordinary moral language." In another form, it is the view that morality, like the law, consists of a system of specific rules or decrees which vary according to social conditions because they contain an arbitrary element based upon the welfare needs of the particular society. As stated by Baier,

> There is no a priori reason to assume that there is only one true morality. There are many moralities, and of these a large number may happen to pass the test which moralities must pass in order to be called true. For there will be many different moralities all of which are true, although each may contain moral convictions which would be out of place in one of the others. Thus, 'Lending money for interest is

wrong,' 'A man ought not to marry his brother's widow,' 'It is wrong to take more than one wife,' and so on, may be true moral convictions in one set of social conditions, but false in another (Baier, 1965, p. 114).

Clearly, such a modified or methodological nonrelativism is an improvement over the metaethical orientation of Jaye. When the stage 5 recognition of the formal properties of law (universality, impartiality) is extended to define criteria for moral rules and choice, it constitutes the neo-Kantian formalistic criterion of "moral principle" most recently and clearly elaborated by Hare (1963). In a somewhat broader formalistic way, the "moral point of view" may be equated with "qualified attitude" criteria of moral judgment, criteria including various checks or tests in making moral rules or moral judgment as elaborated by Brandt (1959) and Baier (1965). Such formal criteria are primarily "procedural" or "methodological," and rule utilitarianism, while more substantive than formalistic principles, also functions primarily as a methodological principle. Brandt (1968), who combines a "qualified attitude" and a "rule-utilitarian" approach, says rule utilitarianism can be viewed either as a "a true principle of normative ethics or as a rule for valid inferences in ethics," but in actual use it is a methodological principle, "a rule of valid inference" to guide persons making laws and social rules rather than a true substantive principle. "Rule-utilitarian" approaches to normative ethics qualify some claims of law, and extend the legal perspective to extralegal role obligations, but remain procedural principles for generating rules of a quasi-legal variety rather than representing substantive principles comprehensively defining individual moral obligation. Accordingly, the particular rules and obligations generated by "rule-utilitarian" views, like those generated by formalistic "qualified attitude" views, will still be arbitrary or culturally relative.

To document these points, we shall quote two moral philosophers who rely heavily upon combinations of "qualified attitude" and "rule-utilitarian" reasoning to resolve the "Heinz steals the drug" story.

Philosopher 1: What Heinz did was not wrong. The distribution of scarce drugs should be regulated by principles of fairness. In the absence of such regulations, the druggist was within his legal rights, but in the circumstances he has no moral complaint. He still was within his moral rights, however, unless it was within his society a strongly disapproved thing to do. While what Heinz did was not wrong, it was not his duty to do it. The crucial questions are (1) Does a wife (or friend) have a right to the drug? (2) Does the druggist have a right to withhold the drug? (3) Does Heinz have a duty to help his wife (or friend)? In this case it is not wrong for Heinz to steal the drug but it goes beyond the call of duty, it is a deed of supererogation.

(Should Heinz be punished by the judge, if caught?)

The judge's role is to apply the law. Unless there are very strong reasons for setting aside the law, he must do what the law prescribes. The circumstances are not so fully described that I would be confident in saying that they warrant the judge in setting aside the law, thereby creating a precedent entitling people in such conditions to steal.

Philosopher 2: Yes, he should steal the drug. It was right. Although there is a duty in general to obey the law, and to form in oneself the habit of law-abidingness (because it is nearly always harmful to disobey it) there obviously are cases (e.g. protection of Jews in Nazi Germany) in which the law ought to be broken. These are, for the most part, cases in which one can prevent harm to other innocent people which is very much greater than the harm which comes of breaking the law. The present case appears to me to be one of these.

(Did the druggist have the right to charge that much if it was not against the law?)

I think that in matters of life and death like this, common opinion is right to expect a degree of benevolence which is not expected in the ordinary line of business; more good than harm comes of the general observance of the principle that one should save others from grave harm at small cost to oneself, if one can easily do so. It is a husband's duty to steal the drug. The principle that husbands should look after their wives to the best of their ability is one whose general observance does more good than harm. He should also steal it for a friend, if he were a very close friend (close enough for it to be understood that they would do this sort of thing for each other). The reasons are similar to those in the case of wives. If the person with cancer were a less close friend, or even a stranger, Heinz would be doing a good act if he stole the drug, but he has no duty to.

(Should Heinz be punished by the judge, if caught?)

He should let him go free or give him a nominal sentence, if he has the descretion to do so. More good than harm comes of judges observing the principle of letting people off lightly who have broken the law for good moral reasons. A nominal sentence might be justified in order to maintain the principle that law breakers are to be punished.

Now, we note in these responses that the claims and bases of law and social contract are left much as they were in nonphilosophical stage 5 subjects who have not elaborated a consistent moral point of view. Philosopher 1 says that while the druggist has a legal and moral right to withhold the drug, he has no moral basis to complain of its theft. Heinz is not wrong for doing it, but he has no obligation to do it. There seems to be no clear basis *for obligation* here beyond law, although there is a clear distinction between legal violation and moral condemnation of the violator. There are fairly clear criteria of utility and justice in making laws ("distribution of scarce drugs should be regulated by principles of fairness"), but these principles have little effect in determining individual behavior. (They do not obligate the husband to steal, they do not exempt the judge from the obligation to punish.)

For Philosopher 2 law obedience is itself a moral rule to be viewed by rule-utilitarian criteria, but the criteria or circumstances under which the balance of harm over good would justify disobedience of law is not worked out in any clear or general way. The resolution of the conflict between legal and moral obligation is relatively vague. Rule utilitarianism does, however, define for Philosopher 2 a very definite set of moral "principles," that is, those rules "whose general observance does more good than harm." But they are not universal across actors (they dictate that a husband has an obligation to steal, but not a friend or a stranger). "Principles" here seem to be behavior prescriptions similar to what sociologists call "role expectations," that is, they refer to specific classes of persons and prescribe general intentions, and so are not suitable to be enacted as laws. (The way in which these principles are formulated, however, is similar to the way in which laws are formulated.)

Our discussion and our case examples suggest that stage 5 and its extensions cannot yield a universal morality on which all men could agree. It yields a set of procedural principles on which men could agree, but it does not yield substantive moral obligations or choices on which men will agree, any more than do the two philosophers quoted. A morality on which universal agreement could be based would require a different foundation. It would require that moral obligation be directly derived from a substantive moral principle which can define the choices of any man without conflict or inconsistency. This, of course, was the original intent of Kant's categorical imperative as well as the intent of the earlier act utilitarianism. In practice, however, both the categorical imperative and act utilitarianism could not provide plausible weights to either institutionalized rules or substantive justice in their determinations. Accordingly, as embodied in current ethical thinking, they function as "stage 5" procedural principles limiting concrete rules and laws.

There is, however, a more universalistic, moral orientation, which defines moral obligation in terms of what may alternately be conceived as (*a*) the principle of justice, (*b*) the principle of role taking, or (*c*) the principle of respect for personality. We call this orientation stage 6. It is represented by the response of Philosopher 3 to the Heinz dilemma:

> Philosopher 3: Yes. It was wrong legally, but right morally. I believe that one has at least a prima facie duty to save a life (when he is in a position to do so), and in this case, the legal duty not to steal is clearly outweighted by the moral duty to save a life.
>
> It is my belief that systems of law are valid, only insofar as they reflect or embody the sort of moral law which most rational men recognize and all rational men can accept.
>
> In the case of conflict between the imperative of a specific law and a moral imperative, one can often "see" or intuit that one "ought" to break a law in order to fulfill a moral duty. If this is not convincing, and it still is not clear why one ought to break the law against stealing in order to save a life, one can appeal to reason as well as to

intuition. First of all, recognition of the moral duty to save a life whenever possible must be assumed. If someone claims not to recognize this duty, then one can only point out that he is failing to make his decision both reversible and universalizable, i.e., that he is not viewing the situation from the role of the person whose life is being saved as well as the person who can save the life, or from the point of view of the possibility of anyone filling these two roles. Then one can point out that the value of property and thus the authority of the law protecting that property are subordinate to the value of a human life and the duty to preserve that life, respectively. Since all property has only relative value and only persons can have unconditional value, it would be irrational to act in such a manner as to make human life—or the loss of it—a means to the preservation of property rights.

One might deem it sufficient to weigh the amount of good produced by saving a life against the harm (pain) of stealing the drug. On the other hand, one might wish to refer-solely to the results of everyone's acting on the rule, "Steal to save a life if necessary." Such things as the existence of an implicit social contract which allows men to act civilly to one another and the effect of a violation of the conditions of that contract would then be considered. But then if one went this far, *I think that one must take one more step and consider the personal justice involved in the situation—an even more basic root of the same social contract,* but hardly a utilitarian consideration. Not only can laws conflict but also laws can in some situations tend to contradict the ultimate ground of the purposive act of creating and maintaining a social institution. This ground is that of individual justice, the right of every person to an equal consideration of his claims in every situation—not just those which happen to be codified in law. It is a fact that all situations cannot be codified in law, and even if they could, it would not alter the fact that such laws would still be derivative from and express the "higher," "more basic," "absolute," etc. law of justice perhaps best formulated for the purpose here in Kant's "formula of autonomy," "treat each person as an end, not a means."

(Did the druggist have the right to charge that much when there was no law actually setting a limit to the price? Why?)

As the legal system is set up in this country, the druggist had the legal right to charge that price. But I do not believe he had the moral right to do so. Because he is treating human life as a means rather than an end in itself—in this case, a means to making a profit.

(If the husband does not feel very close or affectionate to his wife, should he still steal the drug?)

Yes. The value of her life is independent of any personal ties. The value of human life is based on the fact that it offers the only possible source of a categorical moral "ought" to a rational being acting in the role of a moral agent. All other possible ends of action and the value accorded to them must take only a subordinate, derivative position to that of human life for a rational, moral agent because they are hypothetical in the sense that they are contingent on either irrational interests and desires or heteronomous commands (e.g. from God or human law). The decision of what to do in such a situation must be a principled one, i.e., must be made from a disinterested point of view that allows one to make a decision that can be justified and that is consistent with the decision of any rational agent in a similar situation.
(Should the judge send Heinz to jail for stealing?)

The judge is put into the position of having both to uphold the laws of the state and to witness that the laws of the state are imperfect maninfestations of a higher law. Given this position (and overlooking other, perhaps decisive factors), the judge should convict Heinz on the count of stealing and then suspend sentence for explicit, public reasons.

Philosopher 3 clearly spells out a stage 6 position. He accepts stage 5 rule-utilitarian and social-contract reasoning in its place, but asserts two moral principles as defining a higher "moral law." These two "higher" principles, he holds are ones from which the claims of civil law can be derived. The *first principle* is that "*persons are of unconditional value,*" translatable into the Kantian principle "act so as to treat each person as an end, not as a means." *The second related principle* is individual *justice,* "the right of every person to an *equal* consideration of his *claims* in every situation, not just those codified into law." He treats the two principles as logically equivalent, and claims that they are higher than "consider the amount of good and harm produced by stealing the drug" (act utilitarianism) or "consider the results of everyone's acting on the rule" (rule utilitarianism). He says the utilitarian principle is not higher than law and social contract, it is at the same logical and moral level; hence, there is ambiguity when the two are played off against one another. In contrast, the principles of justice and respect for persons as ends in themselves are "*higher than the law,*" *because the claims of law and contract may be deduced from them.* Finally, he says, from the two principles of justice and respect for ends, *an unconditional duty may be derived, the duty to save a life whenever possible.* To do otherwise is to irrationally treat a human life as a means (that is, not to view the situation from the role of the person whose life is being saved).

These substantive notions of "justice" and "respect for personality" are clarified by some additional features of the response. In marked contrast to the rule-utilitarian, social-contract philosophers, Philosopher 3 holds that the obligation of the husband is that of an ideal moral agent. It is an obligation to steal the drug for anyone whose life can only be saved in this way if no one else will, or can, act to save the person. For Philosopher 1, it is not a duty for the husband to steal; for Philosopher 2, it is a duty for the husband, but not for someone less close. For them, obligation is what may be "legislated" or expected for the natural man in a given role in a given society. Philosopher 2 thinks one can expect husbands to risk jail for their wives (not for less intimate friends); Philosopher 1 thinks one cannot even expect it of husbands. Their definitions of moral obligation depend upon their different views of the psychology and sociology of roles in a particular society. In contrast, Philosopher 3 defines obligation in terms of a "rational being acting as a moral agent," deciding from "a disinterested point of view that allows one to make a decision consistent with the decision of any rational agent in a similar situation."

Philosopher 3's conception is *not only "ideal," it is universalistic.* The husband's act is to be determined by the fact that he is in a certain role, but this role only defines the situation within which he must act, not the values, rules, or considerations that should determine his choice. The considerations determining his choice are those which "any rational agent in a similar situation" should consider. Philosopher 3 uses universality as a positive "principle" of individual choice, making it a principle of role taking, that is, "consider what any human should do in the situation." This leads to a different notion of universality than the Kantian categorical imperative, "act only on that maxim which you can at the same time will to become a universal law." Clearly, the maxim to be universalized is not a principle at the same level as the categorical imperative. When taken in isolation, the universality of the categorical imperative has a conservative rule-maintaining force, exemplified in Kant's conclusion that it is wrong to lie to save a life because to universalize lying for good causes is to negate the meaning of truth telling. The common-sense embodiment of this is stage 4's "You can't make exceptions to rules, what if everyone started doing it." For stage 4, universalization is used in a rule-maintaining rather than a rule-creating perspective. As used by the rule utilitarian and the Kantian, universalization becomes a rule-creating perspective, for example, Philosopher 2's statement "the principle that husbands should look after their wives . . . is one whose general observance does more good than harm." In contrast to such rule universality in given roles, Philosopher 3 uses a more extensive notion of universality ("any moral agent in his place"), and posits that such universality is to be a conscious guide to the actor in making a decision. (If it is something anyone should do in my place, it is an obligation for me, Philosopher 3 claims, so that a person who fails to recognize his duty to save a life "fails to make his decision reversible and universalizable.")

Philosopher 3's primary principles—Kant's "treat each person as an end, not a means," and the principle of justice ("the right of every person to an equal consideration of his claims in every situation")—can be universalized in a different sense than a "maxim" or rule, like "tell the truth" or "help your wife." They are universal because they explicitly refer to "humanity in the person of yourself and every other"; they state what all of us always owe to every other human being. Such principles referring to all humanity are logically implied by the universalization of the actor's decision. To act in a way you want all humanity to act is to recognize the claims of all humanity. The requirement of reversibility implies that a universalizable moral act must have a universalizable object of action.

The maxim "tell the truth" need not be universalized in either sense, but the principles mentioned must be, they are *substantively universal.* One owes it even to the criminal seeking to murder "to treat him never simply as a means," one owes him "an equal consideration of his claims in every situation"; but one does not owe him the truth about the whereabouts of his victim.

We (and Philosopher 3) claim that full universalization of moral judgment requires more than a formalistic claim, it requires substantive moral principles. These principles are themselves limited to those which are fully universalizable. Philosopher 3 restricts his use of the term "principled" to an orientation to moral decisions which is universalizable to all moral actors in all moral situations. The substantive principles meeting this claim are "justice" and "respect for personality." They are more or less equivalent: If everyone is to be treated as an end, then they are to be treated equally. While Kantian universality is identical to formal justice or impartiality, substantive principles (justice, equality, respect for persons) add additional requirements, and make the "ends in themselves" formulation workable. What the principle of justice adds is the specification that treatment of humans as "ends in themselves" is to be defined in terms of rights or claims. This implies that duties are correlative to rights (Raphael, 1955, p. 49), a notion which in turn implies that obligations are always to specific individuals or persons. These two notions lie behind the general claim of deontological intuitionists like Ross (1930) that there is a set of *prima facie* duties not reducible to utilitarian considerations, a "heap of unconnected obligations" which have something to do with the general notion of justice.

We saw that at all stages, the fundamental content of obligation, the fundamental norm of relationship between man and man, was justice, that is, reciprocity and equality. At stage 5, the core of justice was (*a*) liberty or civil rights, (*b*) equality of opportunity, and (*c*) contract. These three ideas were united by respect for the freedom of others, as this freedom is embodied in civil law and civil rights. At stage 6, the sense of justice becomes clearly focused on the rights of humanity independent of civil society, and these rights are recognized as having a positive basis in respect for the equal worth of human beings as ends in themselves. This implies that (*a*) civil rights represent the basic ends of humans to be respected, (*b*) equality of opportunity means a fundamental treatment of all persons as of equal basic worth, and (*c*) contractual relations are not just agreements, but the fundamental form of a community of ends in themselves as defined by trust.

Just how can these stage 6 principles be used to achieve an integrated moral choice in concrete situations of conflict? The key to this is seen in

Philosopher 3's equation of "universalizability" with "reversibility," which is the fundamental statement of equilibrated role taking. At stage 3, we saw that Golden Rule ideal role taking does not achieve an equilibrated solution, that is, one that is completely reversible so that, in case of a dyad, both actors can switch places and get the same solution. (If a richer man gives all he has to the poor, he has followed the Golden Rule but he has not arrived at an equilibrated solution.) In contrast, equality or justice, is a reversible solution to problems of distribution, of when and how much one person gives to another. One element of such reversibility is contained in the notion that duties are correlative to, or reciprocal to, rights. One has no duty where a corresponding person has no right. Another element of reversibility is the recognition that a right implies the duty to recognize that right in others. Only claims which are reversible are valid. Stage 5 recognizes this in the notion that (*a*) the rights (liberty) of others limit the rights (liberty) of the individual, and (*b*) an individual who transgresses the rights of others can make no claim to have his own parallel rights respected. But at stage 6, these notions are developed in a more positive sense. A just solution to a moral dilemma is a solution acceptable to all parties, considering each as free and equal, and assuming none of them knew which role they would occupy in the situation (Rawls, 1971). As an example, in the "Heinz steals the drug" story the husband can take the role of the wife or the druggist. But the druggist's claim to withhold property at the expense of a life is not reversible, he could not recognize this claim in the wife's role. The wife's claim to life at the expense of property rights, however, is a valid claim which could be recognized were she to switch roles with the husband or the druggist. In general, then, in situations of conflicting claims, the only valid claims are those consistent with recognition of the related claims of others. A claim is final only if one would uphold it as final no matter which role in the situation one were to play, and only such claims define duties.

In the sense just outlined, a universalizable decision is a decision acceptable to any man involved in the situation who must play one of the roles affected by the decision, but does not know which role he will play. This perspective is not that of the greatest good, nor is it that of an ideal spectator. Rather, it is a perspective sharable by all persons, each of whom is concerned about the consequences to him under conditions of justice.

V. Our Stages Form an Order of Moral Adequacy: the Formalist Claim

Let us review our article: We have presented evidence of a culturally universal, invariant moral sequence, as well as evidence that this sequence represents a cumulative hierarchy of cognitive complexity perceived as successively more adequate by nonphilosopher subjects. We then outlined the logical structure of each stage, showing the way in which each higher stage (*a*) had new logical features, (*b*) incorporated the logical features of lower stages, and (*c*) addressed problems unrecognized by, or unresolved by, lower stages. We have attempted to show that a justice structure organizing patterns of role taking in moral-conflict situations is the common core at every stage, culminating in the stage 6 capacity to consistently derive moral decisions from the generalized principle of justice, that is, to use it as a consistent guide to situational role taking independent of the arbitrary specifications of the particular cultural order of the moral judge. These ideas outline our psychological theory of moral judgment, a theory which assumes certain philosophical postulates for the sake of psychological explanation. We must now consider what philosophic support we can give to these postulates themselves.

Commenting on the built-in normative implications of our theory, Alston says:

> What is crucial is the claim that the processes involved in stage transition involve the person's coming to realize that certain modes of thinking are more adequate ways of handling the subject matter, that they represent a more finely articulated grasp of the field in question. Thus, the kind of psychological explanation of stage sequence favored by Kohlberg has built into it claims about the relative worth of the stages as ways of moral thinking. . . . The crucial question, then, is as to just what claims of superiority Kohlberg makes, and whether he has adequately justified them (*pp. 273–274*).

We must now take up the "crucial question(s)" raised by Alston. We will first clarify the sense in which we are claiming that the higher moral stage is the philosophically better, and then turn to the "is" to "ought" issue, that is, the sense in which it is permissible to use psychological findings and concepts to support philosophic claims.

First, note that our "claims of superiority" for higher stages are not claims for a system of grading the moral worth of individual persons, but are claims for the greater adequacy of one form of moral thinking over another. In our view, the basic referent of the term "moral" is a type of *judgment* or a type of *decision-making process*, not a type of behavior, emotin, or social institution. Second, note that stage 6 is a *deontological* theory of morality. The three primary *modes* of moral judgment, and the corresponding types of ethical theory, deal with (*a*) duties and rights (deontological), (*b*) ultimate aims or ends (teleological), and (*c*) personal worth or virtue (theory of approbation). Our claims of superiority, then, are claims for the superiority of stage 6 judgements of duties and rights (or of justice) over other systems of judgments of duties and rights. We make no direct claims about the ultimate aims of men, about the good life, or about other problems which a teleological theory must handle. These are problems beyond the scope of the sphere of morality or moral principles, which we define as principles of choice for resolving conflicts of obligation.

The general criterion we have used in saying that a higher stage's mode of judgment is more adequate than a lower stage is that of morality itself, not of conceptions of rationality or sophistication imported from other domains. Stage 6 is not necessarily more cognitively complex (by nonmoral criteria of complexity), nor need it be based on a philosophically more congenial metaethical position. Accordingly, a philosopher may not judge stage 6 as more adequate than lower stages because it is not more scientifically true, is not more instrumentally efficient, does not reflect more metaethical or epistemological sophistication, or is not based on a more parsimonious set of normative ethical postulates. Only a philosophical formalist who views morality as an autonomous domain, with its own criteria of adequacy or rationality, is likely to evaluate moral arguments by moral criteria rather than by philosophical criteria of rationality imported from nonmoral domains. We assume a metaethic which says that moral judgments are not true or false in the cognitive-descriptivist sense, that higher moral conceptions cannot be judged more adequate by technical–economic criteria of efficiency, for example, as better means for maximizing the happiness of the self or of society.

We are arguing that a criterion of adequacy must take account of the fact that morality is a unique, *sui generis* realm. If it is unique, its uniqueness must be defined by general formal criteria, so our metaethical conception is *formalistic*. Like most deontological moral philosophers since Kant, we define morality in terms of the formal character of a moral judgment, method, or point of view, rather than in terms of its content. Impersonality, ideality, universalizability, preemptiveness, etc. are the formal characteristics of a moral judgment. These are best seen in the reasons given for a moral judgment, a moral reason being one which has these properties. But we claim that the formal definition of morality only works when we recognize that there are developmental levels of moral judgment which increasingly approximates the philosopher's moral form. This recognition shows us (*a*) that there are formal criteria which make judgments moral, (*b*) that these are only fully met by the most mature stage of moral judgment, so that (*c*) our mature stages of judgment are more moral (in the formalist sense, more morally adequate) than less mature stages.

Moral judgments, unlike judgements of prudence or aesthetics, tend to be universal, inclusive, consistent, and grounded on objective, impersonal, or ideal grounds. Statements like "Martinis should be made five-to-one, that's the right way" involve "good" and "right," but lack the characteristics of moral judgments. We are not prepared to say that we want everyone to make them that way, that they are good in terms of some impersonal ideal standard shared by others, or that we and others should make five-to-one Martinis whether we wish to or not. In similar fashion, when a ten-year-old at stage 1 answers a moral question, "Should Joe tell on his younger brother?" in terms of the probabilities of getting beaten up by his father and by his brother, he does not answer with a moral judgment that is universal or that has any impersonal or ideal grounds. In contrast, stage 6 statements not only use moral words, but also use them in a specifically moral way: "regardless of who it was," implies universality; "Morally I would do it in spite of fear of punishment" implies impersonality and ideality of obligation, etc. The individual whose judgments are at stage 6 asks "Is it morally right?" and means by morally right something different from punishment (stage 1), prudence (stage 2), conformity to authority (stages 3 and 4), etc. Thus, the responses of lower-stage subjects are not moral for the same reasons that responses of higher-stage subjects to aesthetic or other morally neutral matters fail to be moral. In this sense, we can define a higher-stage judgment as "moral," independent of its content and of whether it agrees with our own judgments or standards.

This is what we had in mind earlier when we spoke of our stages as representing an increased differentiation of moral values and judgments from other types of values and judgments. (For example, with respect to the moral value of the person, the stage 6 argument has become progressively disentangled from status and property values (stage 1), from his instrumental uses to others (stage 2), from the actual affection of others for him (stage 3), etc. With each stage, the obligation to preserve human life becomes more categorical, more independent of the aims of the actor, of the commands or opinions of others, etc.) This is why we appealed to two of the formal criteria of moral judgment—prescriptivity and universality—and paralleled these to the criteria of differentiation and integration which entail a better equilibrium according to developmental theory (*see p. 184*). We tried to develop this in detail in the preceding section, where we showed that the stage 6 response, being more prescriptive and more universal, generated a more stable and consistent response. In contrast, each stage 5 philosopher (qualified attitude and rule utilitarian) generated a somewhat different solution to the dilemma, stopping at varying points in asserting the universal and prescriptive nature of obligation.

What we are claiming is that developmental theory assumes formalistic criteria of adequacy, the criteria of levels of *differentiation* and *integration.* In the moral domain, these criteria are parallel to formalistic moral philosophy's criteria of *prescriptivity* and *universality.* These two criteria combined represent a formalistic definition of the moral, with each stage representing a successive differentiation of the moral from the nonmoral and a more full realization of the moral form.

Our developmental definition of morality is not a system for directly generating judgments of moral worth, just as Piaget's developmental definition of stages of intellectual adequacy is not a system for grading single acts of persons as better or worse along an IQ scale. A developmental definition seeks to isolate a function, like moral judgment or intelligence, and to define it by a progressive developmental clarification of the function. Thus, intelligence, as defined by Piaget, is both something present from the start of life (in the infant's adaptive sensory motor behavior) and something whose ultimate structure or form is only given in the final stages (for example, the formal operational thought of the adolescent as experimenter and theorist). Similarly, in our view, there is a moral judgmental function present from age 4–5 onwards in judgments of "good and bad" and "has to" (our stage 1), but this function is only fully defined by its final or principled stages.

What we are stressing is that our developmental *metaethical* conception of the higher or later as the more moral is not a *normative ethical* principle generating moral judgments. Some formalistic philosophers, notably Kant, have attempted to construct rules of punishment or blame, and a theory of the good or of virtue from deontological principles. But we make no such claims and do not think a stage 6 normative ethic can justifiably generate a theory of the good, a theory of virtue, or rules for praise, blame, and punishment. In order to engage in moral education and social control, society may need rules of punishment and reward, and rules for labeling virtues and vices (stage 5). But stage 6 principles of justice do not *directly* obligate us to blame and punish, even though it is necessary or expedient in terms of social utility.

We have been arguing that, both by stage 6 normative ethical standards and by formalist metaethical criteria, stage 6 is a more moral mode of judgment than stages 5 or 4. One may define an act as moral if it is in accord with stage 6 principles in a particular situation, but this does not generate rules for grading the worth of individual men or of actions. Nor does our formalist metaethic answer questions like "Why be moral?" or "What good is justice?" Such questions cannot be answered by a normative ethical theory or by using moral concepts. Just as a theory of formal logic is a theory of what logical inference is and ought to be, but does not answer the question "What good is logic?" or "Why be logical?" so answers to these metaethical questions are not given by a stage 6 normative ethical theory. A formalistic normative theory says, "Stage 6 is what it means to judge morally. If you want to play the moral game, if you want to make decisions which anyone could agree upon in resolving social conflicts, stage 6 is it." It cannot give a justification of stage 6 morality in nonmoral terms.

In the present section, we have clarified our claim that stage 6 is the most adequate exemplification of the moral, supporting it with a few of the many arguments advanced by formalist (deontological) theories. In this connection, Alston's comment that "it is notorious that moral philosophers agree no more about what is distinctive of the moral than about anything else" (*p. 276*) is somewhat misleading. While there are an infinite variety of definitions of the moral, there is a fairly high degree of agreement among formalists as to the formal properties of moral judgment (compare Frankena, 1963). Philosophers who offer alternative definitions of morality do so because they ignore formal features of morality, and define it instead in terms of the particular content of the normative morality they advocate. To my knowledge, those who object to a formalist definition of morality have no positive alternative to offer except (*a*) morality is what is in accord with my own system, or (*b*) morality is relative. Regardless of psychology, then, our conception of morality has a strong philosophical base. Anyone who tries to criticize it must provide a stronger positive alternative.

VI. The Claim for Principles of Justice

We now turn to the defense of our substantive definition of stage 6 in terms of principles of justice. While every domain of thought, from grammar to music, implies "principles" (that is, abstract rules), moral principles have unique features and functions. If a "bad" painting is made according to principle, so much the worse for the principle. But the whole notion that there is a distinctively moral form of judgment demands that moral judgment be principled, that is, that it rely on moral principle, on a mode of choosing which is universal, which we want all people to adopt in all situations.

By "principle" we mean something more abstract than ordinary moral rules of the Ten Commandment variety. Conventional college students say, in regard to the drug stealing story, "the principle of loyalty to your family comes ahead of obeying the law here," etc., but, on the face of it, they do not wish to universalize these rules. For one thing, not everyone has families; for another, it is doubtful that if one's uncle were Hitler one could claim loyalty to be a relevant or *prima facie* principle. We know it is all right to be dishonest and steal to save a life because a man's right to life comes before another man's right to property. There are always exception to such rules. By "moral principle," all thoughtful men have meant a general guide to choice rather than a rule of action. Even our college student who talks of "the principle of loyalty to your family" means something like "a consideration in choosing," rather than a definite rule prescribing a class of acts.

It has sometimes been thought that principles like the utilitarian maximization of happiness, or Kant's categorical imperative, are not only universalizable to all men and all situations, but are also absolutely definitive of right action in any situation. Thus far we have never encountered a live human being who made moral judgments in terms of principle in this sense. On the other hand, we do find people judging in terms of principles in a weaker sense that is illustrated in the writings of the principled institutionists, such as Sidgwick and Ross. In this weaker sense, a person may consistently hold more than a single principle of moral judgment, and these principles may not be definitive of a choice in all situations (that is, alternative choices may be derived from them). In our empirical work, we considered the term "principles" to refer to considerations in moral choice, or to reasons justifying moral action. We found empirically that almost all these reasons easily fall into the categories outlined by principled intuitionist philosophers.

Accordingly, in our detailed coding of categories of moral judgment, we have the following categories of "principles," which correspond to those of Sidgwick, except that we add the psychological category of "respect for authority": (*a*) prudence (and self-realization); (*b*) welfare of others; (*c*) respect for authority, society, or persons; and (*d*) justice. As we suggested in preceding sections, all of these "principles" are present in one form or another from stage 1 onward, except that prudence and authority have dropped out as reasons by stage 6. From the start, these reasons have two characteristics: they refer to states of affairs which seem right or good in themselves, and they refer to states of affairs which are involved in all moral situations and are potentially relevant to all people. Still, benevolence and justice do not become genuine moral principles until stages 5 and 6. At the conventional stages, the reasons for choices include considerations of benevolence and justice, as well as of prudence and social authority. But not until stages 5 and 6 is there an effort to systematically and consistently derive *prima facie* rules or obligations from these principles, or to view obligation as fundamentally directed by them rather than by concrete rules.

In our view, mature principles are neither rules (means) nor values (ends), but are guides to perceiving and integrating all the morally relevant elements in concrete situations. They reduce all moral obligation to the interests and claims of concrete individuals in concrete situations; they tell us how to resolve claims which compete in a situation, when it is one man's life against another's. If our formal characterization of the functioning of mature principles is correct, it is clear that only principles of justice have an ultimate claim to being adequate universal, prescriptive principles. By definition, principles of justice are principles for deciding between competing claims of individuals, for "giving each man his due." When principles, including considerations of human welfare, are reduced to guides for considering such claims, they become expressions of the single principle of justice.

The only general principle of content, other than justice, seriously advanced by philosophers, has been the principle variously termed utility or benevolence. While benevolence can be universalized (that is, everyone should care for the welfare of all other humans), it cannot resolve a conflict of welfares, except by quantitative maximization. The content of moral concerns and claims is always welfare, but maximization is no true moral principle, as we attempted to show in our analysis of stage 5 rule utilitarianism. Concern for the welfare of other beings, "empathy," or "role taking," is the precondition for experiencing a moral conflict rather than a mechanism for its resolution. The moral question is "Whose role do I take?" or "Whose claim do I favor?" The working core of the utilitarian principle is the maximization principle. As everyone knows, and our studies document, "Consider everyone's happiness equally" is not a working principle of justice. Stage 6 subjects will say "Steal the drug for anyone, whether it's his wife or not, every man has a right to live," but they do not claim that a husband should treat the happiness of his wife and of a stranger equally. Neither do they rationalize the husband's preference for his wife's happiness on "rule-utilitarian" grounds. Instead, they speak of a marriage tie, or "contract," or relationship of reciprocal trust and love, that is, a claim of commutative reciprocity or justice, not one of utility.

My argument for justice as the basic moral principle is then as follows:

1. Psychologically, both welfare concerns (role taking, empathy) and justice concerns, are present at the birth of morality and at every succeeding stage, and take on more differentiated, integrated, and universalized forms at each step of development.

2. Of the two, however, only justice takes on the character of a principle at the highest stage of development, that is, as something that is obligatory, categorical, and takes precedence over law and other considerations, including welfare.

3. "Principles" other than justice may be tried out by those seeking to transcend either conventional or contractual–consensual (stage 5) morality, but they do not work either, because they do not resolve moral conflicts, or because they resolve them in ways that seem intuitively wrong.

4. The intuitive feeling of many philosophers that justice is the only

satisfactory principle corresponds to the fact that it is the only one that "does justice to" the viable core of lower stages of morality.

5. This becomes most evident in situations of civil disobedience for which justice, but not other moral principle, provides a rationale which can cope with the stage 5 contractual–legalistic argument that civil disobedience is always wrong.

6. The reason that philosophers have doubted the claims of justice as "the" moral principle is usually that they have looked for a principle broader in scope than the sphere of moral or principled individual choice in the formal sense.

Denial that justice is the central principle of morality thus tends to coincide with a refusal to accept a formal deontological concept of morality, but is not backed by an alternative positive definition of morality.

In identifying the core of principled morality with justice, we follow a line of normative ethical argument advanced recently by Raphael (1955) and Rawls (1963, 1971). Formalists who disagree with the primacy of justice usually do so because they wish to keep morality completely content-free. In one sense, justice is itself content-free; that is, it merely prescribes that principles should be impartially applied to all. However, we have also argued that the stage 6 form implies justice as equity, that is, as a treatment of persons as morally equal (compare Frankena, 1963). Second, we have argued that it also implies commutative justice as reciprocity, contract, and trust. In this article, we cannot show that the moral form of universality, tied to the notion that obligations are to persons, logically implies the principle of justice, a task which Raphael (1955) has attempted. We simply point to the fact that no principle other than justice has been shown to meet the formal conception of a universal prescriptive principle.

Let me briefly consider Alston's criticism that

> What Kohlberg really wants most to recommend to our acceptance is the principle of justice (in his interpretation) as a supreme moral principle. But stages of prescriptivity will not advance that cause. A judgment based on a principle of racial destiny, or on no principle at all, can be just as prescriptive as a judgment based on an application of Kohlberg's principle of justice (*p. 277*).

For most of us, it is counterintuitive to believe that racial destiny could be held as a universal prescriptive principle. This is because no human being held it or similar beliefs as such a principle, at least none in our research studies. Hitler himself explicitly said "Might makes right," that is, his judgments were nonprescriptive, and he explicitly held that Nazi morality was nonuniversal, that is, it was not designed to govern the decisions of Jews or others. The fact that psychological study shows that no one does use unjust "principles" in a formally principled way, is no proof that they cannot. However, it is of more moment that no philosopher ever has seriously attempted to demonstrate that an alternative substantive principle to justice could function in a universal prescriptive fashion in a satisfactory way. Alston is correct in saying that I have not proved that justice is the only possibility, but he neglects to point out that no one has successfully argued for an alternative.

In summary, if a formalistic definition of moral principle is unjustified, no one has proposed a better definition. And if an equation of moral principle with justice is unjustified, no one has proposed a satisfactory alternative. In that sense, it is clear that my definition of stage 6 as the way people ought to reason is more than what Alston suggests, namely "some arbitrarily selected criterion . . . [based on] congeniality to his predelictions" (*p. 277*).

VII. From "Is" to "Ought"

Let us consider the sense in which our description of what morality is tells us what it ought to be. To begin with, there are two forms of the "naturalistic fallacy" we are not committing. The first is that of deriving moral judgments from psychological, cognitive–predictive judgments or pleasure–pain statements, as is done by naturalistic notions of moral judgment. Our analysis of moral judgment does not assume that moral judgments are really something else, but insists that they are prescriptive and *sui generis*. The second naturalistic fallacy we are not committing is that of assuming that morality or moral maturity is part of man's biological nature, or that the biologically older is the better. The third form of the "naturalistic fallacy" which we *are* committing is that of asserting that any conception of what moral judgment ought to be must rest on an adequate conception of what it is. The fact that our conception of the moral "works" empirically is important for its philosophic adequacy. By this we mean first that any conception of what adequate or ideal moral judgment *should be* rests on an adequate definition of what moral judgment *is* in the minds of men. If Ph.D. philosophers showed a stage 6 concern for universal and autonomous moral principles, while all other men were Durkheimian asserters of the authority of the group, or were Benthamite hedonists, it would be, I believe, impossible to construct a plausible account of why men should adopt a stage 6 morality. Contrariwise, neither a Benthamite construction nor a Durkheimian construction of what morality ought to be, based as they are on the assumptions that morality really is stage 2 (Bentham) or stage 4 (Durkheim), is viable, because both ignore the reality of what morality is at stages 5 and 6. Every constructive effort at rational morality, at saying what morality ought to be must start with a characterization of what it is, and in that sense commits "the naturalistic fallacy."

What we are claiming about the relation of "is" to "ought" in moral development comes to this:

1. The scientific facts are that there is a universal moral form successively emerging in development and centering on principles of justice.

2. This Kantian moral form is one which assumes the fact value distinction, that is, the moral man assumes that his moral judgment is based on conformity to an ideal norm, not on conformity to fact.

3. Science, then, can test whether a philosopher's conception of morality phenomenologically fits the psychological facts. Science cannot go on to justify that conception of morality as what morality ought to be, as Durkheim attempted to do. Moral autonomy is king, and values are different, from facts for moral discourse. Science cannot prove or justify a morality. because the rules of scientific discourse are not the rules of moral discourse.

4. Logic or normative ethical analysis can, however, point out that a certain type of moral philosophy, for example, stage 4, does not handle or resolve certain problems which it acknowledges to be problems that it ought to handle, whereas another type of morality (for example, Stage 5) can do so. Here, factual investigation of men's beliefs must support internal logical analysis of why the developmentally higher philosophy can handle problems not handled by the lower ones. Science, then, can contribute to a moral discourse as to why one moral theory is better than another.

5. The scientific theory as to why people factually *do* move upward from stage to stage, and why they factually *do* prefer a higher stage to a lower, is broadly the same as a moral theory as to why people *should* prefer a higher stage to a lower. In other words, a psychological theory of why people move upward in moral ideology is not like a psychological theory of why they move from the anal to the genital stage. It is the naturalistic fallacy to say that a Freudian theory of an instinctual progression is an ethical justification of why genitality is better than anality. But the theory of *interactional* hierarchical stages of cognition and morality, and the theory of *maturational* embryological stages are critically different in their logic, as I have discussed in detail elsewhere (Kohlberg, 1969).

Claims 1–4 are simply claims that moral psychology and moral philosophy should work hand in hand. This unexciting conclusion is represented in this article, where we have tried to give normative ethical answers to problems set by developmental findings. Since Alston regards my claim that any constructive effort at rational morality must start from a characterization of what it is as "a very innocuous sense" of the "naturalistic fallacy" (*p. 273*), he probably does not object to them. Alston does object to claim 5, and thinks that I am trying to "pull a moral philosophy out of a hat" (*p. 277*). What is not completely clear to me is whether he means that it is logically impossible to derive anything for moral philosophy out of a hat of developmental facts, or whether he is arguing that I have not been completely successful in a logically possible enterprise, because it is a hard trick to pull off. (I agree with his latter conclusion; if my argument were completely successful, it would have solved the basic problems of moral philosophy.) The former notion, that is, that facts of development cannot be of any use in arguing for moral "oughts," because the distinction is absolute and "Thou shalt not use facts in the development of principles," is an untenable position, as Scheffler (1953) seems to me to have demonstrated.

At any rate, it should be noted that even the claim that normative theories need to be grounded on a firm view of the facts of moral judgment carries us quite a way. First, our findings indicate that philosophical analysts are justified in asserting universal features, as against the arguments of ethical and cultural relativists. They also show that the philosopher's task cannot be merely to clarify moral language or moral common sense, since there are six such systems of moral language. Further, since the highest stage includes the basic positive features of lower stages, only a normative ethical theory which includes all these features can tell us how we ought to make moral judgments. This rules out most ethical theories, for example, utilitarian and nonprincipled intuitionistic theories.

However, we do hold a stronger position, claiming that while psychological theory and normative ethical theory are not reducible to each other, the two enterprises are isomorphic or *parallel*. In other words, an adequate psychological analysis of the structure of a moral judgment, and an adequate normative analysis of the judgment will be made in similar terms. In the context of our work, psychological description of moral stages corresponds to the "deep structure" of systems of normative ethics. The logical relations between stages represent indifferently the structure of an adequate theory of moral judgment development, or the structure of an adequate theory as to why one system of moral judgment is better than another. Thus, we have argued for a parallelism between a theory of psychological development and a formalistic moral theory on the ground that the *formal psychological* developmental criteria of differentiation and integration, of structural equilibrium, map into the *formal moral* criteria of prescriptiveness and universality. If the parallelism were correct in detail, then formalist philosophers could incorporate an equilibration concept as part of their normative ethical theory, and vice versa. The ultimate result would be a theory of rational moral judgment like that now present in economics, in which the theory of how people ought to make economic decisions and the way they do make decisions are very closely linked.

What can warrant such a "parallelist" claim is only the fruitfulness of its results. I have argued that the fruitfulness of the parallelist assumption is revealed in the clear success of the psychological work based on it. Its fruitfulness in solving philosophic problems will, I optimistically believe, be apparent when moral philosophers begin to use the new moral psychology to help pose and solve their problems.

Let me be concrete about the way in which our stage psychology provides guidance for the moral philosopher's task. Critical or analytic moral philosophy sees its task as the clarification of ordinary consciousness. But if there are six stages, and each stage is a reconstruction of moral "principles" of lower stages, then moral principles are active constructions, and moral philosophy must construct, not merely analyze or clarify. Confronted by the task of constructing a rational morality, philosophers have usually taken one of two metaethical positions: that a rational system for moral choice must consist of deductions from principles which are self-evident to an actor who accepts nothing but rational methods of inference and of optimizing choice (the classic Benthamite utilitarian stance, leading to a naturalistic form of descriptive metaethic); or that moral principles are dimly intuited by the common man (ordinary morality), and the philosopher's task is simply to codify and make consistent the morality derived from these principles (Kant or Sidgwick). How far off this was is documented by the Rest (1968) study, which shows the lack of comprehension of subjects at conventional stages for even the most concrete and palatable statements of Kant's categorical imperative. On the basis of our research, we reject both the Benthamite (naturalistic) position and the Kantian notion that principles are innate, universal *a prioris*.

From our developmental perspective, moral principles are active reconstructions of experience; the recognition that moral judgment demands a universal form is neither a universal *a priori* intuition of mankind nor a peculiar invention by a philosopher, but rather a portion of the universal reconstruction of judgment in the process of development from stage 5 to state 6. An analogy to grammar may clarify our point. Kantian moral intuitionists see their task as like that of Chomsky, who attempts to delimit the principles, the deep structure transformations, which define competent syntax in any language. In grammar, the codification of these principles does not, however, transform syntax itself. Chomsky speaks the same syntax he spoke at age five. It is for this reason that he is able to hold a Kantian epistemology of grammar. There is only one grammatical system of intuition, known to all children of five. In contrast, we are arguing that the codification of principles is an active reconstruction of morality, that stage 6 principled morality is a radically different morality rather than a codification of conventional stage 4 morality. The task of both the psychologist and the philosopher, then, is very different in the sphere of morality than in grammar. If our position is correct, the only "competent moral speakers" are the rare individuals at stage 6 (or more tolerantly at stages 6 and 5), and normative ethical codifications and metaethical explanations of conventional moral speech will miss their true task. Like neo-Kantian intuitionists, ordinary language moral philosophers, particularly formalists like Hare, think their task is to analytically define and clarify ordinary (stage 4) moral language. If the form of ordinary moral language is, however, qualitatively different from that of the language of a normative ethical philosopher, the problem is different.

Another implication of our stage psychology for moral philosophy is that arguments for a normative ethic must be stepwise. Rawls (1971) has taken a formal set of assumptions which I term stage 5, namely, that society is ordered by a constitution defined by a social contract, and he shows how such a society must be based upon principles of justice, or of equal rights, because these are the only principles to which rational individuals in the imaginary original state could consent. These principles are, in a sense, prior to law and social institutions, and in certain conditions justify civil disobedience. In other words, Rawls has used a formal argument to derive stage 6 morality from stage 5, and to systematize stage 6 morality insofar as stage 6 morality is defined by socio–political choices. In contrast, one of the classical arguments for stage 5 morality has been that of deriving it from stage 2 morality. Assuming an instrumental egoistic man (stage 2), moral theory attempted to show that it is rational for him to create a social contract with social welfare conditions. This argument fails to be fully convincing because it ignores the stage 4 to which it "ought" to be addressed. From this, one can conclude that there is no one line of argument for stage 6 (or stage 5) morality, but only a family of arguments which move from one stage position to the next.

In essence, there is a "deep logical structure" of movement from one stage to the next; a structure tapped by both a psychological theory of movement and by families of philosophical argument. If these contentions are correct, they provide a new definition of the moral philosopher's task, a definition more exciting than that implied by much recent philosophic work.

VIII. From Thought to Action

A moral decision, we usually think, involves a conscious conflict between two lines of action, and a strong emotional component. Psychology's notion of conscience comes from the prophets through Saint Paul to Freud's conception of the battle between the id and the superego. Saint Paul's "The flesh lusteth against the Spirit and the Spirit against the flesh so that ye cannot do the things ye would," St. Augustine's "O Lord, give me strength to give up my concupiscence, but not just yet," have passed into the clichés of most psychology text books: moral behavior is construed as resistance to temptation, the algebraic outcome of two forces, the lusts of the flesh (needs), and the anticipation of the guilt (superego), mediated by a slightly overwhelmed ego, self, or will.

To get an indication of the battle of conscience, one of my students (Lehrer, 1967) built a ray gun test following Grinder's (1962) rationale. Grinder's gun was preprogrammed to yield a marksmanship score just a little below that needed to get a handsome prize, and the twelve-year-olds tested had the opportunity to fudge their scores. Grinder (1962) reports that 80% of the children end up cheating. Lehrer wanted to tempt the children even more, by improved gadgetry that leads them to the brink of success in a realistic but random fashion. To our surprise, when Lehrer ran 100 children, only 15% cheated (Lehrer, 1967). This was hardly a decision of conscience; the machine obviously struck the children as being a computer which kept its own score, while the Grinder machine did not.

What I am trying to show is what Hartshorne and May showed forty years ago, though it has been ignored ever since, namely:

1. *You cannot divide the world into honest and dishonest people! Almost everyone cheats some of the time.* Cheating is distributed in bell-curve fashion around a level of moderate cheating.
2. *If a person cheats in one situation, it does not mean he will or will not in another. There is very little correlation between situational cheating tests.* It is not a character trait of dishonesty which makes a child cheat in a given situation, if it were, you could predict from one situation to another.

The emphasis on moral virtues which are acquired by habit derives from Aristotle, whose bag of virtues included temperance, liberality, pride, good temper, truthfulness, and justice. Hartshorne and May's bag included honesty, service, and self-control. The Boy Scout bag is well known—a scout should be honest, loyal, reverent, clean, and brave. My quick tour through the ages indicates that the trouble with the bag of virtues approach is that everyone has his own bag. The problem is not only that a virtue like honesty may not be high in everyone's bag, but that my definition of honesty may not be yours. When I have given the circles test to children, I have been lying and cheating them, saying I was testing their aptitude. I cheat and lie to them so that I can catch them cheating me. Nevertheless, I would argue that my cheating does not indicate a lack of consistency between my self-concept as honest and my behavior, but reflects the consistency of this particular kind of cheating with my moral principles. Your moral principles might be inconsistent with giving these tests to children, but you will probably believe that I am generally moral even though I cheated in this situation.

The objection of the psychologist to the bag of virtues should be that virtues and vices are labels by which people award praise or blame to others, but the ways people use praise and blame toward others are not the ways in which they think when making moral decisions themselves. You may not find my cheating children "honest" or moral, but I find it in accordance with my moral principles and thinking. To illustrate the point another way, Edmund Wilson (and Thoreau) failed to pay income taxes as a "matter of conscience," while millions of their fellow citizens fail to do so for reasons of "expedience." The behaviors are the same, and no psychologist can tell them apart; it is only what the people involved think they are doing which sets the behavior apart. There simply is no valid psychological definition of moral behavior, in the sense that no observation and categorization of behavior "from the outside," or "behavioristically," can define its moral status in any psychologically valid sense. But while there is no such thing as moral behavior as such, there is such a thing as behavior which is consistent with an individual's moral principles, or which springs from a moral decision. Before we can know anything about such behavior, however, we must first know what a man's moral judgments or principles are.

We can now relate moral judgment to moral action in light of our earlier contention that the major general individual and group differences in moral judgment are developmental differences. What we are ready to predct is not that people in a moral situation will do what they said they should do outside that situation, but that maturity of moral thought should predict to maturity of moral action. This means that specific forms of moral action require specific forms of moral thought as prerequisites, that the judgment–action relationship is best thought of as the correspondence between the general *maturity* of an individual's moral judgment and the maturity of his moral action. This implies the cognitive-developmental contention (Kohlberg, 1969) that maturity of moral judgment and action have heavy cognitive components, and suggests a broader developmental notion of moral action than that represented by the "bag of virtues."

In our first study (Kohlberg, 1958), 72 Chicago boys aged 10–16 were rated by their teachers on a variety of character traits including conscience strength or internalized conformity. The product moment correlation between maturity of moral judgment scores and ratings of conscience was .46. Experimental studies by Krebs (1967) and by Brown, Feldman,

Schwartz, and Heingartner, (1969) bears these correlational trends out. In the latter study, a short form of my moral judgment instrument was administered to 35 undergraduates, who could then be divided into two moral judgment levels, the conventional and the principled. Principled subjects appear much less likely to cheat than conventional subjects. Only one of nine principled subjects cheated while about one-half of the conventional subjects did so. The former study reports similar results with 120 sixth-grade children (20% of the principled subjects cheated as compared to 67% of the subjects at lower stages).

On the usual attitude test measures of cheating, principled subjects were no more opposed to cheating than conventional subjects; those strongly opposed to cheating were just as likely to cheat as those who were indifferent. So the greater resistance to cheating of the principled subjects was not due to their greater endorsement of conventional rules about cheating. To understand why the principled subjects did not cheat, while many of the conventionals did, one must remember that the experimental situation is Mickey Mouse (it does not matter much whether one cheats or not), and that it is fishy (the experimenter explicitly leaves the child unsupervised in a situation where one would expect supervision). Even if the conventional subject is taken in by the experimenter, there is the more basic ambiguity as to whether anyone cares or not. The experimenter indicates he does not care whether cheating goes on, he almost suggests its possibility and desirability. If an adult experimenter takes a casual attitude, not only is the possibility of punishment minimized, but a far more important thing is minimized, *the concept that the authority or the group is damaged or that it cares whether you conform or not.*

While the conventional child cares about maintaining social expectations and order regardless of punishment, his reasons for not cheating (it is wrong, you should do your own work, the other fellow may not have the right answer, etc.) carry no force as soon as they are not supported by the expectations and sanctions of the authority or of the group. In contrast, a stage 5 or 6 person defines the issue as one of maintaining an implicit social contract with the tester and the others taking the test. The more unsupervised, the more trusting the experimenter, the more contractually obligated this principled person is. Also, the principled person defines the issue of cheating as one of inequality, of taking advantage of others, of deceptively obtaining unequal opportunity, that is, in terms of justice.

This interpretation implies *that moral judgment determines action by way of concrete definitions of rights and duties in a situation.* Moral attitudes as measured by attitude tests do not indicate the way an individual defines moral conflict situations. Since "Cheating is always wrong," means "You always get caught" for stage 1, but "It's good to be honest because nice people are honest" for stage 3, a stage 1 subject cheats when there is no punishment, a stage 3 subject when other nice people are cheating. Implicit in stage 3's definition of "good" is a stereotypical conception of "what most people do" and "expect," which is much more potent in defining the situational conditions of cheating or not cheating than are variations in the intensity of his statements about the value of honesty.

Since moral stages are defined as *structure* of values, not as *content* of values, choice on our dilemmas is not always determined. A stage 4 law and order subject may opt for not stealing the drug out of respect for law and property rights, as he may opt for stealing out of respect for marital responsibility and for the value society puts on human life. We call the choice "content" and the stage characteristics "structure." But many aspects of value hierarchy are determined by stage structure. Stage 2 recognizes nothing higher than individual needs, so he says he will steal. Stage 4 places social order over individual needs, but it is uncertain whether law and property or an individual human life is more primary to the social order. Stage 6 again has a clear hierarchy in which moral principles demanding respect for life are higher than the social order. Prediction to action thus requires that the alternatives are ordered by a hierarchy related to the individual's basic structure. In the case of stage 4, we could only predict how a subject would choose when social order stands clearly on one side and other values on the other, as in civil disobedience. Again, however, if authority is on the side of civil disobedience, as it is in Southern racist areas, the choice becomes ambiguous.

An even more basic way in which stage defines choice is by bringing sensitivity to new aspects of the moral situation, while ruling out other aspects of the situation. Principled subjects are sensitive to justice aspects of the cheating situation which are ignored by conventional subjects. In the case of cheating, there is no conflict between "law and order" and justice, so the principled subject is not required to choose justice over law and order. It is, however, the principled subject's sensitivity to justice which gives him a reason to not cheat when "law and order" reasons have become ambiguous or lost their force because of the confusion and indifference involved in the experimental situation.

We are arguing that moral judgment dispositions influence action through being stable cognitive dispositions, not through the affective changes with which they are associated. Textbook psychology preaches the cliché that moral decisions are a product of the algebraic resolution of conflicting quantitative affective forces. Though efforts to predict moral decisions by this model have yielded slim results, the metaphor continues to have currency. We are claiming instead that the moral force in personality is cognitive. Affective forces are involved in moral decisions, but affect is neither moral nor immoral. When the affective arousal is channeled into moral directions, it is moral; when it is not so channeled, it is not. The moral channeling mechanisms themselves are cognitive. Effective moral channeling mechanisms are cognitive principles defining situations. It is no more inspiring to find that cognitive moral principles determine moral choice in a cheating situation, than it is to find that cognitive physical principles determine choice in a situation dealing with physical objects. In playing billiards, you do not follow the principles of physics because of your affective identification with them. While more than truth value is involved in moral principles, the analogy is that you follow moral principles in a situation because you feel they correctly define that situation, not because of an abstract affective identification with these principles as verbal abstractions. The motivational power of principled morality does not come from rigid commitment to a concept or a phrase. Rather, it is motivated by awareness of the feelings and claims of the other people in the moral situation. What principles do is to sort out these claims, without distorting them or canceling them out, so as leave personal inclination as the arbiter of action.

This leads us to an even more basic point about moral action. The conception that difficult moral choices are difficult because of the conflict between the flesh and the spirit, the id and the superego, is misleading. If we attend to literature and history instead of textbook personality psychology, it appears that real moral crises arise when situations are socially ambiguous, when the usual moral expectations break down. The traditional social psychology example is the mob. The *Lord of the flies* is a better example, a group of well-behaved young British boys who became moral savages when left on a desert island. It is apparent that maintenance of morality in such situations depends upon principles which make sense in spite of the fact that external social definitions do not support them. We have interpreted our experimental cheating situation as simply the most trivial of such situations, claiming that conventional subjects cheat, not because their restraint of impulse is less than that of principled subjects, but because their cognitive definition of right and wrong is less independent of what other people think.

Psychology has assumed that action is determined by emotional and social forces associated with belief, that the relation of belief to action is independent of the cognitive adequacy of the belief, that a rational or cognitively mature moral belief affects action in the same way as an irrational belief. If this is not the case, we must start theorizing about thought and action in a new way. While the way is new, it seems clear. The study of the relation of social cognitive structures to social action seems in principle much like the study of the relation of physical cognitive structure to actions upon physical objects, including the fact that both take place in social fields. The issue of sacrifice, however, raises a fundamental difference in the moral area. Because much morality involves basic sacrifice, it has been consigned to the realm of the irrational by Nietzsche, Freud, Kierkegaard, and their followers. If, however, a mature belief in moral principles in itself engenders a sacrifice of the rational ego, apart from other personality and emotional considerations, we are faced with a conception of the rational and of cognitive structure which has no parallel in the realm of scientific and logical thought.

To summarize, I have found a no more recent summary statement of the implications of our studies than that made by Socrates:

> First, virtue is ultimately one, not many, and it is always the same ideal form regardless of climate or culture.
>
> Second, the name of this ideal form is justice.
>
> Third, not only is the good one, but virtue is knowledge of the good. He who knows the good chooses the good.
>
> Fourth, the kind of knowledge of the good which is virtue is philosophical knowledge or intuition of the ideal form of the good, not correct opinion or acceptance of conventional beliefs.

Most psychologists have never believed any of these ideas of Socrates. Is it so surprising that psychologists have never understood Socrates? It is hard to understand if you are not stage 6.

References

Alston, W. P. Moral attitudes and moral judgments. *Noûs*, 1968, **2**, No. 1, 1–23.

Asch, S. E. *Social psychology*. Englewood Cliffs, New Jersey: Prentice-Hall, 1952.

Baier, K. *The moral point of view: A rational basis of ethics*. New York: Random House, 1965.

Baldwin, J. M. *Social and ethical interpretations in mental development*. New York: Macmillan, 1897.

Baldwin, J. M. *Thoughts and things*. New York: Macmillan, 1906. 3 vols.

Bar-Yam, M., & Kohlberg, L. Development of moral judgment in the kibbutz. In L. Kohlberg and E. Turiel (Eds.), *Recent research in moral development*. New York: Holt, 1971.

Berkowitz, L. *Development of motives and values in a child*. New York: Basic Books, 1964.

Blatt, M. The effects of classroom discussion on the development of moral judgment. Unpublished doctoral dissertation, Univ. of Chicago, 1969.

Blatt, M., & Kohlberg, L. The effects of classroom discussion on the development of moral judgment. In L. Kohlberg and E. Turiel (Eds.), *Recent research in moral development*. New York: Holt, 1971.

Bradley, F. H. *Ethical studies*. London and New York: Oxford Univ. Press, 1962.

Brandt, R. B. *Ethical theory*. Englewood Cliffs, New Jersey: Prentice-Hall, 1959.

Brandt, R. B. *Value and obligation; systematic readings in ethics.* New York: Harcourt, 1961.
Brandt, R. B. Toward a credible form of utilitarianism. In M. D. Bayles (Ed.), *Contemporary utilitarianism.* Garden City, New Jersey: Anchor Books, 1968.
Bronfenbrenner, U. The role of age, sex, class, and culture in studies of moral development. *Religious Education,* 1962, **57,** 3–17.
Brown, M., Feldman, K., Schwartz, S., & Heingartner, A. Some personality correlates of conduct in two situations of moral conflict. *Journal of Personality,* 1969, **37,** No. 1.
Child, I. Socialization. In G. Lindzey (Ed.), *Handbook of social psychology.* Reading, Massachusetts: Addison-Wesley, 1954.
Dewey, J. *The logical conditions of a scientific treatment of morality.* Chicago, Illinois: Univ. of Chicago Press, 1903.
Dewey, J., & Tufts, J. H. *Ethics.* (Rev. ed.) New York: Holt, 1932.
Durkheim, E. *Sociologie et philosophie.* Paris: Alcan, 1924.
Durkheim, E. *Moral education: a study in the theory and application in the sociology of education.* (MMM ed.) New York: Free Press, 1961. (1st ed., 1925)
Erikson, E. *Childhood and society.* New York: Norton, 1950.
Eysenck, H. J. *Handbook of abnormal psychology: An experimental approach.* New York: Basic Books, 1961.
Feuer, L. S. *Psychoanalysis and ethics.* Springfield, Illinois: Thomas, 1955.
Flugel, J. C. *Man, morals, and society: a psycho-analytical study.* New York: International Universities Press, 1955.
Frankena, W. K. *Ethics.* Englewood Cliffs, New Jersey: Prentice-Hall, 1963.
Frankena, W. K. Recent conceptions of morality. In H. Castaneda & G. Nakhnikian (Eds.), *Morality and the language of conduct.* Detroit, Michigan: Wayne State Univ. Press, 1965.
Freud, S. *The basic writings of Sigmund Freud.* New York: Modern Library, 1938.
Grinder, R. Parental childrearing practices, conscience, and resistance to temptation of sixth grade children. *Child Development,* 1962, **33,** 802–820.
Hare, R. M. *Freedom and reason.* London and New York: Oxford Univ. Press, 1963.
Hartshorne, H., & May, M. A. *Studies in the nature of character.* (Columbia University, Teachers College). Vol. 1: *Studies in deceit.* Vol. 2: *Studies in service and self-control.* Vol. 3: *Studies in organization of character.* New York: Macmillan, 1928–1930.
Hobhouse, L. T. *Morals in evolution.* London: Chapman & Hall, 1906.
Holstein, C. Parental determinants of the development of moral judgment. In Kohlberg & Turiel, 1971.
Homans, G. T. *The human group.* New York: Harcourt, 1950.
Josselyn, I. M. *Psychosocial development of children.* New York: Family Service Association, 1948.
Kohlberg, L. The development of modes of moral thinking and choice in the years ten to sixteen. Unpublished doctoral dissertation, Univ. of Chicago, 1958.
Kohlberg, L. Moral development and identification. In H. Stevenson (Ed.), Child psychology. *62nd yearbook of the national society for the study of education.* Chicago, Illinois: Univ. of Chicago Press, 1963. (a)
Kohlberg, L. The development of children's orientations toward a moral order: I. Sequence in the development of moral thought. *Vita Humana,* 1963, **6,** 11–33. (b)
Kohlberg, L. Stages in conceptions of the physical and social world. Unpublished monograph, 1963. (c)
Kohlberg, L. Cognitive stages and preschool education. *Human Development,* 1966, **9,** 5–17. (a)

Kohlberg, L. A cognitive developmental analysis of children's sex-role concepts and attitudes. In E. Maccoby (Ed.), *The development of sex differences.* Stanford, California: Stanford Univ. Press, 1966. (b)

Kohlberg, L. Early education: A cognitive-developmental approach. *Child Development*, 1968, **39**, 1013–1062. (a)

Kohlberg, L. The child as a moral philosopher. *Psychology Today*, 1968, **2** (4), 27. (b)

Kohlberg, L. Stage and sequence: the cognitive-developmental approach to socialization. In D. Goslin (Ed.), *Handbook of socialization theory and research.* New York: Rand McNally, 1969.

Kohlberg, L. Stages of moral development as a basis for moral education. In C. Beck and E. Sullivan (Eds.), *Moral education.* Toronto: Univ. of Toronto Press, 1970. (a)

Kohlberg, L. Education for justice: A modern statement of the Platonic view. In T. Sizer (Ed.), *Moral education.* Cambridge, Massachusetts: Harvard Univ. Press, 1970. (b)

Kohlberg, L., & De Vries, R. Relations between Piaget and psychometric assessments of intelligence. Paper presented at the Conference on the Natural Curriculum, Urbana, Illinois, 1969.

Kohlberg, L., & Kramer, R. Continuities and discontinuities in childhood and adult moral development. *Human Development*, 1969, **12**, 93–120.

Kohlberg, L., & Turiel, E. *Recent research in moral development.* New York: Holt, 1971.

Krebs, R. L. Some relationships between moral judgment, attention and resistance to temptation. Unpublished doctoral dissertation, Univ. of Chicago, 1967.

Kuhn, D., Langer, J., & Kohlberg, L. Relations between logical and moral development. In L. Kohlberg and E. Turiel (Eds.), *Recent research in moral development.* New York: Holt, 1971.

Lehrer, L. Sex differences in moral behavior and attitudes. Unpublished doctoral dissertation, Univ. of Chicago, 1967.

Malinowski, B. *The sexual life of savages.* New York: Halcyon House, 1929.

Mead, G. H. *Mind, self, and society.* Chicago, Illinois: Univ. of Chicago Press, 1934.

Piaget, J. *The moral judgment of the child.* (MMM Ed.) Glencoe, Illinois: Free Press, 1948. (1st Ed., 1932)

Raphael, D. *Moral judgment.* London: Allen & Unwin, 1955.

Rawls, J. The sense of justice. *Philosophical Review*, 1963, **72**(3), 281–305.

Rawls, J. *Justice as fairness.* Cambridge, Massachusetts: Harvard Univ. Press, 1971. (in press)

Rest, J. Developmental hierarchy in preference and comprehension of moral judgment. Unpublished doctoral dissertation, Univ. of Chicago, 1968.

Rest, J. Comprehension preference and spontaneous usage in moral judgment. In L. Kohlberg and E. Turiel, (Eds.), *Recent research in moral development.* New York: Holt, 1971.

Rest, J., Turiel, E., & Kohlberg, L. Relations between level of moral judgment and preference and comprehension of the moral judgment of others. *Journal of Personality*, 1969, **37**, 225–252.

Ross, W. D. *The right and the good.* London and New York: Oxford Univ. Press (Clarendon), 1930.

Royce, J. *The religious aspect of philosophy; a critique of the bases of conduct and of faith.* Boston, Massachusetts: Houghton, 1885.

Scheffler, I. Anti-naturalistic restrictions in ethics. *Journal of Philosophy.* 1953, **1**, No. 15.

Selman, R. The importance of reciprocal role-taking for the development of conventional moral thought. In L. Kohlberg and E. Turiel (Eds.), *Recent research in moral development.* New York: Holt, 1971.

Sidgwick, H. *Methods of ethics.* London: Macmillan, 1887.

Sumner, W. G. *Folkways.* Boston, Massachusetts: Ginn, 1906.

Thrower, J. Effects of orphanage and foster home care on development of moral judgment. In L. Kohlberg and E. Turiel (Eds.), *Recent research in moral development.* New York: Holt, 1971.

Tillich, P. *Love, power and justice; ontological analyses and ethical applications.* London and New York: Oxford Univ. Press, 1966.

Turiel, E. An experimental test of the sequentiality of developmental stages in the child's moral judgment. *Journal of Personality and Social Psychology,* 1966, **3,** 611–618.

Turiel, E. Developmental processes in the child's moral thinking. In P. Mussen, J. Langer and M. Covington (Eds.), *New directions in developmental psychology.* New York: Holt, 1969.

Weber, M. *The methodology of the social sciences.* Glencoe, Illinois: Free Press, of Glencoe, 1949.

Westermarck, E. *Ethical relativity.* Paterson, New Jersey: Littlefield, Adams, 1960. (1st ed., 1932)

MORAL DEVELOPMENT: A Plea for Pluralism [1]

R. S. Peters

I. Introduction

Much of moral philosophy in the past has been unconvincing because it has not dwelt sufficiently on the different views that can be taken about what is morally important. It has been bedeviled by monistic theories such as Utilitarianism, or some version of Kant's theory, in which the attempt is made to demonstrate that one type of justification can be given for everything which there are reasons for doing or being. Keeping promises, telling the truth, the pursuit of poetry rather than of push-pin, being courageous, and being just have all been fitted into a monolithic mold provided by some fundamental principle. The result has been an artificial type of theory that has never quite rung true. Utilitarians, for instance, who have usually been decent people with developed moral sensitivities, have invented highly dubious, and quite untested empirical speculations to demonstrate that their conviction that they should be just and truthful, which they would never really dream of giving up, rests on alleged consequences to human welfare.

There is a danger of a similar fate befalling theories of moral development. It may well be that some generalizations have been established about certain aspects of moral development; but these may be peculiar to the limited range of phenomena studied. It would be unfortunate if these generalizations were erected into a general theory of moral development without account being taken of the differences exhibited by the phenomena that have not been studied.

[1] My thanks are due to the Australian National University for the facilities provided for me as a Visiting Fellow which enabled me to write this article, and to Geoffrey Mortimore of the Philosophy Department of A.N.U., whose thesis on *Virtue and vice* put me on the track of some important differences between virtues, and whose comments helped me to revise a first draft of this article.

In developing this thesis I shall use Kohlberg's cognitive stage theory as my point of departure; for his work in this field seems to me to be by far the most important which has been done to date. Yet I have certain doubts about it. Some of these derive from his failure to spell out certain points in more detail; others derive from the thought that there is much more to morality than is covered by his theory, and that his generalizations may be true only of the area of morality on which he has concentrated his attention. My article will be divided, therefore, into five main parts: exposition of Kohlberg's theory; some doubts about details; virtues and habits; is Kohlberg prescribing a morality?; and Freud and moral failure.

II. Exposition of Kohlberg's Theory

Kohlberg claims, like Piaget, that there are invariant sequences in development which hold in any culture. He produces evidence to show, for instance, that in any culture children begin by being unable to distinguish dreams from real events. They then grasp that dreams are not real; then that they cannot be seen by others, and take place inside the dreamer; then that they are immaterial events produced by the dreamer, like thoughts (Kohlberg, 1968b, pp. 1024–1029). He makes two points about this sequence which, he claims, hold for all proper developmental sequences. First, he claims that this sequence could not have a different order. It depends upon the relationships of concepts such as "unreal," "internal," "immaterial," which it would take too long to explicate. Second, he claims that this sequence cannot be fully explained in terms of the teaching of adults; for if adults taught anything about dreams, they would tend to use concepts about them appropriate to a much later stage, which would not explain how children go through the earlier stages. Also, the same sequence can be observed in cultures where adults have different beliefs about dreams.

Piaget has, of course, extensively illustrated this thesis about invariant order depending upon relationships between concepts in the case of mathematics and elementary physics, and, to a more limited extent, in the moral sphere, where Kohlberg has elaborated this thesis. He holds that, though there is a difference between cultures in the *content* of moral beliefs, the development of their *form* is a cultural invariant. In other words, though there is variation between cultures about whether or not people should, for example, be thrifty or have sexual relationships outside marriage, there are cross-cultural uniformities relating to how such rules are conceived—for example, as ways of avoiding punishment, as laid down by authority. Children, Kohlberg claims, start by seeing rules as dependent upon power and external compulsion; they then see them as instrumental to rewards and to the satisfaction of their needs; then as ways of obtaining social approval and esteem; then as upholding some ideal order; and finally as articulations of social principles necessary to living together with others—especially, justice. Varying contents given to rules are fitted into invariant forms of conceiving rules. Of course, in many cultures there is no progression through to the final stages, the rate of development will vary in different cultures, and in the same culture there are great individual differences. All this can be granted and explained. But Kohlberg's main point is that this sequence in levels of conceiving rules is constitutive of moral development and that it is a cultural invariant.

How, then, does Kohlberg think that this type of development occurs if it is not the result of teaching? He rejects maturation theories as non-starters except in the case of abilities such as walking. He also rejects three types of socialization hypotheses. First, he claims that a whole mass of empirical studies have failed to confirm the findings of the psycho-analytic school. There are no correlations, for instance, between parental modes of handling infantile drives and later moral behavior and attitudes. There are no correlations between the amount of reward given and moral variables. Findings on parental attitudes give no clear support for the theory that early identifications are central to a moral orientation. The only established correlation, he claims, is between what he calls "induction," which often goes along with the withdrawal of love, and moral guilt. By "induction" he means cognitive stimulation connected with the awareness of the consequences of actions. Similarly, there is a correlation between maternal warmth and the development of conscience. But this operates, he maintains, by only providing a climate for learning (Kohlberg, 1964).

Second, he maintains that the evidence from the classic Hartshorne–May study shows overwhelmingly that the theory of habit generalization put forward by psychologists with a learning theory type of orientation has no validity. What came out of this mammoth enquiry was that the traits such as honesty are situation-specific. Moral learning of this sort can only bring about specific forms of behavior conformity. It cannot bring about predictable behavior over a wide range of situations, such as is found in a person who has emerged to the principled stage of morality. He also claims that learning theorists have produced no evidence whatever about the influence of early forms of habit training on later adult behavior.

Third, Kohlberg rejects Piaget's hypothesis, which he got from Durkheim, that the peer group plays a decisive role in moral development in the sense that its norms are internalized by the individual. There is a correlation between the development of a principled morality and peer-group participation. But Kohlberg argues that this is because of the stimulation which such a group provides for the individual to reflect upon situations (Kohlberg, 1968a).

How then does Kohlberg think that these Kantian categories, which provide forms of conceiving of rules at the different stages, evolve? He rejects Kant's own view that they are innate molds into which specific experiences are fitted (Kohlberg, 1968b, p. 1023). He argues that they develop as a result of interaction between the child and his physical and social environment. To understand how this happens it is necessary, therefore, to analyze, first, the universal structural features of the environment; second, the logical relationships involved between the concepts; and third, the relationship between the particular child's conceptual scheme and the type of experience with which he is confronted. In order for development to take place there must be an optimal amount of discrepancy between the two.

This interactionist theory of development is applied to the moral sphere. Kohlberg thinks that the stages of development represent culturally invariant sequences in the child's conception of himself and his social world.

> It implies, then, that there are some universal structural dimensions in the social world, as there are in the physical world. . . . These dimensions are universal because the basic structure of social and moral action is the universal structure provided by the existence of a self in a world composed of other selves who are both like the self and different from it (Kohlberg, unpublished manuscript).

He follows Baldwin and Mead in ascribing great importance to role taking and the dawning of reciprocity in the development of this understanding of the social situation in which we are placed. Social and moral understanding develop *pari passu* with other forms of cognitive development. And just as contact with the physical world gradually stimulates the child, for example, to classify it in terms of objects having causal relationships with others, so also in the social and moral case, the child is led gradually to grasp principles which must obtain if individuals are to live together and to satisfy their claims as social beings who are both similar to and different from others.

In support of his thesis, Kohlberg claims that the main factors which have been shown to correlate with the development of a principled, predictable morality are intelligence, moral knowledge (that is, knowledge of the rules of a society), the tendency to anticipate future events, the ability to maintain focused attention, the capacity to control unsocialized fantasies, and self-esteem. The major consistencies in moral conduct represent decision-making capacities rather than fixed behavior traits (Kohlberg, 1964).

It is difficult to know where to begin in criticizing a theory which is so varied in its claims, but an obvious strategy which matches Kohlberg's manner of presentation suggests itself. Questions can first be asked about the acceptability of his positive theory. Then, as he puts this forward as an alternative to theories which stress habit formation and to Freudian theory, questions can be raised about his grounds for dismissing theories of this sort. It might well be, for instance, that if morality is not as unitary an affair as he suggests, there is some place for habit formation in some of the areas of morality which he rather disregards. Similarly, he assumes that Freud was trying to answer the same sorts of questions about moral development as those on which he and Piaget have concentrated. But if Freud was in fact concerned with a different range of questions, then Kohlberg's criticisms of Freud might not be altogether apposite. This is the strategy which I will, in fact, use in commenting upon Kohlberg's theories. Doubts will first be raised about some of the details of his positive theory; doubts will then be raised about his dismissal of other theories in the field; and these doubts derive from the thought that Kohlberg adopts too simple and too monolithic an approach to moral development.

III. Some Doubts about Details

If Kohlberg's cross-cultural claims are confirmed, they are the most important findings in the psychology of morals since those of Piaget, which have often been criticized for being culture-bound. Most people, on reflection, would be prepared to concede that there is some kind of culturally invariant order of development in the case of mathematical or scientific forms of experience; but they would regard morality as much more relative to culture both in its form and in its content. Nevertheless, leaving aside the validity of the empirical findings, there are some conceptual difficulties about Kohlberg's account which could, perhaps, be dispelled if he were to spell out in more detail what he has in mind.

Let us start by probing into what he claims to be the two main features of all proper developmental sequences as applied to this particular case, namely that the order of conceptual development could not be otherwise for logical reasons and that development does not depend upon teaching.

A. Order of Development and Logical Relations between Concepts. In his account of stages of moral development, Kohlberg has, for a variety of reasons, elaborated Piaget's three stages of egocentric, transcendental, and autonomous morality into six stages by making a subdivision within each stage. The egocentric stage, for instance, is subdivided into the stage when rules are seen as dependent upon power and external compulsion, and the stage when they are seen as instrumental to rewards and to the satisfaction of the child's needs. He claims that this order of stages could not be otherwise than it is because of the logical relationships between the concepts. What can this mean in this particular case? In a general way the claim might seem to hold of Piaget's three stages. For instance, it is difficult to see how an autonomous morality could come before a transcendental one, for an autonomous morality implies that one can raise questions about the validity of rules and accept or reject then after reflection. Unless, therefore, one already has been introduced in some way to rules and knows, from the inside, what it is to follow a rule, there would be no content in relation to which one could exercise one's autonomy. But surely a similar point cannot be made so easily about connecting rules with power and external compulsion as distinct from connecting them with rewards and with the satisfaction of needs. It may be empirically true that children do conceive of rules in these different ways in this order. But what is there in the concepts concerned which might convert this discovered order into some kind of logical order? That there must be some explanation of this sort seems a reasonable hypothesis; how else could the culturally invariant order be explained? For instance, one might plausibly suggest that the conceptual structure required for seeing rules as means to getting rewards must be more sophisticated than that required merely for seeing them as ways of avoiding things that are unpleasant. Children have, for instance, to have a more determinate conception of the future; they have to be able to conceive of things as positively pleasant, rather than as things which either hurt or ease an unpleasant condition of need. As a matter of empirical fact, their behavior can be influenced by external compulsion and interference much sooner than it can be influenced by offering them rewards, and it could be shown that this is no accident, because of the conceptual structure required to see things as rewards. A similar analysis could probably be given of why seeing rules as connected with rewards must come before seeing them as connected with approval, for, conceptually speaking, "approval" is a much more sophisticated notion than "reward." I have no doubt that some detailed work on the concepts concerned could reveal the kind of connections that have to be revealed. Kohberg links these stages of moral development with a theory of role-taking and with more general features of a child's developing understanding of other people in relationship to himself. It may well be that he can, by means of this type of analysis, make it intelligible why the child *must* conceive of rules in the order in which they in fact conceive of them. But it is incumbent on Kohlberg to spell out these connections explicitly at every point. Otherwise his theory fails to carry conviction; for it does not manifestly satisfy one of the two main conditions which, on his own view, a proper developmental theory must satisfy, namely, that the temporal order of the stages should reflect some kind of logical order in the forms of conception characterizing each of the stages.

B. Teaching and Moral Development. The second condition which a proper developmental theory must satisfy is that the progression from stage to stage is not brought about by the teaching of adults. Kohlberg claims that the transition from one level of understanding to another can be aided by cognitive stimulation which helps to establish an optimal amount of discrepancy between what the child has already mastered and what he has yet to master. But this cannot be brought about by explicit teaching.

This seems, at first, to be rather a startling point which has a counter-intuitive thrust to it, to put it mildly. Surely Kohlberg cannot mean, it might be said, that saying things to children such as "That's not fair" plays no part in helping them to develop the concept of "fairness." How could children ever learn such a complicated concept unless the word was used by someone in situations in which the concept had application? It is difficult to be sure what Kohlberg is asserting because he gives no account of what he means either by "teaching" or by "cognitive stimulation," with which he contrasts teaching. He suggests that much of the *content* of morality is passed on by example and instruction, but the *form* is something which the individual has to come to understand for himself with appropriate stimulation from others and from typical concrete situations. This, he claims, provides the appropriate psychological rationale for Socrates' conception of education, in which the learner is gradually brought to see things for himself—not haphazardly, but in a tightly structured situation (Kohlberg, 1970).

In making this sort of contrast, Kohlberg surely displays an over rigid conception of what teaching is. Socrates was teaching the slave all right even though he was not telling him things. He was asking him leading questions, getting him to concentrate on some things rather than on others, putting questions in sequences so that the slave came gradually to make certain crucial connections. "Teaching" surely can be applied to a great variety of processes which have in common the feature that something is marked out, displayed, made plain so that someone can learn. Information, skills, and attitudes are taught in different ways. But, if they are taught, there is always some process by means of which attention is drawn to the different types of things that have to be mastered. In the case of the learning of principles, which is what Kohlberg is talking about, this marking out can also be present. But it can only take the learner a certain way. If information which has to be memorized is being imparted, the teacher can instruct the learner explicitly in what has to be learned; in teaching a skill the particular movement can be demonstrated explicitly for the learner to copy and practice. But when what is being taught is a principle which provides some kind of unity to a whole number of previously disconnected items, the teacher can only put the matter this way and that until the learner comes to "see" it or understand it. If, therefore, the teacher is trying to get the child to "see" something that is characteristic of one of the developmental stages, all he can do is to draw attention to common features of cases and hope that the penny will drop. He cannot get him to memorize some explicit content, or practice some movement, as in the case of imparting information or training in a skill.

There is another feature, too, of this kind of learning which makes the notion of *specific* teaching inapplicable. A child may be brought to grasp a principle by being confronted, in a variety of ways, with particular examples. But once, as Wittgenstein put it, he knows how to go on, there is no limit to the number of cases that he will see as falling under this principle. There is a sense, therefore, in this sort of learning, in which the learner gets out much more than anyone could possibly have put in. Kohlberg's objection to *specific* teaching is therefore readily explained; for, in this sense, principles just are not the sorts of things that can be regarded as applying to only a specific number of items which could be imparted by a teacher.

It looks, therefore, as if Kohlberg's thesis about the impossibility of adults bringing about conceptual development by teaching is either false or a conceptual truth. It is false if a normal, nonrestrictive concept of "teaching" is being employed; for it is manifestly the case that children's understanding can be accelerated by a variety of processes such as presenting them with examples and so on. Kohlberg may call this "cognitive stimulation"; but most people would call it "teaching." It is a conceptual truth if a restricted concept of "teaching" is being employed, which rules out the processes by means of which adults help to get the child into a position where he can grasp a principle. Understanding a principle is just not the sort of thing that can be imparted by instruction, example, training, and other such processes.

There is a further point, perhaps, about the actual effectiveness of leaving the child alone to make his own connections, as distinct from trying to lead him to the brink as Socrates did with the slave. My guess is that what one says about this will depend very much on the types of principles that are being learnt. If one takes, for instance, the forms of conception that are features of the different developmental stages, it is not obvious what can be done about these—for example, coming to see a rule as connected with approval rather than with rewards. Kohlberg, however, like

Piaget, regards other principles as of equal developmental importance—for example, that actions should be assessed in terms of their intentions rather than in terms of their objective consequences, as in the case of the child who thinks that what is crucial about breaking cups is whether the breaker intended it, as distinct from the number of cups that are in fact broken. In a sense, both these are "formal" notions, but in very different ways, and it could be that the teaching of adults, in the nonrestrictive sense of "teaching," could play a larger part in helping children to grasp the latter principle than the former.

Kohlberg's thesis about the learning of principles, however, though it looks like some kind of conceptual truth about learning, is a very important one to emphasize at a time when there is much pointless controversy between those who emphasize "activity" and "discovery" methods and those who emphasize more traditional methods of instruction and training. The general point must first be made that the method used is limited severely by what it is that has to be learnt. Discovery methods have little application to the learning of skills or to the acquiring of information. However, insofar as there are principles which have to be understood in the type of learning that is taking place, the sorts of methods included by Kohlberg under "cognitive stimulation" have manifest application. They also apply to the grasping of those principles—for example, of causality or of the relevance of intended consequences in morality—which constitute *one* type of what Kohlberg calls the "form" of experience. Instruction, training, and learning by example seem much more appropriate in learning what he calls the "content." This is a particular example of the general thesis that there need be no conflict between these different approaches to learning. The possible methods will depend largely on the details of what has to be learned (see Peters, 1969).

IV. Virtues and Habits

Kohlberg maintains not only that character traits such as honesty are comparatively unimportant in morals, but also that processes of habit formation, by means of which they are assumed to be established, are of secondary significance. The considerations which led him to this somewhat surprising view are as follows:

1. The Hartshorne–May investigation cast doubt upon the existence of stable character traits. In the case of honesty, low predictability was shown of cheating in one situation from cheating in another. The tendency of children to cheat depended on the risk of detection and the effort required to cheat. Noncheaters thus appeared to be more cautious rather than

more honest. Peer-group approval and example also seemed to be an important determinant (Kohlberg, 1964, pp. 386–387).

2. Kohlberg claims that his own studies show that the decision not to cheat has something to do with the awareness of universal moral principles, not with principles concerned with the badness of cheating *per se*. Other good predictors of resistance to cheating are factors to do with ego strength. He concludes that the crucial determinants of moral development are cognitive. There are different conceptual levels in morality, and stability of character depends upon the level attained by the individual.

A. Traits and Principles. Before discussing the role of habit in morality, something must first be said about the dichotomy which Kohlberg makes between traits and principles. In his account of moral development a principled morality is contrasted with a morality of character traits. This is a strange contrast. Surely, being just or fair are paradigm cases of character traits. They are as much character traits as being honest, which is the virtue with which justice is often contrasted in Kohlberg's work. Yet fairness and justice are also paradigm cases of moral principles. To call something a "trait" of character is simply to suggest that someone has made a rule—for example, of honesty or of justice—his own. Whether a rule, which can also be regarded as a trait of character if it is internalized, is a principle depends on the function which the rule or consideration, which is personalized in the trait, performs. To call justice or concern for others principles is to suggest that backing or justification is provided by them for some more specific rule or course of action. We might, for instance, appeal to considerations of justice to back up a decision to give women the vote; gambling might be condemned because of the suffering which it brought on the relatives of gamblers. In these cases, justice and concern for others would be functioning as principles. Honesty, too, often functions as a principle in that it can be appealed to in condemning fraud and many other forms of deceit. The contrast, therefore, between traits of character and principles rests on no clear view of how the term "principle" functions.

There is, however, an important contrast which Kohlberg does not make between traits, such as honesty and justice, and motives such as concern for others. As we shall see, there are important differences between virtues which are motives and those which are character traits. But one obvious difference needs to be noted at this point: that concern for others develops much earlier in a child's life and does not require the same level of conceptual development to be operative as does justice or even honesty. *Prima facie*, too, there are grounds for thinking that it can be learnt or encouraged by the example of others. Of course, concern for others can be exhibited at different levels which vary according to a person's imagination and sophistication about what constitutes harm or welfare. But it certainly can get a foothold in a person's moral life earlier than justice, because it is not necessarily connected with rules and social arrangements, as is justice. This was one of the reasons which led Hume to distinguish the artificial from the natural virtues. It may, of course, take time for children to grasp that reasons for rules can fall under it *as a principle*. Kohlberg's stage theory may apply to it insofar as it comes to function as a principle—that is, as providing considerations that give backing to rules. But a different account must be given of how children become sensitized to such considerations than is given of how they come to be concerned about justice.

In talking about a principled morality we must not only distinguish motives from character traits such as justice and honesty. We must also note the peculiarities of a certain class of character traits that are both content-free and which do not, like motives, introduce teleological considerations. These are traits such as consistency, persistence, courage, determination, integrity, and the like. They are of a higher order and relate to the ways in which rules are followed or purposes pursued; they prescribe no particular rules or purposes, as do honesty and ambition. In ordinary language this group of character traits is intimately connected with what we call "the will." Kohlberg suggests that "ego-strength" variables correlate with the development of a principled morality. But this must necessarily be the case, for part of our understanding of a "principled morality" is that people should stick to their principles in the face of temptation, ridicule, and the like. But a different account must surely be given of their development than of that of a virtue like justice, for though it may be a necessary condition of a stable, principled morality that people should both be able to understand what justice is and assent to it, and that it should come to function as a principle for them in the sense of providing justifying reasons for a whole range of behavior, it is nevertheless not sufficient. There are many who can do all this but who still lack the courage, determination, integrity, and persistence to carry out what they see as just.

It looks, therefore, as if there is little validity in Kohlberg's distinction between principles and character traits. But a more positive finding of this brief examination is that there are distinct classes of virtues, the differences between which may prove to be important in considering the relationships between virtue and habit. To summarize, there are (*a*) highly specific virtues, such as punctuality, tidiness, and perhaps honesty, which are connected with specific types of acts, and which lack any built-in reason for acting in the manner prescribed—that is, are not motives, unlike (*b*) virtues, such as compassion, which are also motives for action. There are, then, (*c*) more artificial virtues, such as justice and tolerance, which involve more general considerations to do with rights and institutions. Finally, there are (*d*) virtues of a higher order, such as courage, integrity, perseverance, and the like, which have to be exercised in the face of counter-inclinations.

When, therefore, Kohlberg criticizes a character trait type of morality on account of the specificity of character traits, it looks as if his criticism is based on the peculiar features of the character trait of honesty, on which most research has been done. Dishonesty has to be understood in terms of fairly specific situations such as cheating, lying, and fraud. This is a feature of all type (*a*) virtues. Other virtues and vices, however, such as benevolence, cruelty, and integrity, are not tied down in this way to specific types of action, although about all such virtues the more sophisticated point could be made that what is to count as cases of them will vary from culture to culture. Kohlberg's criticism, therefore, depends on the peculiarities of a particular class of character traits.

In general, however, this criticism follows analytically from the meaning attached to a principled morality; for principles pick out very general considerations, such a unfairness or harm to people, which can be appealed to in support of a number of rules. As many type (*a*) character traits, such as thrift, punctuality, chastity, and the like, represent internalized social rules whose justification depends upon appeal to more general considerations picked out by principles, their specificity, when compared with principles, is not surprising, for it is implicit in what we mean by a principle. But here again this depends very much on the examples taken. Punctuality and thrift manifestly require some further justification in terms of principles. Fairness and unselfishness, on the other hand, are also character traits, but there is nothing particularly specific about them. Indeed, they are internalizations of considerations which would normally be appealed to as principles. Consistency, integrity, determination, and the like are, as we have seen, character traits as well, but of a higher order and in no way tied down to specific acts.

It is important to realize too, that although principles pick out abstract considerations that can be appealed to in contexts of justification and moral uncertainty, for the most part they enter into our lives in a much more concrete, specific way. For most of us, for instance, the principle that we should consider people's interests is to be understood by reference to specific roles such as that of a father, teacher, citizen, etc., with the specific duties that are constitutive of them, and in following the more general rules that are internalized in the form of punctuality, tidiness, thriftiness, and the like. This was a point well made by Mill in his stress on the role of "secondary principles" in morality.

B. The Role of Habit. Kohlberg's contention that specific character traits, such as honesty, which function as habits, are of little significance in the moral life, is paralleled by his claim that learning theorists have produced no evidence of the influence of early forms of habit training on adult behavior (Kohlberg, 1966). Most of the evidence is negative—the effect of exposure to Boy Scouts, Sunday School, etc., and of the effect of earliness and amount of parental training on habits such as obedience, neatness, etc. (Kohlberg, 1964, p. 388). This type of learning seems to be short-term, situation-specific, and reversible.

This lack of importance assigned to habit goes against a whole tradition of thought about moral development stemming from Aristotle. He too assigned a central place to cognitive factors in moral development insofar as he characterized this in terms of the gradual emergence of practical reason. But he conceded a major role to habits in morals and in moral education. He maintained (Aristotle, Bk. 11, Chap. 1) that the capacity given to us by nature to receive virtue is brought to maturity by habit. We acquire virtue by practice. Just as we become builders by building houses, so "we become just by doing just acts, temperate by doing temperate acts, brave by doing brave acts" (Aristotle, Bk. 11, Chap. 1). It is therefore of great importance to see that children are trained in one set of habits rather than another. In their early years they cannot, of course, act bravely or justly in a full sense for they lack the appropriate knowledge and dispositions. But through instruction, praise and blame, reward and punishment by men who are already courageous and just, they can acquire action patterns which gradually become informed by a growing understanding of what they are doing and why.

How then is habit related to virtue in the life of a developed person, and how can a morality, which is firmly rooted in habit, provide the appropriate basis for a more rational reflective type of morality? An examination of the concept of "habit" may indicate answers to these questions which are also compatible with Kohlberg's contentions about habit formation; for it may well be the case that his contentions depend upon a limited conception of "habit" and on the peculiarities of the facets of morality on which he has concentrated his attention.

In order to raise questions about the role of habit in morality, it is necessary to distinguish three applications of the concept of "habit." (See also Peters, 1963; Kazepides, 1969.) We can speak, first, in a descriptive way about a person's habits or what he does habitually. Second, we can use explanatory phrases such as "out of habit," "from force of habit," and "a matter of sheer habit." Third, we can talk of certain things being learnt by a process of "habituation." Let us consider each of these applications of the concept of "habit" in relation to the types of virtue already distinguished in Section IV A.

Habits. When we use "habit" as a descriptive term, we are making certain suggestions about behavior. We are claiming, first, that it is something that the individual has done before and is likely to do again. It implies repetition arising from a settled disposition. Second, we suggest that it is the sort of thing that the individual *can* carry out more or less automatically. He does not have to reflect about it before he does it, to plan it in any way, or to decide to do it. But he may. If one of a man's habits is to get up early, it does not follow that he will not reflect about it on a particular occasion. It only suggests that he will not *have to* reflect on what he is doing on a particular occasion, that he *can* do this more or less automatically. Needless to say, also, there are many manifestations of automatic behavior that are not usually habits—for example, automatic writing.

What forms of behavior can be termed "habits"? Etymologically, the word suggests forms of behavior that one has in the way in which one has clothes. Habits, like clothes, express how a man holds himself. They thus can refer to his demeanor as well as to his clothes. Nowadays, we tend to confine the word to a person's settled dispositions which manifest themselves in behavior which, like clothes, he can put on or take off at will. We do not, therefore, call dreaming a habit, nor do we speak in this way of stomach aches and facial tics. We thus can say that a man is in the habit of going for a walk before breakfast, that talking philosophy in the pub is one of his habits, or that he is habitually punctual and polite.

There are some forms of behavior which may be exercises of dispositions which we do not call "habits." For instance, we do not talk about sympathetic or angry behavior as "habits." This is because these forms of behavior are too deeply connected with our nature; they are not the sorts of behavior that we can put on and take off at will, like clothes. Also they are not the sorts of behavior which, even if repeated, we tend to perform automatically. If we did, they would cease to qualify as being sympathetic or angry in a full-blooded sense.

It might be thought that there is an incompatibility between habits and intelligence or reasoning. But if there is such a clash, it is not with this application of the concept of "habit." Ryle (1948, pp. 42–43), for instance, sees such an incompatibility. But that is because he does not distinguish between the three applications of the concept of "habit." He slides between talking descriptively of habits, which he regards as single-track dispositions, and the use of explanatory phrases such as "out of habit." He also seems to think that all habits are developed by a particular form of habituation, namely drill, and incorporates this mistaken empirical assumption into his concept of "habit." In actual fact, not all habits are single-track dispositions. Playing bridge or chess could be regarded as among a person's habits, and there is nothing single-track or unintelligent about activities of this sort. Indeed, there are writers who go to the opposite extreme. Oakeshott, for instance, regards plasticity as one of the main features of habits. To use his own words: "Like prices in a free market, habits of moral behaviour show no revolutionary changes because they are never at rest" (Oakeshott, 1962, p. 65). Habitual forms of behavior can involve reasoning as well as intelligence in the sense of adaptability. Indeed, we can talk about a habit of reflecting upon conduct.

Is there any reason, then, why virtues should not be described as habits, and are they of much importance in morality? Surely the importance of established habits in the moral life is manifest. Life would be very exhausting if, in moral situations, we always had to reflect, deliberate, and make decisions. It would also be very difficult to conduct our social lives if we could not count on a fair stock of habits such as punctuality, politeness, honesty, and the like, in other people. This applies particularly to those type *a* character traits, such as punctuality and tidiness, which are internalized social rules.

Habits, however, are not sufficient for the conduct of a person's moral life for at least three reasons. The first reason is that the different classes of virtues distinguished in Section IVA differ in their relation to habit, and it is important to understand what underlies Kohlberg's claim that only some situation-specific types of virtue, which form part of the "content" of morality, can be habits. Type *a* virtues, such as punctuality, tidiness, and perhaps honesty, seem to be the most obvious class of virtues which can be called habits, because they are connected with specific types of acts; so there seems to be no difficulty about the condition of automaticity being sometimes fulfilled. They also lack any built-in reason for acting in the manner prescribed. They are to be contrasted with type *b* virtues, such as compassion, which are also motives for action. It seems essential to the exercise of such virtues that feelings should be aroused, that one's mind should be actively employed on bringing about specific states of affairs. The concept of "habit" therefore cannot get a grip on virtues such as these. Nor can it get a grip on type *c*, more artificial virtues, such as justice and tolerance, for a rather different reason. Being just, tolerant, or prudent involves much in the way of thought. Considerations have to be weighed and assessed. The suggestion, therefore, that acting justly might be one of a man's habits sounds strange. Finally, type *d*, higher-order virtues, such as courage, integrity, perseverance, and the like, would also be incongruously described as habits, because such virtues have to be exercised in the face of counterinclinations. It is, of course, part of our understanding of what can be considered a virtue that there should be counterinclinations which might be operative. Otherwise there would be no point in the virtue in general. But it is only essential to some virtues, namely, those that involve some kind of self-control, that counter inclinations must be present when they are exercised. Now insofar as this condition is realized, as it is in the case of virtues such as courage, it seems inappropriate to think of them as habits, for they require active attention. This would not be true, however, of all higher-order virtues—for example, consistency, which might be regarded as a habit.

The second reason for the insufficiency of habit in the moral life is that those virtues which we can call habits have an incompleteness about them because the reason for behaving in the ways which they mark out is not internal to them, which is why we do not call virtues such as thrift, punctuality, and politeness motives. It is not surprising, therefore, that the Hartshorne–May enquiry found that children saw being honest as a way of escaping punishment or gaining approval. These may not be particularly good reasons for acting honestly, but some reason is required; people do not act *out of* honesty, as they act out of jealousy or compassion. Honesty, in other words, is a trait of character, not a motive. Ideally, acting honestly should be connected with considerations which provide a rationale for being honest, rather than considerations which are manifestly extrinsic to this form of behavior, such as the avoidance of punishment or the obtaining of approval. But such a rationale is beyond the understanding of young children. So it is not surprising that, insofar as they are honest, they are honest for some extrinsic reason, as Aristotle saw in his account of how virtues are acquired under instruction.

This introduces a third point about the insufficiency of habits—when people are in nonroutine situations, habits, by definition, can no longer carry them through. The question then arises, with virtues such as honesty and punctuality, as to what considerations become operative. If, as in the case of the children in the Hartshorne–May enquiry, or that of the Spartans when they went abroad, the sanctions of punishment and social approval are withdrawn, they may not continue to be honest. In their case the extrinsic considerations which supported their honesty were not such that honesty seemed sensible to them when being dishonest had no manifest disadvantages and some short-term advantage. Suppose, however, that, as Aristotle put it, "they understand the reason why of things," and connect being honest with some more general principle about human relationships—for example, respect for persons, concern for finding out what is true. They might then link particular manifestations of honesty, such as not cheating, or not lying, with further considerations falling under these principles. This would be what Kohlberg calls having a principled morality which, he claims, is the only stable sort. He usually links this with the acceptance of the principle of justice, but this is only a particular case of such a morality. What is important is that considerations deriving from such principles are reasons which always exist for various ways of being honest. Possible censure or punishment, on the other hand, do not always exist and they depend on the attitude of people generally to breaches of rules such as that of honesty. They provide reinforcements for rules rather than a rationale. If people have no rationale for rules, and only keep to them in conditions where there is positive or negative reinforcement for them, then they are ill equipped to deal with situations of a nonroutine sort where the usual reinforcements are absent. This points to the necessity for the development of reason in morals to provide a rationale for habit. Reason is a supplement to habit but not a substitute for it.

Out of Habit. It was noted that there seems to be no incompatibility between "habit," when used as a descriptive term, and intelligence and reasoning. But there is a clash when explanatory terms such as "out of habit" are used of behavior; for this phrase and others, such as "from force of habit," do suggest routine types of situations to which the concept of "intelligence" is not applicable. The condition of automaticity, of a stereotyped form of behavior, seems more strongly implied. They also rule out the possibility that the individual who has done something has deliberated before he did it, has reflected or gone through any process of self-criticism or justification, or has seen what he does as a means to a further end. Of course he might, in the past, have formed this particular habit by some series of decisions involving deliberation, planning, justification, and other such exercises of reason. But if we say that a man does something, for instance, calls someone "sir" out of habit, we are denying that in this case any of the processes typically associated with reason have taken place. He might be able to give *a* reason for this if asked afterwards, but on this particular occasion he did not act with the end in view which he might specify if so pressed; it was not *his* reason.

"Out of habit" also rules out explanations of behavior which relate to features intrinsic to the behavior so explained. In other words, it rules out the suggestion that the individual did what he did for enjoyment, because of the satisfaction which it brought him, or for fun. It also rules out any suggestion of its being done out of a sense of duty. It claims nothing more than that this is the sort of thing that the individual tends to do because he has done it often before. To put it more technically, the explanation is in terms of the old psychological law of exercise.

In the life of any man, however rational, it is important that a great many things should be done out of habit. His mind is then set free to pay attention to things that are novel and interesting, and for which he has no established routine. Any complex skill, for instance, presupposes a number of component movements that are performed out of habit, and conversation would flag at meal times if most of our eating maneuvers were not performed out of habit. But what about the sphere of morality? Has this application of the concept of "habit" much relevance to this sphere?

Everything that was previously said about virtues which can be called habits would apply also *a fortiori* to the suggestion that they might be exercised out of habit. The only difference would be that more might be ruled out because the condition of automaticity seems to be more strongly suggested. To say that something is a habit is to say that it is the sort of behavior that an individual *could* perform without giving his mind to it, but to say that he performed it out of habit is to suggest that he did not give his mind to it. Obviously, therefore, type (*b*) virtues, which are motives, type (*c*) virtues, which involve much in the way of thought, and type (*d*) virtues, which involve self-control, would be ruled out. But even some type (*a*) virtues might seldom be exercised out of habit. Honesty, for instance, is exercised by means of a specific range of acts such as telling the truth, not cheating, and so on. But it would not often be exercised out of habit, because people are usually honest in the face of some sort of temptation, though they might be so disciplined that they become almost oblivious of this aspect of the situation. Honesty does not *have* to be exercised in the face of some counterinclination as does a type (*d*) virtue such as courage. Thus, in a particular case, a man might be honest without being troubled much by counterinclinations, and it might be said of him that he was honest out of habit. But this explanation of behavior is appropriate, in the main, to the more conventional virtues such as politeness, punctuality, and thrift.

Habituation. Thus far I have considered only one problem raised both by Aristotle and by Kohlberg, namely, that of the relationship between virtue and habit in the moral life. We must now address ourselves to another problem, that of the development of a rational morality out of a basis provided by early habit formation. In other words, we must study the relationship between the development of virtues and various forms of habituation.

Kohlberg, like Plato, emphasizes that the most important features of moral education are cognitive. The individual has to come to the grasp of principles and to connect particular rules like that of honesty with these instead of with extrinsic reinforcements such as praise and blame, reward and punishment. A grasp of principles, he maintains, cannot be directly taught; it can only develop with appropriate environmental stimulation, like the grasp of the causal principle or of the conservation of material things. This confirms Aristotle's point that children cannot, in the early stages of their lives, behave like the just man. This means two things: first, that they cannot grasp the principle of justice, which is very abstract and difficult to grasp; and second, that they cannot raise questions about the validity of rules, that they cannot see that principles, such as that of justice, might provide a justification for other rules. As Piaget (1932) showed, it takes quite a time in the development of children before the notion of the validity of rules makes any sense to them, before they realize that they might be otherwise, and those rules they accept should depend upon the rationale which can be provided. Thus, in their early years, they cannot accept rules in a rational way or be taught rules by processes, such as explanation and persuasion, which depend upon the ability to grasp a rationale.

What, then, is to be said about early moral education? Must children first of all become habituated to following certain rules, as Aristotle suggested, and can we conceive of a form of behavior which is learned in this way, developing into the rational form of behavior of Aristotle's just man or into Kohlberg's principled type of morality? We must first ask what is meant by "habituation." We use the term to describe a wide class of learning processes in which people learn by familiarizing themselves with, or getting used to, things, and by repetition. For instance, a boy might learn not to be afraid of dogs by a process of habituation, by being constantly in their presence and getting used to their ways. This type of learning might be contrasted with being instructed or with learning by insight. Drill is another obvious example of habituation.

Ryle, as has already been mentioned, not only thinks that habits are formed by the particular process of habituation known as drill, but incorporates this belief into the meaning of "habit." This raises the question whether habits must be formed by *some* process of habituation, even if it is not the particular process of drill. It does not look as if this is a conceptual truth. Indeed, the *Oxford English Dictionary* explicitly states that there is no etymological ground for supposing that a habit must even be an acquired tendency. One might be led to think this because part of our understanding of "habit" is that a form of behavior should be repeated. We might therefore conclude that it was learned by repetition. But this is not necessarily the case. After puberty, for instance, one of a boy's habits might be to look long and lingeringly at pretty girls. He did not have to learn to do this. He just found himself doing it. The explanation would be in terms of the maturation of the sex organs and consequent sensitization to girls, rather than in terms of any process of habituation, let alone drill.

Most habits, however, as a matter of empirical fact, are learned by some process of habituation. Not all of these are characterized by the sort of mindlessness that we associate with drill. If this was the case, the emergence of any rational type of morality out of processes of habituation would be a mystery. For instance, after reflection on the unsatisfactoriness of his daily pattern of life, a man can make a resolution to get up early; he can decide to make this one of his habits. In the early stages, when the alarm sounds, he may have to exhort himself, to rehearse his reasons for getting up early, and so on. When he has formed the habit, none of this deliberation and decision is necessary; but this is one way of forming a habit. Similarly, we can form habits intelligently in the context of an activity which has some overall end, such as a game of tennis. We may have to drill ourselves in particular movements, but we can learn also to make the movements in the context of a more widely conceived objective—for example, putting the ball where the opponent is not. Indeed, practice in situations where movements have to be varied in the light of changes in the situation is regarded by many as one of the best ways of forming habits, for this prevents too stereotyped a pattern of movements developing. Important, also, in the development of adaptable habits are the higher-order scruples connected with reason, such as having regard to whether what is done is correct, taking care, checking, and thinking of objections. These scruples are learned mainly by taking part in situations where actions and performances are criticized. Gradually, through a process of role playing, the learner becomes a constant critic of his own performances.

These ways of forming habits, in which reason and intelligence are involved, can be contrasted with other processes of habituation where a habit is "picked up" in ways which are explicable only in terms of laws of association, such as contiguity, recency, and frequency. In these cases, the learner may not be trying to master anything; there may even be a suggestion of automaticity. Something is done, for instance, which is associated with something pleasant, and it is repeated as in operant conditioning. Or some constant conjunction leads the individual to expect something without any connection being consciously noted—for example, the part played by serial probability in learning to spell. Alternatively, some mannerism, or form of behavior, is picked up by some process of imitation without any conscious modeling or copying. These principles may also be at work in cases where habits are deliberately formed, or where a person's mind is on what is being learnt. This is not being denied. For instance, in learning to spell, one can attempt to learn in a rational way by formulating rules. This can help learning; but at the same time one may also learn through "picking up" combinations of letters which frequently occur together. The point is that there are some processes of habituation where people fall into habits in ways which are explicable purely in terms of associative principles. But not all cases of habituation are like this.

Learning the content of morality [type *a* virtues]. What then is to be said about the role of "habituation" in the moral sphere? Surely, it cannot refer to a process in which learning is explicable purely in terms of the principles of association. For, as in all cases of learning, one cannot apply some general theory of learning without paying careful attention to what it is that has to be learnt. And this is very complicated in the moral case, even if we take some type *a* virtue, such as honesty, which is to form part of the content of morality. Learning to be honest is not like learning to swim. It could not conceivably be picked up just by practice or by imitation; for a child has to understand what honesty is in order to behave in this way, and this presupposes all sorts of other concepts such as truth and falsehood, belief and disbelief, and so on. Such understanding cannot grow just by repetition and familiarity, though they may aid it. Similarly, extrinsic reinforcements, working by principles of association, may strengthen a tendency to behave in accordance with a rule, but the child has to understand what particular feature of his behavior is being singled out for attention. Parents often punish children for stealing, without appreciating that the child has not yet the grasp of concepts such as property, ownership, lending, giving, and the like which enable him to understand that it is stealing for which he is being punished. Such extrinsic reinforcers may help to mark out the relevant features of behavior by, as it were, underlining some aspect of it. But it is impossible to conceive how they could be sufficient to bring about understanding. Neither could understanding develop just through untutored "learning from experience"; for "honesty" can only be exercised in relation to socially defined acts such as cheating and lying, and these could not be understood without initiation into a whole network of social practices. There must, therefore, be some kind of teaching of rules for moral education to get started at all. The content has to be exhibited, explained, or marked out in some way which is intrinsically rather than extrinsically related to it. This is a central feature of any process that can be called a process of teaching. Moral education is inconceivable without some process of teaching, whatever additional help is provided by various processes of habituation.

Although at an early stage there is no possibility of reason in the sense of justification being operative, there is ample scope for intelligence, for learning to apply a rule like that of honesty to a variety of situations which are relevantly similar. In other words, the rule can be taught in such a way that children gradually come to see the similarity between actions like that of lying and cheating. Parents can relate rules to their point even if children do not yet grasp the idea that their validity depends upon their point. And, surely, drawing attention to the consequences of their actions will help them to understand that actions have consequences. This at least will prepare the way for the stage when they grasp that the reasons for some rules of action depends upon consequences.

SENSITIZATION TO PRINCIPLES [TYPE *b* AND *c* VIRTUES]. Kohlberg maintains that the assessment of actions in terms of their consequences is an important feature of a developmental stage in morality that cannot be taught by any kind of direct instruction. Children, like Socrates' slave, must come to see it, which is true enough; for this is not just a matter of information, like the height of St. Paul's cathedral, which simply has to be remembered rather than understood. But he also claims that "cognitive stimulation" can aid this process of coming to understand. And what else is that, apart from presenting some kind of content in different ways until eventually the appropriate connections are made? And, in the case of rules, this is surely done by teaching them intelligently, that is, by linking rules with other rules and with consequences which will eventually come to be seen as providing some point for them. Kohlberg also argues that some features of the situation in which rules are learned, for example, parental warmth, aid cognitive development because they provide a favorable climate for it. It may also be the case that some sorts of extrinsic aids, such as punishment, may encourage a rigidity or lack of intelligence in rule following that may become compulsive. These, however, are empirical questions which are largely still a matter for speculation. All I have been trying to do is to show how it is intelligible that acquiring habits in ways that are possible at an early stage should develop into a more rational way of following rules. I have been putting the same kind of case in the sphere of morals that I previously put when discussing the general relationship between forming habits and intelligence. It is not the case that habits have to be formed by a process like that of drill. They can be formed in the context of an activity which is more widely conceived. My argument is that learning habits in an intelligent way can be regarded as providing an appropriate basis, in the moral case, for the later stage when rules are followed or rejected because of the justification that they are seen to have or lack.

The encouragement of intelligent rule following, however, in relation to what Kohlberg calls the content of morality, is not the only thing that can be done in the early stages to prepare the way for principled morality. For, although a child may not be able, early in life, to connect rules with those considerations which are picked out by principles, he can become sensitive to considerations which will later serve him as principles. Psychologists such as Piaget and Kohlberg have failed to draw attention to this because of their preoccupation with type *c* virtues such as the principle of justice, which picks out very abstract considerations that are very difficult for a small child to grasp. If, however, instead of justice, we consider the status of type *b* virtues such as concern for others, I think that we may look at moral education in a very different light. The plight of others is much easier to grasp, and concern for it develops much earlier in children. If such concern is encouraged early in children, it can come to function later on as one of the fundamental principles of morality, when the child reaches the stage of being able to grasp the connection between many rules and their effect on other people.

Can anything be done early by training to sensitize children in this respect? Habituation seems the wrong sort of term to use in this context; for the last thing we want is to habituate children to the sight of suffering. Possibly, however, by exposing them a bit to the sight of suffering in others, or rather by not shielding them from situations where they will be confronted by it in a first-hand way, their sensitivity to it may be sharpened. It might also be argued that children can be encouraged to form the habit of paying attention to people's suffering rather than just concentrating on their own projects. This habit of mind would not itself be a virtue. But it might predispose children to be influenced by compassion on specific occasions. Again, this is a matter of speculation, but this sphere of the cultivation of appropriate forms of sensitivity is certainly one of the most crucial areas in the development of a principled form of morality. It is pointless to encourage children to reflect about rules, and to link them with general considerations of harm and benefit, if these considerations do not act as powerful motives for the person who can perform such calculations.

THE DEVELOPMENT OF SELF-CONTROL [TYPE *d* VIRTUES]. When Aristotle spoke of the importance of habituation in moral education, perhaps he had in mind the particular type *d* virtues which are intimately connected with self-control. Indeed, Von Wright (1963, Chap. VII) has explicitly suggested that *all* virtues are forms of self-control. Habituation may be very important in the development of this particular class of virtues in that it may be necessary for people to be tempted, or made fearful, by situations which appear to them in a certain light. The more familiar they become with such situations, and with the internal commotions which they occasion, the more likely people are to be led by a variety of considerations to control their immediate responses. In the case of small children, the proper reasons for self-control are not readily apparent, and they are unable to link the manner of behavior with its proper justification. If, however, children are exposed to, for example, danger, and praised when they do not run away in terror, they may learn to control themselves for such extrinsic reasons. There is, of course, the danger that later on they will only display courage when the reinforcing conditions associated with the manner of behavior are present. But it could be argued that familiarity with both the external features of dangerous situations and with the internal commotions, which such danger occasions in them, carries over into situations in later life when they appreciate the proper reasons for being courageous. Like Aristotle's child, who learns to be temperate by behaving temperately under instruction, they are preparing themselves, by going through the motions of self-control, for the stage when they will have a more inward understanding of the reasons for the pattern of behavior that they are exhibiting. Habituation is important both in familiarizing children with the features of such situations and in developing the relevant action patterns that will enable them to deal practically with the emotions that may be aroused instead of being overcome by them. Habituation may thus help to lay down a pattern of response that may be used in the service of more appropriate motives at a later stage.

Kohlberg nowhere deals with the development of this class of virtues which necessarily involve self-control. He might well claim, however, that even if people do learn to be courageous by some such process of habituation, there is no evidence of transfer. Like the Spartans they might display their courage only in very specific types of situations. Or people might become physically brave but moral cowards. To which it might be replied that, if moral courage is thought a desirable character trait to develop, it is difficult to conceive how it could develop without some kind of practice. Maybe there is not necessarily much transfer from situations requiring physical courage to those requiring moral courage, but some account must be given of how moral courage is developed. In this sphere the individual has to learn to accommodate himself not to dangers that threaten him in a palpable physical way, but to social threats and pressures such as ridicule, disapproval, ostracism, and so on. These sorts of reactions on the part of others can be evoked by a wide range of moral stances taken up by an individual. It is therefore possible for an individual to learn to cope with typical patterns of response on the part of others on the basis of a very limited number of issues on which he may make a stand. In other words, there is a built-in type of generality about this type of moral training. The English public school system of character training, derived from Thomas Arnold, is usually associated with team spirit and moral conformism. But equally strong in this tradition is the insistence that the individual should stick up for principles connected with "fair play" in the face of group pressure. Does Kohlberg think that an individual can in fact adhere to his favored principle of justice, when the screws are put on him, without some such training? And does he think that generations of British administrators, who, like the Romans, were able to maintain the rule of law with a fair degree of impartiality in situations where they were comparatively isolated and subject to social pressures, bribes, flattery, etc., were quite unaffected by the type of character training to which they were subjected at school? This seems, on the face of it, a most implausible assumption, but, of course, it would be an extremely difficult one to test.

Morality and the development of motivation. Sticking to a principle such as justice, however, should not be represented in too negative a light, as it might be by those who are overinfluenced by the Puritan tradition. There is also strong positive aspect to it which is of great importance in considering the phenomenon of "will." This links with another central aspect of morality, to which Kohlberg pays too little attention, namely, the intimate connection between knowing the difference between right and wrong, and caring. It is not a logical contradiction to say that someone knows that it is wrong to cheat but has no disposition not to cheat, but it could not be the general case; for the general function of words like "right" and "wrong," "good" and "bad" is to move people to act. If there is no such disposition to act in a particular case, we would say that the person is using the term in an external sort of way, or that he is not sincere, or something similar to that. There is neither need nor time to defend such a generally accepted point about moral knowledge, though there has been no general acceptance, ever since the time that Socrates first put it forward, about the precise relationship between moral knowledge and action (see Ryle, 1958).

Now, as Hume pointed out, justice is an artificial virtue which only gets off the ground when reason gets to work in social life. Hume equated "reason" with reasoning of the sort that goes on either in logic and mathematics or in science, and was led to think, therefore, that reason of itself provides no considerations that move people to act. On a broader view of "reason," however, it becomes readily apparent that there are a cluster of "passions" closely connected with it without which its operation would be unintelligible. I am referring not just to the passion for truth, but also to other passions which are intimately connected with it such as the abhorrence of the arbitrary, the hatred of inconsistency and irrelevance, the love of clarity and order, and, in the case of nonformal reasoning, the determination to look at the facts. These passions both provide point to theoretical enquiries and transform the pursuit of practical purposes.

When Kohlberg talks of the principle of justice, it is not clear whether he means the formal principle that no distinctions should be made without relevant differences or more particularized versions of this in distributive or commutative justice. But any application of this principle must involve some kind of abhorrence of arbitrariness and of inconsistency if it is to be operative in any individual's life. Also, as Kohlberg maintains that it presupposes becoming aware of some "universal structural dimensions in the social world," some focused attention to the facts of the social world is also involved. How do such rational passions develop? What helps to foster them? Kohlberg, like Piaget, postulates some kind of intrinsic motivation which leads children to assimilate and accommodate to what is novel and to develop their latent capacities. But there is a great difference between sporadic curiosity and the passions which cluster round the concern for truth. Does not the encouragement and example of adults and older children play any part in their development? Without them a child's understanding of justice would be very external. He might know what justice is, but might not care about it overmuch. To apply the principle seriously, the child has to develop not only an abhorrence of the arbitrary, but also a more positive concern for the considerations that determine relevance. How do children come to care? This seems to me to be the most important question in moral education; but no clear answer to it can be found in Kohlberg's writings.

V. Is Kohlberg Prescribing a Morality?

In discussing the adequacy of Kohlberg's account of the role of habit in moral development, distinctions were made between different classes of virtues. These seemed to be of some significance in assessing his account of processes of development. But they are of even more fundamental significance if we survey Kohlberg's conception of moral development from an overall ethical standpoint; taking these distinctions seriously might lead us to reflect that Kohlberg is really prescribing one type of morality among several possibilities. "Morality" can be used as a classificatory term by means of which a form of interpersonal behavior can be distinguished from custom, law, religious codes, and so on. But in ethics and in the practical task of bringing up children, this does not take us very far; for it would involve us in the most feeble form of the naturalistic fallacy to argue that, because we term a form of behavior "moral," this behavior is one which should be pursued or encouraged. Nothing about what ought to be or to be done follows from the empirical fact that we use a word in a certain way. It might well be, for instance, that a form of behavior, in which justice plays such a prominent part, might accord very well with our usage of "moral." But that is neither here nor there if anyone is troubled by the general question, "What are there reasons for doing?" or by more particular questions about how he is to bring up his children.

Even within this principled form of morality considered thus far, there are, in fact, different emphases open. For instance, one might think that the most important things to encourage in children were sympathy, compassion, concern for others, and the like. One might not be particularly concerned about consistency or about the virtue of justice, which one might think of as being a rather niggardly one. Similarly, one might think that courage, integrity, autonomy, or other such excellences ought to be encouraged without being overly concerned about the substantial rules or purposes in relation to which these higher-order traits were exercised. Finally, one might not be too impressed with the interpersonal realm. One might go along with Gauguin and say that painting pictures was the thing, or advocate some other type of worthwhile activity. This form of activity, it might be said, is so valuable that considerations of an interpersonal sort would have to be set aside. All of these are possible moral positions in the general sense that reasons could be given for behaving in the ways suggested and for bringing up one's children accordingly. Of course, an attempt might be made to introduce some kind of unity into the moral life either by attempting to show that all such considerations were derived from one type of consideration, as did the Utilitarians, or by arbitrarily demarcating the sphere of the moral, as did Kant. But *prima facie* it appears to be a difficult enterprise, and it is certainly not one upon which Kohlberg has embarked. His account of moral development might therefore be considered to be one-sided in that it has been erected on the features of a limited interpretation of morality.

A further point must be made, too, about any moral system in which justice is regarded as the fundamental principle: it cannot be applied without a view, deriving from considerations other than those of justice, about what is important. This point can be demonstrated only very briefly, but it is one of cardinal importance. When we talk about what is just or unjust, we are applying the formal principle of reason—that no distinctions should be made without relevant differences, either to questions of distribution, when we are concerned about the treatment which different people are to receive, or to commutative situations, when we are concerned not with comparisons but with questions of desert, as in punishment. In all such cases some criterion has to be produced by reference to which the treatment is to be based on *relevant* considerations. There must therefore be some further evaluative premise in order to determine relevance. Without such a premise, no decisions can be made about what is just on any substantive issue. In determining, for instance, what a just wage is, relevant differences must be determined by reference to what people need, to what they contribute to the community, to the risk involved, and so on. To propose any such criteria involves evaluation. This opens up obvious possibilities for alternative emphases in morality in addition to those already mentioned. But are these emphases to be put on the "formal" or on the "content" side of Kohlberg's account of moral development? When we begin to look at his system in this more detailed way, it must become apparent that it is either implicitly prescriptive or so formal that it is of only limited significance for those who are interested in moral education, or moral development, in a concrete way. His findings are of unquestionable importance, but there is a grave danger that they may become exalted into a general theory of moral development. Any such general theory presupposes a general ethical theory, and Kohlberg himself surely would be the first to admit that he has done little to develop the details of such a general ethical theory. Yet without such a theory the notion of "moral development" is pretty insubstantial.

VI. Freud and Moral Failure

It would be impossible in a short space to do justice to Kohlberg's massive examination of theories deriving from Freud which explain moral development in terms of identification (Kohlberg, 1963). But one main point can be made which is in line with the general thesis of this article: Kohlberg assumes that Freudians must be in some way producing an alternative theory to his own Piagetian theory of moral development. No doubt, many Freudians have thought that they were doing this, and some of Freud's speculations in this area might support such a view. But, as I have maintained elsewhere (see Peters, 1960), it is equally plausible to maintain that, in fact, Freud was attempting explanations of a rather different realm of phenomena.

Rieff (1959) makes much of what he calls Freud's ethic of honesty and of his uncompromising egoism. He suggests that Freud's "education to reality" and his explicit advocacy of "the primacy of the intelligence" amounted to a prudential type of morality in which self-honesty played a large part. This, as a matter of fact, is a disputable interpretation of Freud's own moral standpoint. He actually said of himself, "I believe that in a sense of justice and consideration for others, in disliking making others suffer or taking advantage of them I can measure myself with the best people I know" (Jones, 1955, p. 464), which looks very much like the confession of a rational Utilitarian sort of code that one could find in Sidgwick—or indeed in Piaget. But what is not disputable is that Freud subscribed to some sort of a rational morality, which his practice as a therapist also presupposed; for the aim of psychoanalysis was to strengthen the ego by making unconscious conflicts conscious and by helping people to stand on their own feet with full cognizance of the sources of their irrational promptings and precepts. But in his theory of moral development there is no explicit theory about the development of the ego, which, in Freud's rather pictorial terminology, represented a rational level of behavior. Indeed, he was later criticized by Freudians such as Erikson, Hartmann, and Rapaport for neglecting the development of the autonomous ego, the stages of which were mapped in Piaget's theory.

What, then, did Freud's theory of moral development explain? This is not at all a simple question, for Freud's theory underwent many transformations (see Flugel, 1945). One might say, for instance, that the early theory of the ego ideal was meant to explain simply how some kind of cultural *content* was passed on from parents to children by the rather mysterious process of identification. And even this limited interpretation would not be inconsistent with Kohlberg's theory in that Kohlberg is not much interested in content; from his point of view identification might be as good or as bad an explanation of the transmission of *content* as habit formation. For Kohlberg, it will be remembered, argues that it is the *form* of moral experience rather that its content which is of crucial developmental significance. But Freud was not basically concerned with a simple theory of content transmission in his theory of the ego ideal, let alone in his later speculations about the superego. On the one hand, he was trying to explain the fact that some children seem to develop more rigorous standards than those demanded by their parents; on the other hand, he tried to explain the fact that many people have a picture of themselves—what Adler later called a "guiding fiction"—which is quite out of keeping with the traits which they in fact exhibit. In other words, Freud's theory of the superego was basically a theory of moral failure—of why people become obsessional, unrealistic, and aggressively self-punitive in the moral sphere. It therefore can be seen as a supplement to Piaget's type of theory rather than as a substitute for it.

The same sort of point can be made about Freud's theory of character traits. This does not begin to look like a theory of how traits such as honesty, which were studied in the Hartshorne–May enquiry, are developed. Nor is it a theory about the development of higher-order traits such as consistency, determination, and courage, to which we are usually alluding when we speak of people *having* character. Rather, it is in the tradition of characterology, which goes right back to Theophrastus, in which a type of character is portrayed. Either there is a subordination of traits to a dominant one, as in the sketch of the penurious man; or a whole range of traits are shown as being exercised in an exaggerated or distorted manner, as in the case of a pedantic person. Jones (1955, p. 331) explicitly speaks of Freud's *Character and anal erotism* as a contribution to this sort of speculation, and he notes its literary style. Freud thought that he spotted a similarity between types of character and various forms of neuroses, and assigned a common cause to both in his theory of infantile sexuality. Here again we do not have a competing explanation of the sort of phenomena in which Kohlberg is interested, namely, the determinants of a rational, principled form of morality. Rather we have an attempt to explain types of character that fall a long way short of this in some systematic way.

To discuss the status of the evidence for Freud's type of explanation, even for this realm of deviant phenomena, would require another article—and it would not be the sort that a philosopher would be expected to write. But these phenomena exist, and they certainly cannot be explained in terms of either Kohlberg's or Piaget's type of theory. Therefore, insofar as Freud and his followers have been attempting explanations, however far-fetched, of phenomena of this sort, they are providing a much needed supplement to the work of the Piaget–Kohlberg school. It is not doing justice to them to represent them as providing merely a competing theory of moral development.

References

Aristotle, *Nichomachean ethics*. See J. A. K. Thompson (Ed.). Harmondsworth: Penguin, 1955.

Flugel, J. C. *Man, morals and society*. London: Duckworth, 1945.

Jones, E. *Sigmund Freud, life and works*. Vol. II. London: Hogarth Press, 1955.

Kazepides, A. C. What is the paradox of moral education? *Philosophy of education 1969*. Proceedings of the twenty-fifth annual meeting of the Philosophy of Education Society, Denver, 1969.

Kohlberg, L. Moral development and identification. In H. Stevenson (Ed.), *Child psychology*. 62nd Yearbook Nat. Soc. Stud. Educ. Chicago: Univ. of Chicago Press, 1963.

Kohlberg, L. Development of moral character and ideology. In M. L. Hoffman (Ed.), *Review of child development research*. Vol. I. New York: Russell Sage Foundation, 1964.

Kohlberg, L. Moral education in the schools. *School Review*, 1966, **74**, 1–30.

Kohlberg, L. Stage and sequence: The cognitive–developmental approach to socialization. In D. Goslin (Ed.), *Handbook of socialization*. New York: Rand McNally, 1968. (a)

Kohlberg, L. Early education: A cognitive developmental view. *Child Development*, 1968, **39**, 1013–1062 (b)

Kohlberg, L. Education for justice. In N. F. Sizer & T. R. Sizer (Eds) *Moral Education*. Cambridge, Massachusetts: Harvard Univ. Press, 1970.

Kohlberg, L. Stages in the development of moral thought and action. Unpublished manuscript.

Oakeshott, M. (Ed.) The tower of babel. In *Rationalism in politics*. London: Methuen, 1962.

Peters, R. S. Freud's theory of moral development in relation to that of Piaget. *British Journal of Educational Psychology*, 1960, **30**, 250–258.

Peters, R. S. Reason and habit: The paradox of moral education. In W. R. Niblett (Ed.), *Moral education in a changing society*. London: Faber, 1963.

Peters, R. S. *Perspectives on Plowden*. London: Routledge, 1969.

Piaget, J. *The moral judgment of the child*. London: Routledge, 1932.

Rieff, P. *Freud, the mind of the moralist*. New York: Viking Press, 1959.

Ryle, G. *The concept of mind*. London: Hutchinson, 1948.

Ryle, G. On forgetting the difference between right and wrong. In A. I. Melden (Ed.), *Essays in moral philosophy*. Seattle: Univ. of Washington Press, 1958.

Von Wright, G. H. *The varieties of goodness*. London: Routledge, 1963.

COMMENTS ON KOHLBERG'S "FROM IS TO OUGHT"[1]

William P. Alston

I hope that Peters will forgive me if I direct my comments largely to Kohlberg's article. Since Peters' article itself is so largely concerned with a discussion of Kohlberg's views, it does not provide an ideal target for comment, except by way of taking up the cudgel in Kohlberg's defense. In fact, I feel that Peters' points are almost invariably well taken, and so rather than spending my time squabbling with him over fine points, I shall direct my comments to Kohlberg's views as they are presented in his contribution to this volume. At certain points I shall be touching on issues raised by Peters, but I shall strive to avoid merely duplicating what he has said.

First I must voice some doubts as to the extent to which the articles are concerned with the topic of symposium. Of course, topics are born to be honored in the breach, and I should not want to discuss the matter in such a way as to lead to my being classified at stage 4, with an orientation toward fixed rules and the authority of the conference chairman, but it is well to be clear as to what we are and are not doing at a certain time. It is, of course, quite clear that Peters has devoted practically all his attention to aspects of the development of moral character other than the acquisition of moral concepts, and that Kohlberg has devoted most of his article to questions of metaethics and normative ethics. However, Kohlberg's theory of stages is in either the forefront or the background of most of these discussions, and since it is easy to suppose that this theory is a theory of concept acquisition, it may be worthwhile to point out the extent to which this is not the case. A careful scrutiny of the descriptions of Kohlberg's

[1] Editor's note: Alston's comments are based on the early version of the article which Kohlberg prepared prior to the conference. Page references have been changed so as to correspond to the revised Kohlberg article printed above, but it must be kept in mind that Kohlberg has thoroughly revised his paper in light of these comments and discussions at the conference.

stages, and of the basis on which a subject is assigned to a stage, will reveal that what is being so classified is what might be called a person's habitual style of moral reasoning—the kind of moral judgments he is inclined to make and the way in which he is inclined to support such judgments. Thus, a person is classified as stage 3, for example, on the grounds that he more often than not responds to questions about moral dilemmas by bringing in considerations as to what conduct would be generally approved of by others. This is taken to indicate that he typically or habitually reasons about moral problems in this way.

But can we also construe these stages, as so described and so identified, as stages of conceptual development? Certainly the assignment of a person to a given stage has some implications as to his conceptual repertoire. That is, if a person utilizes certain concepts in a piece of reasoning, whether this is habitual or not, it follows without more ado that he has those concepts. Thus, a stage 3 person will necessarily have the concepts, for example, the concept of disapproval, that are essentially involved in stage 3 reasoning. However, this is not sufficient to make these into stages of conceptual development. It would also have to be the case that a person's habitual mode of moral reasoning embodies his highest or latest conceptual acquisitions in the moral sphere; that is, that he does not possess any concepts that are distinctive of higher stages of reasoning. And this we cannot infer just from the fact that he habitually or typically reasons about moral problems in a way that features stage 3 concepts. He might conceivably possess the concepts of stage 4, 5, or 6, even though he does not habitually employ them in his moral thinking. This conclusion is simply a particular application of a fundamental conceptual point about the concepts of having a concept, on the one hand, and of using a concept (or habitually or typically using a concept) on the other. One cannot use a concept in a given situation without having it, but one can have a concept without using it in a given situation (or perhaps without using it at all, though this is more controversial). Possession of a concept is something more latent than a habit, trait, or tendency, and all the more latent than an actual performance, whether covert or overt.

Kohlberg certainly recognizes this point, for he makes explicit that the "modal" state of a person, in terms of which he is classified, will typically be reflected in only about 50% of his statements, the others extending both above and below this stage, though more heavily below (Kohlberg, 1968, pp. 386–387), and he explicitly distinguishes testing for use (which is what the assignment to a stage is based on) from testing for comprehension (Kohlberg, 1968, p. 386). The data on which the assignment to stages are based thus do not in any straightforward way support a corresponding assignment to a stage of highest conceptual attainment. This means that the hypotheses that are confirmed by empirical studies using these stage assignments, hypotheses concerning the causes and consequences of stage membership and stage transition, cannot themselves be construed as hypotheses about the causes and consequences of stages of conceptual development. Let me illustrate this. Kohlberg reports (*p. 229*) an experiment in which only one of nine "principled" subjects cheated when apparently given an opportunity to do so without chance of detection, while about one half of the "conventional" subjects did so. (This was a cruder stage discrimination, which contrasts, roughly, stage 4 with stages 5 and 6.) Does this mean that subjects who have attained only the *conception* of conventional morality are more likely to cheat than subjects who have gone further and acquired the concepts of general abstract moral principles that go beyond conventional rules in their scope and status? Not necessarily. We still do not know how the subjects are distinguished with respect to their level of *conceptual* development. For all we know, given the detection devices used, all or most of the "conventional" subjects may *have* the concepts of abstract moral principles that go beyond convention, but not choose, or find it natural, to reason about moral problems in those terms. Again studies show (*p. 190*) that "middle-class children were found to be more advanced in moral judgment than matched lower-class children." For the same reason these results cannot be interpreted without further data as showing that middle-class children are more advanced *in their stage of conceptual development* than their lower-class contemporaries.

I have been pointing out that Kohlberg's research on the causes and consequences of stage membership and transition cannot be interpreted without more ado as research into the causes and consequences of membership in and transition between stages of conceptual development. But nothing that I have said has any tendency to show that there is not in fact a sequence of stages of conceptual development corresponding to that sequence of stages of habitual moral reasoning. That is, for all that I have just said, it may well be the case that there is a culturally invariant sequence from the acquisition of the concept of a sanction of punishments to the acquisition of the concept of a sanction of rewards, and so on. Kohlberg presents some indirect reasons for believing in the existence of such a sequence. He reports research showing that though one assigned to a certain stage can readily comprehend statements at his own stage and below, he comprehends statements above his stage much less well, and in proportion to their distance above (*p. 181*). This suggests that one's currently preferred mode of reasoning embodies the "highest" mode of conceptualization that one has thoroughly mastered to date, and that the concepts of lower stages, but not those of higher stages, are secure possessions. Again there are *a priori* arguments, to be considered later, to the effect that the logical relations of the concepts in the various stages are such that if one acquires moral concepts, he must necessarily acquire them in the order that is reflected in the order of stages of moral thought. However, it would obviously be desirable to have some more direct way of showing a developmental sequence in concept acquisition. A more direct demonstration would require the development of a test for *possession* of moral concepts, analogous to the test of typical mode of moral reasoning. It goes without saying that such a test is much more difficult to develop. Here we are not tapping tendencies, we are not simply trying to determine what is most likely to emerge under certain institutable conditions; rather we are trying to determine what latent capacities a person does, and, most difficult, *does not* have. We have to find a way of surveying his whole field of moral conception so as to see what is and what is not present. It is no wonder that such instruments have not been the first to be developed.

Moreover, even if we could establish the existence of a culturally invariant unique sequence of moral conceptual development corresponding to the sequence of stages of preferred modes of moral reasoning, it would be a further question whether these sequences go along in parallel fashion; that is, whether one adopts a mode of reasoning roughly at the same time as that at which he acquires the concepts needed for that mode, rather than the latter trailing behind the former, perhaps at a pace varying widely from case to case. Let's call the assumption of such a parallel the "Principle of Parallelism." As we shall see later, Kohlberg assumes this principle without seeming to see the necessity for any justification of it. Indeed, it may seem that the principle is ruled out by some facts to which we have already alluded, namely, that a person typically understands, and even uses concepts at stages above his "modal" stage. But a rejection on those grounds would be overhasty. One can always interpret these partial understandings of higher concepts as incipient beginnings of a movement to a higher stage of reasoning. We cannot expect to catch our subjects squarely in the middle of a developmental stage. The more usual case will be that of the person at one or another point of a transition. Such a person will exhibit greater or smaller traces of stages above the one in which he predominantly fits. This consideration, plus the usual allowance for imperfections of the instruments and for the idealization involved in any workable theory, will allow us to maintain parallelism in the face of such facts.

Next I should like to make some remarks on Kohlberg's attempt to move from "is" to "ought." In order to come to grips with his contentions, I shall have to look into the exact claims he is making for his stages of moral thought.

First we should clear out of the way an unfortunate mischaracterization Kohlberg gives of his position. In introducing his "is to ought" argument he says, "The third form of the 'naturalistic fallacy' which we *are* committing is that of asserting that any conception of what moral judgment ought to be must rest on an adequate conception of what it is" (*p. 222*). And again, "Every constructive effort at rational morality, at saying what morality ought to be must start with a characterization of what it is, and in that sense commits 'the naturalistic fallacy' " (*pp. 222–223*). This is a very innocuous sense indeed, as is clearly indicated by the fact that in this sense the "fallacy" is committed by "every constructive effort at rational morality." Indeed, more generally, any attempt to evaluate anything, whether a bottle of wine or the Viet Nam war, must proceed on the basis of a conception of the nature of what we are evaluating; to the extent that out conception is mistaken our evaluations are likely to be off. If this were all that Kohlberg's argument from "is" to "ought" came to, there would be nothing to discuss. But fortunately, for the commentator, his project involves considerably more than that. He gives a much better characterization of his position when he writes, "The scientific theory as to why people factually *do* move upward from stage to stage, and why they factually *do* prefer a higher stage to a lower, is broadly the same as a moral theory as to why people *should* prefer a higher stage to a lower" (*p. 223*). Let us see what there is in the psychological theory that Kohlberg supposes to have these normative implications, and let us consider what we should say about the matter.

First note that it is an *explanation* of the stage sequence, rather than its mere existence, that is claimed to have moral implications. I believe that Kohlberg is well advised to set the matter up in this way. Even if the facts did clearly indicate a unique sequence, the normative implications to be drawn would still depend on how this is to be explained. This dependence can be shown by considering a fantastic "possibility," namely, that the sequence is to be explained by a genetically determined progressive deterioration of mental powers after age eight. If that were the explanation, then no one would be tempted to make an inference from "later" to "morally superior." What sort of explanation would provide a basis for the moral implications claimed?

Kohlberg characterizes his explanation of the sequence as "interactional." The precise processes that he takes to be crucial for this interaction involve role taking in a variety of groups in the person's environment. However, this aspect of the theory is not crucial for the normative implications, and we shall say no more about it. What is crucial is the claim that the processes involved in stage transition involve the person's coming to realize that certain modes of thinking are more adequate ways of handling the subject matter, that they represent a more finely articulated grasp of the field in question. Thus, the kind of psychological explanation of stage sequence favored by Kohlberg has built into it claims about the relative worth of the stages as ways of moral thinking. It is perhaps not so surprising that "the scientific theory as to why people factually *do* move upward from stage to stage . . . is broadly the same as a moral theory as to why people *should* prefer a higher stage to a lower"; this is just because the "scientific" theory has built into it claims about the relative worth of the various stages. The crucial question, then, is as to just what claims of superiority Kohlberg makes, and whether he has adequately justified them.

The criteria to which Kohlberg appeals in making these judgments are "the *formal* criteria which developmental theory holds as defining all mature structures, the criteria of increased differentiation and integration" (*p. 184*). "These combined criteria, differentiation and integration, are considered by developmental theory to entail a better equilibrium of the structure in question. A more differentiated and integrated moral structure handles more moral problems, conflicts, or points of view in a more stable or self-consistent way" (*p. 185*).

Before raising any critical questions about this hierarchical evaluation, I want to say something about the closely associated claim of a logical necessity to the order of development, a claim already discussed by Peters. "The sequence represents a universal inner logical order of moral concepts . . . each new basic differentiation made by each stage logically depends upon the differentiation before it; the order of differentiations could not logically be other than it is" (*p. 187*).

With respect to this claim several points are in order.

1. If justified, it would be a conclusive reason for holding that there is a sequence of concept acquisition *corresponding* to Kohlberg's sequence of habitual modes of thinking. (Though it would still not establish the principle of parallelism.) If the concepts involved in stage 3 thinking logically presuppose the concepts involved in stage 2 thinking, as, for example, the concept of a violation of a rule logically presupposes the concept of a rule, then it is clear that one could not acquire the former set of concepts before acquiring the latter.

2. So far as I am aware, the only reason Kohlberg gives for imputing such an order is tied to the above-mentioned claims concerning differentiation. Since the stage 3 conception of the value of human life involves a differentiation of "the value of human life, as based on social sharing, community and love" from "the instrumental and hedonistic value of life applicable also to animals" that is characteristic of stage 2, the former conception logically depends on the latter. How could we have the concept of a differentiation of X and Y unless we also had the concept of Y? I will grant that this does follow from the interpretation of the stages as neces-

sarily involving a series of hierarchical differentiations, but I shall dispute that claim shortly.

3. In any event, the necessary logical order thesis in itself, though highly inflammatory from the standpoint of other concerns, has absolutely no bearing on the question with which we are presently concerned. The mere fact that one concept logically depends on another has no tendency to show that moral thinking involving the former is superior to moral thinking involving the latter. The concept of arbitrary exceptions to rules logically depends on the concept of rules, but it enjoys no moral superiority on those grounds.

To return to the main stream of the discussion, we have seen that Kohlberg considers his stages to be ordered in terms of increasing differentiation, integration, and capacity to give definitive resolutions to moral problems. I shall confine my remarks to the first of these.

In setting out the sequence of stages, Kohlberg, after giving a positive characterization of each stage, adds that it involves a differentiation of its characteristic content from that of the preceding stage. It would follow from this that the sequence of stages involves a sequence of increasingly complex (differentiated) conceptual fields. Note, however, that we are justified in characterizing the stages in this way only if we are justified in accepting the principle of parallelism. To say that each stage "involves" a differentiation of its distinctive concepts from the distinctive concepts of the preceding stage is to say that one's acquisition of the distinctive concepts of stage n is contemporaneous, at least roughly, with one's adopting (or falling into) that mode of moral reasoning as dominant. I suggested earlier that Kohlberg has, to my knowledge, not presented adequate evidence for that claim. Now I may add that common-sense considerations make the assumption seem implausible, especially with respect to the higher levels, where the real controversies in moral philosophy center. (I take it that the lower levels do not really constitute serious alternatives for moral philosophy.) The most striking fact here is that many philosophers who are surely at least as conceptually sophisticated as Kohlberg's stage 6 subjects take positions in moral philosophy that reflect stage 4 or 5. Many highly sophisticated theologians, for example, have espoused a subjection-to-the-will-of-God morality that I suppose would be classed by Kohlberg as stage 4. What is Kohlberg to say about such cases? He might suggest that the moral philosophy of these people does not accurately reflect their actual moral reasoning, which would be classified as stage 6. Or he might treat them as cases of "culturally induced regression," that is, cases that had reached stage 6 in both respects (concepts and habits of reasoning), and then had regressed to stage 4 in habits of reasoning because of cultural pressure or emotional needs. It would certainly be interesting to test such suggestions.

Suppose it could be shown that, with appropriate subsidiary explanations of deviant cases, conceptual development does proceed in tandem with the dominance of modes of reasoning. Stage 6 moral reasoning would then, by hypothesis, "involve" the most finely articulated conceptual scheme. Is this a moral recommendation? Does the cognitive superiority of a more elaborate conceptual scheme imply the moral superiority of the associated mode of resolving moral problems? Kohlberg's argument for the moral superiority of the more differentiated stage is tied to his account of what makes a moral judgment a *moral* judgment, as distinguished from factual judgments, as well as from other species of value judgments. He seems to be of two minds about this, but one of his inclinations is to take a "formalist" approach and separate out moral judgments in terms of their prescriptivity and universality, and it is this view that plays a role in the "is" to "ought" argument.

> The increasingly prescriptive nature of more mature moral judgments is reflected in the series of differentiations we have described, which is a series of increased differentiations of "is" and "ought" (or of morality as internal principles from external events and expectations). . . . The series [of stages of conceptions of the moral worth of human life] is a series toward increased prescriptivity, because the moral imperative to value life becomes increasingly independent of the factual properties of the life in question. First, the person's furniture becomes irrelevant to his value, next, whether he has a loving family, and so on (*pp. 184–185*).

Now insofar as I understand this, which, I fear, is not very far, I take Kohlberg to be saying that, as we go through the stages, moral judgments are increasingly distinguished from factual judgments and therefore conform more exactly to the pure type. It almost sounds as if he is saying that this differentiation goes along with a separation of moral reasoning from any dependence on factual considerations at all, but of course he cannot mean this. If I interpret him correctly, he is simply saying, with respect to the differentiation of this dimension, that the further we go along in the stages, the more we get distinctively moral judgments. There are two problems about this. First, unless Kohlberg can do more than he has done to show that his choice of a definition of "moral" is based on something more than a personal preference among the variety of definitions that have been proposed, the fact that his later stages conform more exactly to his conception of a moral judgment has no objective significance. It is notorious that moral philosophers agree no more about what is distinctive of the moral than about anything else; and a large number of distinct accounts of what makes a judgment, a reason, an attitude, a rule, or a principle, *moral* have been put forward. Kohlberg chooses one of these (or rather, I suspect, two of these at different places in the article), but fails to do anything by way of showing that this is more than a choice of what seems most congenial or interesting to him. That is quite acceptable if it is just a matter of carving out a subject for empirical research. If Kohlberg wants to investigate the development of moral reasoning according to some arbitrarily selected criterion of "moral," well and good; he may come up with something interesting. But if he wants to use the developmental approximations to the purely moral in his sense as a basis for pronouncements as to how people *ought* to reason in their action-guiding deliberations, that is another matter. If these pronouncements are to carry any weight, he will have to show that this sense of "moral" which is functioning as his standard has itself some recommendation other than congeniality to his predilections.

The second point is this: Even if the superior conformity of later stages to certain formal features of moral judgments shows them to be "so far forth" superior, that does not get us very far. What Kohlberg really wants most to recommend to our acceptance is the principle of justice (in his interpretation) as a supreme moral principle. But stages of prescriptivity will not advance that cause. A judgment based on a principle of racial destiny, or on no principle at all, can be just as prescriptive as a judgment based on an application of Kohlberg's principle of justice.

For these reasons, and others, I do not feel that Kohlberg has fully succeeded in showing what he set out to show, namely, that the facts of the order of moral development and its explanation reveal his stage 6 of moral reasoning to be a morally superior way of resolving moral problems. Nevertheless, when all this is said, I do think that the evidence Kohlberg adduces goes far toward breaking down the popular contrast between factual and scientific judgment as objective, and moral judgment as subjective. It does at least strongly suggest that one's modes of moral judgment universally tend to develop in certain directions under the impact of objective dimensions of its subject matter.

Turning aside now from attempts to pull a moral philosophy out of a hat, I should like to consider Kohlberg's theory of moral thought in the general context of moral psychology. More especially, I would like to raise the question as to the place of an account of moral thought in a complete psychology of morals, which amounts, I suppose, to the same thing as raising the question as to the place of moral thought in moral life. I am aware that Peters has made many useful comments on this score, but I should like to add just a few remarks of my own.

First, since I have been unrelievedly critical up to this point, let me say how much I think Kohlberg's work has enriched moral psychology in this country. For me, at least, it has opened up a number of new perspectives on the subject. More generally, he is to be given a great deal of credit for doing some very hard and very unfashionable thinking on moral thought as a subject of interest in its own right, and for producing evidence that should force psychologists to take the cognitive aspects of morality seriously as an important influence on behavior. However, like all champions of the neglected, Kohlberg has not been able to resist the temptation to overstate his case. From being the outcast stepdaughter, moral thought must be not only restored to its rightful place as a princess of the court; it must be elevated into an absolute sovereign. Feeling himself, with ample justification, in an embattled position in contemporary American psychology, he has been led into exaggerated claims for his favored variables, and into unwarranted denigration of the more fashionable variables. I believe that we can fully recognize the importance of developmental stages of moral thinking without condoning the excesses of Kohlberg's dismissal of other kinds of variables. I shall now try to document these points with respect to Kohlberg's discussion of affect and habit.

Kohlberg opposes "irrational emotive theories of moral development such as those of Durkheim and Freud," but draws the contrast between "cognitive" and "emotive" theories with such a broad brush, that I do not know exactly what his views are on the role of affect. From what he says about the dynamics of moral development, I would suppose that he is opposed to the idea that anything like a Freudian superego plays a crucial role. As to the motivation of moral behavior, he says

> . . . moral judgment dispositions influence action through being stable cognitive dispositions, not through the affective changes with which they are associated. Textbook psychology preaches the cliché that moral decisions are a product of the algebraic resolution of conflicting quantitative affective forces. . . . Affective forces are involved in moral decisions, but affect is neither moral nor immoral. When the affective arousal is channeled into moral directions, it is moral; when it is not so channeled, it is not. The moral channeling mechanisms themselves are cognitive (*pp. 230–231*).

This makes it clear that he is insisting that cognition has a role, and it is tolerably clear what role he is assigning it. What is quite unclear is *what* role he is assigning to affect. In the absence then of sufficient indications from the text, I am going to formulate two propositions that I suppose Kohlberg would deny, suggest that nothing in his theory or the empirical results on which it is based has any tendency to show that they are mistaken, and then see what he has to say now about the matter.

The first proposition has to do with moral development.

1. A necessary condition of a person's taking a principle or rule to be moral is that it either be part of, or be associated with, a certain set of

rules which he has internalized in early childhood in the special kind of way and with the special kind of emotional intensity that Freud describes as the establishing of the superego.

This I take to be a rough statement of the Freudian position in a form in which it is compatible with all of Kohlberg's positive contentions. We can admit that the "form" of moral thinking develops just as Kohlberg claims, and that one's behavior and feeling will be powerfully altered by this development. Even if all that is true, proposition 1 insists that these are cognitive developments in *moral* thinking because they are developments of an original core, the essential elements of which are highly affectively charged self-destructive tendencies (guilt feelings) contingent on the violation of certain rules. Incidentally it will be clear from these remarks that I do not agree with some of the other authors of this volume that Freudian superego theory, insofar as it is distinctively useful, is an explanation of the morally tinged components of psychopathology, not a theory of the development of universal or normal features of morality. I regard it as, at heart, an account of a developmentally necessary condition for an attitude, judgment, concept, or piece of reasoning to be distinctively moral. No doubt, as it stands it is by no means a complete theory of moral development; it at the very least requires supplementation along the lines of Kohlberg's exploration of cognitive structural features of moral thought, and, I should think, in other ways, as well. Nevertheless, I do not agree that it is limited to moral pathology. I do not know whether anything like the Freudian account is true (or better, how close an approximation it is), but I do maintain that as a specification of one necessary condition for the acquistion of moral concepts, principles, attitudes, and emotions it is quite compatible with both the theory and the evidence that Kohlberg presents.

My second proposition has to do with moral motivation. It naturally goes with the preceding but is logically independent of it.

2. In order for one to be motivated to act in accordance with a moral principle, rule, or judgment it must be the case that one anticipates (not necessarily consciously of course) that feelings of guilt would ensue on one's failing to act in accordance with it.

(Of course one might weaken the principle so as to claim only that this is one of the major sources of moral motivation.) So far as I can see, this proposition too is quite compatible with Kohlberg's theory and with the evidence on which it is based. His theory certainly tells us a lot about the modes of variation of such judgments, and he certainly has given us reason to think that very general structural differences in moral reasoning and judgment make a difference to behavior. But I fail to see that any of this shows that the motive to avoid guilt feelings does not play a major or even an essential role in the transition from thought to action. Granting all of Kohlberg's contentions, it still may be the case that when one does not act in accordance with one's moral judgment, it is because the judgment lacks the extra push that comes from an association between violation of it and guilt feelings.

Kohlberg does advance certain very general theses concerning the relation of affect and cognition, and he may very well take them to imply an insignificant role for affect in the moral life, and, more especially, to show that my two propositions are mistaken. He maintains that so far from being "different mental states," " 'cognition' and 'affect' are different aspects, or perspectives, on the same mental events, that all mental events have both cognitive and affective aspects, and that the development of mental dispositions reflects structural changes recognizable in both cognitive and affective perspectives" (*pp. 188–189*). This formulation may make it appear that there is something like a parity between the two aspects, but in fact Kohlberg's view is that "the quality (as opposed to the quantity) of affects involved in moral judgment is determined by its cognitive-structural development" (*p. 189*). In other words, pure affective arousal without concepts is blind and has no distinctive function in the guidance of behavior. I am wholeheartedly in sympathy with this claim, and have in fact argued along the same lines (Alston, 1968). What differentiates fear from embarrassment from shame from remorse is not some simple phenomenal quality peculiar to each, nor yet some distinctive pattern of autonomic arousal, but rather the way the felt autonomic arousal is interpreted by the person.

However, this general doctrine of the interrelation of cognition and affect would run counter to propositions 1 and 2 only if those propositions were stated in terms of a "blind" view of the nature of affect. Their proponents have often done so, but it is not necessary to conceive them in such oversimplified terms. One can unreservedly embrace the thesis that any distinctive emotional state will have a cognitive side, by virtue of which it is the kind of emotional state it is, and still insist that emotional states, to which an affective side is also essential, play crucial roles in moral development and moral motivation as specified in propositions 1 and 2. We should beware of supposing that the nonsufficiency of pure affect for a certain process entails the nonnecessity of pure affect for that process.

Peters has already discussed at some length the place of habit in the moral life, but I will take this opportunity to add a few points, particularly with reference to what Kohlberg says in his article. Kohlberg speaks contemptuously of the "bag of virtues" conception of morality and rejects concepts of traits based on cultural norms as useless in psychology. Although he does not explicitly discuss the habit category in its full generality, the impression one receives is that he feels such concepts have no place in moral psychology. As against this I would like to argue that not only are habit concepts indispensable in psychology, moral or otherwise, but that, once more, none of Kohlberg's positive theses or the evidence on which they are based, have any tendency to show that this is not the case.

It is easy to become so preoccupied with some particular class of habits, for example, those defined in terms of cultural norms (honesty and chastity), or those with a particular kind of content, for example, stimulus–response, as to lose sight of the generic features of the habit category, as contrasted with other broad categories of psychological characteristics, such as abilities, desires, and attitudes. To attribute a habit to someone is simply to say that he is presently so constituted that in a certain specified type (or types) of situation(s), he is more or less likely to do so and so. Habits can be of the most widely varied sorts, and still fit this general paradigm, depending on how the type of situation and the "so and so" done are specified. Thus, in a physiological reflex the situation is defined in terms of a kind of stimulus, and the do "so and so" in terms of a kind of bodily movement. But with the personality traits (including traits of character) that can be construed as habits, the situation is in practice defined, despite the programmatic asseverations of behavioristically minded personologists, in terms of the individual's "psychological field," what he takes the situation to be, and the response in terms of rather abstract action categories. This is true of such varied terms as *cooperative*, *sociable*, *domineering*, *conscientious*, *sympathetic*, and *polite*. Or the response category may not range over overt actions but over emotional responses, as in *excitable* or *anxious*, or over cognitive operations, as in *analytical* or *superstitious*. I have already implicitly underlined this indefinite variability in the content of habit concepts by claiming that Kohlberg's stages are properly conceived as stages of habits of moral reasoning. To be in a given stage is, in the first place (whatever else it may involve), to have a habit, the situational side of which is something like "recognizing that there is a problem as to what someone ought to do," and the response side of which is defined in terms of "thinking about the problems in terms of such and such considerations." Thus, even if one were able to get along in moral psychology without any reference to habits of behavior, and this *may* be Kohlberg's aspiration, his own example illustrates the difficulty of getting along without using habit concepts at any level. I do regard habit concepts as embodying a relatively superficial way of describing persons; they simply impute a *de facto* situation–response regularity (usually a very rough regularity) without specifying what explains this regularity. (This is one of the points made already by Peters.) If we were ever in a position to give a sufficiently comprehensive and adequate description of the more basic underlying features of persons, whatever those may turn out to be, perhaps we could dispense with habit concepts in personality description. But I fear we are a long way from that consummation. This is evidenced by Kohlberg's falling back on habit concepts at the level of cognitive operations, and I shall now go on to try to show that nothing Kohlberg has done shakes the prior presumption that we cannot get along without talking about behavioral habits either.

Kohlberg objects to traditional concepts of virtues on the grounds that they do not divide the population into dichotomous groups and that a given individual is not consistent in his responses (*p. 227*), that is, such traits are not tightly organized. His most fundamental point, which presumably he adduces in explanation of the Hartshorne–May results is (to put it in my own terms) that the response categories in virtue concepts are defined by cultural norms, which may very well not correspond to effective response categories in the psychological structure of many members of the society, and which are useless in specifying concepts that can be usefully applied to all subjects across cultures. One may readily admit that virtue concepts have all these defects, without drawing the conclusion that they have no place in moral psychology. One can easily be led into overgeneralizations from the Hartshorne–May results. There is a potential infinity of habit concepts, corresponding to the potential infinity of conceptual possibilities for the specification of situation and response categories. Hartshorne and May took some common-sense concepts that many expected to display certain kinds of distributions across individuals and occasions. Those expectations were disappointed. But (*a*) there may very well be other habit concepts from that potential infinity that will show such distributions in a similar sample; (*b*) even if a given habit concept does not show the distribution in question throughout the population, it may be very useful in describing some members of that population. I am here, of course, alluding to G. Allport's distinction between "common traits" and "unique traits." It is certainly the beginning of wisdom to recognize that not all members of a society, especially not all members of as diverse a society as ours, organize their behavior in terms of the same set of situational and response categories. But this simply complicates the task of specifying situation–response regularities; it does not obviate the task. One's "bag of virtues" does not have to be as conceptually crude as the ones Kohlberg enumerates.

In the preceding paragraph I have been contending that the arguments and data presented by Kohlberg do not suffice to show that our need to identify (at least roughly) situation–response regularities in "moral behavior" must remain unsatisfied. Clearly, I was presupposing that there is such a need. Perhaps Kohlberg believes that there is not, or at least that there will not be, when we have gained a penetrating enough understanding of moral thought. Now once more, just as in the discussion of affect, I want to maintain that though Kohlberg has filled a serious gap with his treatment of moral thought, he would be unjustified in supposing that his favored variables do the whole job. Let us grant that his moral stage assignments do a better job of predicting to, for example, cheating or not cheating, than do either ratings of conventional character traits, or direct expressions of moral attitudes couched in terms of conventional character traits. Nevertheless, there is no reason to think that it will do the whole job. In fact, there is every reason to think that it will not. So long as there is any significant discrepancy between the moral judgment a person makes about a situation (or would make if the question arose) and what he actually does, there will be a need, in describing persons, for an account of what they are likely to do as well as what they are likely to think. And Kohlberg has given us no reason to suppose that there is no such significant discrepancy. To put it in the bluntest terms, in choosing a wife, if I were capable of doing so in cold blood, I would want to know more, on the moral side, than how she reasons about moral dilemmas. Her conceptual sophistication and invocation of principles of justice and welfare may be exemplary, but I will also want to know how likely she is to have my dinner ready for me in the evening, and how she is likely to respond to flattering attentions from other men. Again, let me repeat that if we knew enough about the deeper sources—cognitive, emotional, etc.—on which situation–response regularities depend, we would probably not need to conceptualize the person, even partly, in habit terms. But until that millenium arrives, talking about one's capacities and proclivities for moral reasoning will not do the whole job.

I have been arguing that habit concepts, including concepts of behavioral habits, are indispensable in the description of moral character. One of Kohlberg's objections to them, as we have seen, is that they are useless for cross-cultural comparisons and culturally invariant descriptions. This may well be. If it is, it just shows, I suppose, that not all of what we need to know about a person to fully understand his moral character is culturally invariant. But this is hardly a surprising conclusion, even if we fully grant Kohlberg's contentions about the cultural invariance of the structure of moral reasoning. After all, morality is content as well as form, and to understand a particular person's moral character we need to know both.

To sum up, I have been arguing that however important Kohlberg's theory may be as a theory of moral thought and reasoning, and however important it may be to insist, as against dominant trends in American psychology, on the significance of this side of morality, his theory and his evidence do nothing to show that affect and habit are not also important in morality in ways which Kohlberg seems to deny. Perhaps one thing that is responsible for Kohlberg's unwarranted slighting of these other aspects of morality is his concentration on moral dilemmas in his research. Kohlberg's special subject is moral reasoning, and if you want to find out what sort of moral reasoning a subject does, you have to get him to do some, which means that you have to present him with a problem (real or imaginary) that calls for reasoning. It has to be a situation that has no obvious solution in terms of dominant cultural standards; otherwise it will not evoke hard thinking. Now there is no doubt that it is just situations of this kind in which reasoning looms largest, as over against affect and habitual response, both in terms of relative contributions to the determination of behavior, and in terms of phenomenological prominence. We tend to *feel* strongest about the matters we feel most certain about (which seem less problematical), and it is in just the cases that do not seem at all problematical that our habits function in an unimpeded fashion. Thus, one may see the neglect of the affective and the habitual as, in part, a sort of "methodological artifact," as springing from a preoccupation with that range of cases, surely a minority in terms of gross frequency, in which those factors are relatively less salient. This is also connected with Kohlberg's astounding statement that "The conception that difficult moral choices are difficult because of the conflict between the flesh and the spirit, the id and superego, is misleading . . . real moral crises arise when situations are socially ambiguous, when the usual moral expectations break down" (*p. 231*). Surely there are plenty of difficult moral situations of both kinds, and it is only a kind of intellectual "vested interest" that could lead one to award only one of these kinds of situations the label of "real moral crisis."

References

Alston, W. P. Moral attitudes and moral judgments. *Noûs*, 1968, 2, 1–23.

Kohlberg, L. Stage and sequence: The cognitive–developmental approach to socialization. In D. Goslin (Ed.), *Handbook of socialization*. New York: Rand McNally, 1968.

Part II

Basic Issues in the Psychology of Cognitive Development

C. The Motivation of Cognitive Development

EARLY COGNITIVE DEVELOPMENT: Hot or Cold?

William Kessen

It requires little in the way of imperial disposition to see all psychology in the motivation of early cognitive development. Classic disjunctions of impulse and thought, instinct and intelligence, drive and habit come at once into view. Even if you see children behind the conceptual issues (as you should!), significant questions remain. On one side, it seems as strange to ask "What motivates a baby to walk?" as to ask "What motivates a flower to bloom?" On the other, the ordered development of the baby demands some response to questions about the sanctions, directions, and sources of human action. To control somewhat the vast domain of possible discourse, I will impose several limitations on my task. First, I will sketch roughly and in an exaggerated fashion the two major twentieth-century alternatives to Piaget's theory of motivation and development—psychoanalysis and stimulus–response–reinforcement theory. Along the way, a collection of troubling general questions will emerge; of especial interest is the tendency of the theories to root thought in impulse—the dimension of "hotness." Next, I will present an opinion about what Piaget maintains as a motivational theory—a "cold" theory, of course—in full recognition that the today's exegete may be confounded tomorrow by new scripture. The resulting contrasts may help to illuminate those special issues in the development of thought where motivational assumptions seem particularly pertinent, and where we are most sadly ignorant.

Throughout, examples will be drawn from and proposals will be directed toward the behavior of the newborn and very young infant. In part, this restriction of scope springs from my research involvement with babies, but it also has a higher justification. Views of man held by philosophers and, derived from them in often garbled and antic forms, by psychologists can also be most sharply differentiated by noticing the mental apparatus that they assign to babies. The pages that follow will be chiefly concerned with varying theoretical *ascriptions of early mind.*

I. The Psychoanalysis of Early Cognition

Freud did not merely propose that there was a mind behind conscious ratiocinations; he put the source of all thought in somatic demand. His inversion of traditional attitudes produced the "hottest" theory of cognitive development; for Freud, all cognition is chilled impulse. To be sure, Freud's vision of the baby is a subtle and complex one, too easily reduced to false simplicity. However, Rapaport (1959) has managed to extract the essence of the psychoanalytic position without destroying the plant, and I follow him closely here.

The infant is started toward thought with the occurrence of "restlessness"; commonly under these conditions, the infant will be able to suck, and as a result, the restlessness will subside (the *model of primary action*). The critical event, both for the development of cognition and for the development of affect, is the withholding or postponement of the appropriate gratifying event (here, sucking). On such occasions, the infant will hallucinate earlier gratification and will often show affect discharge (crying, visceral change, and so on).

Model of *primary action:*

Restlessness → Sucking → Reduction of restlessness

Model of *primary cognition:*

Drive → Absence of drive object → Hallucinatory "image" of previous gratification

Model of *primary effect:*

Drive → Absence of drive object → Affect discharge

Model of the *role of thought* in ego-controlled gratification:

Drive → Structures of delay → Experiments in thought → Detours in route to direct gratification → "Acceptable" satisfaction

Experiments in thought ⇄ Anxiety signals

Fig. 1. An expression of the relation between impulse and thought in psychoanalytic therapy. (After Rapaport, 1959.)

Infantile hallucination of the breast or bottle (or, better, of certain critical aspects of the situation in which he has sucked) is the beginning of mind, the origin of thought. Cognition is, thus, from the outset in the service of the gratification of impulse and is palely hallucinatory.[1] As the child grows, maturational changes occur in the instinctual drives, and the child enters into a series of conflicts (first between child and the world, and before long, between different institutions within the child) that jointly produce a pattern of relation between drive and thought that remains appropriate for adults. An abbreviated account of the development is shown in Fig. 1.

Put in another way, when an impulse or derivation of an impulse presses for gratification, the older child and the adult will restrain the expression of the impulse, try out (in thought) possible ways of solving the "problem" under a guidance system that feeds back anxiety if the solution is dangerous, and take action in compromise of the impulse and restraining external and intrapsychic dangers. In Rapaport's summary, the central factors underlying developmental change are "instinctual drives and the structures restraining them." As originally laid out by Freud, the task of the student of cognitive development is to chart the course of growth of these compromising mental structures.[2]

My reduction of Freud's abstraction can only hint at the possibilities for talking about human thought in the terms of psychoanalytic theory, but a quick look may have been sufficient to show that Freud posed many of the problems that continue to concern us in attempting to understand cognitive development. Let me list them as an agenda for stimulus–response–reinforcement theory and for Piaget.

II. A Group of Central Questions

A. Structures and Strategies. What Do We Assign to the Infant? The most determining move in the psychology of thought is the initial assignment of characteristics to the human infant. Once a decision has been made about the contents and functions to be assumed for the baby, he is irretrievably put into a particular line of development. For

[1] Freud's language hardly overlaps Piaget's, but the notion of hallucinated gratification can be put in close parallel with Piaget's description of the schema of sucking in the absence of the nipple. For both theorists, early changes in sucking are the beginning of psychology.

[2] Modern psychoanalysis, of course, has expanded Freud's doubts about the impulse origin of all thought to include, even in the infant, a conflict-free area of autonomous ego functions.

example, the psychoanalytic child is provided with, at least (*a*) two drive systems, (*b*) a set of reflex structures, and (*c*) a tendency to seek low levels of stimulation.[3] Every theory of development, aloud or by implication, posits a parallel (though obviously differing) definition of the child's strategies and structure.

The strategic assignment—the *functions* ascribed to the child—has been rather more explicitly treated than has the assignment of structures. The psychoanalytic child is biased to be aroused by tidal expressions of sexual impulse and to be calmed by gratifying reflexes; the learning theorist's child is assigned the primary function of a tendency to associate environmental events presented in particular ways; and so on. But the definition of the nature and dimension of cognitive structure remains perhaps the most irksome and persistent problem in the psychology of thought.

What do we assert when we say that the child has mental structures?[4] For limited aspects of psychology—in particular, for perception—sound structural notions have been developed (Garner, 1962). But theorists of development have been remarkably casual in their assignment of mental structures. Almost everyone will agree that there are reflex structures, many will agree that there are preformed maturational structures that will unfold under very low and nonspecific levels of environmental support, a few will accept instinctual structures in the baby [for example, Bowlby's (1969) treatment of the grounds of maternal attachment], but there is little uniformity in the conceptual forms of the assignment. Two issues are embedded here. First, because there is no general theoretical language having to do with mental structures, it is impossible to make systematic comparisons among theorists. The problem is amplified, of course, by the reluctance of developmental theorists (Koffka and Piaget, perhaps, aside) to face the task of laying out their presuppositions on the issue. Second, developmental psychologists, like their colleagues of other special interests, have been shamefully unwilling to talk about a *psychology of content.* It matters a great deal not only that the infant has reflexes, but that he has particular reflexes that are interconnected in a particular way and subject to influence by particular conditions of the environment. To take another instance, it matters not only that the child approaches his surroundings

[3] Again, I make no effort to be complete in this account, to reconcile the conflicting views of psychoanalytic theorists. Rather more important is the fact that the initial assignment of structures and strategies often has more a philosophical than a psychological basis. This may be the point, in fact, where the considerations of philosophers and psychologists become most entangled and most susceptible to joint address.

[4] Two controversies are ignored in the present discussion—whether it is possible to have a psychology that does not use the notion of "mental structures" (I think not), and the existence characteristics of "mental structures" (for me, they are in the mind of the child, but they can be lodged in the mind of the theorist if one wishes).

under certain general *perceptual strategies*, but also (and mightily) that he is a finely tuned perceiver, more sensitive to some aspects of his surroundings than others. In brief, mental structures have content as well as form, and many psychologists, in search of the commanding and essential general principle, have been perilously inattentive to the distinction.

As we look at stimulus–response–reinforcement theories of cognitive motivation, and especially as we look at Piaget's proposals, the absence of a formal (or, for that matter, hesitant and informal) metapsychological account of mental structures will become increasingly painful.

B. Stimulus and World. How Shall We Conceive the Environment? A short step separates consideration of the nature of mental structures and consideration of the curiously mixed problem of the postulations we must make about the nature of the child's environment. In what terms should we "describe" the world of the child? Here again the epistemological and the psychological problems are knotted together, and we cannot easily unpack the distinction between philosophical warrant and empirical justification in the use of words like *stimulus, thing, gestalt, presentation,* or *somatic demand,* to start a list. To be sure, developmental psychologists seem able to proceed with their empirical work without distress about how they define the surround of infants, and it may be useful to speculate about how we manage such insouciance.

Several explanations, all partial, can be proposed. First, psychologists often adopt an attitude of naive realism decorated with the concepts of Newtonian physics. Thus, the category *stimulus* typically contains common objects and such exotica as wavelengths and intensities. Freud probably saw the world of the infant in this way, although he was clearly sensitive to the constructive aspects of early perceptual development. A harsh critic may see the solution as a scientistic evasion of the problem of defining the environment. A second, and much more widespread justification of our relative lack of concern with the problem can be expressed in a combination of conventionalism and the optimism of method. Briefly, one may assert that the terminological systems we use to describe the environment are all flawed to one degree or another. Therefore, one should adopt a set of definitions or assumptions that is personally comfortable or in the traditions of one's research, and then find out *if they work*. Here the optimism of method enters. We will try out our conventions about the environment in empirical studies and see if they permit us to comprehend our obtained data. If they do, all is well; if they do not, then we may examine whether or not we have made the proper assumptions about the nature of the baby's reality. The wisdom of the position is in its recognition that we must make *some* initial assumptions about environment in order to get on with the business of research, and in its further recognition that no single system of description will withstand all criticism. The weakness of the position can be seen in the common observation that the review or reconsideration of postulations almost never takes place. What starts as a conventional ascription quietly becomes (as it probably must) so interconnected with assumptions about mental structure and method that it can no longer be examined without putting the whole conceptual apparatus in jeopardy. And sadly, of course, psychologists of infancy understand relatively so little of the mind of the baby (in another language, have assigned so little variance in his behavior) that partial—even misleading—assumptions about the baby's environment can continue to be used and believed in. It is rather like using only color to organize the variations among animals; elephants will be uniformily differentiated from tigers, and crows from antelopes, but the system would be woefully insufficient even for a descriptive account.

In spite of the ability of empirical workers to proceed with their studies generally undisturbed by epistemological questions, the psychology of infancy will suffer if we do not, philosophers and psychologists together, continue the elaboration of *theory of the environment.* As I have pointed out before (Kessen, 1966), the psychologist of adult perception can get good agreement on useful ways to understand the surround of his subjects; the developmental psychologist will miss several of his most interesting problems if he adopts a conventional and unyielding definition of environment. It is both appropriate and exciting to ask about the child's initial organization of his surround, and to ask how that organization changes and is changed toward adult modes. Just as each major theory of development makes assignments of strategies and structures, so it makes (intricately related) assumptions about the nature of the baby's world.

C. Cognitive Development as Problem-Solving: What Is the Locus of Demand? Consider *infans psychoanalyticus,* equipped with structures (for example, perceptual apparatus) and strategies (for example, the "instruction" to seek certain levels of stimulation), embedded in an environment containing, for example, somatic demands and external presentations. How will he change? Or, to put the question in a form closer to our present task, what is the motivation for cognitive development? One can at least imagine circumstances under which gratification of impulse would be always appropriate and instantaneous. Under such circumstances, cognitive change would not be expected nor, for that matter, would the development of affect. Change, it seems, requires the imposition of a demand, the occurrence of a disequilibrium, or the posing of a problem. These are not equivalent ways of establishing the problem of motivation, but for the moment, I would like to consider cognitive development in general as a form of problem-solving. For the case in hand, the baby's need to suck may not be met fast enough or in quite the correct manner, and a problem is set for him. Looking at cognitive development in this fashion permits the formulation of several subquestions about motivation which can order our examination of developmental theories.

1. What constitutes a demand for change? How is the cognitive problem set?
2. What strategies or functions are brought to bear on the problem? How are particular strategies selected from the ones available to the baby?
3. What changes in mental structure result from the operation of particular strategies on presented problems?
4. What constitutes a solution to the problem posed? How is the problem resolved? To put the question in volitional terms, how does the child know when to stop seeking a solution?

The first of these questions is the one that heads the present section—what is the locus of demand?—and it represents a dimension on which developmental theories of cognition show marked variation.

As noted earlier, the presence of a biological impulse is necessary for a psychoanalytic account, but it is by no means sufficient. Only when the environment does not gratify the somatic demand will a call for change be heard and, as Freud recognized much more clearly than some of his early admirers in psychology, the environment will surely fail to gratify. Baldwin's image of "the insisting self" and "the resisting world" is realized. In brief, the locus of motivational demand in psychoanalytic theory lies in the imbalance between, on one hand, a congenital strategy acting through a congenital structure and, on the other, an arrangement of the environment that does not permit the completion of the strategic move without modification of the structure. Thus, one can see, even in the abridgment of Fig. 1, that new structures (in the first instance, hallucinations of gratification) are formed from the demand—the problem—which is posed by imbalance. Psychoanalysis presents a *disequilibrium* theory of the motivation of cognitive development, and it shares with all other such theories the profound difficulties of specifying in more than a metaphorical way the parameters of imbalance.

Two particularities of Freud's account of the locus of demand should be noted, not only for themselves, but for the light they throw on Piaget's assumptions about motivation. First, the "resisting world" which is essential to disequilibrium in our psychoanalytic baby is critically the world of *other human beings*. The developing cognitive organization of the baby is shaped in substantial measure by the actions of people, especially as they attempt to limit or modify the operation of his initial biological strategies. Second, *anxiety* is given high rank in the explanatory machinery of psychoanalysis. Anxiety, with its several sources, serves as a fundamental agency in guiding the child toward the resolution of disequilibrium.[5]

D. Cognitive Development as Problem-Solving: What Is the Locus of Resolution? We can turn now to the question of what constitutes a solution to a presented problem. What is the event or the arrangement of circumstances which reduces or ends, at least for a while, the demand placed on the baby? Once more, as we shall see, developmental theories diverge impressively. Resolution occurs in the psychoanalytic account when the balance disturbed by a discrepancy between demand and gratification is restored. Crudely put, strategies are applied and structures changed so as to achieve the most gratification that is possible under the prevailing conditions. Impelled by the gratificational strategies, constrained by the limitations of social partners, biased by whatever structures (congenital and acquired) exist, and guided by variation in anxiety, the baby finds a new equilibrium.

It is interesting to note, in anticipation of other theories, that equilibrium in psychoanalytic theory may be reestablished in several ways. The press for expression of impulse may diminish either through gratification or cyclic diminution, the resistance of the constraining environment may decrease, and both of these "problem solutions" may occur through the operation of existing structures. However, the most interesting mode of equilibrium in comprehending cognitive development is the formation of new structures (usually lodged in Ego) that compromise the demand-constraint conflict in a more or less stable way.[6] Mental structures formed in this way—the structures of postponement, sublimation, defense, and effective thought and action—comprise the development of cognition in psychoanalysis.

Of course, in parallel to the difficulties of specifying precisely what constitutes a disequilibrium for the baby are the difficulties of specifying precisely (and, particularly, of predicting) what constitutes an equilibrated solution. Any acquired compromise or balance can be seen as one of an infinite set of combinations of demand and constraint. Unless resolution is

[5] Psychoanalytic theory makes a strong maturational postulation, both in regard to psychosexual development and in regard to the development of ego apparatus. In psychoanalysis, as in other developmental theories, it is difficult to understand the regularity and apparent directionality of cognitive change without appealing to determining physiological influences as well as to the effects of posing cognitive problems to be solved.

[6] Wolff (1960), in his comparison of psychoanalysis and Piaget, has made extensive use of the distinction between procedures to handle cyclic short-term demand and long-term structural change.

made equivalent to the reduction to nihil of one component of the conflict [as Freud occasionally, and Dollard & Miller (1950) uniformly proposed], the theorist is under some obligation to tell us what rules govern the elaboration of a particular compromise. Again, to put the question in more troublesome language, how does the baby (or the set of mental apparatuses that we assign him) recognize that he has solved the presented problem and reachieved equilibrium? We will meet exactly the same *formal* problems in Piaget's design, although the elements that enter into the psychoanalytic and Piagetian disequilibria seem of utterly different constitutions.

III. Stimulus–Response–Reinforcement Theories of Early Cognition

Psychological theories rooted in simple learning are not, strictly speaking and in their own terms, developmental; whatever the age or present cognitive structure of the child, the theories (after the usual nod toward maturation) provide a prescription for producing different behavior. Such innocence of the development of one set of mental structures from preceding ones most agitates Piaget's contempt for learning theories of cognition. Nonetheless, the recent desire of child psychologists to escape the dead grasp of behaviorism as metaphysics has almost certainly diminished our appropriate appreciation of the power and simplicity of a learning-based analysis of early cognitive development, especially in the hands of a sophisticated practitioner (see, in demonstration, Gewirtz, 1961). Here, as in the case of psychoanalysis, my exposition will be introductory and evocative; I want only to expose the major divergences on early cognition and its motivation.[7]

Learning theories are generally free of concern for "mental structure"; they avoid the language of mind and they strain for expression in the language of common observation. Skinner's *tour de force* of explaining the acquisition and use of human language with a basic theoretical vocabulary of three words must stand as model and memorial. But, of course, learning theorists make assignments of structures and strategies to the infant just as other men; the use of an impoverished language—and the constant evasion of its limitations in metaphor, the vernacular, and cumbersome translations—only tends to hide the precise nature of the assignments.

[7] Learning theories can be seen as members of the same category only from a great distance. There are so many variations among the heirs of Spencer, Pavlov, Ebbinghaus, and Thorndike that any summary assertion about "learning" will be either uselessly vague or productive of disagreement. Still, there is enough of a shared attitude toward issues of general method and enough shared divergence from Piaget to justify the risk of categorical treatment.

Consider the most obvious case in point. In order to apply a learning analysis, one must postulate for the child a strategy—the tendency to make associations—and a structure—the representation of associations in habit or memory! Examples can be produced at length; what has not been produced is a systematic survey of the mental apparatus—strategy and structure—implicitly given to the child in the learning theorists' discussion of acquisition and extinction, generalization and differentiation, memory and forgetting. These capacities or activities are not part of the environment and they are not (solely) part of the theorist's own cognitive equipment; somehow or other, "learning" (together with other essential explanatory notions) is an activity of the child which implies the possession of certain modes of dealing with the world and certain ways of representing and preserving the results of such interaction. But the answers of the learning analyst to questions about mental structure and strategy are clear and simple. The subject matter of development is change in behavior over age, and the empirical domain for the study of cognitive development consists of the topographically describable responses that the baby makes. The sole "strategy" required, if one could persuade the learning folk to use so uncongenial a term, is the tendency to make associations, the strategy of learning.

As I suggested earlier, learning analysts of development have cared little about the epistemological problems that lie under the definition of the environment. With a commitment to reliable and ultimately physicalistic description, and with an apparent unreadiness to recognize how determining of one's observations are the first assumptions made about the nature of the baby's world, the associationists have plainly not encountered the puzzles of the constructivists. If the baby's environment is stipulated to contain wavelengths and intensities, then questions cannot even be asked about how he comes to develop the adult's view of reality.[8] So straightforward an attitude toward the psychoepistemological tangle may, in fact, move us more quickly toward a better understanding of cognitive development; psychologists have in the past paused at their peril to consider interesting philosophical questions. But of the basic proposition of the learning analysts there can be no doubt. The categories and dimensions that are used (with whatever efficacy) to describe the environment of the adult are the categories and dimensions that will be applied in the study of children, even of the newborn infant.

The essentially motivational issues for learning analyses are once more the locus of demand for change and the procedures for resolving a presented

[8] The use of the highly abstract dimensions of physical measurement as a *first postulation* of the baby's environment seems curious in any case, even if we agree that the world of the child is not our world.

problem; in the terms of a learning analysis, how are cognitive problems posed and how are they resolved? Accounts based on different theoretical attitudes vary, of course, but the key to them all is the ingenious, fluid, and powerful concept of *reinforcement.* In starkest form, the argument may be advanced that problems are set by whatever operations, events, or circumstances make the effective application of reinforcement possible; problems are resolved when the child consistently behaves so as to make the delivery of reinforcement appropriate. The position is neither circular nor trivial. To be sure, the argument would be stronger if an independent definition had been achieved for the setting operations that make reinforcement effective, but neither specifications based upon physiological considerations (for example, the reduction of need) nor upon critical considerations (for example, the lowest possible level of stimulation) have proved satisfactory. But even without independent specification of *drive* or other setting operations, the notion of reinforcement remains the single most important idea in twentieth-century psychology.

Let me repeat in slightly modified form the strong argument advanced earlier. Whatever "problem" is posed for the child to solve (and I will consider the matter shortly), it is to some degree "solved" when reinforcement is forthcoming. Take the following example: A baby is being taught to turn his head to the right when a bell sounds. Whenever he in fact turns his head, he is reinforced by a taste of milk. The degree of his "problem solution" is measured by the conformation of his behavior to the demand made, and his behavior is changed as a function of the intensive and temporal characteristics of the reinforcing event. In generalized form, the questions of problem setting and problem solution are answered elegantly by the learning theorists. With sufficient control over setting operations and reinforcing events (together with skill in procedures for shaping behavior), any demand can be made and any behavioral (and, implicitly, any mental) change can be effected.

The obvious insufficiency of simple physiological needs or drives as problem-setting occasions for human beings has required an emphasis, in learning accounts of cognitive development, on the *social partner* and on *fear.* By association with primary reinforcement of various sorts, the mother (and, by generalization, other human beings) becomes a potent reinforcing event. There is an interesting and developing literature of what particular aspects of the human being come to serve as the focal source of reinforcement, but there is general agreement that approval of the other (sometimes subtly conveyed) is a major factor in changing the behavior of children. Learning theories, as has often been noted, turn out to be teaching theories, and the power of the teacher is in his ability to control reinforcing events.

The role of fear in changing the behavior of children has not been so often or so explicitly noted. Presumably, the absence or disapproval of the adult produces or comes to produce concern and fear in the child which can be used (however unintentionally) as a motivation for cognitive change. Thus, other human beings (particularly, parents and teachers) play a crucial *double* part in development. By a number of procedures (frowning, turning away, harsh words) the other person sets the critical occasions where social reinforcement will be effective. Then, when the learner has brought his behavior to a satisfactory level of conformity with the desires of the teacher, the teacher can become the reinforcer of the desired behavior by smiling, accepting, approving behavior. For all its simplicity, the view that sees another human being as the central locus of demand *and* the primary locus of resolution in the problem-solving of cognitive change represents well the fact that much teaching, from crib to graduate school, is a complex social act that involves bringing the behavior of the learner into line with the expectations or desires of the teacher.

Two somewhat surprising implications can be drawn from the foregoing account. In the first place, there is no obvious expectation that *development* (or, in a more limited sense, change over age) will be as regular and uniform as common observation attests. Only by making heavy use of maturationally determined sequencing of behavior and of readiness to learn, or by assuming implicitly some kind of simplicity–to–complexity movement by the child, or by maintaining that all children are exposed to much the same kind of demand–reinforcement occasions, can the strict learning analyst make sense of the fact that remarkable regularities exist, across time and culture, in the cognitive development of the very young child (see, for the case of language, Lenneberg, 1967). Any one of these assumptions either flaws the elegance of a learning analysis, puts a demand on the theorist to state the exact relations connecting the conditions of learning with the additional assumptions, or both.

Equally consequential is the second surprising implication. In a learning account of development—at least, in the exaggerated portrait I have drawn—there is no necessary relation between the cognitive (or behavioral) change achieved and the procedures used to control the change. A child may learn problems in physics to please his parents; he may memorize a poem to be let out of the schoolroom; a baby may avoid the bookshelves because they are associated with the displeasure of the parents. This discrepancy between the posing of a problem and the means of its solution has been examined closely by Merleau-Ponty (1963); for him, the separation of problem and solution produces "meaningless" behavior. Only when there is a connection among the child's present mental structures, the demand put on him, *and* the nature of the solution can behavioral or mental change be seen as "meaningful."[9]

Perhaps the point can be sharpened by comparing the role of the social partner in a learning account with that role in psychoanalysis. For the psychoanalytic child, the parent poses problems for the economy of gratification. He does not so much determine the shape of a solution (as the learning analyst will); rather, his behavior (anger, anxiety, a caress) makes a demand on the child's cognitive apparatus which he must use or modify in order to reestablish a demand–constraint equilibrium. In the sense that the problem and its solution are relevant to the impulse under which the child is operating and to his present defensive structures, the change he makes will be meaningful. The opposition can nowadays be best seen in the disagreement about the symptom conceived as part of a complicated cognitive and affective mental organization, and the symptom as something that can be changed by the manipulation of reinforcement events, a disagreement which fundamentally separates traditional psychotherapists from behavior therapists. Although it is easy to overdraw the distinction that Merleau-Ponty makes, we will better see Piaget's peculiar contribution if we keep in mind the fact that a learning analysis sees a cognitive problem as a goal to be reached rather than as a demand for change in current structure.

To the degree that the learning analysts see all behavior as motivated by primary drive and its derivatives, to that degree does the learning position represent a "hot" theory of cognitive change. However, as renovations are made in the definition of setting operations for the effectiveness of reinforcement, the learning attitude comes to depend less and less on somatic demand as source.[10] In another sense, of course, the theory is very "cold"; if what can be learned is independent of present need and present structure, cognitive change is a fact of the world rather than a fact of the person.

The great conceptual advantage of the older learning attitude is its

[9] It matters, for Merleau-Ponty, "whether the response has a meaning and is related to the very essence of the problem, or whether, on the contrary, it is a stereotyped reaction evoked by an aspect of the situation which is abstract and external to it" (1963, p. 101).

[10] The most far-reaching attempt to encompass cognition in the frame of learning theory is Berlyne's (1960). By calling on a wider range of motivating conditions (for example, "epistemic curiosity") and by expanding enormously the compass of the concept "response," Berlyne can plausibly talk about (say) Piaget's observations on infants. But, as Piaget (1964) points out, Berlyne has thereby run into "learning theory" homologs of the traditionally uncomfortable notions of "mental operations" and "equilibration."

relative freedom from the staggering problems of equilibration. Routine procedures can be used to define effective reinforcements and the strong assertion can be made that change will occur when properly arranged reinforcements occur. It is an advantage that will keep the learning position strongly connected with the explanation of cognitive development. The cost of simplicity may be high—is only meaningless change explained?—but the power of the assertion cannot be ignored.

IV. Piaget on the Motivation of Cognitive Development

Piaget comes on stage as liberator from the chains of the flesh. Although he explicitly declares the contribution to cognitive development of society, experience, and maturation—and once (Piaget, 1959) proposed a six-factor taxonomy of acquisition—he puts his most forceful arguments in support of *equilibration* as a mechanism for change. Neither physiological deficit, fear, nor the approval of a social partner is necessary for cognitive change. In his exhilarating conception, the child can move from the primitive beginnings of the newborn inevitably, but without the pressing force of impulse, toward the epistemological theories of the adult in a coherent sequence of mental structures.

At the beginning of life, the child is possessed of a set of reflex structures which organize his world in the acts of sucking, looking, grasping, and "phonation." Piaget describes these structures (or schemata) as groups of "elements joined together in a totality" and, as we shall see, the definition of "elements" is a central problem for Piaget. In any case, they cannot be thought of as "responses" in the traditional sense, and seem rather to be approximately what, for adults, would be considered environmental events, behavioral events, and the relations linking them.[11] One possible reading of Piaget is to see a schema as made up of an operation or function and the domain of elements or events over which the operation is effective. Take, as an example, the child who has sucked effectively when presented with his mother's breast; the relevant schema may be represented thus:

$$\mathrm{Sc}_{\alpha}\begin{Bmatrix} x_1 & \cdot & \cdot \\ \cdot & \cdot & x_n \end{Bmatrix},$$

where x_1 stands for "the breast" in the baby's current perceptual system,

[11] My extraction of Piaget is confined to sensory-motor—that is, preverbal—development. It remains open whether or not so simplified a treatment can be transformed easily to account for conceptual change.

and Sc_α stands for the activity of sucking which is appropriate to x_1 and, it may be guessed, to other suckable elements as well. Piaget assigns a number of such structures to the newborn child and then makes a case for their standing at the origin of thought.

In addition to the primitive structures, as every student in introductory psychology has learned over the last decade, Piaget assigns two strategies to the baby—conservative *assimilation* and innovative *accommodation.* In simplest and strongest statement, Piaget's theory of cognitive development deals with the enlargement, differentiation, and combination of congenital reflex structures and their successors constructed under the rules of assimilation and accommodation. The strategies are as much a part of our biological heritage as are the structures, and their operation governs the development of man from first breath to logic.

Piaget's conception of the baby's environment is also contained in the proposal of *elements in a structure.* How is the environment represented in elements? Much of Piaget's work on perception, summarized in translation (Piaget, 1969), bears on the empirical aspects of the question, but it is more to our present purpose to indicate Piaget's sensitivity to the complicated epistemological issues and his remarkable neutrality about the "ultimate" nature of the world. More than any other psychologist outside the Gestalt school, Piaget has understood that philosophical stands determine the direction and eventually the outcomes of research; even so, he has provided a model which permits a wide range of choice in the specification of environment. His advantage is great in not making dogmatic claims about reality from which no escape can then be found. However, it is worth noting that his position demands of a theory of development a tandem epistemology and an associated perceptual theory. Clearly, for Piaget, the world is constructed rather than given or "learned in the strict sense"; beyond that giant first step, the issue is for research.

When we come to the motivation of cognitive change, we find that Piaget has cast the problem in unusual terms. There is no motivating event comparable to impulse or drive; no physiological or social demand is put on the child. The call for a cognitive change is *a perturbing event,* an event which puts a current structure into a condition of disequilibrium. Consider our breast-sucking infant. When offered an artificial pacifier, the sucking schema may be placed in disequilibrium. The fundamental mechanism of cognitive change for Piaget—the "motivation" for cognitive development, if you will—is the occurrence of such disequilibrium. Faced with a perturbing event, the child may follow one of three paths. He may assimilate the event to an existing scheme with consequent enlargement of its domain. Or he may, under certain circumstances, accommodate to the event, thereby changing the schema currently in effect. Or he may not show any change in cognitive structure at all. If the perturbing event (x_p) is a pacifier experienced for the first time, one may expect assimilation and a simple addition to the domain of Sc_α thus:

$$\mathrm{Sc}_\alpha \begin{Bmatrix} x_1 & \cdot & \cdot \\ \cdot & \cdot & x_n \end{Bmatrix} \xrightarrow{\overset{x_p}{\downarrow}} \mathrm{Sc}_\alpha \begin{Bmatrix} x_1 & \cdot & \cdot \\ \cdot & x_n & x_p \end{Bmatrix}.$$

A more "demanding" perturbation (say, his thumb) may require the child to accommodate his sucking schema. Note that, when the breast is next presented, one may expect that the new schema will assimilate it:

$$\mathrm{Sc}_\alpha \begin{Bmatrix} x_1 & \cdot & \cdot \\ \cdot & \cdot & x_n \end{Bmatrix} \xrightarrow{\overset{x_p}{\downarrow}} \mathrm{Sc}_\beta\{x_p\} \xrightarrow{\overset{x_1}{\downarrow}} \mathrm{Sc}_\beta\{x_p \quad x_1\}.$$

Finally, the case of "impossible perturbations" must be listed. If Sc_α is confronted with the onset of a ceiling light in the baby's room, no change in the sucking schema can be expected. Of course, light onset can, strictly speaking, be considered a perturbation only if it is related to the domain of the looking schemata available, but the problem is an interesting one in its forecast of later interschematic assimilation.

Before addressing the worrisome questions of what constitutes the locus of demand and what constitutes the locus of resolution in the Piagetian system, let me underline the observation that the sequence *schema, perturbation, assimilation/accommodation* can be seen as a motivational arrangement. Piaget does not mean for it to apply to all cognitive change, but it has certain unique properties. Mention has already been made of its independence of tissue deficit or social reinforcement. Perhaps as important is the intimate relation between the problem-setting event, the structural change, and the problem termination. In Merleau-Ponty's sense, cognitive change of the kind described here is meaningful, and development can truly be considered ". . . not as a fixation of a given force on outside objects which are also given, but as a progressive and discontinuous structuration . . . of behavior" (Merleau-Ponty, 1963, p. 177). A change is made in mind that is directly related to the demand for change. The baby does not suck the pacifier because he is gratified or because he is reinforced for so doing; sucking the pacifier is the inevitable consequence of the relation between his cognitive (here, sensory–motor) structures and a presentation in the environment. Incidentally, this reading of Piaget frees the theory somewhat from the demands of *telos* and suggests that the inevitability of development is not based on preformed structures.[12]

But what constitutes a perturbation? And what determines whether the consequence of a perturbing event is assimilation, accommodation, or no change? Piaget has approached the questions several times (Piaget, 1957, 1960, 1967, in particular) and several characteristics of his answers can be found. Foremost, the locus of demand is neither in the person nor in the world. A problem is posed by the exigency of an environmental event *in relation to* present mental structure. Piaget describes the connection between demand and structure for the case of infantile looking:

> . . . the subject looks neither at what is too familiar, because he is in a way surfeited with it, nor at what is too new because this does not correspond to anything in his schema. . . In short, looking [is] . . . put to use progressively in increasingly varied situations (Piaget, 1952, p. 37).

On another occasion, Piaget speaks of an "optimal zone of interest for what is neither too well known nor too new," and the theme of productive novelty is found often in his pages. Plausible and appealing, the concept of optimal novelty leads inexorably toward several fundamental conceptual difficulties. In order to be more than a way of speaking, Piaget's proposal about the setting of problems must be given some quantitative statement, however primitive. Piaget has emphasized, particularly for the very young child, the primacy of assimilation—the essentially conservative character of early mind. He has also reminded us that some mental structures are more resistant to change than others, just as, in precise analogy, some conceptual schemata are more capable of reversibility than others. He has proposed a distinction between actual intrusions (or perturbations) and virtual intrusions (Piaget, 1967). He has noted, as has Wolff (1960), the need to consider separately short-term recurrent demands and problems that require permanent change. Yet, each of these dimensions represents a new call for refined statement, for parametric analysis.

Of particular interest to a group of philosophers and psychologists is the epistemological problem alluded to earlier—how shall we conceive of the

[12] American critics have tended to leave Piaget with no out on the issue of inevitability. We have maintained both (*a*) that his expectation of regularity of sequence makes Piaget a preformist, and (*b*) that the sequences are not that regular after all! Piaget finds the charge of preformism peculiarly off the mark; there exists, under his reading, the possibility of alternative patterns of development when problems are presented in untypical ways. However, there is a biologically determined fit between given and got; human beings *belong* in this world and have been selected for it. We will be hard pressed, particularly for the child in the first months of life, to devise alternative and basic problem presentations for the young infant.

elements that enter cognitive structure and the operators or functions that govern them? In his works on infancy, Piaget (1951, 1952, 1954a) has given brilliant and detailed illustrations of his conception at work in teasing apart psychoepistemological problems; what remains incomplete is the systematic and dimensional explication of the different structures that infants maintain. One group of solutions can be based on the assumption of common elements—present structures begin to assimilate a presentation because it has elements already in the domain, and they are put in disequilibrium when novel elements are encountered among the old. Dramatically, this group of solutions requires attention to the definition of element and operator. I am reluctant to fuss at Piaget overmuch in this matter, because his concern with such root questions is so much greater than that of his contemporaries, but it may not be amiss to suggest two potential sources of incompleteness. Piaget, too, may underestimate the content-relevant variety that exists in the structures of early mind, and further, his occasional ambiguity about conceptual point of view—whether he stands with the observer or with the baby—has kept him from becoming deeply committed to specifying the dimensions of problem posing, of disequilibration.

Once a problem has been posed to the child in a perturbation, it is resolved, according to Piaget, by the reestablishment of equilibrium through the process of *equilibration*. Piaget is richly aware that the notion of equilibration troubles many of the people who study him, and he has devoted many pages of the serial *Études d'épistémologie génétique* to a discussion of the process. Mischel's fine analysis of Piaget on equilibration affords me the chance to be brief in summarizing several aspects of Piaget's proposals and in addressing a few questions to them.

Piaget once more and properly makes much of the relational character of equilibration; equilibrium is a system of activities and its reestablishment is based on the baby's active compensation for disequilibrating events. Moreover, except for the structures of logic, no human system is in permanent equilibrium, and it is especially the case for the preverbal child that equilibrium is only gradually approached and is always incomplete. But, given a set of congenital reflex structures, the rules of assimilation and accommodation, and a surround that contains perturbations, the baby will show progressive and inevitable cognitive development. If schemata are changed to accommodate the just novel, the barely assimilable, each accommodation and equilibration will lead to another problem, to another equilibration, and so on. So long as problems are posed to existing structures which do not permit easy assimilation but which are not beyond accommodation, change will occur and each successive structure will represent a cognitive gain. The traditional problems of the "motivation" of cognitive development—either in push (impulse) or pull (reinforcement) form—are plainly and simply vacated!

But what are the rules of equilibration? Like any other balance theorist, Piaget cannot escape a distressing onrush of nonunique problem resolutions unless he tells us how one solution comes about rather than another—the problem, if you like, of choice. Again, Piaget gives his answer in several places in several ways, but the heart of that answer has two parts—a general strategy and some comments on tactics. The basic strategy is *a principle of least effort.* That equilibrating change will occur which permits a maximum of activities and a maximum openness of exchange among structures. The process of equilibration tends toward a set of structures which have as their domain the largest possible field of presentations and which permit the most mobility through the field with the simplest mental transformations.[13] The ideal and only perfectly equilibrated structures are, thus, logic.

The tactical considerations that determine the selection of a particular problem resolution are frankly economic. When both assimilation and accommodation are possible, or when two possible schematic solutions are incompatible, an assessment is made of "gain and loss." The gain of new mobility and new simplicity must be measured against the cost of accommodatory change. Consider the young infant:

> . . . one of two schemata produces only a slight cost in accommodation but results in only a slight gain (from the point of view of an easy success or already acquired knowledge) while the other either produces a more difficult success that reinforces the feeling of one's own power or it produces a gain in new knowledge: in this case the question is of knowing if these anticipated values sufficiently balance the effort (the cost) of accommodation (Piaget, 1959, p. 48).

An important and, for me, worrisome passage. Although Piaget points toward dimensions of an economic analysis, he also speaks to two remarkable assumptions. First, he jeopardizes the independence of his theory from traditional motivational conceptions in his allusion to the reinforcement value of "a more difficult success." The words can easily be read as a species of White's (1959) competence motivation. Second, and more important, he makes a staggering assignment of cognitive ability to the infant in his reference to "anticipated values." Is the pattern of accommodation to be determined by the *baby's* assessment of cost and gain? If so, we will need a powerful theory indeed to understand a (say) twelve-month-old child who can assemble, compare, and choose among alternative paths

[13] The contrast between the basic strategy of psychoanalysis and Piaget's is here focused. The psychoanalytic child builds compromise structures which maximize gratification; Piaget's child builds compromise structures which maximize fast simple access to information.

toward the overall goal of mobile thought. If not—if Piaget refers rather to the observer's assessment of anticipated values—it is not obvious how that assessment becomes relevant to the baby's problem solution. But, however we interpret parts of the quotation, it fairly represents Piaget's general commitment to equilibration as an economic process. It also fairly represents the great distance we must go before equilibration becomes sufficiently subtle and detailed an idea to guide specific research and to generate specific predictions about the course of cognitive development.

Having proposed a variation in conceptual temperature among theories of cognitive development, I am tempted to overdraw the "coldness" of Piaget's position. One can make due allowance for the occurrence of maturational change and simple learning, and then stake out a major claim to understand much of cognitive development without recourse to traditionally motivational, affective, or energetic postulates. Problems posed in the "optimal zone" would carry the child forward without distress, and the adult who achieved the kind of mobile balance which is postulated for logic across a wide range of his cognition would be ultimately "cool"—without strong affect and, incidentally, without Unconscious. Whatever event he encountered—the rise of cyclic drives, variation in the behavior of others, a problem in natural science—our ideal cognizer would have available a solution or a way toward a solution that would not demand the occurrence of affect. So radical a position warrants further exploration, particularly as it bears on implications for child-rearing practice, education, and psychopathology. Mandler's (1965) proposals about the affective and motivational consequences of interrupting well-organized patterns of behavior are on the way toward a "cold" theory of affect. He suggests a conceptual apparatus that allows us to imagine a cognitive theory of many affective phenomena currently cast into an impulse–demand or a drive–reinforcement language.

But, however we may extend in imagination certain implications of Piaget's position, it must be made clear that Piaget does not draw them. He rejects as "at the antipodes of our position" the kind of "intellectualist" argument I have presented to justify exploration of the cognitive basis of affect. Certainly one can make polar contrasts between the energetics of affect and the structures of intellectualization, just as one can make polar contrasts between use values and knowledge values, but the relation between thought and affect is, for Piaget, intimate and pervasive. He writes of a year-old child's behavior:

> . . . action has value, . . . it is desirable because it is difficult, because it presents a resistance to the habitual power of one's activity. . . . When the difficulty is not too great, [and] does not seem insurmountable to him, the obstacle itself creates a value [for the child] in the form of a need to overcome it (Piaget, 1954b, p. 41).

For Piaget, "affectivity" shows a developmental course parallel to and invariably intertwined with cognition.

Other human beings, and especially the parents, have two chief parts to play in Piaget's account. They are problems to be solved, aliment to the child's schemata, and they will be "constructed" over the first year of life as are other parts of the environment. In addition, other people serve as posers of problems. They function not primarily as objects of gratification or as reinforcing agents; rather, they introduce perturbations of existing structures. If the other person is a skillful teacher, he will introduce the perturbations at exactly the correct place in the optimal zone of accommodation and thereby advance—even speed—the development of the child. Thus, Piaget can, in his own strict terms, account for variation in the rate and the asymptotes of cognitive development.[14]

Piaget has contributed more to our knowledge about the course of cognitive development than any other man, and in my view, he has added more to the narrow land between philosophy and psychology than any psychologist since Baldwin. In a way, it is a pity that Piaget—probably because he has so well-tuned a sense of the child thinking—has been unwilling to enounce a radically cognitive theory of development. Even so, Piaget's theory is the best worked out "cold" theory we have, and it is textured and suggestive enough to warrant extension in detail.

V. A Last Word

The sharply drawn divisions among three theoretical attitudes that organize the present article were meant only to form a frame within which more detailed and subtle analysis could be carried on. My dogmatic and necessarily superficial summaries can, at best, serve to structure a fairly large group of questions about the motivation of cognitive development that philosophers and psychologists can profitably approach together.

[14] The problem of *error* in theories of cognitive development needs close study. The cognitive mistakes of the psychoanalytic child must be motivated; that is, related to his attempts to achieve gratification. The learning theorist's child can presumably learn error as easily as truth if the contingencies of reinforcement are properly arranged. The position is saved from absurdity, of course, by the fact that much early learning is not based on socially mediated reinforcement, but is dependent on setting operations and reinforcements arranged by nature. Piaget, on first glance, suffers from the peculiar problem of not being able to account for cognitive error at all. Mental structures may be incomplete or partial, but they cannot be wrong if the child possesses structures in a state of tentative equilibrium. Piaget must not only assume that early structures are less well equilibrated than later ones, but also that degrees of equilibrium mark degrees of error.

Somehow we must come closer to an understanding of what constitutes mental structure, of how we can conceive the enormous variety of mind, of the nature of error and superstition, and of the development of will. Obviously, no single theoretical account will be adequate to the tasks; we require both openness and the expectation of theoretical diversity. And, even more, we require the working through of particular developmental phenomena in detail sufficient to justify comparison of varying theoretical accounts.

References

Berlyne, D. E. Les équivalences psychologiques et les notions quantitatives. In D. E. Berlyne & J. Piaget (Eds.), *Théorie du comportement et operations.* Études d'épistémologie génétique, 12. Paris: Presses Univ. de France, 1960.

Bowlby, J. *Attachment and loss.* Vol. 1. London: Hogarth, 1969.

Dollard, J., & Miller, N. E. *Personality and psychotherapy.* New York: McGraw-Hill, 1950.

Freud, S. *The outline of psychoanalysis.* New York: Norton, 1949.

Garner, W. R. *Uncertainty and structure as psychological concepts.* New York: Wiley, 1962.

Gewirtz, J. L. A learning analysis of the effects of normal stimulation, privation, and deprivation on the acquisition of social motivation and attachment. In B. M. Foss (Ed.), *Determinants of infant behavior.* Vol. 1. New York: Wiley, 1961.

Kessen, W. Questions for a theory of cognitive development. In H. W. Stevenson (Ed.), The concept of development. *Monographs of the Society for Research in Child Development,* 1966, **31,** Whole No. 107.

Lenneberg, E. H. *Biological foundations of language.* New York: Wiley, 1967.

Mandler, G. The interruption of behavior. In M. R. Jones (Ed.), *Nebraska symposium on motivation.* Lincoln: Univ. of Nebraska Press, 1965.

Merleau-Ponty, M. *The structure of behavior.* London: Methuen, 1963.

Piaget, J. *Play, dreams, and imitation in childhood.* New York: Norton, 1951.

Piaget, J. *The origins of intelligence in children.* New York: International Univ. Press, 1952.

Piaget, J. *The construction of reality in the child.* New York: Basic Books, 1954. (a)

Piaget, J. *Les relations entre l'affectivité et l'intelligence dans le développement mental de l'enfant.* Paris: Centre de Documentation Univ., 1954. (b)

Piaget, J. Logique et équilibre dans les comportements du sujet. In L. Apostel, B. Mandelbrot, & J. Piaget (Eds.), *Logique et équilibre.* Études d'épistémologie génétique, 2. Paris: Presses Univ. de France, 1957.

Piaget, J. Apprentissage et connaissance. In P. Gréco & J. Piaget (Eds.), *Apprentissage et connaissance.* Études d'épistémologie génétique, 7. Paris: Presses Univ. de France, 1959.

Piaget, J. The general problems of the psychobiological development of the child. In J. M. Tanner & B. Inhelder (Eds.), *Discussions on child development.* Vol. IV. London: Tavistock, 1960.

Piaget, J. Development and learning. *Journal of Research in Science Teaching,* 1964, **2,** 176–186.

Piaget, J. The role of the concept of equilibrium in psychological explanation. In J. Piaget, *Six psychological studies.* Edited by D. Elkind. New York: Random House, 1967.

Piaget, J. *The mechanisms of perception.* New York: Basic Books, 1969.

Rapaport, D. The structure of psychoanalytic theory: A systematizing attempt. In S. Koch (Ed.), *Psychology: A study of a science.* Vol. III. New York: McGraw-Hill, 1959.

Skinner, B. F. *Verbal behavior.* New York: Appleton, 1957.

White, R. W. Motivation reconsidered: The concept of competence. *Psychological Review,* 1959, **66,** 297–333.

Wolff, P. H. The developmental psychologies of Jean Piaget and psychoanalysis. *Psychological Issues,* 1960, **2,** Whole No. 5.

PIAGET: COGNITIVE CONFLICT AND THE MOTIVATION OF THOUGHT

Theodore Mischel

I. Introduction: Human Motives and Theories of Motivation

A. The Concept of Motivation. To say that someone had a motive for doing X is, ordinarily, to imply that he did X in order to achieve certain ends; it is to explain his conduct by connecting it with his desires and beliefs, with what he wants to achieve or avoid and how he thinks this can be done. If we claim that someone had a motive for what he did, we are thus ruling out various other possible explanations of his behavior—for example, that it was done absentmindedly; or that it was simply a habit, the sort of thing he regularly does in such circumstances; or that he was overcome by some passion, or by some nervous agitation, etc. Instead, we account for his behavior in terms of what Peters (1958) has called the "purposive rule-following model," that is, by relating what he did to the context of aims, beliefs, desires, plans, norms, and the like, that is operative in the conduct of socialized human beings.

It has also been pointed out that we do not ordinarily raise questions about a man's motives, unless the conduct in question is of some importance, and is up for assessment because there is a suspicion that the person "is not sticking to the standard moves" (Peters, 1958, p. 34), that is, that his reasons differ from those which are typical and socially acceptable for such conduct. This may well make it advisable to focus a general discussion of motivation on the way wants are used to explain conduct rather than on our more restricted use of "motives" (Alston, 1967b, pp. 400–401). But even if we think of motivation in this wider sense, some connection with justification seems to emerge again when we turn to the motivation of thought, as contrasted with action; for there is an important difference between the situations in which we appeal to a man's desires in order to explain his deeds, and those in which such an appeal is made in order to explain his thoughts. If we are told that someone did X because he wanted A and thought that this was the way to get it, this is no way suggests that his doing X was unjustified, or involved a departure from the "standard moves"; far from it, this sort of explanation usually enables us to understand which standard move he was making, which of the normal reasons for acting were operative in this case. But if we are told that he thought P because he wanted A, this surely does suggest that P is not what one would normally think in such a context, or that his thinking P may not be justifiable in terms of the intellectual requirements of the situation. Ordinarily, "Why does he think P?" is answered by giving the evidence and line of reasoning that led him to think P, and insofar as evidence and reasoning justify his thinking P, his desires, whatever they may be, are simply irrelevant. It is only insofar as his thinking P cannot be justified by evidence and reasoning that we look to his desires in order to explain why, nevertheless, he thought it.

There is, of course, "wishful thinking" in which the criteria of logic and evidence operative in our normal thinking are suspended. In such cases, as in daydreams and the like, what a man wants does, indeed, determine what he thinks. Again, thoughts sometimes simply occur to someone in ways that seem unrelated, or incongruous, to the context; a person may be haunted by certain thoughts, etc., and in such cases we do look to his desires and emotions for an explanation. But such explanations seem inappropriate when a man is capable of justifying his thinking on the basis of evidence and reasoning.

This does not mean that common sense fails to recognize motivational factors in directed ("logical") thinking. For, in the first place, the constraints on such thinking are rarely so tight as to allow only one possible conclusion. There is often more than one way of selecting and interpreting the facts, more than one way of seeing similarities and differences, more than one way of weighing the relative importance of various factors. We know that there can be legitimate disagreement about the cogency of certain bits of evidence, about the way the evidence is to be interpreted, and about the inferences that can be drawn from it, and we often attribute such differences between people to their different wants and interests—they differ because they are committed to different theses about these phenomena, because they want to establish different theories. It is no strain on ordinary language to say that certain thinkers adopted, for example, the Marxist interpretation of history, or stimulus–response behavior theory, from among the theories that seemed possible *because* they wanted to prove that. . . When reasonable people can arrive at different conclusions about the same situation, an appeal to their different motivations seems to be an appropriate way of explaining why they differ. Second, we also recognize that if such desires are strong enough, they can lead thinkers to jump to unwarranted conclusions; they can even make a man manipulate the evidence and twist the inferences that can be drawn from it, without realizing that this is what he is doing. We know that a man's desire that P be true may be great enough to make him treat the evidence for P as much stronger than it actually is, and so deceive himself. Directed thinking is subject to many distortions, and such distortions are often explained in terms of the thinker's wants and emotions.

There is another range of questions related to motivation which arises in our ordinary thinking about thinking. We know that people have different interests, that some find it fascinating to think about matters which others find totally dull, that some persist in their efforts to solve difficult problems while others quickly lose interest, and so forth. And we may want to know why what interests some fails to interest others, what keeps people interested in something and what makes them lose interest, and so on. Here there seem to be at least two sorts of answers that are normally given. One has to do with the person; it appeals to the intellectual background and training which enable him to appreciate the nature of the issue or problem, etc., and to such character traits as persistence, curiosity, etc. A second kind of answer that is ordinarily given has to do with structural properties of the situation about which the person is thinking; here one might talk about such things as its novelty, or complexity, the challenges it presents and the surprises it holds, etc. No doubt, this raises all sorts of further questions about the reasons for such individual differences, about why novelty and complexity should be appealing and about the extent to which they are in the eye of the beholder, etc., but these further questions are rarely pushed very far in our ordinary, common-sense accounts.

The foregoing is, of course, sketchy. It is intended only as a rough reminder of some of the general features of the framework in which we ordinarily think about human motivation.

B. Psychological Theories of Motivation. This framework contrasts sharply with that involved in most psychological theorizing about motivation. For most experimental psychologists, motivation has to do, first, with the instigation and energizing of behavior—that is, what triggers behavior and what controls the degree of its vigor. Second, psychologists see motivational questions as related to the factors that are thought to determine the "direction" of behavior—that is, what "internal factors" determine approach or avoidance, as well as the selection of the specific responses that occur in such behaviors; these questions are connected with questions about "reinforcement," the "rewards" that can strengthen responses, and related matters of "learning" (see, for example, Hunt, 1965, pp. 191–194). The cognitive structures, which are the core of our commonsense accounts of human motivation, have no natural place in such psychological theories of motivation.

In order to understand why the framework in which psychologists think about motivation differs so radically from that which we ordinarily use, one must recall the historical context in which the concept of motivation was introduced into experimental psychology. Pavlov, Thorndike, Watson, and many of the theorists who followed them, took the reflex arc as their model for the explanation of behavior. Given this model, motivation would really be unnecessary if a given stimulus always elicited a given response. But since it does not—for example, food does not trigger eating if the animal is sated—an additional inner trigger for behavior had to be introduced. Motivation thus came to be regarded as an inner state of tension which sets off the response to an outer stimulus, and it seemed natural to identify these inner states with various physiological deficits or needs. In this way motivation became an inner state of "drive" which provides the "dynamism," the energy or force, that explains the vigor of the response triggered by the outer stimulus. Woodworth, who introduced the term "drive," explained it by analogy to a machine:

> The drive here is the power applied to make the mechanism go. . . The material and structure of the mechanism determine the direction that shall be taken by the power applied. . . . But the mechanism without the power is inactive, dead, lacking in disposable energy (Woodworth, 1918, p. 37).

So, while motivation ordinarily has to do with the goals toward which behavior is directed, the drive state which psychologists came to equate with motivation was, so far forth, a directionless activator of behavior, used only to explain its initiation and vigor.

"Learning" was supposed to explain the direction of behavior, but in order to account for learning one had to explain why rewards (for example, food when the animal is hungry) serve to strengthen the responses that are rewarded. Theorists like Hull (1943) did this by assuming that these rewards reduce an internal tissue deficit or need, and such drive reduction reinforces the response that has been made to the stimulus, thus stamping in the connection. Moreover, since drive can hardly be a completely general activator of behavior—after all, the hungry animal is not "driven" to drink—Hull also postulated an internal drive stimulus (S_d) which, together with the external stimulus, played a role in the selection of the response. Drive ("motivation") thus came to be connected, via learning, with reinforcement and internal factors that determine the "direction" of behavior. But this, of course, did not involve any notion of a goal towards which the animal directs its behavior; on the contrary, such "cognitive" notions were deliberately avoided by these theorists as "unscientific" and "anthropomorphic," and the intent was to sketch a mechanism that could explain how seemingly goal-directed behavior gets stamped into the animal.

The account of motivation provided by stimulus–response behavior theory has, of course, become vastly more sophisticated and complex than this—Hull himself introduced "secondary reinforcement" and other refinements, others elaborated various "acquired drives," and the like. Still, behavior theory has not departed far from these historical roots in its basic conceptualization of human motivation. As one psychologist recently put it, Hull and Thorndike

> . . . led several generations of academic theorists to persist in the attempt to deal with motivation without reference to cognition as such. We have, in fact, continued to hope that we could do away with motivational problems by explaining all behavior in terms of instigation by stimuli, merely noting that the conditions of instigation include the prior influence of what we call positive and negative reinforcement on the formation of habits (Prentice, 1961, p. 505).

But the motivation of socialized human beings seems to be inextricably connected with complex cognitive structures. As the child grows up, many of his primitive desires are transformed because they are cognitively elaborated in various ways. Our desires come to depend in essential ways on the beliefs we acquire; they come to be stabilized and connected with related desires and beliefs, and so can persist over long periods of time, need not be felt as special states of consciousness, and can take the form of plans and projects for the future. Such desires have conceptual dimensions not found in simple transient animal urges for food, or sex. To desire the good of one's children, or the success of a business venture, to desire to keep a promise one has made, or to find a way of checkmating one's opponent in three moves; to elaborate plans for the future and to anticipate what might prevent them from going the way one wants and how this could be circumvented; to set oneself goals one wants to achieve and to figure out ways of attaining them—these clearly are performances which presuppose the use of complex systems of concepts, concepts which one learns in being brought up in society. Such conceptual elaborations are not only presupposed in much human motivation, but they are also frequently the main locus of its expression: the various social, economic and intellectual desires, needs, or interests, which come to mind when one thinks of what motivates the normal conduct of adult human beings, are manifested, not primarily in the triggering or energizing of bits of behavior, but in the conceiving of plans for future action. This is where our ordinary notion of doing something in order to achieve an end, that is, having a motive, is rooted. And this is the context which much recent philosophical discussion of motivation takes for its point of departure.

It would, no doubt, be surprising if there were no anticipations of such human conduct in the behavior of higher animals; perhaps even the behavior of Tolman's rats at the choice point of a maze is, in some ways, analogous. But other animals are not concept users, and such behaviors cannot appear in their full and characteristic form until the animal can conceptually elaborate his desires, conceive plans for the future, and the like. So it is easy to see why psychologists, who approach motivation by extrapolating from theories about the factors that determine the energizing and "direction" of animal behavior, come to see problems of human motivation in a way so different from that in which it presents itself to philosophers, who start out from common sense and our ordinary ways of construing the motivation of our fellow men.

Against this background, Piaget's views have special significance. Piaget takes as his point of departure the "dual nature of intelligence as something both biological and logical" (Piaget, 1950, p. 3). On the one hand, Piaget has spent much effort and ingenuity in diagnosing and describing the way people think when confronted by problems at various stages of their intellectual development, in a way that brings out how the subject himself tries to cope with the problem, how he tries to justify the various moves he makes, the rationale that informs what he says and does, and the like. Where other investigators have tried to give an account of human thinking in terms of Hullian, Freudian, or other psychological theories, Piaget holds that, at least for the adult, logic is "an ideal 'model' of thought" (Piaget, 1950, p. 29); the aim of Piaget's investigations has been to show how thinking develops towards "operations" which, ideally, correspond to the structures of logic. But he also insists that "intelligence is a particular instance of biological adaption" (Piaget, 1952, pp. 3–4), and tries to show how these complex cognitive structures are gradually developed and built up, through a series of connected stages, in an organism that starts out with little more than a few inborn reflex mechanisms. In other words, Piaget takes seriously both the biological emphasis on the organism and its energy regulations, which underlies the experimental psychologists' approach to motivation, and the cognitive emphasis on the conceptual elaboration of desires, plans, norms and the like, which underlies the approach taken by philosophers. We might, therefore, hope to find in Piaget's account of motivation a serious attempt to bridge these two divergent approaches.

II. Piaget on the Motivation of Thought

Piaget's most sustained treatment of this topic is to be found in *Les relations entre l'affectivité et l'intelligence dans le développment mental de l'enfant* (1954a), though he also touches on these matters in most of his other works. As the title suggests, Piaget uses "affect" in a very broad sense, to cover feelings, emotions, desires, needs, interests, values, and will (Piaget, 1954a, pp. 2, 29, and *passim*), just as he uses "intelligence" broadly to cover all sorts of cognitive structures. The general thesis Piaget defends is that affect and intelligence are complementary facets of mental development, distinguishable but inseparable "aspects" of all conduct (Piaget, 1954a, p. 2). For all conduct has both "structure" and "energy"; affects provide the latter, while the structures of intelligence constitute the former (Piaget, 1954a, pp. 6–7, 123). As Piaget puts it, "in all behavior the motives and energizing dynamisms reveal affectivity, while the techniques and adjustments of the means employed constitute the cognitive sensory–motor or rational aspect" (Piaget, 1967, p. 33). Or "one could say that the energy of conduct depended on affectivity while the structures depend on cognitive functions" (Piaget, 1954a, p. 6).

As the dynamic or energizing aspect of intellectual life, affectivity can influence intellectual functioning, it can speed up or slow down intellectual development, but "it does not of itself engender cognitive structures, nor does it modify the structures in whose functioning it intervenes" (Piaget, 1954a, p. 5). Of course, affective behavior always has structure, but the structures involved are the cognitive structures of intelligence—there is no special "logic of feelings" whose structures differ from those of ordinary intelligence (Piaget, 1954a, pp. 9, 117, 155). On the other hand, every intellectual performance, no matter how abstract—for example, the thought of a mathematician trying to establish a novel theorem—always requires "energizing" by affective elements. Piaget's general thesis thus has two parts which I will discuss separately: (*a*) "There are no purely affective states without cognitive elements" to provide "structure," and (*b*) "there are no cognitive mechanisms without affective elements" to provide "energy" (Piaget, 1954a, p. 3).

A. The Cognitive Structuring of Affects. Piaget tries to show that "in the normal development of the individual we observe, at each level, a sort of parallelism or strict correspondence between the transformations of affectivity and the transformations of cognitive functions" (Piaget, 1954a, p. 154). The child's affects are not, so Piaget argues against Freudian notions of libido, something "given" that can be cathected to different objects; rather, the construction of objects first makes possible new feelings connected with these objects (Piaget, 1954a, pp. 33–38). For example, the infant does not have the cognitive structures which make it possible to distinguish self from not-self; consequently, his narcissism can only be a "narcissism without Narcissus" that corresponds to the intellectual egocentrism of the early sensory–motor period (Piaget, 1954a, p. 35). And the achievements of the sensory–motor period—for example, construction of objects in space, objectification of causality, awareness of one's own actions—not only transform the child's intellectual life from a neonatal stage of undifferentiated chaos to a stage where he can manage his immediate environment with considerable skill; they also transform his affective life from a chaos of fluctuating and undifferentiated feelings to something "much more structured, and equally more stable, through an affective systematization parallel to the cognitive structuring" (Piaget, 1954a, p. 66).

Thus, when it becomes possible for the child, toward the end of the second year, to represent what is not immediately present, feelings can also become "representative like thought, that is, they acquire an existence independent of the presence of the affective situation" (Piaget, 1954a, p. 73). As it becomes possible to remember, or evoke through language, satisfactions previously received, there now develops a tendency towards "affective conservation"—that is, feelings of gratitude and reciprocity towards others can appear—a tendency which parallels the start of "cognitive conservation" in representative thought (Piaget, 1954a, p. 79). Similarly, where successful or unsuccessful actions could previously give rise to momentary feelings, such feelings can now last and become feelings of self-confidence or self-doubt (Piaget, 1954a, p. 82)—valuations of self which could not occur at earlier levels of cognitive development. Further, as the socialization of intelligence progresses, behaviors learned in relation to others come to be applied to oneself. For example, the child starts by blurting out whatever ideas he has and finds that these may conflict with the ideas of another; he thus learns to discuss with others and finally becomes capable of discussing with himself (Piaget, 1954a, p. 87). Again, the child first learns to make promises to others and later comes to make promises to himself, to oblige himself (Piaget, 1954a, p. 106).

Since the affects which appear in a given period depend on the intellectual developments of that period, it would be a mistake to suppose that "in early childhood interpersonal feelings are capable of attaining the level of what we shall call affective operations (by comparison with logical operations)" (Piaget, 1967, pp. 36–37). That is, the loves, hates, etc. of the sensory–motor period are not those of the normal adult, or even of an older child, because affective life is again transformed on the basis of the intellectual transformations that occur in the operational period. For the development of reversible operations, of conservation concepts, and others, not only eliminates contradictions from the child's thought, but also allows the formation of systems of values which are "reversible in the sense of a return to previous values, a permanence of values which allows the comparison of a new situation with past and future situations" (Piaget, 1954a, p. 116). This becomes possible because at this level the child develops his will power, and willing is an affective operation which, according to Piaget, "acts exactly like the logical operation" (Piaget, 1967, p. 60). Just as the development of logical operations allows the child to resolve a conflict between rational considerations and appearances by "decentering" so as to take past and future appearances into account, so willing allows him to resolve the conflict of desires, or of desires and duty, by "decentering" from the immediate situation so as to take past and future values into account (Piaget, 1954a, pp. 128–130). Moral feelings, like truthfulness, justice, treating similar cases in similar ways, become the "invariants" of affective life, and the child develops a stable system of values which is, says Piaget, "the logic of values or of action among individuals, just as logic is a kind of moral for thought" (Piaget, 1967, p. 58)—an ideal logic of action, to be sure, which is only approximated in fact, but this is equally true of logical thinking (Piaget, 1954a, p. 120). The greater stability, integration and "reversibility" which characterize intelligence in the period of concrete operations are thus reflected in the affective life of that period.

The development of formal ("hypothetico-deductive") thought, with its shift of emphasis from the real to the possible, again transforms affective life in adolescence, since it is "the source of the living responses, always so full of emotion, which the adolescent uses to build his ideals in adapting to society" (Piaget & Inhelder, 1958, p. 314). Formal thinking makes possible the adolescent's new interest in abstract collective ideals like social justice, political reform, etc., ideals which presuppose an understanding of possibilities rather than actualities. The child can have no such feelings because he cannot understand the relevant concepts. In adolescence, when such abstract concepts can be understood, they also become new sources of interests and values (Piaget, 1954a, pp. 147–151).

In sum, Piaget finds that "there is egocentric thought, just as there is egocentric affectivity, and there is socialized thought adapted to reality just as there is socialized affectivity adapted to reality" (Piaget, 1954a, p. 191)—in tracing the development of the former we also trace the development of the latter. We must, therefore, so Piaget contends, rid ourselves of the "romantic prejudice which makes us suppose [that affects are] immediate givens," and recognize instead that "there is, in truth, as much construction in the affective as in the cognitive domain" (Piaget, 1954a, p. 11).

Piaget's conclusions are based on his empirical studies of development, but his point is strikingly similar to one which philosophers have recently made on conceptual grounds. Analyses of the way "fear," "anger," "love," and other "affective" terms are ordinarily used, have led to the rejection of both the classical identification of emotions, desires, etc., with specifiable mental states which are immediate givens and of behavioristic analyses into dispositions towards specifiable patterns of behavior. The difficulty that has been found in behavioristic analyses is not only that the dispositions involved seem indefinitely complex, but also that there seems to be no way of deciding whether or not certain behaviors are, for example, expressions of anger, without taking into account the person's state of mind—his thoughts, wishes, feelings—as well as the social practices which constitute the background of his behavior. The classical identification of affects with immediate givens of consciousness, on the other hand, not only makes it hard to see how we can use our affective terms meaningfully; it also runs counter to the fact that we cannot, normally, distinguish between our wants, feelings, and emotions by specifying the different phenomenal states they involve, as well as the fact that no particular conscious state need be present whenever we want something, are angry, and the like. Affects do, indeed, manifest themselves both in behavior and in conscious states, but there seems to be no way of identifying them either with specific behavior tendencies or with specific mental states. Philosophers thus came to see that emotions, desires, and even feelings have a previously unsuspected conceptual complexity; these concepts were found to be such that their application normally presupposes temporally extended and complex patterns of intelligent social life. This has led to the rejection of both behavioristic and mentalistic analyses as overly simple, and to a focus on attempts at mapping the "logical geography" of the mind—that is, attempts to exhibit the complex conceptual interrelations between our emotions, desires, thoughts, feelings, and actions in their social settings (see, for example, Alston, 1969; Kenny, 1963; Melden, 1969; Peters, 1961–1962, 1969).

Such a "logical geography" corresponds roughly to what Piaget calls the "cognitive structure" of affects, and the mind being mapped is that of an adult who, after all, has learned the concepts he now has in the course of being raised in society. Piaget's empirical studies of how children, at various stages of development, respond to other persons, their attitudes towards rules, towards telling lies, and so forth, are, in effect, studies of the geological strata that underlie this logical geography. Whether such developmental studies are relevant to the logical mapping that interests philosophers, and conversely, is part of the larger issue explored by Toulmin and Hamlyn in their contributions to this volume.

B. The Affective "Energizing" of Cognition. The second part of Piaget's thesis, namely that "affectivity assigns value to activities and distributes energy to them" (Piaget, 1967, p. 69), is more troublesome. On the one hand, Piaget holds that affects have some connection with energy regulations because vague feelings of effort and interest, or fatigue and disinterest, etc., regulate the energy expended in behavior, and control its activation and termination (Piaget, 1954a, pp. 25–28). But, on the other hand, Piaget explicitly denies that "affectivity can be reduced to energy regulations" on two grounds: First, even the earliest inchoate feelings presuppose some rudimentary comprehension and so cannot be separated from cognitive structures (Piaget, 1954a, p. 23). Second, such "internal regulations of forces" cannot explain why, for example, a young child who accidentally succeeds in a certain motor task, will keep at the difficult business of trying to accomplish the same thing again until he has mastered the task (Piaget, 1954a, pp. 28–29, 40–41). In order to understand the child's intellectual development, we must assume, so Piaget argues, that a "system of values" develops and that "it is value which will determine the energies to employ in action" (Piaget, 1954a, pp. 38–39). This system of values differs from the system of energy regulations because "it is the value of the goal that determines the energy employed in attaining it and not the available energy that determines the value or nonvalue of the goal" (Piaget, 1954a, p. 69). The value system makes its first appearance at the third stage of the sensory–motor period (that is, at an age of four to eight months), and, when it is made stable and precise with further development, becomes a system of "norms for action" (Piaget, 1954a, p. 39).

The trouble with this is that "value" and "energy" are concepts belonging to such radically different frameworks. No doubt, an appeal to a person's values may enable us to understand better why he engages in some activities rather than others, why he gives much thought to some questions and little to others, but such explanations do not tell us anything about the underlying physiological mechanisms that energize his behavior. Since value is a concept that belongs to the "rule-following purposive model," it is hard to see what connection it can have with a mechanical model of energy regulations. In what sense can values be "the motor of conduct, or its mechanism of acceleration?" (Piaget, 1954a, p. 154).

Piaget evidently finds it necessary to appeal to values in order to account for the child's intellectual development, at least after the earliest two stages. But there is an obvious conceptual gap between a "system of values," or of "norms for action," on the one hand, and a biological model of energy regulations on the other. Piaget makes a stab at bridging this gap by suggesting that "the notion of interests [is] the point of juncture between these two distinct systems" (Piaget, 1954a, p. 33). While the precise meaning of this suggestion is far from clear,[1] there are good reasons for holding that Piaget does not really regard affects, *qua* psychological phenomena, as "energizers" of behavior in any literal, physiological sense. For one thing, he insists that "consciousness seen as energy seems to us a fallacious metaphor" (Piaget, 1954b, p. 142). Since affects, as psychological phenomena, fall under what Piaget calls the "point of view of consciousness," it would be "fallacious" to identify them with the energies that activate the organism. Further, Piaget repeatedly maintains that "comprehension is no more the cause of emotion than emotion is the cause of comprehension" (Piaget, 1954a, p. 23), because it simply makes no sense to ask whether affective developments cause cognitive developments, or conversely (Piaget, 1954a, pp. 56, 150). Since affect and cognition are correlative aspects of one and the same psychological phenomenon, the relation between them is not an external causal relation between separately identifiable entities. Finally, when Piaget deals with needs, interest, and other affects, he explicitly rules out consideration of their physiological conditions (Piaget, 1954a, p. 30) and focuses instead on their "functional significance." And "from such a functional point of view, need is essentially an awareness of momentary disequilibrium, and the satisfaction of need, that is awareness of re-equilibration" (Piaget, 1954a, p. 44). We must turn to Piaget's account of equilibration if we are to understand the sense in

[1] Following Claparede, Piaget defines interest as "the affective relation between a subject experiencing needs and objects which permit their satisfaction" (Piaget, 1954a, pp. 29, 46). He holds that interest is the point of juncture between value and energy because interest has degree or intensity (linking it with energy), while its contents—that is, our different interests—are values which are ordered in such a way that one interest depends on another, is subordinate to another, etc. (Piaget, 1954a, pp. 29–31, 43). In an important paper on the problem of consciousness, Piaget says:

> From the physiological point of view, interest is a causal process that can be described by regulation of energies: interest facilitates action by freeing available energies. From the point of view of consciousness, this means that certain values are being attached to certain objects, persons or actions. None of these values is determined by law of cause and effect, but by implied relationships. Here is an example: a child may be interested in drawing: therefore he attaches value to pieces of paper that he would otherwise disregard. The value attached to drawing (value of goal), entails or implies value attached to paper (value of means). Here we have a relationship of implication rather than causality (Piaget, 1954b, p. 144).

But just how is the relation between the "physiological point of view," which is causal, and the "point of view of consciousness," which deals with "implication rather than causality," to be understood? Piaget says he rejects both psychophysical parallelism and causal interactionism in favor of "another concept of consciousness" (Piaget, 1954b, p. 145), but the people discussing Piaget's paper found it hard to get clear about just what that concept is (Piaget, 1954b, p. 147). Fortunately, this matter need not be pursued here.

which he regards needs, interests, and the like, as motivations for intellectual development and activity.

III. The Equilibrium Model of Thinking

A. Cognitive Development as Equilibration. What Piaget means by "equilibration" is, roughly, a process of self-regulation which maintains a balance between "assimilation" and "accommodation," compensates for internal and external disturbances, and in so doing leads to the development of more and more complex, integrated and balanced structures. Since Piaget wants to construe intelligence as a form of biological adaptation, he puts a good deal of emphasis on the continuity between equilibration as a psychological process and biological processes which, in his view, are the root out of which psychological equilibration develops. Thus, assimilation and accommodation are "the functional invariants of intelligence and biological organization," they are "the invariants common to all structuring of which life is capable" (Piaget, 1952, p. 3). What Piaget means by this is that mental life involves both an interpretation of the "given" in relation to the "schemas" which are the subject's cognitive organization (that is, assimilation), and an adjustment of the subject's cognitive system to novel features of the given (that is, accommodation). But biological life also involves both assimilation and accommodation—for example, in chewing up and digesting foodstuffs, the organism is modifying the ingested materials to fit its own structures, while at the same time its structures adjust to the ingested material. So intelligence and biological functioning are both "adaptions" to the environment, which depend not only on the environment but also on the "organization" of the system interacting with the environment. Just as intellectual adaption is an equilibrium of assimilation and accommodation involving the subject's cognitive structures, so biological adaption is an equilibrium of assimilation and accommodation involving the organism's physiological structures (see, for example, Piaget, 1950, pp. 7–9). These are the sort of analogies Piaget likes.

But such analogies obscure crucial differences between physiological and cognitive "structures," they slur over the very different senses in which physical and mental "organizations" can be said to "assimilate" and "accommodate" their very different "materials." Biological equilibria are maintained by the causal interaction of specifiable physical forces, but psychological equilibration cannot be understood in terms of such homeostatic models. For Piaget defines psychological equilibrium "very broadly as the compensation resulting from the activities of the subject in response to external intrusion" (Piaget, 1967, p. 101), and he characterizes psychological equilibration in ways which make any analogy to physical processes, in which the behavior of an organism, or mechanism, compensates for environmental changes which are independent of it, extremely thin.

In the first place, the "external intrusion" to which the subject responds is not a physical stimulus; what he responds to, and whether there is anything at all for him to respond to, depends on the cognitive schemas to which the stimulus must be assimilated. This is clear in one of Piaget's basic criticisms of stimulus–response behavior theory: that theory fails to see that "there is a system of interaction without stable frontiers" between stimuli and responses, because "objects don't intervene except relative to the structures through which the subject introduces their proper bearings," while "responses are nothing other than the actualization of schemas giving stimuli their meanings" (Piaget, 1959, pp. 27–28). But in that case, we are not dealing with a physical or biological process of compensation. For what influences behavior is not feedback from physical stimuli but only the subject's cognitive assimilation of it; what he responds to is his construal of the external intrusion, and he is also the one who interprets the outcome of his compensatory activities. Equilibration thus depends, from start to finish, on the subject's *cognitive* schemas. If he is at a stage where a given stimulus cannot be cognitively assimilated, then there simply is nothing for him to respond to.

Further, Piaget holds that after early sensory–motor development, equilibration becomes a matter of compensating for "virtual" rather than "actual" intrusions (Piaget, 1967, p. 101). At the operational level, the intrusions to which the subject responds "can be imagined and anticipated by the subject in the form of the direct operations of a system . . . the compensatory activities will also consist of imagining and anticipating the transformations but in an inverse sense" (Piaget, 1967, p. 113). So we are not talking about any interaction between internal mechanisms and actual occurrences in the environment, but about the subject's "precorrections for anticipated errors" (Piaget, 1967, p. 108), that is, his "logical" (operational) thinking about the situation confronting him. Piaget adds that these "virtual transformations exist in the mind of the subject" (that is, they are his system of operations), and that equilibration can serve as an explanatory concept in psychology because "the mind is the proper domain of psychology" (Piaget, 1967, p. 114, 1957, pp. 40–41).

Finally, there need be no "external intrusions" at all in order for there to be equilibration. For example, the acquisition of conservation concepts is, in Piaget's view, "not supported by anything from the point of view of possible measurement or perception . . . it is enforced by logical structuring much more than by experience" (Piaget, 1967, p. 154, 1957, p. 106). Such conceptual developments are, in Piaget's view, due to "internal factors of coherence . . . the deductive activity of the subject himself" (Piaget, 1959, p. 32), so that equilibration is here a response to *internal* conflict between the subject's conceptual schemas rather than a response to any disturbance from outside. In such cases, equilibration is more a matter of achieving what Piaget calls the "accord of thought with itself" than it is a matter of establishing the "accord of thought with things" (Piaget, 1952, p. 8).

While Piaget frequently speaks of the "mechanism of equilibration," it should now be clear that this is a rather misleading metaphor for the cognitive processes he is analyzing. In point of fact, Piaget himself warns against interpreting equilibration as the operation of a causal process (Piaget, 1957, pp. 30-31, 40–41), and explicates it instead by reference to a series of four "strategies" adopted by the subject, such that the consequences of adopting one strategy increase the probability of his adopting the next, until he reaches the last strategy and succeeds in establishing a more stable and permanent cognitive equilibrium than was achieved by any of his preceding strategies. For example, in learning conservation concepts the child begins by reasoning on the basis of one or the other of the two transformed dimensions (for example, there is more because it is longer). But, after a while he is likely to become dissatisfied with this strategy and to reason on the basis of the other dimension which "he had, of course, perceived . . . but had conceptually ignored" (that is, he now reasons that there is less because it is thinner). After a period in which "he will oscillate between the two," it becomes probable that he will begin "discovering the interdependence of the two transformations." The child now "starts to reason about the transformations," and the probability increases that "he will discover that the two variations are inverse to each other . . . the child now finds a reversible system, and we have reached the fourth phase" (Piaget, 1967, pp. 154–157). Piaget does not want to say that the child necessarily goes through conscious calculations in adopting these strategies, but he does insist that their adoption must be seen from the subject's point of view and that it is always the "failures or insufficiencies" of one strategy that lead to the adoption of another, more "equilibrated," strategy (Piaget, 1957, pp. 58–59). Moreover, in explaining the probability of the successive strategies, Piaget constantly talks about "consideration by the subject," his "choice" of strategies, his "doubts" and "reasonings," what he "conceives," "asks himself," "imagines," "discovers," and the like (Piaget, 1957, pp. 62–72).

Now this psychological process of equilibrating, that is, of adopting, again and again, a succession of strategies for coping in more and more effectively organized ways with cognitive perturbations or problems of increasing complexity, is Piaget's explanation for cognitive development.

That is, beginning with the infant's earliest copings, "every schema tends to assimilate every object," but runs into the "resistance of objects to assimilation" (Piaget, 1959, p. 43). This produces "perturbations" which the child equilibrates in two complementary ways: by accommodation, which is "not dictated by the object . . . but is still an activity consisting in differentiating a schema of assimilation"; and by coordinating the differentiated schemas through "reciprocal assimilation" (Piaget, 1959, pp. 44–50, 1957, p. 74). In the early phases of development "a schema is only a practical concept and not a concept of thought" (Piaget, 1959, p. 43). But "logical structures result from the progressive equilibration of the pre-logical structures" (Piaget, 1967, p. 105, 1957, pp. 93–97). As mental representation, language, and the socialization of thought take hold, actions are internalized, and perturbations can be "anticipated" before they occur. The prelogical structures which the child develops in coping with his problems during the sensory–motor period make it possible for him to appreciate problems which could not arise before he had these structures, and in his efforts to deal with these new perturbations he equilibrates concrete operations; these in turn do not suffice for coping with "the problems encountered by a pre-adolescent" and the equilibration of these new problems leads to the development of formal operations (Piaget, 1957, pp. 97–98). The entire process of cognitive development "consists of reactions of compensation to perturbation (relative to previous schemas) which make necessary a variation of the initial schemas" (Piaget, 1959, p. 50), so that equilibration continues until the "permanent equilibrium" of formal (logico–mathematical) structures is achieved.

So understood, Piaget's account of cognitive development has interesting similarities to accounts of the development of scientific thought as pictured by writers like Hanson (1958), Kuhn (1962), and Toulmin (1961). There is the same stress on the thought-impregnated character of observation and experimentation, on how what is observed depends on what is expected, and what is anomalous depends on what is accepted. In both cases the "normal" tendency to assimilate anomalies to accepted paradigms through minor accommodations provides for the continuity of thought; and the development of novel systems of thought, which differ in important ways from those which preceded (Kuhn's "scientific revolutions" and Piaget's major "stages"), is explained in terms of a need for reconstructing the accepted system of concepts so as to coordinate new insights with the intellectual gains of the past. No doubt, Piaget, who sees developmental psychology as directly relevant to "genetic epistemology" and the history of science, would be pleased by the similarity.

B. Motivational Aspects of Equilibration. Our primary concern here must be with what Piaget calls the "dynamism" of equilibration.

What motivates the subject to adopt the successive strategies which lead to the development of more and more equilibrated thought structures? And what motivates him when he applies conceptual structures which he has already achieved?

It has been noted that Piaget connects the motivation of intellectual activities with needs, holding that "need as such is the motive power for all activity" (Piaget, 1952, p. 44). On the one hand, Piaget points out that no matter how useful "corporeal needs" may be in explaining animal behavior, "in the young child the principal needs are of a functional category"; such needs cannot be separated from schemas and "the basic fact is therefore not need but the schema of assimilation of which it is the subjective expression" (Piaget, 1952, p. 45). But, on the other hand, Piaget's biological orientation leads him to stretch the concept of need so as to cover both organic and functional needs. He writes:

> We do not act unless we are momentarily in disequilibrium . . . [which manifests itself as] awareness of a need. Conduct ends when the need is satisfied: the return to equilibrium is thus marked by a feeling of satisfaction. This schema is very general: no nutrition without alimentary needs; no work without needs; no act of intelligence without a question, that is without a felt lacuna, therefore without disequilibrium, therefore without need (Piaget, 1954a, pp. 3–4).

This use of "need" to cover both alimentary needs (for example, hunger) and questions, makes it sound as if the latter were "cognitive" or "functional" needs in the same sense of "need" as that in which we speak of "organic needs." This has led Wolff (1960) to suggest that Piaget and psychoanalytic theory might be reconciled by allowing that behavior can be "motivated both by drive discharge tendencies and needs to function"; neither classic psychoanalytic theory, which emphasized the discharge of instinctual drive tensions, nor Piaget in whose theory "the need to function is [the] sole motivational concept," is sufficiently "comprehensive," and Wolff suggests a synthesis which will postulate the operation of both of these needs (Wolff, 1960, especially pp. 120–123). Again, Flavell connects Piaget's views with theories like those of Berlyne, in which curiosity and exploratory behavior are attributed to a special drive (Flavell, 1963, p. 410).

While Piaget's biological analogies and mechanical metaphors may invite such interpretations, they run counter to his claim that "values" rather than "energy regulations" motivate intellectual functioning. I have already cited some textual reasons for holding that Piaget does not construe affects as "energizers" of behavior in any literal sense (see Section IIB). It may, however, be useful to show in another way why one cannot make sense of Piaget's account of motivation along the lines suggested above. Let us agree that for Piaget "there is an intrinsic need for cognitive organs or structures, once generated by functioning, to perpetuate themselves by more functioning" (Flavell, 1963, p. 78). Can such "needs to function" figure in explanations of the same type as are provided by need-reduction theories? The latter conceive needs as organic conditions that "energize" behavior, conditions that can not only be detected apart from the behaviors they energize, but that are also conceptually independent of them[2]—that is, drives can, in principle, be identified without reference to the behaviors they "drive"; what activates the behavior is the occurrence of an organic need state, and whether or not the animal is "aware" of, or "recognizes," what it needs has nothing to do with the case. By specifying, for example, hunger drive in terms of hours of food deprivation, such theories conceptualize drive as an antecedent causal condition (for example, of tissue deficit) which has a merely contingent connection with the behavior to be explained, that is, the persistence and intensity with which the animal sniffs, moves about the box, and finally, feeds. This conceptual independence of drives (needs) and behavior is essential to any drive theory of motivation, because such theories purport to provide causal ("mechanistic") explanations which, like the explanations characteristic of the physical sciences, make no use of "purpose," "cognition," or other "intentional" factors. Since behavior theory makes it a matter of "fundamental principle" to rule out teleological explanations in terms of "purpose" or "goal" (Skinner, 1953, p. 87), it must conceptualize drives, or needs, as conditions that can be specified without reference to the behaviors they "motivate." If needs could not be specified without reference to what behavior is needed—if, for example, hunger drive could only be identified in terms of various activities aimed at getting food (sniffing for it, looking for it, etc.)—then to say that the animal behaves in these ways because it is hungry (needs to eat) would be to indicate its aim, the end towards which its behavior is directed. But, in that case, we would be giving an intentionalistic explanation in terms of the animal's purpose or goal. Drive theory can manage to "do away with motivational problems" by replacing questions about the goals of behavior with questions about the conditions of its instigation, it can succeed in its "attempt to deal with motivation without reference to cognition" (see Section IB), only if the needs to which it appeals are conceptually independent of the behaviors they motivate—without this it would cease to be a "drive theory" of motivation.

But Piaget not only fails to provide such independent specification of needs and behavior; what is crucial is that in his theory "functional needs"

[2] See the Postscript at the end of this article for further discussion of this point.

cannot, in principle, be specified independently of the cognitive behaviors they motivate. Piaget, therefore, differs sharply from drive theorists in the way he conceptualizes "needs" and in the role which he assigns to "functional needs" in the explanation of cognitive processes. To see this, consider Piaget's criticism of the role of motivation in stimulus–response learning theory. He argues that a focus on needs like hunger and thirst, which can be treated as independent variables in "simplified laboratory experiments," has led theorists of this persuasion to decompose learning into external structures and internal motivations which activate their acquisition. But this is a false "previous decomposition, introduced by the observer, between cognitive factors (stimulus–response) and affective factors (motivation)" (Piaget, 1959, pp. 30–31). The (human) subject's needs are not "internal factors" that can be identified apart from his cognitive schemas, just as the stimuli that influence his behavior are not "external factors" that can be identified apart from those schemas. In support of this, Piaget argues that the child's needs and interests depend on his level of development: as he acquires new cognitive structures he also acquires new interests which could not have existed before he had these structures (Piaget, 1959, p. 30; see also Section IIA). Indeed, "interest is nothing but the affective aspect of assimilation" (Piaget, 1959, p. 45)—the different needs and interests that motivate the child to apply and develop his schemas are conceptually dependent on those schemas because novelties that occur in his environment are "accepted by accommodation and considered as 'interesting' to the extent to which they allow the resumption of an enlarged accommodation through this differentiation of prior schemas" (Piaget, 1959, p. 46). Similarly, what can "reinforce" the child's behavior, that is, satisfy or reduce his needs, is not identifiable apart from his schemas, so that both need and satisfaction are motivations which are "indissociable from cognitive structure" (Piaget, 1959, p. 33).

So while the "needs" of need-reduction theory are organic conditions which are conceptually independent of the behaviors they motivate, the functional "needs" and interests which motivate cognitive activity in Piaget's theory are needs *for*, interests *in*, activities that cannot be identified without reference to just those schemas whose use these needs motivate. That is, at a certain point in his development the child is motivated by an "interest" in discovering new means by active experimentation ("tertiary circular reaction"), or by a "need" to search for novelty, etc.; but these aims, which are characteristic of the child at a certain stage, are a function of the schemas available to him at that stage. To put it another way, a "functional need" is, for Piaget, "an awareness of momentary disequilibrium," that is, the recognition of a discrepancy between one's schemas and the situation one encounters—this is what motivates the child to deploy and develop his schemas, he needs to accommodate those schemas in order to assimilate the situation he has encountered—but such needs are conceptually dependent on the schemas whose activation they explain. Again, Piaget argues that, beginning early in sensory–motor development, much of what the child does cannot be motivated by primary needs like hunger, but must rather be motivated by a "need to understand."[3] But just what the child needs to understand can be specified only by reference to the conceptual structures which are the basis of his understanding.

In short, Piaget holds that it is

> . . . not necessary for us to have recourse to separate factors of motivation in order to explain learning, not because they don't intervene . . . but because they are included from the start in the global conception of assimilation. . . . To say that the subject is interested in a certain result or object thus *means* that he assimilates it or anticipates an assimilation, and to say that he needs it *means* that he possesses schemas requiring its utilization (Piaget, 1959, pp. 46–47; italics mine).

But for this very reason, Piaget's functional needs and interests cannot be properly assimilated to anything like the needs that are thought to be reduced in various drive-reduction models of motivation. The latter are assumed to be separate "internal factors," independent variables which are conceptually distinct from the behaviors which they are thought to explain and which are, at least in principle, specifiable without reference to these behaviors. But this is precisely what Piaget's functional needs are not—because Piaget includes "needs" in his "global conception" of assimilation they cannot, in principle, be conceptually independent of the relevant assimilatory schemas. Since the needs of need-reduction theory are conceptually independent of the behaviors they motivate, while Piaget's functional needs are not, Piaget's concept of "need" differs from that of drive-reduction theorists; he has an entirely different theory of motivation because his functional needs to explore and understand, to attain greater coherence or "reversibility," and the like, are really goals which behavior is intended to achieve, not antecedent conditions involved in its instigation. That is why Piaget's account differs sharply from theories like Berlyne's; this is why it cannot be reconciled with drive- or need-reduction theories by adding "functional needs" to the usual "organic needs."

How, then, are we to understand Piaget's account of the way in which needs, and the like, motivate intellectual activities? As we have seen,

[3] Piaget (1959, p. 48) holds that only such a need can explain why the baby keeps trying to reproduce a result, which first occurred by accident, until it has mastered the motor task in question. The point corresponds to the distinction between "values" and "energy regulations" noted earlier (see Section IIB).

Piaget identifies need with "awareness of momentary disequilibrium"; he says that intellectual activity is prompted by "questions . . . felt lacuna," and he describes equilibration as the process in which the subject's intellectual activities compensate for actual or anticipated "perturbations" of his cognitive system. Moreover, in showing how the child's ideas of movement, force, weight, etc. develop, Piaget repeatedly stresses the role of cognitive conflict in these developments. The child attempts to assimilate reality to his developing schemas: for example, initially he thinks that the clouds move because they follow him when he walks, later that they obey the orders of God or other people, later still that the sun acts on the clouds as a policeman acts on a thief, and so forth, until mechanical explanations begin to appear and develop. What leads the child to give up one of his solutions in favor of the next is that his cognitive assimilations keep running into difficulties because they conflict with "facts" available to the child, or with his other beliefs, or with what other people say, etc. (Piaget, 1930, *passim*). Thus, whatever resists assimilation to the child's schemas generates cognitive conflict, and the child's recognition of this "disequilibrium" motivates him to resolve the conflict: he accommodates his schemas in order to assimilate it.

So understood, cognitive conflict (that is, "awareness of a momentary disequilibrium" in the system of schemas), the "need" for establishing cognitive consistency ("equilibrium") between the schemas one has and the novel feature that has introduced disequilibrium, would be the motivation for cognitive activities. The general motive, both for applying a schema one already has and for elaborating new schemas in the course of development, would be, in effect, the "need" to make sense of present problems by fitting them coherently to schemas used in past solutions—this is what motivates the process of "equilibrating," or striking a balance, between construing the novel in terms of the schemas one has (assimilation) and modifying one's schemas to accommodate the novel. But, in this context, to speak of what the child "needs" is to speak of what he "should do" to achieve a goal; the latter makes this desirable for him to do, or harmful not to do. The child "needs" to equilibrate his schemas (that is, to develop greater consistency, etc., in his thinking) in a sense similar to that in which he may "need" to practice arithmetic, or do piano exercises. Talk about such needs points to what the activity accomplishes, its value or significance, not to the conditions that may energize it.

Such an interpretation is clearly consistent with Piaget's account of cognitive development as a process of equilibration in which the subject adopts "strategies" for coping, based on his prior schemas, and the "failures and insufficiencies" of one strategy make more probable the adoption of another, involving "more equilibrated" schemas. We can now see why no motive other than "the error to which the first strategy led" (Piaget, 1957, p. 72) is needed to understand the subject's adoption of the next strategy, and the new "problems" which keep arising at various levels of development will be the "disequilibria" that keep cognitive development going (Piaget, 1957, p. 97).[4] As Piaget himself points out, the notion that "perturbations introduced into the subject's system of prior schemas" lead to "the adoption of a strategy" is the key difference between the theory of equilibration and associationistic learning theories (Piaget, 1957, pp. 108–109). For the latter, what is learned depends on what is given from outside, and the motives that facilitate learning are inner (physiological) states of the organism (needs). But for Piaget, what is learned depends on what the learner can take from the given by means of the cognitive structures available to him, and what motivates his learning are the cognitive disequilibria (functional needs)—the "questions" or "felt lacunae"—that arise when he attempts to apply his schemas to the given. The cognitive conflicts which the child himself engenders in trying to cope with his world, are then what motivates his cognitive development; they are his motives for reconstructing his system of cognitive schemas, when different schemas ready for new coordinations become available to him, until he reaches the "stable equilibrium" of logico–mathematical thought.

Similar considerations apply to the utilization of schemas already developed. "When the difficulty is not too great, does not seem insurmountable to him," the child is motivated to apply his schemas because "the obstacle itself creates a valuation in the form of a need to conquer" (Piaget, 1954a, p. 41). The child thus takes an interest in what generates cognitive conflict, that is, in what he sees as an anomaly because it is neither so far out as to be totally unassimilable, nor so obvious and routine as to require no thought. There is, says Piaget, a "zone of optimal interest for that which is neither too known nor too new" (Piaget, 1959, p. 47), and whatever falls within that zone is found "interesting," that is, motivates the subject to attempt an application of his schema. This is why "a need is nothing but the conative or affective aspect of a schema, claiming . . . objects which it can assimilate" (Piaget, 1959, pp. 46–47).

On this interpretation it is easy to see why "we cannot begin by splitting into two the affective and cognitive aspects of behavior" (Piaget, 1957,

[4] I share Flavell's uncertainty about whether "all instances of 'equilibration' have to do with processes one would comfortably label as 'cognitive conflict' " (*p. 125*), because talk about "problems," "strategies," and the like, clearly become odd when pushed down to what the child does during the first few months of his life. On the other hand, it is not clear just where the line should be drawn here, since this whole approach involves an attempt to trace the various stages of proto-concepts, proto-problems, and proto-strategies in relation to the mature thought processes into which they develop.

p. 34), why "the same schema of assimilation can be simultaneously the source of needs and interests and of knowledge" (Piaget, 1959, p. 33). As manifestations of disequilibria in the system of cognitive structures, the functional needs and interests that motivate intellectual activity are simply the subject's (more or less clear) awareness of some conflict or discrepancy between his schemas and a novel situation he encounters; recognition of the discrepancy is the motive for trying to reassimilate the incongruous item. Piaget's "functional" needs thus turn out to be much like the scientists' need to explain anomalies; his account of the motivation for cognitive change is like that which historians of science give when they appeal to paradigm-induced anomalies in order to explain what motivates the activities involved in "normal science"—that is, the scientist's attempt to make apparent deviations consistent with accepted paradigms—as well as those involved in "scientific revolutions," that is, in reconstructions of the conceptual framework of science designed to again produce a proper "fit" between theory-based expectations and encountered facts (see, for example, Kuhn, 1962). This is, of course, entirely in line with Piaget's frequent references to parallels between the cognitive development of the child and the historical development of the sciences (see, for example, Piaget, 1930, *passim*).

Now if an historian of science makes clear to us just how and why there was a conflict between what scientists observed (or thought they observed) and what they expected, then we do, of course, understand their interest in that phenomenon—if it conflicted with their conceptual scheme, then, of course, they had a motive for trying to assimilate it through some accommodation of that scheme. But by now we have, indeed, come a very long way from any biological model concerned with the energizing of behavior. What we have instead is a form of cognitive consistency theory in which intellectual activities are motivated by the "need" to establish "the accord of thought with things," and the "accord of thought with itself"—this is the general aim of such activity and, in this sense, its "motive."

IV. Cognitive Conflict and Motivation

Since Piaget's concept of equilibration provides, if the preceding discussion is right, an account of the motivation for cognitive activities, it may seem surprising that in the opinion of many psychologists, motivational questions "have not occupied a prominent place in [Piaget's] thinking" (Flavell, 1963, p. 78). Thus, Kagan says that "the noteworthy flaw in Piaget's prodigious output is the absence of any set of theoretical statements that accounts for how or why a child passes from one stage of operations to another" (Kagan, 1966, p. 98); and Bruner, after dismissing Piaget's account of equilibrium as "surplus baggage," criticizes him for neglecting motivational questions like "the nature of the unfolding and development of his [the child's] drives" (Bruner, 1959, pp. 365, 369). The reason for such appraisals by American psychologists is, I think, the special meaning given to the concept of motivation in experimental psychology (see Section IB). If an account of the motivation of behavior is an account of the conditions that instigate and "energize" it, then talk about resolving cognitive conflict or inconsistency does not tell us what motivates behavior, but instead raises the question recently asked by Singer: "Why is such inconsistency motivating?" (Singer, 1966, p. 52). While "cognitive dissonance" and related concepts have become common in American psychology, it must be remembered that Festinger, whose work helped make it so, regarded dissonance as a drive similar to hunger (Festinger, 1957, pp. 3–4). The fact that Piaget rejects the need- or drive-reduction model may help explain why he is thought to have neglected motivational issues. This may also be what lies behind Berlyne's attempt to "reinterpret Piaget's view by regarding what he calls equilibrium as a class of hitherto overlooked sources of drive and reward propelling the learning process" (Berlyne, 1960, p. 302).

I have already argued that this is not what Piaget intends and that Piaget's theory cannot be successfully "reinterpreted" along such lines. But leaving this aside, let us see whether the attempt to explain the cognitive phenomena with which Piaget deals in terms of the motivational framework of stimulus–response behavior theory is plausible in its own right. Since the most systematic and sophisticated recent effort along these lines is due to Berlyne, my discussion will be concerned only with his theory.[5]

A. The Inappropriateness of Cognitive Drive Concepts. Berlyne's aim is to deliniate, within the framework of stimulus–response theory, the "factors that determine when a bout of directed thinking will start, what course it will take, and when it will come to an end" (Berlyne, 1965, p. 240). He recognizes that the account of thinking provided by theorists in the Watson–Hull tradition is inadequate on two counts. First, this account, true to its historical roots (Mischel, 1969), saw the direction of thought as determined by associations. But this fails to recognize the basic difference between "directed" and "autistic" thinking. Since "directed thinking is thinking whose function is to convey us to solutions of

[5] Efforts in a similar direction have also been made by Hunt (1965) and others.

problems" (Berlyne, 1965, p. 19), it cannot consist of just *any* chain of thoughts leading from the representation of some initial situation to the representation of a terminal situation (as in, for example, free association, or wishful thinking). Rather, in directed thinking, each thought in the chain "must be joined to the last by a *legitimate step*," so that there must be, so argues Berlyne, not only representations but also "legitimate steps" by which the thinker moves from one representation to the next: "what constitutes a 'legitimate step' will vary with the type of problem" –in logic it will be "an operation that obeys the rules of inference," in chess a "permissible move," in practical thinking "a representation of an action that could change one stimulus situation into another," etc. (Berlyne, 1965, p. 108). In order to account for this characteristic of directed thinking, Berlyne suggests that behavior theory must be extended so as to include not only "situational thoughts" (that is, representations of external stimulus situations), but also "transformational thoughts" which

> . . . will constitute the 'legitimate steps' that must link each situational thought with the next if the aims of directed thinking are to be fulfilled. The necessity of inserting an appropriate transformational thought or series of transformational thoughts between any two situational thoughts will thus be the factor that differentiates directed thinking from autistic thinking (Berlyne, 1965, p. 115).

The difference between wishful thinking about getting rich and directed thinking about it will then be that in the latter, but not the former, thoughts representing external situations will be linked by "legitimate steps," that is, thoughts of actions that are "appropriate" for bringing these situations about.

A second difficulty in behavioristic accounts of thinking, which Berlyne notes, is their exclusive reliance on "extrinsic motivation" (that is, hunger, thirst, etc., and secondary drives which can be "derived" from these primary ones). But it is clearly wrong to say that thinking is energized by extrinsic drives which can be reduced only by external agencies—since such drive reduction would come only when thinking stops and gives way to action, this could not explain what keeps the thinking process going. If, on the other hand, it is held that "symbolic responses" (that is, thoughts) can reduce extrinsic drives, then one cannot explain why, for example, the thirsty man is motivated to work out a realistic plan for getting water, instead of simply imagining himself drinking. Similarly, the mathematician who is motivated to prove a formula cannot reduce his "drive" by just repeating the formula to himself; yet when he gets to the formula at the end of his proof the "drive" is reduced (Berlyne, 1960, pp. 277–280).

To meet these difficulties, Berlyne suggests that conceptual conflict is "drive inducing" and so constitutes an "intrinsic motivation" that must be added to the extrinsic motivations long recognized in behavior theory

(Berlyne, 1960, pp. 286–287). In his view,

> . . . epistemic behavior must generally be initiated by a specific dissatisfaction, and knowledge, which marks the successful completion of epistemic behavior and supplies its reinforcement, can hardly be rewarding, or even identifiable, apart from its power to assuage the original dissatisfaction (Berlyne, 1963, p. 324).*

The aversive drive state which, allegedly, sets people off in quest of knowledge is conceptual conflict, and knowledge is a "reward" which "reinforces" such behavior because it reduces this drive. According to Berlyne, this "intrinsic motivation depends primarily on the collative properties of the external environment" (Berlyne, 1965, p. 253)—properties like novelty, surprisingness, incongruity, complexity, etc. (Berlyne, 1965, p. 245). When we encounter such properties there arises "a state of high drive induced by conflict traceable to disharmonious symbolic processes," and "this is a condition that can be relieved by the acquisition of knowledge and that therefore leads to epistemic behavior" (Berlyne, 1965, p. 254). Directed thinking is thus assimilated to the drive-reduction model on the ground that it is instigated by a drive aroused by "collative properties of the environment," and that such thinking serves to "bring the drive or arousal down again" (Berlyne, 1965, p. 253).

Since this strange theory is, as Berlyne himself admits, "based largely on extrapolation from general principles of behavior theory" (Berlyne, 1965, p. 261), we must ask what makes this extrapolation appropriate. What is the justification for the claim that a "drive to solve the problem" (Berlyne, 1965, p. 325) propels one's thinking whenever one is working out some problem or other? In line with the role assigned to motivation in general behavior theory, Berlyne argues that the use of such drive concepts is "appropriate" because they are needed in order to explain three sorts of phenomena: (*a*) "activation," that is, the energies that control the starting, stopping, and intensity of thinking; (*b*) the "direction" of thought insofar as it is determined by "internal factors" rather than external stimuli; and (*c*) "reinforcement," that is, the "rewards" that can strengthen thinking and make it "resistant to extinction" (Berlyne, 1963, pp. 298–306, 1965, pp. 237–242). Berlyne's point is that thinking is a form of behavior ("symbolic" or "epistemic" behavior), and drives are needed to explain it in much the way in which they are needed to explain, for example, maze learning in rats—"the motivational problems that concern directed thinking," so Berlyne tells us, "are essentially those that confront behavior in general" (Berlyne, 1965, p. 239). Since the usual organic drives clearly will not do, conceptual conflict must arouse drive and so be the "intrinsic motivation" that explains "epistemic behavior."

* From *Psychology: A Study of a science*, S. Koch (Ed.). Copyright © 1963 by McGraw-Hill Book Company. Used with permission of McGraw-Hill Book Company.

But just what is the evidence that such cognitive drives are in fact operative in normal human thinking? Just how does this theory improve our understanding of what goes on in appropriate thinking that "conveys us to solutions of problems"?

First, consider the claims made for (*a*). Berlyne makes much of the fact that "as many writers have remarked, thinking does not occur when things follow a smooth, accustomed course" (Berlyne, 1965, p. 279)—rather, it begins with some sort of "problem," "question," or "gap," and continues until the problem is solved, the gap filled (Berlyne, 1965, pp. 279–289). But this is hardly evidence for the claim that conceptual conflict is a drive-inducing state which "activates" thinking, since it simply restates what the behavior is which this drive must, allegedly, explain. To say that in a question "the interrogative adverb provides a motivating perplexity conflict; it implies an information space, with some attendant uncertainty in the questioner" (Berlyne, 1960, p. 289) is to bombinate a bombastic truism, not to give evidence for a drive which serves "to keep the epistemic process moving, and to determine in what direction it will turn at each choice point" (Berlyne, 1960, p. 290). Again, in a section entitled "Evidence for motivating effects of conceptual conflict," Berlyne cites experiments showing that when "conceptual conflict" over some subject is aroused, people tend to report more "epistimic curiousity" (that is, they want to know more about it), children tend to evince greater "interest" in the subject and to be more eager to learn about it, etc. (Berlyne, 1965, pp. 261–269). Since Berlyne identifies conceptual conflict with "doubt," "perplexity," "confusion," and the like (Berlyne, 1965, pp. 257–258), this amounts to the not very startling "discovery" that when people find themselves confused or in doubt about something, they may want to know more about it. Surely such truisms fail to do what Berlyne wants them to do, namely, give "credibility to the postulated drive-inducing power of conceptual conflict" (Berlyne, 1965, p. 269).

If the claim that directed thinking is instigated by an antecedent state of drive is to be substantiated, then there must be a way of identifying that drive without making reference to the goal-directed thought processes (for example, solving the problem, clearing up the confusion) whose occurrence this drive is to explain. This, as was argued earlier (Section IIIB), is essential for any drive theory of motivation. How could this be done? Berlyne reports evidence showing that various "indices of arousal" (for example, alpha waves, muscle tensions, skin resistance) are higher when someone is thinking than when he is sitting and relaxing (Berlyne, 1965, pp. 294–299). This shows what few would doubt, namely, that various physiological processes occur when people think. But evidence for a general state of arousal during thinking is hardly evidence for a specific drive state which sets off thinking. Besides, since this drive is held to "depend primarily on the collative properties of the external environment"—even "how much conflict there will be at any particular times depends largely, we may surmise, on the collative properties of the stimuli that are acting on the organism" (Berlyne, 1963, p. 351)—its link with physiological processes must be, as Berlyne himself points out, via the influence of such "collative stimuli" on arousal (Berlyne, 1963, p. 313). So the drive state which allegedly "activates" directed thinking should be specifiable in terms of those "collative properties of the external environment" on which it is supposed to depend. And if this alleged drive were really specifiable in terms of properties of the external environment, then there would be a way of identifying it in conceptual independence from the thought processes it is to motivate, so that we would have the sort of motivational state needed for a drive theory of thinking.

Unfortunately, it is very hard to see how such independent specification can be given, for collative properties are properties like novelty, complexity, incongruity, surprisingness, and Berlyne gives them that name because "they all depend on collation or comparison of information from different stimulus elements"; these need not be simultaneously present but may be "elements belonging to the present and the past" (Berlyne, 1965, p. 246). But this, surely, amounts to saying that these are *not* "properties of the external environment." Berlyne himself admits that while it is "convenient and usual to talk of them as properties of stimulus patterns," they can also be regarded as "relations between properties of the stimulus field and properties of the organism" (Berlyne, 1963, p. 290). But are these physical properties of the organism? Since characteristics like novelty, complexity, and the like are judged in relation to a person's cognitive expectations, the relation in terms of which of these collative properties are to be identified seems to be, not a relation between physical stimuli and physiological states of the organism, but the relation between a man's expectations, beliefs, and so forth, and a situation he finds thought-provoking on the basis of these expectations, etc. No wonder Berlyne finds that the attempt to measure collative properties "lands us in all kinds of perplexities from the outset" because of the difficulty of "knowing what exactly we ought to be looking at in both [organism and environment]" (Berlyne, 1963, p. 291). On this showing, the collative properties, in terms of which this drive is to be specified, cannot be identified without reference to the very thoughts for whose occurrence that drive is supposed to be a (conceptually independent) antecedent condition.

Piaget makes a related point, in his discussion of Berlyne's theory, when he says that a subject at a certain level of development

> . . . will ask himself different questions and will therefore experience needs different from those of a subject who has not attained this level. And above all, he will feel different

compatabilities and incompatabilities and will therefore experience different 'conflicts', as well as 'uncertainties' and novel 'surprises' (Piaget, 1960, p. 117).

As we have seen, considerations of this sort lead Piaget to hold that the "functional needs" which motivate thinking are conceptually "indissociable" from it, and to conceptualize the motivation for cognitive activities in a way that differs sharply from drive theory (see Section IIIB).

In sum, Berlyne contends that "collative properties" are a source of intrinsic motivation because they produce conceptual conflict which arouses drive. But the drive-inducing conflict, which is supposed to depend on "collative properties of the external environment," turns out not to be identifiable by reference to the stimulus field because it is a function of the subject's cognitions. And as long as the drive that is, allegedly, operative in directed thinking is not identified without reference to the directed thought processes it is to explain, there can be no substance to the claim that we have even the barest outline of a drive theory of thinking—that is, an account of its "motivation," not in terms of aims or goals, but in terms of antecedent conditions involved in its instigation. So far, the claim that conceptual conflict arouses a drive which sets off epistemic behavior adds nothing to our knowledge, but simply translates into the jargon of behavior theory the fact for whose explanation that theory was supposed to be indispensable: namely, when a person finds something doubtful or surprising, when he has some question or problem—that is, when there is "conceptual conflict"—he is likely to look for answers or solutions.

Next, consider (*b*), the direction of thought. I do not intend to examine in any detail Berlyne's account of how in directed ("transformational") thinking "the steering function may be exercised by some kind of conflict reduction" (Berlyne, 1965, p. 338)—an account which he himself characterizes as "flagrantly speculative" (Berlyne, 1965, p. 303). However, one general point concerning the character of this whole enterprise should be noted: Normally, talk about "directed thinking" that proceeds according to "legitimate," "appropriate," or "permissible" steps implies that the thinker has an aim, namely, to solve some problem or difficulty, and that he has criteria, certain rules, norms, or maxims, prescribing what *should* be done, which define what can be an "acceptable" solution to his problem or difficulty. Berlyne wants his "transformational responses" to account for this, but at the same time he wants them to be located in the same conceptual space as "situational responses," that is, within the framework of a behavior theory which has no room for rule-following actions. And it is very hard to see how both of these things are possible. If, as Berlyne tries to show, there are "mechanisms" which "impel" the occurrence of transformational thoughts, then it is hard to see how the thinker can be following rules, how the notion of recognizing and correcting mistakes can be applicable to his behavior, how there can be any room for concepts like "legitimate." If, on the other hand, such concepts are to apply, then it would seem that thinking must be in the thinker's control and so cannot be explained by elaborating the mechanisms that account for simple conditioning, that is, for behaviors that are not in the animal's control.[6] The fact that Berlyne wants it both ways may be what prompted Piaget's comment, that Berlyne fails to "choose without equivocation" between two very different models: that of behavior theory, and that provided by Piagetian 'operations' " (Berlyne & Piaget, 1960, p. 113). In effect, Berlyne's attempt to account for transformational thinking in terms of stimulus-response drive theory negates the distinction between "appropriate" directed thinking and thinking which is "driven," for example, by some overpowering wish, the very distinction which he seeks to recognize by bringing in transformational responses and a special drive due to conceptual conflict.

Finally, let us turn to (*c*). "The relief of conceptual conflict," so Berlyne claims, "will mark the point at which the thought process has reached a solution and can appropriately end; its reinforcing power will cause the products of the thought process to be retained" (Berlyne, 1965, p. 294). So the reduction of conceptual conflict is to help explain the "piecing together of a sequence of 'legitimate steps' or acceptable transformations" (Berlyne, 1965, p. 306)—removal of the conflict is to signal arrival at the "solution" with which thinking can "appropriately end"—and conflict reduction is to be the reward which reinforces such behavior—"knowledge is welcomed . . .If we are right, for its power to relieve conflict" (Berlyne, 1965, p. 324).

Berlyne admits that "there have been regrettably few experiments directly aimed at the hypothesis that . . . dimunition of conceptual conflict will reinforce learned responses" (Berlyne, 1965, p. 269), but he does cite a few studies in which, for example, children remember more facts when they are asked questions to which these facts are answers than when they are just presented with a list of these facts (Berlyne, 1965, p. 269, 1960, p. 296). But do we need experiments to establish that "questions heighten epistemic curiosity," and do we need drive theory in order to explain why asking questions facilitates "the retention of facts that answer the questions" (Berlyne, 1960, p. 297)?

As for the piecing together of "legitimate steps," Berlyne gives us an odd analogy and a label. The analogy is that just as in rescuing a drowning man one can build a chain by having "each person grasp the legs of the

[6] A similar point is discussed in detail by Toulmin in his criticism of "verbal conditioning." See Toulmin (1969, especially pp. 87–94).

next until the last one can secure a firm grip on the victim," so in thinking one "begins with a represented stimulus situation that he recognizes as real" and then

> . . . establishes a transformation, and the represented situation that results from this transformation is thereby invested with the same status of truth and reality that belongs to the initial situation. . . This same status of truth or reality is then transmitted to yet another represented situation by the next transformation and so on (Berlyne, 1965, p. 307).

Berlyne calls this "recursive anchoring," but the label is about the only thing the two cases have in common. If whatever happens to reduce a person's conceptual conflict is to count as a "solution," then the distinction between directed and autistic thinking, which Berlyne is trying to explain, has again been lost. If, on the other hand, the solution is to have the "status of truth and reality," then the thinker must have criteria for recognizing the initial situation as "real" and the transformations as "appropriate." Unless the question is begged from the start by presupposing such criteria, the analogy to the chain of rescuers does not even begin to suggest a "mechanism" that could explain how the thinker can use such criteria in order to find a "solution [with which directed thinking] can appropriately end."

As if aware that his "recursive anchorings" are slipping, Berlyne goes on to say that

> . . . we are still far from the time when we shall understand the exact psychological mechanism, let alone the physiological mechanism, of recursive anchoring, which conveys the sanction of validity from the starting point to the end point of a solution chain and relieves conceptual conflict (Berlyne, 1965, p. 307).

But what is at issue is whether this is because we lack empirical knowledge, or because there is a conceptual absurdity in trying to get a "psychological mechanism" to crank out the "sanction of validity." How could one possibly explain why the mathematician's formula "has a reward value when it occurs as the final stage of a valid proof that it lacks when performed in other contexts" (Berlyne, 1960, p. 280), without bringing in the criteria in virtue of which his performance is a valid proof?

B. Cognitive Conflict and Common Sense. Since the prospects for explaining the motivation of directed thinking in terms of drive theory do not seem promising, we must return to the question: Why is cognitive conflict motivating? If someone becomes aware of some conflict, inconsistency, or dissonance between his beliefs, then he surely has a reason for trying to reduce the conflict or inconsistency, for trying to achieve a better fit, a greater coherence, among his cognitions. Since to have a reason for doing something is, in one sense, to have a motive for doing it, we can properly say that cognitive conflict may motivate a person to change his beliefs, or to modify his cognitive system, so as to reduce the conflict.

What sort of explanation are we giving when we cite cognitive conflict as the motive for intellectual activities? Are "needs" like the need for consistency (that is, for equilibrating cognitive perturbations), for understanding what is novel and assimilating what is surprising, needs to answer questions, solve problems, clarify perplexities, and the like, are these antecedent conditions whose occurrence is only contingently correlated with the behaviors they explain? No matter how much a man's beliefs may conflict, he has no reason to change them if he fails to see that they do. Only the recognition of cognitive conflict can be motivating, and if a man faces such a conflict, then, of course, he needs to resolve it; questions need answers and problems need solution for the person to whom they are problems or questions. But do we have to engage in empirical investigations in order to discover this? It is hard to see how someone could understand that something is a problem without understanding that it needs to be solved—though he might, in fact, see this and yet himself not be interested in solving that problem. Could someone have the concept of "consistency" and yet fail to grasp that inconsistent beliefs need to be reconciled? No doubt, one could recognize an inconsistency between one's beliefs, and so have a reason for trying to make them consistent, yet fail to do so because one has stronger reasons for not changing these beliefs. But could one, having recognized an inconsistency, simply fail to see that this is *any* reason for making one's thinking more consistent?

It is clearly a factual, rather than conceptual, question whether or not a given person will see a certain situation as problematic or perplexing, whether or not he will recognize that certain beliefs are inconsistent or conflicting, and the like. It is also a question of fact whether or not a given problem or perplexity interests a certain person, in certain circumstances, sufficiently so that he tries to solve or clarify it; or whether or not this inconsistency, encountered in that context, is a sufficient reason for this person to try to remove the inconsistency. But when we say that inconsistencies need to be removed, perplexities need to be clarified, dissonant cognitions need to be adjusted to fit better, novelties need to be assimilated to what is known, and so forth, we are not enunciating empirical discoveries but are stating the prescriptions that guide directed thinking. To say that problems need solutions, cognitive conflicts need to be reconciled (equilibrated), etc., is to say that they should be solved, reconciled, etc. And if someone asks why they should be, the answer one would ordinarily give is that norms like consistency, clarity, coherence, and the like, govern directed thinking; to say that they "should be" is to acknowledge the normative force of these rules over our thinking, to recognize that deviations from these norms are mistakes that need correction. This system of norms defines the social practice with which we are dealing, and there is no way of saying what constitutes "directed thinking" without appealing to these norms.[7]

Piaget, unlike drive theorists, recognizes that one cannot provide an adequate account of intellectual development and activity without bringing in such norms ("values"). But Piaget discusses the "process" of equilibration as if he were presenting an empirical theory about the workings of the mind, a theory which is continuous with biological theories about organic processes of assimilation and accommodation. Now, I want to suggest that Piaget's *general* account of equilibration, of the way in which the child's awareness of cognitive perturbations (conflicts) motivates his intellectual development and functioning, does not constitute a theory to be confirmed or refuted by facts; it is an analysis, or rational reconstruction, of how we think in accordance with the norms that govern directed thinking—an analysis which Piaget uses as a framework for an empirical mapping of the stages through which the child passes in coming to think in accordance with the norms of adult logic.

Piaget's general account of the equilibration of cognitive perturbations is, in fact, rather like the analysis of problem solving which Dewey gives in *How we think* (1910).[8] Both stress the notion that directed thinking starts with some specific "problem" or "perplexity," some "obstacle," "felt difficulty," or "conflict" (Dewey, 1910, pp. 9, 64, 72). Both note that the "object of thinking is to introduce congruity" between the conflicting elements (Dewey, 1910, p. 72), to "link together into a consistent whole apparently discrepant" elements (Dewey, 1910, p. 76). Both hold that this aim—that is, to solve a specific problem or conflict by working out an appropriate "fit" between the dissonant element and the cognitions relative to which it appeared problematic or conflicting—is what guides directed thinking (Dewey, 1910, p. 12 and *passim*). Both insist that thinking is always selective (Dewey, 1910, p. 103), and that what is selected

[7] One might, of course, want to know why this practice came into being. And here the fact that it has survival value—that is, people need some degree of order, clarity, etc. in their thinking if they are to survive, let alone be rational members of society—is surely relevant. But these matters are at a different level; one does not, typically, solve problems, or remove inconsistencies in one's thinking in order to survive.

[8] It may be worth noting that Piaget refers to Dewey in connection with his own discussion of how interests motivate intellectual activities. See Piaget (1954a, p. 43).

depends on the "acquired habitual modes of understanding" with which someone approaches the matter (Dewey, 1910, p. 106)—that is, on what Piaget calls "assimilatory schemas." For both, "only the novel demands attention, which, in turn, can be given only through the old" (Dewey, 1910, p. 222), so that the interests which motivate a person's thinking are a function of his cognitive schemas.

An analysis of this sort provides us with a framework in which the various calculations and deliberations that are specific cases of directed thinking can be located and explained in relation to the thinker's aims and the norms that guide directed thinking. Within this framework it is possible to investigate empirically questions about what children at various stages of development recognize as problematic, what sort of conflicts they experience, and what sort of inconsistencies or dissonances, in what sort of situations, are usually sufficient to motivate them to change their beliefs, and the like. Dewey, who did no empirical studies of children, could say that "the baby's problem determines his thinking" (Dewey, 1910, p. 157), which is easy enough, since it follows from the (nonempirical) claim that directed thinking is guided by a specific problem which the thinker faces. Piaget's important empirical contribution lies in the ingenious ways in which he has managed to answer a question which Dewey regarded as "unanswerable in detail" (Dewey, 1910, p. 157)—namely, just what is the baby, or at least the young child, thinking? Piaget has traced in great detail the stages through which the child passes in coming to think as we do; by showing us what the child is able to understand at various stages of development, what his aims and interests are, he shows us the sort of considerations that can have weight for the child, the "calculations" he is able to construct, in short, the way he thinks. Whether his account of these stages—that is, of what, typically, interests the child at various levels of development, what sort of conflict and cognitive perturbations he encounters, and which of these are, typically, sufficient for him to make changes in his cognitive system—is correct, is a question of fact. To put it in terms of Flavell's distinction, Piaget's "stage-dependent contributions" (Flavell, 1963, p. 411) are empirical; but, so I am arguing, Piaget's "stage-independent" account of how cognitive conflicts (perturbations) motivate the "equilibrations" through which the child moves from one stage to the next, is not. The conflicts and perturbations which motivate the child to adopt more coherent, reversible, etc. modes of thought are essentially logical—they are conflicts and perturbations that arise when the child is thinking about a specific subject and attempts to achieve a more adequate grasp of its structure. It is only by applying logical concepts like consistency, relevance, and others, to the specific subject matter with which the child is coping that we can interpret what Piaget says about cognitive "perturbations" and the restoration of "equilibrium."[9] To say that cognitive conflict motivates the transition to more equilibrated ("rational") modes of thought thus turns out to be rather like saying that the recognition of a mistake in adding is what motivates one to change the addition.

But this does not denigrate the value of Piaget's work. Where investigators like Festinger have been primarily concerned, not with thinking that is "responsive to the real world," but with distortions of thinking that may result from attempts to reduce "cognitive dissonance" (Festinger, 1958, p. 71), Piaget is concerned with normal, appropriate, directed thinking. And the key characteristic of such thinking, in the adult, is precisely that it can normally be explained by the same considerations that justify it in relation to the thinker's problem or perplexity and the logical requirements of the situation—this is why a request to explain why one thought such and such in this situation is, normally, answered by citing the evidence and reasoning that justify one's thinking it. Piaget has set himself the task of understanding the genesis of such thinking, and to this end he has sought to discover the stages through which the child, typically, passes in coming to think as we do. In order to account for the transitions from one such stage to the next, Piaget gives us, so I am arguing, a rational reconstruction of the "calculations," the "aims," "strategies," and "reasonings," which could, typically, lead the child from one way of thinking about objects, or physical transformations, and the like to the next, which is less liable to "errors" and "perturbations." The direction of development is thus towards greater "rationality," seen in light of the mature, adult logic towards which it tends; and the explanation for the transitions that are found in this development coincides with their justification—it consists in exhibiting the "failures and insufficiencies" of the earlier way of thinking, the greater coherence, "reversibility," etc., which thinking achieves at the next stage.[10]

Such rational calculations can, indeed, help us to understand why the child gives up one way of thinking in favor of another. But they do this in a way similar to that in which, for example, historians can explain why a statesman changed his point of view, or a scientist came to see his

[9] Flavell has pointed out that sometimes Piaget also characterizes equilibration in terms of the principle of "least action," but here again it seems clear that this has to be cashed in logical terms—for example, something like what Mach and others have called the "economy of thought."

[10] It is interesting to note that the conclusion for which I am here arguing is like one to which Kohlberg is led by his studies of the development of (normal) moral reasoning—namely, that a "scientific theory as to why people factually *do* move upward from stage to stage . . . [coincides with a] theory as to why people *should* prefer a higher stage to a lower" (*p. 223*). See also *p. 154*.

problem in a different way—by setting forth the considerations, known to be available to this person, which he could have used to justify this change in his thinking. If we are puzzled by why someone should have thought "so and so" in a certain situation, the puzzle can be removed by exhibiting the pattern of reasons which were his justification for thinking it; but such explanations can be constructed without bringing in a theory of motivation discovered by psychology (see Mischel, 1963). Piaget's main concern is, of course, with the development of rational thinking, and he explains the course of this development by locating its stages in relation to the goal towards which it is directed. When Piaget appeals to the "mechanism of equilibration" in order to account for the transition from one way of thinking to another, his explanation really consists in making clear just what problem the child is trying to solve with the intellectual means available to him, and why the new mode of thinking he adopts is more consistent, clear, reversible—that is, "rational"—than the one that preceded. The transition is thus explained by being located as a definite step in the direction of rational thinking, whose genesis we are trying to understand. The ultimate goal is the rationality of the mature adult, and the considerations that justify the transition to the more rational way of thinking—the smaller number of "errors," "inadequacies," and "perturbations" to which it is liable—are also the considerations that explain the transition.

It is important to notice, in this connection, that Piaget is concerned not only with thinking that is normal and appropriate, but also with thinking that is typical—his theory is "geared exclusively to the normative, 'in general' aspects of cognitive ontogenesis . . . it contains no obvious conceptual machinery for dealing with individual-differences development" (Flavell, 1963, p. 440). If we are trying to account, not for individual differences in the speed or level of development, but only for the normal and typical course which development "in general" takes towards more "rational" ways of thinking, then it is hard to see how, once the greater "rationality" of the new stage is exhibited, any further explanation is needed in order to account for the transition. Once we understand how this new mode of thought gives the child a more coherent, relevant, reversible, etc., grasp of the structure of the subject matter about which he is thinking, what is there left to explain?

It may be suggested that we must postulate something like a "need for rationality" in order to explain what "moves" the child towards being consistent, avoiding irrelevance, and the like. But what could this "need for rationality" be other than just that tendency towards being consistent, avoiding irrelevance, and the like, which it is supposed to explain? And are we really dealing with something that requires, or permits, psychological explanation? Will this child recognize that inconsistency in this context, and if he does, will this be sufficient to lead him, in these circumstances, to alter his thinking in the direction of greater consistency and relevance? These are psychological questions which must be answered by empirical investigation.[11] But if someone asks why there is consistency, relevance, etc. in thinking, he is not asking a psychological question that could be answered empirically by, for example, discovering the existence of "needs" for consistency, or relevance, etc. For it cannot be just a contingent fact that directed thinking has these characteristics. Nothing goes wrong with our concept of (directed) "thinking" if we suppose a thinker who fails to recognize this or that inconsistency in his thoughts, or who does nothing about an inconsistency he has recognized because he is too tired or distracted, or because he believes this inconsistency is "profound," and the like. But we simply could not make sense of a "thinker" who just happens not to care about consistency and relevance, who just does not see that there is ever any need for relevance, consistency, etc. in his thinking; for then, what reason could there be to call the activity in which he is engaged "(directed) thinking"?

What is in need of empirical explanation is the contingent fact that people vary enormously in their cognitive performances. Why do children develop to a given level with different speeds, and why do some children fail to develop past a certain level? What accounts for the great differences in the intellectual goals and aspirations of people, in the persistence with which they pursue their interests, in their sensitivity to irrelevance and in their ability to spot inconsistencies, in the efforts they are willing to expand in learning and thinking, etc.? And what accounts for the various distortions that can occur in thinking, the various deformations that may be found in the development of thought? These matters may, of course, be contingently connected with, among other things, the fact that different people have different "ego needs" (for example, for self-respect), different social needs (for example, for praise, for achievement), different anxieties, and the like—needs which are conceptually independent of the intellectual activities in which they engage—and the role which such extrinsic needs may play in cognitive development and functioning can only be ascertained through empirical investigation.

Piaget readily admits that such extrinsic motivations can accelerate, or impede and decelerate, cognitive activities (Piaget, 1954a, p. 6), but he regards this as a matter of concern for the "psychology of differences"

[11] These are, I think, the "cognitive bridges" leading to, and from, cognitive conflict, to which Flavell refers (*p. 126*); as he points out, such bridges are presupposed by cognitive conflict explanations, and cannot themselves be "explained in cognitive conflict terms."

rather than for "general psychology" (Piaget, 1954a, pp. 67–68) and has not himself devoted much attention to it. Similarly, Piaget recognizes that such motivations can distort directed thinking and deform normal intellectual development (Piaget, 1954a, p. 117). He suggests that these pathological phenomena, to which psychoanalysis has called attention, can be understood as regressions to "feelings or affective states of a different level, generally an inferior level" (Piaget, 1954a, p. 154), but this again is outside the "general psychology" which Piaget has taken for his domain.

V. Conclusion

Behavior theorists like Berlyne begin with a paradigm according to which all behavior must be motivated, in the sense that there must be some aversive antecedent state which explains the initiation, energizing, and, in part, the "direction" of behavior; they then try to envisage ways in which directed thinking can be made to fit this model. I have argued that thinking "whose function is to convey us to the solution of problems" does not fit this Procrustean bed, that the motivation of such directed thinking cannot be adequately understood in terms of the drive-reduction model.

Piaget, as I understand him, holds instead that the motivation of typical, appropriate thinking must be understood in relation to the thinker's aim—his "interest" in solving a specific problem, or equilibrating a specific cognitive perturbation—and the norms which guide directed thinking—the thinker's "need" to make sense of the novel in terms of the schemas available to him, in ways that tend towards increasing coherence, clarity, and stability. Though Piaget expresses this in the quasi-biological language of the assimilation–accommodation model of equilibration, I have argued that this *general* account is not an empirical theory but an analysis, or rational reconstruction, of directed thinking. This analysis provides a conceptual framework which Piaget fills with empirical content in his *specific* accounts of the various stages through which the child passes in coming to think as we do.

Piaget thus makes clear to us the genesis of our thinking, the stages through which we typically pass in coming to follow the norms of adult, logical thinking. Since he exhibits the intellectual equipment available to the child at a given stage, and so makes clear what the child can understand, take an interest in, aim at, etc., Piaget also shows us the "considerations" that can be operative for the child and enables us to understand how he thinks—that is, the sort of calculations, reasonings, and justificatory moves that are possible for, and characteristic of, the child at a given stage of development. The growth of logical thinking is thus mapped in relation to the goal towards which it is directed. In order to explain the normal, typical transitions from one stage of development to the next, Piaget points, primarily, to the "failures and inadequacies" of the earlier way of thinking, the "errors" to which it leads. This, so I have argued, explains the transition in terms of the considerations (for example, greater coherence, stability, reversibility) that justify it—much as showing the considerations in terms of which a person justifies the moves he makes in solving a problem also explains why he makes these moves, at least insofar as these moves are appropriate and justifiable on the basis of the information available to him. No other motives are needed to explain the transition from one stage to the next, as long as we are dealing with the normal, "in general" trend of cognitive development. Special motivations are required in order to account for deviations from normal development—for example, "extrinsic" motivations like ego needs, or anxieties, may speed up, or slow down, development. In Piaget's view, however, these matters fall into the domain of the "psychology of differences," while "abnormal psychology" deals with motivations that may distort normal intellectual development. But, in that case, the "general psychology" of intellectual development needs no (empirical) theory of motivation at all.

On this account, which is close to our ordinary view of "normal" (that is, typical and appropriate) thinking, no antecedent states of motivation need to be empirically discovered in order to understand what motivates thinking that is justifiable in terms of rational considerations—no interests other than an "interest" in this particular problem or conflict, no needs other than the "need" to deal with it in consistent, clear, and orderly ways, are required. Since the reasons which justify such thinking are sufficient motives for it, it is not necessary to bring any other motivations into the explanation of such thinking. Other motives, that is, special needs or desires whose influence must be empirically discovered by psychology, may in fact be operative in a given case, and it may turn out to be the case that such motives are of crucial importance when we try to explain individual differences in directed thinking, or the various distortions to which such thinking is liable. But since Piaget relegates these matters to the psychology of differences and pathology, he really needs no empirical theory of motivation for his "general psychology" of thinking. Nor does he, if I am right, have one.

In sum, if, as Piaget contends, "morality is a logic of action, as logic is a morality of thought" (Piaget, 1954a, p. 11), then thinking which conforms to this "morality" can be understood in terms of the reasons that justify it, and no other motivations are needed to explain it. But such appropriate, directed thinking is only one of many different activities that fall under the general rubric of "thinking." And there are many important questions about the relation between the well-ordered, conscious, and appropriate activity of directed thinking, which has been the sole concern of this article, and the confused profusion of mental processes which may be going on simultaneously without the person's being fully, or perhaps even partly, conscious of them—processes which may be motivated in different ways, and which may sometimes have an influence on directed thinking (see Neisser, 1967, Chap. 11). But these questions are beyond the scope of this article.

Postscript

What appears above is a revision of the draft I prepared prior to the conference, and has benefited not only from Ausubel's thoughtful comments, but also from the very helpful ways in which the other participants discussed my draft at the conference. I am grateful to them for enabling me to make what I wanted to say much clearer than it originally was.

But there remains a central point which I did not treat adequately in my article, and which I may be able to bring out by delineating more sharply the issue over which Ausubel and I differ. He agrees that "motivational factors need not be invoked" (*p. 360*) to account for the transition from one stage of development to the next, indeed he places "equally little weight" (*p. 358*) on such factors, so that we do not differ with respect to the sort of motivational explanation that is required for a theory of cognitive development. And even with respect to "contemporaneous" cognitive performances, Ausubel agrees that "motivation is not an indispensable condition" (*p. 359*), though he thinks that both extrinsic and intrinsic motivation "customarily facilitates and energizes such functioning" (*p. 361*). I argued that the motives for appropriate thinking may simply be the reasons that justify it, so that there is no reason to insist, as drive theorists tend to do, that some other motivation *must* be brought in to explain directed thinking. To put it another way, my point was that cognitive conflict has nothing to do with "energizing," and that energetic notions are not appropriate because the conflicts involved are logical. But whether or not extrinsic motivations are "customarily" involved, especially in "long-term learning enterprises," is a question of fact, and I did not intend to argue about facts—especially not with Ausubel, who is, no doubt, much better acquainted with these facts.

So the issue between us pertains to intrinsic motivation and comes down to this: I support Piaget's rejection of the drive-reduction model and argue that cognitive drives are not appropriate for the explanation of directed thinking, while Ausubel holds that "cognitive drive is an independent antecedent motivational factor that is psychologically real, separately identifiable, and accessible to consciousness," even if we do not know much about its neurophysiological basis or how to measure it behaviorally (*p. 359*). But just what is meant here by "cognitive drive"? Ausubel speaks of the "need to know, to understand . . . to obtain tenable solutions to problems" (*p. 358*), and since his basis for claiming that there is such a need is that it is "psychologically real . . . and accessible to consciousness," I assume that he means by "cognitive drive" something like a desire to know, to understand, and the like—this desire is the "intrinsic motivation" that may be operative in cognitive performances.

But such a desire is conceptually dependent on what it is a desire for—we cannot specify what is meant by a "desire for knowledge" without making reference to the knowledge that is desired. Ausubel agrees, but argues that while the "need to know must be separately identifiable from knowledge-acquiring activities" (*p. 358*), just because cognitive needs "cannot be conceptualized apart from cognitive functions, it does not necessarily follow that they . . . [cannot have] separately identifiable status of their own" (*p. 359*)—a point also stressed by Alston. And, in one sense, they are clearly right. For one thing, since the desire for knowledge finds expression in many activities, we can base the claim that Jones desires knowledge (and believes he can best satisfy that desire at the library) on evidence other than his studying at the library, and so can have clear empirical warrant for holding that he studies at the library because he desires knowledge. Further, a man who desires knowledge is not only likely to do, when circumstances are right, what he believes is required in order to get knowledge; he will also, if sincere, avow his desire for knowledge in appropriate circumstances, and typically, his thoughts and conversation are likely to turn, when the context is appropriate, to matters relating to the acquisition of knowledge (see Alston, 1967a, p. 329). In this sense, the desire for knowledge, though conceptually dependent on its object, can be detected apart from knowledge-acquiring activities and so can have "separately identifiable status."

It should, however, be noted that a man who avows his desire for knowledge is not reporting some inner occurrence; normally, we would take him to be telling us that he means to get knowledge—he is, if sincere, expressing his intention to do what it takes, when the circumstances are right, in order to achieve this goal. Again, a man who desires knowledge will, in standard cases, tend to converse with others, when the situation allows, about various problems and issues, books, lectures, and the like, and his thoughts are likely to turn to such matters when he has the chance. But such patterns of talk and thought indicate a desire for knowledge only if they are, in some way, relevant to his acquisition of knowledge, or are expressions of his intent to do so. If they are animated by a different aim—for example, to impress others, or to avoid thinking about some personal problem—then they are not expressions of a desire for knowledge. So while we do, in standard cases, have indicators of a desire for knowledge other than the person's engaging in the acquisition of knowledge, what they indicate is that the person aims to get knowledge.

Talk about a person's "desire for knowledge" thus does enable us to link some of his actions with some of his avowals and with patterns of his thought and conversation, but it does so by connecting these with the goal towards which the agent is aiming. That is, we find an intelligible pattern in what the person does, says, and thinks, in certain circumstances, by seeing that, given his beliefs, these are all relevant and appropriate in relation to his goal of acquiring knowledge. So while we can have good empirical warrant for claiming that a person engages in certain activities, or tends to think and talk about certain things, because he desires knowledge, the "because" here is not causal in the usual sense. We are saying that he does these things *in order to* get knowledge; we are explaining what he does, says, and thinks, in terms of his purpose or intent, in conjunction with his beliefs, and not in terms of a separate condition that precedes and triggers his behaviors. And this is sufficient reason for insisting that a desire for knowledge is not a "cognitive drive." As I argued in my article, the point of drive theory is to provide an account of motivation which makes no appeal to purpose or cognition. If a desire for knowledge explains in terms of the agent's purpose and beliefs, then it is not a "drive," that is, a factor that can account for the motivation of behavior in terms of the conditions involved in its instigation, without bringing in purposes and the like.

Further, the principles which we use when we connect a man's deeds, talk, and thoughts, into a purposive pattern of this sort do not seem to be merely contingent. We do not discover that, as a matter of contingent fact, the various knowledge-getting activities in which a person engages are regularly preceded by a certain condition, or state, which we identify as the "desire for knowledge"; a person who avows this desire is not reporting the occurrence of such a state, and our belief that this desire is, typically, expressed in certain patterns of thought and talk does not rest on the empirical discovery that these are regularly preceded by that state. Rather, we first discover whether or not a man desires knowledge by seeing whether, in proper circumstances, he does what he thinks is required for getting knowledge, whether he sincerely expresses his intent to do so (avows the desire), and whether even in his unguarded thoughts and conversation he expresses this intent and tries to come closer to this goal.

That is, we do not find that there is an empirical correlation between actions, thoughts, and words, on the one hand, and something else—the desire for knowledge—on the other; rather, we attribute that desire to someone because we discern a common intent in his actions, thoughts, and words. Thus, we do not discover that a desire for knowledge is, as a matter of contingent fact, correlated with certain behaviors. Instead, we know to begin with what behaviors are *appropriate*, given the relevant beliefs, if one desires knowledge, and we attribute that desire on the basis of whether or not the person behaves in ways appropriate for someone who desires knowledge. Of course, we may be mistaken in attributing this desire to someone. But if we are, the mistake is not that an empirical generalization correlating these behaviors with a desire for knowledge just happens not to hold; it is that these ways of acting, talking, and thinking did not have the aim, or intent, we thought they had. Such purposive explanations can certainly have empirical content: we can detect that someone desires knowledge and believes that doing X is appropriate to its attainment in certain circumstances, without waiting for him to do X, and so can have empirical warrant when we explain why he does X in terms of his desire for knowledge. But the principles involved in such explanations—for example, the principle linking a desire for knowledge to certain ways of acting, thinking, and talking, when the circumstances are appropriate from the agent's point of view—do not seem to be merely contingent.

No doubt, some of these issues are highly complex and could be debated. But it does seem clear, at least, that if we account for behavior in terms of a desire for knowledge, we are giving some sort of purposive, "intentionalistic," explanation. In fact, Ausubel himself uses concepts that are essentially purposive—for example, "objectives," "positive values," "anticipation of future satisfying consequences" (*pp. 358–359*)—in explicating his notion of "cognitive drive." Since he also says that his use of this concept is "not necessarily in the traditional behavioristic sense of aversive drives and drive-reduction theory" (*p. 357*), he might even agree with the substance of this point. Whether or not he does, I suggest that talk about "cognitive drives" leads us to think about the motivation of directed thinking in terms of a model which simply does not fit.

References

Alston, W. P. Wants, actions and causal explanation. In Hector-Neri Castaneda (Ed.), *Intentionality, minds and perception*. Detroit, Michigan: Wayne State Univ. Press, 1967. (a)

Alston, W. P. Motives and motivation. In P. Edwards (Ed.), *Encyclopedia of philosophy*. New York: Macmillan, 1967. (b)

Alston, W. P. Feelings. *Philosophical Review*, 1969, **78**(1), 3–34.

Berlyne, D. E. *Conflict, arousal and curiosity*. New York: McGraw-Hill, 1960.

Berlyne, D. E. Motivational problems raised by exploratory and epistemic behavior. In S. Koch (Ed.), *Psychology: A study of a science*. Vol. 5. New York: McGraw-Hill, 1963.

Berlyne, D. E. *Structure and direction in thinking*. New York: Wiley, 1965.

Bruner, J. S. Inhelder and Piaget's "Growh of logical thinking." *British Journal of Psychology*, 1959, **50**, 363–370.

Dewey, J. *How we think*. Boston, Massachusetts: Heath, 1910.

Festinger, L. *A theory of cognitive dissonance*. New York: Harper, 1957.

Festinger, L. The motivating effect of cognitive dissonance. In G. Lindzey (Ed.), *Assessment of human motives*. New York: Holt, 1958.

Flavell, J. H. *The Developmental psychology of Jean Piaget*. Princeton, New Jersey: Van Nostrand, 1963.

Hanson, N. R. *Patterns of discovery*. Cambridge: Cambridge Univ. Press, 1958.

Hull, C. L. *Principles of behavior*. New York: Appleton, 1943.

Hunt, J. M. Intrinsic motivation and its role in psychological development. In D. Levine (Ed.), *Nebraska symposium on motivation*. Vol. 13. Lincoln, Nebraska: Univ. of Nebraska Press, 1965.

Kagan, J. A developmental approach to conceptual growth. In H. J. Klausmeier & C. W. Harris (Eds.), *Analyses of concept learning*. New York: Academic Press, 1966.

Kenny, A. *Action, emotion and will*. London: Routledge, 1963.

Kuhn, T. S. *The structure of scientific revolution*. Chicago, Illinois: Univ. of Chicago Press, 1962.

Melden, A. I. The conceptual dimensions of emotions. In T. Mischel (Ed.), *Human action: Conceptual and empirical issues*. New York: Academic Press, 1969.

Mischel, T. Psychology and explanations of human behavior. *Philosophy and Phenomenological Research*, 1963, **23**(4), 578–594.

Mischel, T. Scientific and philosophical psychology: A historical introduction. In T. Mischel (Ed.), *Human action: Conceptual and empirical issues*. New York: Academic Press, 1969.

Neisser, U. *Cognitive psychology*. New York: Appleton, 1967.

Peters, R. S. *The concept of motivation*. London: Routledge, 1958.

Peters, R. S. Emotions and the category of passivity. *Proceedings of the Aristotelean Society*, 1961–1962, **62**, 117–134.

Peters, R. S. Motivation, emotion and the conceptual schemes of common sense. In T. Mischel (Ed.), *Human action: Conceptual and empirical issues*. New York: Academic Press, 1969.

Piaget, J. *The child's conception of physical causality*. London: Routledge, 1930.

Piaget, J. *The psychology of intelligence*. New York: Harcourt, 1950.

Piaget, J. *The origins of intelligence in children*. New York: International Univ. Press, 1952.

Piaget, J. *Les relations entre l'affectivité et l'intelligence dans le développment mental de l'enfant*. Paris: Centre de Documentation Univ., 1954 (my translation). (a)

Piaget, J. The problem of consciousness in child psychology. In H. A. Abramson (Ed.), *Problems of consciousness*. New York: Joiah Macy, Jr., Foundation, 1954. (b)

Piaget, J. Logique et équilibre dans les comportements du sujet. In L. Apostel, D. Mandelbrot, & J. Piaget (Eds.), *Logique et équilibre*. Études d'épistémologie génétique, 2. Paris: Presses Univ. de France, 1957 (my translation).

Piaget, J. Apprentissage et conaissance. In P. Gréco & J. Piaget (Eds.), *Apprentissage et conaissance.* Études d'épistémologie génétique, 7. Paris: Presses Univ. de France, 1959 (my translation).

Piaget, J. La porteé psychologique et épistémologique des essais néo-Hulliens de D. Berlyne. In D. E. Berlyne & J. Piaget (Eds.), *Théorie du comportment et opérations.* Études d'épistémologie génétique, 12. Paris: Presses Univ. de France, 1960 (my translation).

Piaget, J. *Six psychological studies.* Edited by D. Elkind. New York: Random House, 1967.

Piaget, J., & Inhelder, B. *The growth of logical thinking.* New York: Basic Books, 1958.

Prentice, W. H. Some cognitive aspects of motivation. *American Psychologist,* 1961, **16,** 503–511.

Singer, J. E. Motivation for consistency. In S. Feldman (Ed.), *Cognitive consistency.* New York: Academic Press, 1966.

Skinner, B. F. *Science and human behavior.* New York: Macmillan, 1953.

Toulmin, S. E. *Foresight and understanding.* Bloomington, Indiana: Indiana Univ. Press, 1961.

Toulmin, S. E. Concepts and the explanation of human behavior. In T. Mischel (Ed.), *Human action: Conceptual and empirical issues.* New York: Academic Press, 1969.

Wolff, P. H. *The developmental psychologies of Jean Piaget and psychoanalysis.* New York: International Univ. Press, 1960.

Woodworth, R. S. *Dynamic psychology.* New York: Columbia Univ. Press, 1918.

MOTIVATIONAL ISSUES IN COGNITIVE DEVELOPMENT: Comments on Mischel's Article

David P. Ausubel

By way of introduction, I would first like to offer the subjective value judgment that motivational issues in cognitive functioning and development are not of the same order of intrinsic importance and theoretical saliency as some of the other psychological and epistemological issues in these areas that have been discussed in this volume. The latter issues to which I refer include, for example, the value and requirements of an adequate stage theory of cognitive development, the role of language and explicit training in such development, the factors that promote transition from one stage of intellective development to another, the theoretical possibility of accelerating cognitive development, and the extent to which that which is knowable is a function of the developmental status of the knower.

My judgment regarding the relative nonsaliency of motivational issues reflects my partial agreement with Mischel's thesis that "no antecedent states of motivation need to be empirically discovered in order to understand what motivates thinking . . . other than an 'interest' in this particular problem or conflict . . . [or] the 'need' to deal with it in consistent, clear, and orderly ways. . ." *(p. 349)*. According to this analysis, motivation is largely an issue in a negative sense or as a species of theoretical red herring. But what makes my position more psychological and less philosophical than Mischel's is the fact that I interpret the need to cope intellectually with ideational problems as typically constituting an independent motivational factor in cognition, although not necessarily in the traditional behavioristic sense of aversive drives and drive-reduction theory.

In my opinion, the issue of motivation impinges on cognition at two principal points. First, one might ask what role motivation ordinarily plays in such "contemporaneous" cognitive phenomena as the acquisition of concepts and propositional knowledge, problem solving, and thinking. Second, what if any is the role of motivation in the transition from one stage of cognitive development to another? These are distinctly different kinds of problems and call for different kinds of answers. With regard to the first problem, I undoubtedly place greater weight than either Piaget or Mischel on the role of motivation in contemporaneous cognitive functioning. With regard to the second problem, we apparently place equally little weight on motivational determinants, but I place somewhat greater weight on proximate as opposed to more ultimate cognitive determinants of intellective development.

In my view, cognitive drive—the need to know, to understand, to experience or generate clear, stable, and coherent ideas, to obtain tenable solutions to problems—*is* an antecedent motivational or energizing force that is derived from holding these objectives as positive values. It is a nonspecific energizing factor in cognition—intrinsic to the ends of cognitive functioning—that is quite different from extrinsic, aversive, and homeostatic motivational factors that are commonly invoked by behavioristically oriented reinforcement and drive-reduction theorists. The effects of cognitive drive on cognitive functioning are mediated, in turn, by such factors as effort, persistence, concentration, and set. This drive can also be enhanced by those aspects of a cognitive learning or problem situation that for a particular learner are moderately novel, generate ideational conflict or incongruity, or call for accommodation, integration, reconciliation, or synthesis. This does not necessarily imply that the latter novelty, conflict, or incongruity act as aversive stimuli via the familiar stimulus paradigm of drive and drive reduction; it merely assumes that the structural properties of the learning situation *vis-à-vis* the learner can augment the need for cognitive mastery derived from prior satisfying experiences of cognitive learning.

Unlike Piaget and other "intrinsic motivation" theorists, however, I do *not* hold that the need represented by cognitive drive arises simply because it is reflective of an existing capacity, that is, simply because "there is an intrinsic need for cognitive organs or structures once generated by functioning to perpetuate themselves by more functioning." I agree with Mischel that the need to know must be separately identifiable from knowledge-acquiring activities and must reflect more than a capacity for acquiring knowledge. Thus, although cognitive drive is probably derived in a very general way from curiosity tendencies and from related predispositions to explore, manipulate, understand, and cope with the environment, the latter predispositions originally manifest *potential* rather than actual motivational properties, and are obviously nonspecific in content and direction. Their potential motivating power is actualized in expression and particularized in direction both as a result of successful exercise and the anticipation of future satisfying consequences from further exercise, and as a result of adopting knowledge acquisition as a positive value in consequence of this satisfying experience and its related anticipations. Far from being largely endogenous in origin, therefore, specific cognitive drives or interests are primarily acquired and dependent upon particular experience.

Thus, the causal relationship between motivation and learning is typically reciprocal rather than unidirectional. Both for this reason, and because motivation is not an indispensable condition of learning, it is unnecessary to postpone learning activities until appropriate interests and motivations have been developed. Frequently, the best way of teaching an unmotivated student is to ignore his motivational state for the time being and to concentrate on teaching him as effectively as possible. Some degree of learning will ensue in any case, despite the lack of motivation; and from the initial satisfaction of learning he will, hopefully, develop the motivation to learn more and will internalize knowledge acquisition as a positive value. In some circumstances, therefore, the most appropriate way of arousing motivation to learn is to focus on the cognitive rather than on the motivational aspects of learning, and to rely on the motivation that is developed retroactively, so to speak, from successful educational achievement to energize further learning.

I would also maintain that cognitive drive is an independent antecedent motivational factor that is psychologically real, separately identifiable, and accessible to consciousness, even though its neurophysiological substrate is presently obscure, and even though, as a psychological variable, it is probably not currently susceptible to precise behavioral measurement. However, psychological variables do not cease to operate simply because their neurophysiological bases cannot be specified or because they defy current attempts at measurement. And, contrary to Mischel's position, I would argue that simply because cognitive needs are derived from and cannot be conceptualized apart from cognitive functions, it does not necessarily follow that they can be reduced to the latter or accorded no separately identifiable status of their own.

Finally, although one does not have to invoke any kind of motivation other than cognitive drive to explain meaningful learning, and although cognitive drive is potentially the most effective motivational factor in such learning, a proper respect for the realities of the human condition obliges one to recognize the role of extrinsic motivations in long-term learning enterprises. Particularly in our utilitarian, competitive, and status-oriented culture, such extrinsic considerations as ego enhancement, anxiety reduction, and career advancement become with increasing age, progressively more significant sources of motivation for school learning. Although educators theoretically decry the use of aversive motivation, they implicitly rely on it, as well as on other extensive motivations, to keep their students studying regularly for their credits, degrees, and diplomas. They do this because they recognize, at least implicitly, that cognitive drive and anticipated rewards for hard work are not sufficient to overcome both inertia and the typical human proclivity toward procrastination and aversion to sustained, regular, and disciplined intellectual work. Any teacher who imagines that the majority of his students would continue their studies in the absence of assigned work, deadlines, and examinations is, in my opinion, living in a world of fantasy. The motivational force of an examination lies more in the fear of failure than in the hope of success. And much of these same relationships undoubtedly prevail between professorial promotions and scholarly production.

I turn now to consideration of the second principal issue—the possible role of motivation in determining the transition from one stage of cognitive development to another. I would certainly agree with Mischel that motivational factors need not be invoked to account for empirically established progressions along the road to mature cognitive functioning. At a more ultimate level of causal explanation, one can hypothesize that if genic potentialities exist for both less and more advanced particular modes of cognitive functioning, and if the ontogenesis of the more mature level depends on successfully passing through antecedent less mature levels, then both the occurrence and the direction of development are more or less predetermined, provided that a minimally adequate degree of intellectual stimulation prevails in a given individual's cultural environment. Progression in this direction is further enhanced, as Mischel notes, by the occurrence and realization of "the failures and inadequancies of the earlier ways of thinking" and of the advantages and greater efficiency attendant upon later modes of thinking in terms of such factors as coherence, reversibility, precision, generality, inclusiveness, and level of abstraction.

It seems to me, however, that one must invoke the operation of more specific and proximate cognitive determinants to account for the progression through the various stages of cognitive development. Thus, one may hypothesize, for example, that the combined influence of three concomitant and mutually supportive trends accounts for the transition from concrete to more abstract modes of cognitive functioning. First, the developing individual gradually acquires a working vocabulary of "transactional" or mediating terms (for example, conditional conjunctions and qualifying adjectives) that makes possible the more efficient juxtaposition and combination of different relatable abstractions into potentially meaningful propositions and their subsequent relationship to cognitive structure.

Second, he can relate these latter propositions more readily to cognitive structure, and hence render them more meaningful, because of his growing fund of stable, higher-order concepts and principles encompassed within that structure. Finally, it seems reasonable to suppose that after many years of practice in understanding and meaningfully manipulating relationships between abstractions *with* the aid of concrete empirical props, the older child gradually develops greater facility in performing these operations, so that eventually (after acquiring the necessary transactional terms and higher-order concepts) he can perform the same operations just as effectively *without* relying on these props.

In addition, Inhelder and Piaget invoke both general and specific motivational explanations to account for the transition from the concrete operational to the formal stage of logical operations. Desire to obtain greater meaning out of experience may conceivably help hasten the cognitive transition that is taking place, but it cannot convincingly explain by itself why it occurs. Desire to identify with and participate in the adult world—for which the transition to the formal stage is regarded as a prerequisite—has more specific relevance for this age period, but again no amount of motivation would suffice to effect the change in question in the absence of the necessary genic potentialities and of the supportive cognitive growth and experience.

Thus, on balance it would appear that cognitive determinants of intellective *development* are much more salient than motivational factors. But insofar as *contemporaneous* cognitive functioning is concerned, I would hold that although motivation is not indispensable, it customarily facilitates and energizes such functioning in an independent antecedent sense –both in its intrinsic form, as cognitive drive, and in its more extrinsic and aversive manifestations. Energizing factors are particularly important in understanding any form of *sustained* or long-term intellectual activity; short-term cognitive activity, on the other hand, can be carried forward without any need to postulate any independent energization, that is, simply by the need intrinsic within the activity itself to reach a coherent understanding or a satisfactory resolution of the problem. However, where motivational factors do operate, they—typically a combination of cognitive drive, ego-enhancement drive, affiliative drive, and anxiety-reducing drive—explain the *general* problem of how long-term cognitive activity is sustained rather than just the existence of individual differences in such activity. These individual differences are accounted for by the relative weight of the various kinds of drive in different persons.

Part III

Theories of Cognitive Development and the Explanation of Human Conduct

IS A THEORY OF CONCEPTUAL DEVELOPMENT NECESSARY? [1]

P. C. Dodwell

I. Introduction

After a review of the preceding articles in this volume, and with the fruits of an earlier discussion along related lines now available in *Human action* (Mischel, 1969), one begins to wonder how many useful comments there are left to make. One breach remains to be filled, I think, which is opened up by a tendency, in confrontations between philosophers and psychologists, for each group to stick to its own methods of attack on problems about behavior. Psychologists look for the simplest, most powerful or elegant principles and models by which to explain their findings: philosophers argue that psychologists' theories are generally inadequate because they are too crude, neglecting even the mildest subtleties embedded in our everyday language for describing and evaluating behavior. I have some sympathy for both points of view; both cannot be entirely correct, since they are mutually contradictory, yet it seems to me that they each have valid and important things to say about the explanation of behavior. I shall attempt a defense of psychological theorizing, and suggest how the objections of philosophers—or at least some of these objections—can be met.

Theories are devised in order to provide explanations for facts; so the heart of the matter is reached by asking: Why have theories of cognitive development? Is it *necessary* to hold such theories? These are strange questions to ask. What if one put it more broadly: Is *any* psychological theory necessary? Or, for that matter: Is any scientific theory *necessary*? That formulation strikes us as strange because, of course, we should all

[1] This article was planned and most of it written at the Center for Advanced Study in the Behavioral Sciences during tenure of a Guggenheim Fellowship. Support from both sources is gratefully acknowledged.

agree that science as we understand it today would not be science without the underpinning of an elaborate conceptual apparatus which has developed along with, and guided, empirical research. So my answer to the original question must be: Of course a theory of cognitive development is necessary if we want to explain and understand human cognition at a level which is more profound than our everyday, common-sense understanding of what it means to think. Every scientist—and psychologists are no exception—is motivated by the desire to grasp the nature of the phenomena he studies. And this, in very many fields of scientific endeavor, if not in most, has meant *denying* the assumptions and precepts of established orthodoxy, or of common sense. Galileo did it; Darwin did it; Einstein did it, to name three outstanding examples. Therefore, there is a potential danger in criticizing a young science for failing to hold its concepts and theories in line with established everyday usage. That line of argument has too often failed in the past for us to accept it now with equanimity.

My point is not that psychological theorists have always been on the right track—clearly enough they have at times been thoroughly misguided—it is that conformity with everyday usage can scarcely be a sufficient criterion for a valid scientific theory in psychology. And yet there is a puzzle here, expressed aptly by Peters in his contribution to *Human action*. It is the puzzle of "... the relationship between psychological theories and the less specialized knowledge that enables us most of the time to make sense of each other's behavior and of our own" (Peters, 1969).

The facts which psychologists gather do not in themselves usually lead to such puzzles. Establishing antecedent–consequent relations such as that between order of birth and later personality characteristics, or making empirical generalizations about norms of development, or devising more efficient methods of inculcating arithmetical concepts and operations in young children, may be thought to be "neutral" and harmless enough, as far as threatening common-sense understanding of child development is concerned. Yet the fact is that few psychologists are prepared to let the matter rest with simple fact gathering, or with making straightforward empirical generalizations. They want to understand *why* the generalization holds; why one method of instruction is more efficient than another; why children develop in just this way and not that. And here our everyday views may not be especially helpful. It is the desire to "go beyond" these views, in some sense to reach a deeper analysis of the phenomena, which leads to the theories which may seem to offend common sense. What is more, there is—or was—a conviction amongst certain schools of psychology that their theories, because they reached beyond appearances to the true state of affairs, should *displace* common-sense accounts.

II. The Incompleteness of Scientific Theories

That particular form of arrogance—the belief in sufficiently powerful principles of explanation to claim a monopoly, with an unlimited field of application—is reminiscent of the attitudes of physicists in the late nineteenth century who thought that essentially all the problems of the natural world were solved, or at least approaching solution. The physicists were shown to be wrong, and the psychologists have been shown (in a rather different sense, to be sure) also to have erred. But this does not prove in either case that their activities were wrong in principle. Rather it demonstrates a singleness of purpose which characterizes many dedicated scientists, but which may perhaps call for a broadening of perspective, even a little more humility, in assessing a science's contribution to knowledge. There is a major difference between the situations of the two groups. The physicists were shown to be wrong largely because new physical phenomena were discovered which their theories could not handle: psychologists are criticized for *neglecting* vast ranges of already well-known facts about behavior and the ways of appraising and explaining it. The physicists' dilemma arose because of developments within an already successful science; the psychologists' dilemma arises because of developments outside a relatively unsuccessful science. Had the psychology of the twentieth century been as spectacularly successful as the physics of the eighteenth and nineteenth centuries, we should hear less criticism from the armchair, or at least a different sort of criticism, I am sure.

I must hasten to qualify my statement that psychology is a "relatively unsuccessful science." It is true only in the sense of not producing immediate and easily acceptable explanations and predictions about everyday human actions, or if one accepts the philosophers' implicit criterion: A successful science of psychology must explain the ways in which people behave in the same ways that everyday appraisals and descriptions of actions are used to explain behavior. Psychology has not been particularly successful in the sense of providing technological innovations which can improve the well-being of humanity either, and the new technologies it has produced have often aroused antagonism amongst laymen. Yet, it is not true to say that psychology has proved to be unsuccessful according to the psychologists' own criterion. I shall return to this point later; the criterion of what constitutes successful science, or more particularly a valid scientific explanation, poses a fundamental question, and there is no particular reason for psychologists to accept the philosophers' answer to it without further examination.

The argument to be pursued now concerns a major similarity—although one which is seldom stressed—between the fields of physics and psychology, as well as a second difference. Nineteenth-century physicists thought they had solved all the problems of physics because they felt their explanatory principles were correct and comprehensive; and this was true of some psychologists in recent decades too. However, the similarity I want to point to is this: No physicist (then or now) has claimed to be able to give a complete and exhaustive account of *everything* in the physical world, but he has a very clear idea, or at least a well-established tradition, about what needs to be explained. And no psychologist claims (or should claim) to give a complete and exhaustive account of all behavior, but he has a rather less clear idea, despite some well-established traditions, about what needs to be explained. The explanations given in *any* science are incomplete, are abstractions from a richer world of phenomena. Take the example of color and color vision. The physics of light is a highly developed and very successful branch of physics, yet many interesting things about color are simply considered to be irrelevant to the explanations of color which physicists propound (for example, acuity for color differences, esthetic judgments about color combinations, color vision defects). Similarly, the theory of dynamics will not predict or explain in detail why that particular bird I see out of my study window followed precisely that flight path, at a given moment, in getting from one tree to another. (Nevertheless, the physicist will claim correctly that, had the dynamics of the bird's flight been examined, they would have been found to conform to the laws of aerodynamics.) Yet, I have not come across a philosopher of modern times who takes physicists to task for this selectivity. In what sense is the situation of psychology different? Admittedly there have been the brazen few with the temerity to claim that all human behavior could "in principle" be explained completely in terms of a rigid set of general principles, but on the whole, psychologists these days are content to limit their enquiries and attempts at explanation to more modest ends. A psychologist who studies the question of anagram solution, let us say, may be able to devise a model to explain the process of solution which accounts for it in the same way that the bird's flight path can be "accounted for" in terms of aerodynamics. The paradigm case can be understood, but this does not necessarily mean that every outcome in other instances can be predicted with certainty. One may not know what all the relevant factors are, or may not have had an opportunity to measure them. The analogy can be pushed further; the physicist is not interested in the bird's "motivation." Whether it fell from a branch, is seeking food, or a mate, is irrelevant to his description of the aerodynamic situation. Similarly, motivation or "intention," or the initial conditions for the solution of anagrams, might be irrelevant to the explanation of the *process* which the psychologist gives. In this sense, the modern psychologists' explanations are usually incomplete in the same way as the physicists' explanations are, and if so, they simply display a characteristic which is common to virtually all scientific explanations, models, or theories. There is a substantial difference between theoretical physics and theoretical psychology, of course, in the extent to which agreement has been reached on what constitutes an adequate explanation in general.

Philosophers who hammer at the old issue of explaining all behavior on, say, Freudian or Hullian principles, can therefore be said to be tilting at windmills, as far as the activities of most contemporary scientific psychologists are concerned, at least in the field of cognition. We need to shift the argument to new ground; but there are still some thorny issues to be debated, I think.

III. Psychological Models for Thought Processes

Piaget's theory of intellectual development is perhaps an exception to my generalization about contemporary theorizing in cognition. His aim *is* to explain everything—or at least everything about cognitive behavior—in terms of one coherent schema. Unfortunately, the facts do not fit particularly well into the neat pattern which he prescribes, although they often come tantalizingly close—close enough to make one wonder whether the "true" pattern of development is as Piaget suggests, but obscured by extraneous factors which do not in themselves invalidate his basic ideas (Dodwell, 1960a, 1963). Piaget's genius is, to my mind, similar to Freud's in the sense that he opened up a whole range of questions about behavior which no one else had seen in quite the same light, and simultaneously provided a rich conceptual apparatus within which to propose answers to those questions. Just as Freud's ideas, although wrong in detail to a great extent, sparked a new look at human personal and social relationships (as well as at psychopathology), so Piaget's ideas have sparked a great new debate on cognitive development in general. Freud's ideas generated vast amounts of research, and provided the dominant theoretical stance in their field for decades; Piaget's theories seem to be moving into the same sort of dominating position. And just as Freud provides a major talking point for philosophers which will last for half a century or more, so I predict will Piaget. The intellectual excitement which their ideas and theories generate, however, does not guarantee that the ideas, or their methods of research, are completely acceptable to other psychologists, or are typical of all attempts at scientific discovery and explanation of psychological phenomena. Without wishing to belittle the importance of Piaget's contribution in any way, I do suggest that it would be mistaken to think of it as the only one to be taken seriously in discussing theories of cognitive development. It would be a pity if readers of this book were to get the impression that Piaget is the only contemporary source of ideas in cognitive psychology. Some other approaches are worth discussing, both to help keep Piaget in perspective, and also because other, less ambitious, theoretical essays illustrate very well the issues concerning psychological explanations that I shall raise. I hope to be able to show that there is an important sense in which they provide valid explanations of human thinking even if they do clash with everyday usage. This will connect up with the earlier theme of what it is that theories in psychology are aiming at in general, and the sense in which they may yield acceptable explanations despite their possible conflicts with common-sense notions.

The single most powerful influence on psychologists' ideas about cognitive processes at present is the nexus of concepts which has been developed for computer programming. This raises the awful specter of mechanization, which is enough to cause distress in any self-respecting philosopher, so let me say at once that there are few psychologists today—and I am not one of them—who believe that the brain is merely a computer, and that thinking is nothing other than the running of a particular program in the brain–computer. Nevertheless, the influence is clear enough. Perhaps two of the best illustrations of this trend in recent thought are to be found in Reitman (1965) and Neisser (1967), the latter showing also an acute awareness of the limitations of purely mechanical analogies to thinking. What is the seductive power of the computer analogy? First, the digital computer is made up of vast numbers of basically simple elements which interact with each other in simple ways, essentially by switching "on" and "off"; the brain too, is made up of basically simple elements—neurons—which on the whole seem to interact with each other also in simple ways. Just because it is demonstrated in the computer that very large numbers of such elements can be organized to perform complicated operations, it seems plausible to suppose that complicated operations in the brain proceed in much the same fashion. However, it is not the "hardware" aspect of the computer analogy which commands most attention today, but rather the principles of programming ("software") which yield fruitful hypotheses about methods of solving problems which may be applicable as models of human thinking. Here is a nice irony: Philosophers have made much of the fact that human conduct is essentially rule following, and have taken psychologists to task for neglecting this characteristic; philosophers may well scorn the programming analogies to human thought, yet they are fascinating to psychologists (the analogies, I mean) just *because* of their embodiment of rule-following routines! In fact, one of their main inadequacies as models for human thought is that they are only rule-following routines, a point which I shall return to later.

A valid philosophical objection to computer analogies is that the "rule following" of a mechanical system is essentially different from the normal rule following of people, a matter which I will not dispute. However, the point of the computer-program analogy is to make it clear that there is a similarity in the organization of thinking and the organization of a computing routine. It is the *principles* on which a program is based that interest us in the main, not the mechanical, electrical, or other details about how the individual steps of computation are carried out. In this sense, computer programs, or more accurately computer simulations of problem solving, of pattern recognition, or other "cognitive" functions, can be thought of as embodiments of models of the traditional scientific variety (Uhr, 1966). The model itself is formal in the sense that the characterization of its elements and their relations to one another can be made independently of the particular sort of computer on which the program is to be run, or indeed of the particular programming language (a significant phrase) which is used to express the program. Now, I said earlier that no psychologist is likely to assert that such a model will be a perfect and all-embracing *replica* of human cognition; but many will claim that it can characterize important features of some cognitive process, let us say of problem solving in the sense of logic or mathematics.

The two aspects of such a program which appear to be most illuminating are the use of an executive system which controls the sequence of operations, and the "subroutines" which compute specific functions, make use of stored information, and the like, according to the nature of the problem the program is designed to solve. There is no need to go into details here; the point is simply that the "organization" and "directedness," even "goal directedness," of the program is implemented by an executive process which "decides" on the sequence of operations, and this system itself "calls up" specified computing routines to work out each step in a solution. Within such a computing routine there may again be other subroutines which can be called up to make specific computations, so that a sort of hierarchical structure emerges, the operation of each level down the hierarchy being controlled by higher levels. Such a hierarchy does not lead to an infinite regress because, as Neisser (1967) points out, the executive process is the overall controller of what goes on, and is not itself "used" by any higher level—it embodies the "goal" of the whole program.

It might be argued that the computer analogy is trivial, because a program merely codifies a set of operations which are like cognitive operations, but no more *explains* thinking than does writing down a set of rules for solving arithmetic problems, or codifying the grammar of a particular language. The programmer imposes organization of a specific sort on the sequence of steps in his program because he already understands the nature of the problem to be solved, and knows what the principles are by which solutions can be obtained. To say that a computer program can "explain" thinking, then, would have about the same force as to say that a set of logical formulas "explain" the laws of correct deductive argument.

There is more to the concept of computer simulation than this, however. Most psychologists, I suppose, would claim that the structure and organization of a program, together with the possibility of execution in a real computing system, come close enough to the real thing to warrant the term "model of thinking" for some computer simulations. Probably the strongest point in favor of this view would be that explanations of what goes on in problem solving by a computer can be given at several different levels, just as explanations of thinking—or of different aspects of thinking—can be given at different levels. The *implementation* of a program has to be explained in terms of computer hardware, just as, presumably, the implementation of thinking has in some sense to be explained by processes which actually occur in the central nervous system. The subroutines by which particular computations are made can be explained by reference to the "machine language" and the step-by-step algorithms by which solutions are found (say, finding the square root of a number, or the truth value of a logical expression, given the truth values of its component arguments). This looks remarkably like the routine application of "drill" solutions—say, of multiplication tables—in human problem solving. The principle of the subroutine operation is not itself to be understood and explained just by examining the hardware, in just the same way that the point of multiplication tables could not be grasped by examining the brain. Similarly, an understanding of how the subroutines themselves work does not explain the principle of solving problems in terms of a sequence of steps which depend on the subroutine computations, in the same way that understanding multiplication tables does not explain the solution of most types of arithmetical problems. For that, one must look at the executive process, which in the machine embodies the overall organization and goal of the program, and in the human being a less clearly understood "goal directedness." There is a closely parallel set of distinctions (for man and machine) which can be made between solving particular computational problems by set rules, and the sequence of steps in a valid argument which can depend on the outcomes of such computations, the weighing of probabilities, marshalling of evidence, and so on. Looking into the brain will not explain the point of arithmetic and similar operations, and the explication of the concept of algorithmic problem solution will not itself elucidate all the intricacies of organization and presentation of evidence that may occur in a valid argument. In both cases different levels of explanation are appropriate, no one of which is in itself exhaustive. Correct functioning of the "lower-order" processes is a necessary condition for the correct functioning of higher-order operations, and explanations at one level are certainly *relevant* to other levels, even though they are not *sufficient* to explain those other levels. And this, I believe, may be the most important point about the computer analogies in relation to explanations of human cognition.

IV. Cognitive Models and Cognitive Development

I have not said anything about any specific computer program, because it seems to be more relevant here to consider those general features of computerlike "explanations" of cognitive functions which make computer analogies attractive to cognitive psychologists. It should be obvious that a computer type of model of cognition is incomplete in the same way as most other scientific models. It is not designed to take account of affective and motivational factors in cognition, for instance, and, generally speaking, it will also ignore the developmental part of the process. Although there are programs which "learn" how to solve problems and recognize patterns, they seem not to be relevant to questions of cognitive development, because the principles of self-modification are specified by the programmer. Humans, on the other hand, have to learn and develop in a rather different sense. Whereas the self-modifying program is designed so that a particular sort of plasticity in its operations becomes a necessary feature of the way it works, we are reluctant to believe that the only possible sorts of plasticity in human cognitive development are similarly preordained. Human cognitive development is at least in large part a matter of social learning. Yet I am not so sure that the principles of self-modifying programs are irrelevant to our concerns, since the initial conditions from which the young organism develops cognitively are so obviously important, as are the potentialities for growth. To give a banal example; other primates do not learn to talk and think as men do, even when brought up in a human environment, so there must be a "capacity to learn" languages and other cognitive functions which is one part of the built-in initial conditions for human development. Even given the initial conditions, "social learning" does not seem to be a satisfactory or comprehensive label for what goes on in intellectual development. Social learning can be given as a reason for a child's learning this language rather than that one, or for solving problems in one way rather than another, but it fails to take account of the fact that cognitive development occurs in an active human being. Social learning can *mold* the activity in one way or another, it cannot produce the activity out of nothing. So, surely, one of the most important things to do is to look for features, or principles of operation, of the organism that can be molded in this way. It seems to me that this is the most problematic part of any attempt to construct a theory of cognitive development: Piaget is one of the few psychologists who has tried to tackle the question. The self-modifying computer programs are relevant here just because they can help to clarify the nature of a system which undergoes orderly change in the direction of developing "correct" modes of operation. This does *not* mean that one needs to think of the program (or rather its running on a computer) as a replica of human development. Rather, one can think of it as an analog, a model which displays some of the same features as are thought to be important in human development. A successful program may at least suggest the properties one should look for in the real system; perhaps it will display in one form or another some of the necessary conditions which must hold in order for a developmental system to be possible.

We can understand the principles of a program which "learns," but it can be argued that this cannot yield much insight into the problem of human cognitive development just because the process of self-modification *is* designed into the program. A pattern-recognition program, for instance, can be designed to improve its performance by taking into account only those features which most readily differentiate two or more patterns from each other (see Uhr, 1966). The principles by which this is done are specified by the programmer *ab initio*, so that the fact of self-modification requires no additional explanation. While a computer program which simulates cognitive functions may do unexpected things in the sense that the outcomes are not completely predictable in advance, its novel modes of behavior can be explained *post hoc* in terms of the principles on which the program was designed. They are not surprising in the way that new sorts of behavior which cannot be understood in terms of the design principles would be surprising. I suppose this is much like saying that computer-based "cognitive functions" cannot display originality, or creativity, and can only be as clever as the ingenuity which is built into them by the designer allows. Whether human beings display originality of a different order is a difficult question to deal with if we do not know what the "design principles" are. The main point I want to make, however, is this: the self-modifying programs point to the need for specifying both a set of initial conditions and some principles which guide or limit the types of modifications which occur. The external conditions which are then imposed (which set of patterns is used for training, which problems are given for solution, conditions of giving or withholding "knowledge of success") are also relevant, but clearly not as central to understanding the *process* of change as are the internal factors. Psychologists are in the position, generally, of having to infer what the internal factors (principles of operation) may be, on the basis of limited information about sequences of events which are externally imposed, and the system's responses to them. At least the successful self-modifying computer programs can give an indication of the kinds of systems which will work; also, it has been argued that the more closely a simulation approaches human performance (say, in solving logical problems), the greater the likelihood is that its principles of operation are similar to ours. I will not insist on that point too strongly, but I do think that this example is useful in illustrating applications of two points made earlier: First, a model need not predict in detail everything that will happen, although it will be useless if we cannot decide which sequences of events are incompatible with its operations and which are not. Second, a model need not be exhaustive. To understand how a computer program works does not mean that one has to be able to follow step by step every single operation which it performs (far less does understanding human cognition necessarily entail being able to follow, or predict, every single act or thought which contributes to a given cognitive performance). The computer model shares these features in common with other sorts of scientific models.

The question of determinism, or its obverse originality, merits some further discussion. I am not thinking now merely of the fact that the computer operations are rule following; rather I am concerned with the question of how far the rules themselves are inflexibly "wired in." If it be objected that a computer model of cognition is too deterministic to be satisfactory, the simple reply is that many such models include probabilistic functions of one sort or another which make their behavior not fully predictable. On the other hand, a system which obeys a probabilistic law is also deterministic (in a slightly different way), so that this is not an adequate rebuttal of the objection. Unfortunately, it is impossible to judge how relevant the objection is, because we simply do not know how deterministic human cognitive functioning is. Conceivably, there are abstruse statistical regularities in our cognitive behavior, for all its apparent flexibility, which have so far escaped detection. It would be difficult to prove at any stage that the search for such regularities, or laws, had been exhaustive, and despite the evidence of our own introspections, it is not inconceivable that our thinking is far more highly "programmed" than we like to think. This, I believe, is a matter which deserves further debate, since it is an important aspect of the general dispute over the proper field for psychological enquiry and explanation.

V. Models of Cognition and Common Sense

Having looked quite sketchily at some of the ideas which are popular these days among cognitive theorists, and having tried to show why they are popular, I shall now attempt to state my defense of psychological theorizing. Not all psychologists could be expected to agree with me, of course, but I believe that a majority would find the position to be outlined quite acceptable. At least they would agree with my contention that there is an important sense in which psychological theorizing can validly "go deeper than" common sense, and lead to more powerful explanations of cognitive behavior. Parts of the argument have already been presented in the previous sections, but I shall now try to put them together into a single statement.

I have already argued that "failure to satisfy common sense" is not a sufficient criterion for rejecting a scientific theory. Psychological theories, in general, and models of cognitive function, in particular, need not be exhaustive, in the sense that they can account for every quirk and subtlety of human behavior. In this they are not different from other scientific theories and models, for example, in physics or biology; only, in the older sciences, there is often a better appreciation of the significant facts which need explanation, and of the relevant variables which enter into an explanation.

Philosophers often argue that psychologists make a category mistake in attempting to "explain" normative, rule-following or achievement motivated behavior in terms of quasi-mechanical models. I have supported that point of view elsewhere, in trying to show that such models can never be logically sufficient for the deduction of a statement about, let us say, perception or thinking (Dodwell, 1960b; 1970, Chap. XI). But this does not mean that psychologists are necessarily wrong-headed to formulate such models. On the contrary, I argue that this is part of the valid business of the theoretical psychologist. What is wrong, both with the psychologists and their philosopher critics, is their assumption that a scientific explanation must be at least *coextensive* with a common-sense explanation; that it must do the same job, and then some more. It seems to me that the models and theories of psychologists—certainly in the area of cognition—have a different job to do than to ape common sense. One might put it this way: Psychologists who devise models for thinking, memory, or perception are usually attempting to characterize what one might call the *framework*, or structure, within which these activities occur; or one might say that they are attempting to investigate the necessary conditions which govern the occurrence of particular forms of behavior. This can lead, typically, in two rather different directions. On the one hand, it can lead to investigation of physiological properties and the understanding of a system in terms of the physiological constraints on it; the outstanding examples here are, I think, to be found in the field of vision research, particularly in color vision and pattern recognition. On the other hand, it can lead to specifications in terms of the structure and sequence of events of particular kinds which suggest what *type* of system is operative, or as some psychologists might put it, from which the mechanism which controls or generates a particular type of behavior can be inferred. I do not think we should be put off by the word mechanism here: it need have no particular mechanical or quasi-mechanical connotations, and the word "system" would be found equally acceptable. (Indeed, one of the strongest tendencies in modern cognitive psychology is to shift from concepts of the flow of energy in a system to which the mechanical analogy is most appropriate, to the concepts of information flow and control.) Two good examples of this sort of theoretical work which come to mind are in the fields of short-term memory and linguistics. A linguistic theory such as Chomsky's does not attempt to enumerate or describe all the various facets of a language, much less of all languages, but attempts to delineate a basic structure which is common to them all. Models for short-term memory, which are proliferating rapidly these days, do not try to account for all types of remembering; in fact, their range of application is often restricted to a particular type of material and laboratory setting and procedure. They have relatively little to add to the common-sense notions of what it means to remember, of how we ordinarily use memory words. Nevertheless, as scientific models, they can have real value. To take two representative examples: theorists in this area have been concerned with questions about the nature of memory loss, and about the form of "memory coding." The first question revolves largely around the issue of decay versus interference in short-term memory, the second around the possible forms—acoustic, semantic, or structural, for example—which coding might take. Questions of this sort can be answered experimentally (although the answers do not always turn out to be as clear-cut as we should like) by examining people's short-term memory characteristics under rather special and artificial conditions. The results of such experiments, and the models they support or refute, have little enough to do with an understanding of what it means to remember, or of the range of uses to which memory words may legitimately be put. It seems clear to me, however, that they are, or can be, highly relevant to an understanding of some of the *processes* which underly our capacity to remember, in the same ways that experiments in physics are relevant to understanding of such things as gravitation and aerodynamics, without their necessarily having to conform to common-sense ideas about apples falling from trees, the flight of birds, or movements of the celestial bodies.

All this I should like to characterize succinctly by asserting that the job of the theoretical psychologist is to specify as fully as possible the necessary conditions for particular forms of behavior. These may be necessary conditions of the physiological substrate, or of the structure and processes as revealed in laboratory investigations which lead to models in a more formal sense, or sometimes a mixture of the two. Probably some of the most satisfying theoretical developments occur when the two can be combined sensibly [see Dodwell (1970) for examples in the field of perception].

These "necessary conditions" are not of course necessary in the logical sense; one might call them "empirically necessary" conditions, although this suggests too weak a set of constraints, or of concepts. Empirically necessary antecedents to an event may simply constitute the conditions for predicting that event, but this is not the same as an explanation. The sorts of necessary conditions we are talking of in a real sense—although I find it a sense which is difficult to characterize properly—attempt to do more than this. Specifying a model for pattern recognition, for example, might involve choice between a so-called template-matching process and a feature-extraction process. If experimental (or physiological) results give strong evidence for one system rather than the other, the model will be devised so that it belongs to one group of possible models rather than another. The model will have incorporated into it a particular structure which reflects these constraints. Several models may be equally good so far as explaining the available evidence goes, but this situation is common in science, and is not to be deplored as long as new empirical tests to decide between the alternatives are available. The point is that setting up a model of one sort rather than another involves a decision about how the processes—behavior—of the system may be explained, and this is itself an attempt to grasp its underlying nature, or structure.

When a theoretical psychologist talks of structure, or a structural model, he sometimes has in mind a real physiological embodiment within the organism, but more often he is referring to a theoretical construct whose usefulness is independent of whether something can be found within the organism which corresponds to it. Again the program analogy is illuminating. The sense in which we talk of a program's having structure is clear enough, and is much the same as the sense in which we could characterize an argument as having structure, or organization. If the program is entered into a computer, we can then ask: Is there a structure "in" the computer which corresponds to the structure of the program? In the sense that running the program will *demonstrate* the structure, it obviously is "in" the computer. But there is an equally clear sense in which it would be ridiculous to say that there is a structure "in" the computer which corresponds to the program's "behavioral" structure. For example, to look for an hierarchical arrangement within the elements of computer hardware which corresponds to the hierarchical organization of the program would be about on a par with the naiveté of postulating that the brain's "representation" of a square must in some sense itself *be* square (the basic notion of "isomorphism" in Gestalt psychology). I have the distinct impression that when philosophers criticize psychologists for misuse of terms such as structure, they usually have in mind this sort of naive interpretation. If so, they are sadly underestimating the level of sophistication of psychological theory.

The important thing for the psychologist is that a viable model must yield predictions which are subject to verification—an old theme indeed. If these predictions can be made unambiguously, then the question of how far such a model accords with common sense seems to be largely irrelevant. Philosophers are justified in attacking some attempts at psychological theorizing for being too ambitious, too grandiose, too crude; they are not justified in asserting that every psychological theory must be in harmony with common sense and everyday usage. The psychologists' criterion for a successful theory is that it should clarify the *nature* of a behaving system, and should yield insight into the sorts of as yet unexplored behavior of which the organism is capable. As Kuhn (1962) has pointed out, consensus of opinion about the appropriateness of certain problems and explanatory moves amongst scientists themselves is usually an important element in scientific progress. The evaluation of how good, powerful, and elegant a theory is seems to depend on the whole climate of opinion among the relevant group of scientists at a given time (see also Hyman, 1964). Theories of theory construction are not unknown, but it seems to be unnecessary, and perhaps dangerous, for philosophers to try to legislate for psychologists about such matters. Here it appears that the philosopher's appropriate role is more that of critic than innovator. There are innovators enough in psychology already, and to spare in some fields; we often suffer from fads, swings of fashion, and so on (perhaps not surprising in a relatively young discipline), so that help in sorting the gold from the dross should be welcome. Comparatively little of the theoretical work which causes excitement at any one time finds its way into the hard core of permanently useful and successful explanatory concepts. Perhaps this is common to most sciences to a greater or lesser extent; it is a matter which merits more investigation in its own right.

VI. Is a Theory of Conceptual Development Necessary?

The simple answer to this question, as I suggested earlier, is yes. Without a theory, or theories, scientific investigation of cognitive development would be pretty lifeless. The extent to which such a theory or theories can add to our knowledge is much more problematic, and can only be answered I suppose in retrospect. In this regard Piaget's theories are still very much *sub judice*, and as I have tried to show, have active competition from the work of a younger breed of model builders who are heavily influenced by the concepts of systems engineering and the information sciences. At least we can say, in both cases, that the theoretical innovations have led to very active research programs, so that in this sense they have contributed to our knowledge.

To return to Peters' puzzle about the relations between theoretical explanation and common-sense understanding of other people's behavior, I am coming to believe that there is substance to the idea that a scientific theory in psychology often has value chiefly insofar as it is *not* reducible to common-sense language or ideas. After all, the charge that theories in the social sciences are often no more than common-sense ideas in fancy dress is not a new one (Louch, 1966), and to the extent that it is true, such theories tend to be quite misleading. The fact that there are levels of explanation other than those which suffice for everyday commerce with other people is hardly surprising, nor is it unique to psychology to have different forms of explanation and appraisal in scientific, as contrasted to nonscientific, discourse. The builder who has learned to build houses which do not fall down needs no knowledge of the atomic theory of matter, nor will a knowledge of that theory help him to build sturdier or more elegant structures. Obviously, the theory is not *irrelevant* to macroscopic events, but in the vast majority of cases it has no practical significance for them. Just so, perhaps, with many psychological theories. I am not suggesting that Peters' puzzle is unimportant, or not worth further discussion; but it is certainly not unique to psychology.

VII. An Analogy with Art

Perhaps the position as I see it can be clarified by outlining briefly an analogous situation in the artistic sphere, specifically in music, although another art might do equally well by way of illustration. Music as a personal–emotional–intellectual *Gestalt* cannot adequately be explained or represented by one person to another; it must be experienced to be appreciated, and deep appreciation comes only with training and knowledge of several kinds. The language of musical appreciation and criticism is partly technical, but largely drawn from our everyday language for appraisal and description. One can reach a high degree of sophistication as a listener and connoisseur of music without knowing anything much about the scientific and technical bases of sound and music production. Yet, it would be foolish to suggest that the science of acoustics and the techniques of playing and reproducing music are irrelevant because the concepts employed, the explanations for phenomena that are found by common consent to be acceptable, and so on, are not coextensive with those of the esthete.

The grandeur of the opening statement of the second piano concerto of Brahms is not explainable purely in terms of the fine sonority and timbre of the French horn complemented by the limpid quality of the pianist's answering chords. The production and sensed qualities of those sounds are not exhaustively explainable by the science of acoustics either (the correlation between a given sound quality and a certain mixture of sine waves of different frequencies and amplitudes is not an *explanation* of that quality). The techniques of playing are necessary conditions of the production of fine music, but not in themselves sufficient to explain it. Similarly, acoustic laws and phenomena are among the necessary conditions for sound production and instrumental technique, but the latter are not reducible without remainder in terms of the former.

So we can and do talk about music, music production and appreciation at a variety of levels: no one of them exhausts the topic, no one of them can claim to be the single most important level, for all are interdependent. The "lower" levels are necessary conditions of "higher" levels in an obvious sense, but they are not *merely* necessary antecedents to those higher levels. On the other hand, the higher levels cannot be predicted from the lower. The hierarchical structure of the different levels is an essential characteristic of the whole of music; the laws and phenomena of one level can validly enter into the elucidation of the nature of another one without providing adequate explanations of all the phenomena of that level. One level cannot be reduced without remainder to a lower one, and does not provide the (logically) sufficient conditions for deducing statements about a higher one.

The analogy can be pressed in other directions too; in fact, the more one thinks about it, the better it seems. One could talk in terms of development of skills, drills, subroutines; of the development of musical theory, of schools and styles of composition; of methods of achieving particular effects; of history and musicology. All these would have more or less close parallels in more intellectual cognitive activity, and in the story of the attempt to understand it. That, however, is not my present purpose. I simply want to point to the fact that an all-embracing, one-shot attempt to theorize about, and explain, music and musical production would be misguided. Contributions, each in themselves incomplete, can be made at several levels; to understand the whole set of phenomena, one must be able to appreciate this fact. To an equal degree, the same thing is true of cognitive psychology. It is of interest to consider why those concerned with musical production and appreciation should be relatively satisfied with the many-leveled state of their discipline, on the one hand (this is only one of a number of possible examples), those concerned with mental life and behavior thoroughly dissatisfied, on the other (perhaps a unique situation). The reasons are no doubt partly historical, but they also, I suspect, have a lot to do with the general levels of understanding which have been reached in different disciplines, reluctance to see encroachment on a treasured preserve, and a generally misguided belief that explanations of human action need to have a sense of finality and completeness about them. If the history of science and of philosophy have any lesson to teach us, it is surely that that sense of finality and completeness is often illusory and very seldom fully justified. If our investigations of human behavior and mentality are to be scientific, we should do well to bear that lesson in mind.

Postscript

Malcolm's comments (*see pp. 385–392*) seem to me to exemplify just that unwillingness to grant that there may be several valid levels of investigation and explanation of human behavior to which I drew attention in my article. I agree with him that appeals to structure in memory, for example, will not yield a *complete* explanation of remembering; but it is difficult to see why this fact should invalidate the sorts of investigation and model construction to which psychologists devote their efforts. I refer simply to my distinction between levels of explanation, and the necessary and sufficient conditions which may hold between levels, to justify this point.

On Malcolm's view, psychologists would have to restrict their activities to investigations of simple empirical relationships such as that which might hold between memory and sleep deprivation. But it is extremely difficult to see how this restriction could be justified. The factors which psychologists investigate in human memory *are* empirical relationships, although usually of a more complicated sort than the one just mentioned. Who, then, should make the decision on which empirical relationships are to be cleared for investigation? Not philosophers, surely. As a matter of fact, I suspect that should a psychologist propound a theory of sleep and memory which offended the philosopher's conceptual scheme of things, even this kind of investigation would be proscribed. Thus, Malcolm seems to be proposing just that sort of legislation for psychologists which I argued is illegitimate. To accept it would be to restrict the range of psychological enquiry to an absurd degree. It is a fact of life that scientific explanations are not coextensive with common-sense ones, and scientists are in the best position to decide what is, and what is not, worthy of investigation and scientific explanation.

References

Dodwell, P. C. Children's understanding of number and related concepts. *Canadian Journal of Psychology*, 1960, **14**, 191–205. (a)

Dodwell, P. C. Causes of behaviour and explanation in psychology. *Mind*, 1960, **69** N.S., 1–13. (b)

Dodwell, P. C. Children's understanding of spatial concepts. *Canadian Journal of Psychology*, 1963, **17**, 141–161.

Dodwell, P. C. *Visual pattern recognition*. New York: Holt, 1970.

Hyman, R. *The nature of psychological enquiry*. Englewood Cliffs, New Jersey: Prentice-Hall, 1964.

Kuhn, T. S. *The structure of scientific revolutions*. Chicago, Illinois: Chicago Univ. Press, 1962.

Louch, A. R. *Explanation and human action*. Berkeley: Univ. of California Press, 1966.

Mischel, T. *Human action: Conceptual and empirical issues*. New York: Academic Press, 1969.

Neisser, U. *Cognitive psychology*. New York: Appleton, 1967.

Peters, R. S. Motivation, emotion, and the conceptual schemes of common sense. In T. Mischel (Ed.), *Human action: Conceptual and empirical issues*. New York: Academic Press, 1969.

Reitman, W. R. *Computers and thought: An information processing approach*. New York: Wiley, 1965.

Uhr, L. (Ed.) *Pattern recognition*. New York: Wiley, 1966.

THE MYTH OF COGNITIVE PROCESSES AND STRUCTURES

Norman Malcolm

When philosophers and psychologists speak of "cognitive processes" and "cognitive structures" it is not clear what they are talking about. "Cognition" is an esoteric term; but that is not the main difficulty. If we switch to more humble words of everyday language, such as "memory" or "thinking," the talk of "processes" and "structures" remains obscure. This becomes evident if we reflect on such a question as, "What is the process of remembering?" When asked by a philosopher or psychologist, this question assumes that whenever a person remembers something there is a process of remembering. Consideration of a few examples shows that this is not so. Sometimes we go through a process of *trying* to remember. Suppose that you cannot locate your briefcase. You remember that you were carrying it when you left your office. You review in your mind, or aloud, your itinerary on the way home. "I walked to the bank and cashed a check. Did I have the briefcase when I left the bank? I'm not sure. I then went to the bookstore and bought an atlas. Now I know that I *did* take the briefcase into the bookstore, for I remember putting it down when I paid the cashier. And also I remember now that I had the atlas in one hand and my umbrella in the other when I left the store. So I left it in the book store." While saying or thinking these things you may have had feelings of anxiety; images of the streets, the bank, and the store may have passed swiftly through your mind; finally, when the solution came, you may have had a feeling of relief as if a weight had been lifted from you.

Perhaps there would be no harm in calling this combination of utterances, thoughts, images, and feelings, a "process of remembering." We see at once, however, that in a vast number of cases of memory, there is *no* process of remembering, in this sense. We are told to fetch the pliers, and without any effort or trying we remember where we left them. We want a clean shirt, and we go to the right drawer without previously ransacking our mind as to which drawer it is. When asked the way to the museum or the name of a novel we read last week, we often give prompt, confident answers. Thus, in the clearest sense of the words, a "process of remembering" occurs only *sometimes* when we remember.

The same would be true of a "process of pattern recognition." More often than not there is no process; just as when one recognizes a friend on the street there is usually no process of recognition. You see his face in the crowd; you smile at him and say "Hi, John." You do not think, "Now where have I seen that face before?"

There is a real difficulty, therefore, in understanding what a psychologist is talking about when he says, for example, that he wants to explain "the process of pattern recognition" or to construct a model for it. In recognizing patterns, shapes, colors, and people there is usually, or often, no *process* of recognition. So *what* is the model a model of?

I suggest that the assumption that whenever one recognizes something there is a process of recognition, has a purely philosophical origin. The assumption arises in the following way: We consider an ordinary example of recognition, such as recognizing a friend in a crowd. We reflect on what happened: You smiled at him and said, "Hi, John," We then think: "Surely your recognition did not *consist* in that: for you could smile at someone and say those words but not recognize him." True. "So then something else must have occurred; and *it* was the act or process of recognition." But this is a fallacious inference. Although your recognition of your friend cannot be equated with your smiling at him and greeting him, it does not follow that it is identical with *some other event* that occurred when you recognized him. The feeling that it must be, leads us to think that the process of recognition is *hidden*. We are not quite sure whether it is a *mental* process, or a *brain* process; but if we keep the research going, we shall find out someday, we hope.

The kind of muddle we get into here is described with great acuteness by Wittgenstein. One of his familiar examples is that of someone's suddenly understanding how to continue a numerical series of which he has been shown the initial segment (Wittgenstein, 1953, §§ 151–155). Now, what occurred when he suddenly understood? Various things might have occurred. He might have thought of a formula that fitted the initial segment, and exclaimed, "I know how it goes." Or instead of a formula, he might have noticed the series of differences, and cried, "I've got it." Or perhaps he did not think of a formula, or of the series of differences, but simply continued the series a few more places, thinking to himself, "This is easy." In these cases there might, or might not, have been initial feelings of tension and subsequent feelings of relief.

But apparently these various descriptions of what might have occurred have not specified what the sudden understanding *itself* was; for a person could think of that formula, or of the series of differences, or continue the initial segment a few places, but still not understand the series. So we think that the essential thing has not yet been brought to light. As Wittgenstein says: "We are trying to get hold of the mental process of understanding which seems to be hidden behind those coarser and therefore more readily visible accompaniments" (Wittgenstein, 1953, § 153).

The predicament is typical of the attempts of philosophers and psychologists to "analyze" or "explain" the concepts of mind, such as thinking, recognizing, perceiving, meaning, intending, remembering, and problem solving. The feeling that we are dealing with hidden processes gives rise to theories and models. It fosters the desire (of which Dodwell speaks) "to reach a deeper analysis of the phenomena." We feel that when a person recognizes something, in addition to the various manifestations or characteristic accompaniments of recognition something must go on inside. This is the "inner process" of recognition.

The mistake here is easy to state but profoundly difficult to grasp. Recognizing someone is not an act or process, over and above, or behind, the expression of recognition in behavior. But also, of course, it is not that behavior. As we said, your recognizing John in the crowd cannot be identified with your smiling at him and saying "Hi, John." Imagine an eccentric who smiles at and says "Hi, John," to every tenth person he passes; and who has never seen this John before. Given those facts, his smile and utterance on this occasion would not be an expression of recognition. On the other hand, it is easy to imagine a situation in which such a smile and greeting would be an expression of recognition. Thus, it is the facts, the circumstances surrounding that behavior, that give it the property of expressing recognition. This property is not due to something that goes on inside.

It seems to me that if this point were understood by philosophers and psychologists, they would no longer have a motive for constructing theories and models for recognition, memory, thinking, problem solving, understanding, and other "cognitive processes."

I now turn to the notion of "structure," which is so prominent in the thinking of both Piaget and Chomsky. Chomsky has done an impressive job of showing the hopeless inadequacy of a behaviorist account in terms of stimulus–response functions, of linguistic competence. He advocates a "centralist" account. He is struck by the fact that the normal use of language is "innovative," "potentially infinite in scope," "free from the control of detectable stimuli," and "appropriate to a situation" (Chomsky, 1968, pp. 10–11).

> The central fact to which any significant linguistic theory must address itself is this: a mature speaker can produce a new sentence of his language on the appropriate

> occasion, and other speakers can understand it immediately, though it is equally new to them. Most of our linguistic experience, both as speakers and hearers, is with new sentences; once we have mastered a language, the class of sentences with which we can operate fluently and without difficulty or hesitation is so vast that for all practical purposes (and, obviously, for all theoretical purposes), we can regard it as infinite (Chomsky, 1964, p. 50).

> Honesty forces us to admit that we are as far today as Descartes was three centuries ago from understanding just what enables a human to speak in a way that is innovative, free from stimulus control, and also appropriate and coherent (Chomsky, 1968, p. 11).

Chomsky thinks that this normal mastery of language requires that somehow there be *in* a human being "a system of rules," or an "abstract structure," or a "mechanism." This system, structure, or mechanism underlies and explains the multitudinous performances by which the mastery of a language is exhibited. This system is the "grammar" of the language.

> The person who has acquired knowledge of a language has internalized a system of rules that relate sound and meaning in a particular way. The linguist constructing a grammar of a language is in effect proposing a hypothesis concerning this internalized system (Chomsky, 1968, p. 23).

> It seems clear that we must regard linguistic competence—knowledge of a language—as an abstract system underlying behavior, a system constituted by rules that interact to determine the form and intrinsic meaning of a potentially infinite number of sentences (Chomsky, 1968, p. 62).

> It is reasonable to regard the grammar of a language L ideally as a mechanism that provides an enumeration of the sentences of L in something like the way in which a deductive theory gives an enumeration of a set of theorems (Chomsky, 1964, p. 576).

> It appears that we recognize a new item as a sentence not because it matches some familiar item in any simple way, but because it is generated by the grammar that each individual has somehow and in some form internalized. And we understand a new sentence, in part, because we are somehow capable of determining the process by which this sentence is derived in this grammar (Chomsky, 1964, p. 576).

> The child who learns a language has in some sense constructed the grammar for himself on the basis of his observation of sentences and nonsentences (i.e., corrections by the verbal community) (Chomsky, 1964, p. 577).

Lenneberg expresses the same viewpoint:

> It is generally assumed by linguists—and there are compelling reasons for this—that there must be a finite set of rules that defines all grammatical operations for any given language. Any native speaker will generate sentences that conform to these grammatical rules, and any speaker of the speech community will recognize such sentences as grammatical. We are dealing here with an extremely complex mechanism and one that has never been fully described in purely formal terms for any language (if it had, we could program computers that can "speak" grammatically); and yet,

> we know that the mechanism must exist for the simple reason that every speaker knows and generally agrees with fellow speakers whether a sentence is grammatical or not (Lenneberg, 1964, p. 586).

The philosophical assumption behind this postulation of an "internalized" structure, system, or mechanism is easy to perceive. The assumption is that in speaking a person must be *guided.* There must be something at hand that shows him how to speak, how to put words together grammatically and with coherent sense; and how to recognize a combination of words as being ungrammatical or ambiguous or incoherent. What is being explained is knowledge—both knowing that and knowing how. The presence in him of the structure of the language or of its system of rules is supposed to account for this knowledge—to explain *how* he knows.

The inspiration is the same as for the traditional theory of Ideas. A child is taught the words "chair" or "dog." This is done by means of a comparatively few examples. Then he goes on to apply the words correctly to an indefinite number of new instances of chairs and dogs, which differ in various ways from the original examples. How is he able to do this? How does he know that this new creature is a dog when it is so unlike the dogs he previously encountered? One can feel amazed by this ability; just as Chomsky is amazed when he reflects on the normal ability to produce and understand an unlimited number of sentences never previously encountered. How does one know that this new combination of words is a good English sentence and this other one is not?

The solution provided by the traditional theory is to say that the child has in his mind the *Idea* of a dog. Either he formed ("internalized"?) the Idea by abstraction from the original examples, or else it was in him innately, and was activated by the examples. In either case he possesses the Idea, and he uses it as an object of comparison. He recognizes a new creature as being a dog by comparing it with his Idea; that is how he knows.

One can see this notion at work in Locke. Speaking of "the faculty of retention," he says:

> This faculty of laying up and retaining the ideas that are brought into the mind, several other animals seem to have to a great degree, as well as man. For, to pass by other instances, birds learning of tunes, and the endeavours one may observe in them to hit the notes right, put it past doubt with me, that they have perception, and retain ideas in their memories, and use them for patterns. For it seems to me impossible that they should endeavour to conform their voices to notes (as it is plain they do) of which they had no ideas (Locke, Book II, Chapter 10, Section 10).

The birds must be guided in their whistling by internal patterns of the notes. Otherwise, they could not get the notes right, or even *try* to get them right.

There is an obvious similarity between Locke's reasoning and the reasoning by which Chomsky and Lenneberg support their postulation of a structure, mechanism, system of rules, or internalized grammar. The imagery is somewhat different. In Locke's view the Idea is a model or pattern with which one makes comparisons. With Chomsky and Lenneberg the notion seems to be that the deep structure or system is like a set of axioms from which one deduces the sentences one utters.

The criticisms of both views are, or should be, well known. In the first place, this explanation of ability or knowledge is mythological. When I say, "My, that dog is shaggy!" it is not true that I possess a model of a not so shaggy dog with which I compare this one. And it is not true that when I carry on an ordinary conversation I deduce my sentences from a set of rules. One might as well say that when I walk along the street, avoiding people, stepping over curbs, etc., my movements are generated by a system of rules. Or that when I chase a rabbit out of the garden my movements are determined by the grammar of chasing a rabbit out of the garden.

It is reassuring to know that there are linguists who reject Chomsky's conception of generative or transformational grammar. Hall, for example, says the following:

> As anyone can see by direct observation of ordinary people's normal every-day speech-activity, people simply do not talk according to rules, whether they be aware of the rules' existence or not. There are far too many instances of normal speech which cannot be accounted for by any generative rules at all—which constitute, in fact, all kinds of "violations" of rules—but which cannot be neglected or whose existence cannot be denied on that account (Hall, 1969, p. 205).

Hall attacks the notion, of Chomsky and Lenneberg, that a living language is a calculus:

> One cannot establish any set of rules for generating all the possible sentences of a language and none other, because there is no way to determine what is possible and what is not, and because no real language is a closed, well-defined, mathematizable system (Hall, 1969, pp. 207–208).

It is truly surprising that Chomsky should emphasize the "creative" and "innovative" aspect of normal speech, but at the same time conceive of it as the operation of a deductive system. There are rules in language, but it is wrong to suppose that there is some "complete" set of rules governing our utterances. Wittgenstein offers this analogy:

> The regulation of traffic in the streets permits and forbids certain actions on the part of drivers and pedestrians; but it does not attempt to guide the totality of their movements by prescription. And it would be senseless to talk of an "ideal" ordering of traffic which should do that; in the first place we should have no idea what to imagine as this ideal. If someone wants to make traffic regulations stricter on some

point or other, that does not mean that he wants to approximate to such an ideal (Wittgenstein, 1967, § 440).

The conception of an abstract structure or system controlling the questions, answers, exclamations, orders, oaths, jokes, kidding, etc. of ordinary speech activity is erroneous, not only because that is not how we speak, but also because we do not understand what it would *mean*, what it would be like, for there to be some system or structure generating and determining the flow of intelligible, grammatical speech.

The second criticism of this attempt to explain linguistic competence is that either it leads to an infinite regress, or else it leaves one with the same sort of "mystery" that led to the postulating of a system or structure in the first place. We can see how this works in regard to Locke's Ideas. If we say that the way in which a person knows that something in front of him is a dog is by his seeing that the creature "fits" his Idea of a dog, then we need to ask, "*How* does he know that this is an example of *fitting*?" What guides his judgment here? Does he not need a second-order Idea which shows him what it is like for something to fit an Idea? That is, will he not need a model of *fitting*? But then, surely, a third-order Idea will be required to guide his use of the model of fitting. And so on. An infinite regress has been generated and nothing has been explained.

On the other hand, if we are willing to say that the person *just knows* that the creature he sees fits the first Idea (the Idea of a dog), and no explanation of *this* knowledge is needed—if we are willing to stop here in our search for an explanation of how the man knows that this thing is a dog—then we did not need to start on our search in the first place. We could, just as rationally, have said that the man or child, *just knows* (without using any model, pattern or Idea *at all*) that the thing he sees is a dog. We could have said that it is just a normal human capacity (given the initial training) to be able to tell that something is a dog, even if it is quite different from any dog one has previously seen.

That a person knows something cannot be due to his employing an infinite series of models or guides. The explanation of *how* he knows must come to an end. There cannot be an offence to reason here, since the only "alternative" would be the logically impossible performance of consulting an infinite number of models in order to make a single correct identification. Thus, it cannot be a requirement of reason that one should be *guided*.

Obviously this criticism works just as well against the postulation of an abstract structure, or system of rules, or set of principles, that is somehow embedded in a person, and somehow accounts for his linguistic competence, or for his ability to dance the Highland Fling or to whistle Hi-Diddle-Diddle. If the presence of a structure or system is supposed to explain these abilities and performances, then we need to ask, *How* does the person know how to employ the system? Does he have another system that shows him how to use this one? Or does he *just know* how to use it? But if this latter is a rational possibility, then it is also a rational possibility that there is *no* structure or system that accounts for language mastery, or for any repertoire of skills, abilities, or performances. The presence of a guidance system cannot be a general requirement for knowledge.

This point holds for all normal cognitive powers, such as the ability to recognize patterns, or to remember where one parked one's car. The insistence on a structure or mechanism to account for knowledge is a piece of mistaken metaphysics. The error stands out with striking clarity in Lenneberg's remark (previously quoted) in support of the Chomskyan assumption of a system or mechanism of rules in conformity with which a speaker generates sentences:

> We know that the mechanism must exist for the simple reason that every speaker knows and generally agrees with fellow speakers whether a sentence is grammatical or not (Lenneberg, 1964, p. 586).

A mistaken metaphysics lies in this "must." I imagine, however, that Lenneberg is correct in the following remarks:

> Just as we can say with assurance that no man inherits a propensity for French, we can also and with equal confidence say that all men are endowed with an innate propensity for a type of behavior that develops automatically into language and that this propensity is so deeply ingrained that language-like behavior develops even under the most unfavorable conditions of peripheral and even central nervous system impairment (Lenneberg, 1964, p. 589).

What is wrong is the assumption that either the languagelike behavior or the subsequent mastery of language must be under the control of underlying systems or structures, schemes or schemas, processes or principles, plans or isomorphic models. Our understanding of human cognitive powers is not advanced by replacing the stimulus–response mythology with a mythology of inner guidance systems.

References

Chomsky, N. Current issues in linguistic theory. In J. Fodor & J. J. Katz (Eds.), *The structure of language*. Englewood Cliffs, New Jersey: Prentice-Hall, 1964.

Chomsky, N. *Language and mind*. New York: Harcourt, 1968.

Hall, R. A., Jr. Some recent developments in American linguistics. *Neuphilologische Mitteilungen*, 1969, **70**(2), 192–227. For an acute study of Chomskian linguistics, see Hockett, C. F., *The State of the Art*. The Hague: Mouton, 1968.

Lenneberg, E. H. The capacity for language acquisition. In J. Fodor & J. J. Katz (Eds.), *The structure of language*. Englewood Cliffs, New Jersey: Prentice-Hall, 1964.

Locke, J. *Essay concerning human understanding*. A. C. Fraser (Ed.). London and New York: Oxford Univ. Press (Clarendon), 1894.

Wittgenstein, L. *Philosophical investigations*. Oxford: Blackwell, 1953.

Wittgenstein, L. *Zettel*. Oxford: Blackwell, 1967.

WHAT IS INVOLVED IN A GENETIC PSYCHOLOGY?

Charles Taylor

Genetic psychology is dominated by the figure of Piaget, and a philosopher cannot begin to give his comments on the subject without a certain diffidence, as the great man's scathing and uncomplementary remarks about philosophers ring in his ears. So I would like to say something in expiation or extenuation for the lines which follow. The kind of reflection which can be called philosophical cannot simply precede empirical discovery and lay out the field of the possible and the impossible. It can only be a reflection on empirical findings, raising questions about their interpretation, about the connections between them, about the problems they raise or help to solve. In this sense, "philosophy" shades into the kind of reflection and discussion which any innovative empirical scientist must engage in. It can only be distinguished, if at all, in that we like to reserve the term for questions about the more fundamental issues. But wherever one draws the line, I believe that there is a perfectly defensible sense in which one can speak of the philosophical views and ideas of Piaget. And it is in this sense, I believe, that a philosophical reflection on genetic psychology might be useful, even if it loses greatly in value in not being based on the degree and scope of empirical knowledge which searchers in the field have at their disposal.

I. Three Characteristics of Genetic Psychology

What is genetic psychology? The term might be reserved for a certain field within psychology, that containing all questions to do with ontogenesis. But it is much more useful if we take the term to designate an approach or a family of approaches to this subject matter, rather than just a neutral specification of the field. And, indeed, the field of ontogenesis only becomes of salient interest if we do adopt a certain approach to it.

Genetic psychology is then the view that there is a special complex of problems of ontogenesis. This contrasts with a view which has been dominant in Anglo-Saxon psychology for some time; this sees growth in general, and growth of cognitive function in particular, as explicable by very nonspecific mechanisms at work everywhere that "learning," or indeed, behavior change, takes place. Thus, modern behaviorism, the heir to classical empiricism, undertook to attempt to discover an account of all learning by some associative mechanism, in some cases paired with reward, which was thought to operate over the whole field, without discrimination between adult learning and infant development, and without discrimination even between different species. (These two distinctions tend to stand or fall together, as I shall try to outline below.)

The major antagonist to a genetic psychology is thus an incremental view of learning, in which all development is seen as the addition (or sometimes subtraction) of homogeneous units, such as Hull's sHr's, (or "habits" linking stimuli and responses). It was this belief in the ubiquity of simple mechanisms which underlay the *démarche* of behaviorism in approaching a theory of human intelligence by studying rats in a maze or pigeons in a Skinner box. And it was this belief which confined the study of these animals to highly artificial environments, so that really interesting and enlightening discoveries about animal behavior had to come from what was organizationally a separate discipline, ethology. It may be that subsequent generations will stand aghast at these errors (as I believe them to be), but they do not appear so strange or obtuse from within the premises of traditional learning theory. If the same mechanisms underlie all learning, then one can winkle them out anywhere; there is no privileged locus, so why not try the contexts which are easiest to operate with in practical terms, that is, nonhuman organisms in an artificially simplified environment.

In other words, the shape, or structure, of the intelligence or learning capacity of a given species, or at a given maturational stage, does not need to be examined at the outset because it will ultimately be accounted for by a specific differential concatenation of the same fundamental building blocks which underlie the behavior of all other species or stages. On this atomistic view, species and stage differences are *explicanda* which we will ultimately get around to dealing with; they are not the crucial objects of research themselves.

This contrasts sharply with a genetic psychology for which the pattern of intelligence, of learning, of emotional life, and so on is different at each stage in a way which cannot be accounted for by the addition or subtraction of elements. For genetic psychology, these are differences of structure or global organization, and where behaviorism is atomistic, genetic psychology is holistic.

But the difference between these two approaches goes beyond that between atomism and holism. Genetic psychology cannot be satisfied with a simple cataloging of stages; it also wants to go on and account for the differences and hence for growth. But if we are dealing with atomistically irreducible structures, then growth can only be seen as structural transformation; that is, the onset of a new, more developed structure must be explained in terms of the mesh of experience with an earlier structure, when it is not accounted for by the maturation of an innate structure itself. The theory must therefore have among its basic explanatory notions, some features of innate structure, hereditary ways of dealing with the world evident at birth, or arising later through maturation.

Hence, beyond holism versus atomism, genetic psychology tends to differ from traditional learning theory on the issue of innate structures. Behaviorism, faithful to its empiricist ancestry, was generally quite fiercely environmentalistic. Of course, there had to be some spontaneous unlearned activity for there to be association and hence learning, and there were, of course, innate behavioral patterns which we generally call "instincts" (for example, sucking in the human neonate, nest building in certain kinds of birds); but the first offered merely facilitating conditions for learning, whereas the second was thought just to coexist with learning, a set of unlearned sHr's alongside those which are "stamped in" by experience. In either case, there is no question of accounting for the present structure of intelligence or learning by reference, among other things, to innate structure. Innate patterns of behavior were thought, in other words, to play a small role in behavior, and where they were present they were seen merely as elements alongside learned segments of behavior.

Quite different is the place of innate structures in genetic psychology. If higher structures arise through transformation of innate ones, then the instinctive pattern is not interesting just as an original concatenation of elements. More important is the underlying structure which will reappear in the transform. A crucial concept of genetic psychology is therefore that of transformation. This requires some distinction analogous to that between "surface" and "deep" structure, which I borrow here from the transformational syntactics which Chomsky and his associates have developed; the latter provides the identical element underlying what on the surface are two very different structures, and hence allows us to delineate the differential factors which account for the transformation of one into the other. (In Chomsky's theory, of course, the transformations are between deep and surface structures rather than between two surface structures, but the distinction between the two is necessary in either case.)

In Piaget's theory, the notion of transformation comes out in his theory of adaptation. This has two dimensions, assimilation and accommodation;

the former preserves some kind of identity through the changes accorded by the latter. It is this which allows us to see identity, or at least filiation, between schemas at very different levels which are superficially very dissimilar, such as the play behavior of the young infant and his later ability to make deductions as an adolescent. The role of assimilation is what makes the earlier structure essential in the explanation of the later; one is a transform of the other. Because of transformation, the innate is not only interesting as a particular pattern, but even more as a deep structure in which form it combines with experience rather than existing alongside it. In its stark traditional form the nature–nurture controversy is made irrelevant.

The essential role of transformations provide the basis for Piaget's attack on the other three positions, which, along with associationism, he sees as alternatives to his own. Rightly or wrongly, he reproaches Gestalt psychology with a static nondevelopmental notion of form which allows no role for growth in experience; and vitalism opens itself to a related reproach; while "trial-and-error" theory sins in the opposite way—it sees no method in the groping which occurs before a correct solution and hence the acquisition of a new behavior, whereas the notion of transformation implies that these intermediate phases are structured in a way that we can understand from the deep structure involved (that is, the groping behavior is controlled by the schemas which are in the process of undergoing transformation).

For Piaget, transformations ultimately are to be understood in terms of equilibrium theory. There are a number of objections one can make to this as it occurs in Piaget's work, including the familiar one of vacuity: that specification in terms of equilibrium states adds nothing to our understanding of the process which is not already present in our descriptions in terms of contradiction, coherence, etc., for we can only apply the former descriptions via the latter. But the validity of the general approach which we can call transformational does not stand or fall with equilibrium theory.

We thus can single out three important characteristics of genetic psychology, in the sense we are using here: (*a*) it is holistic as against atomistic, (*b*) it is transformational as against incremental, and (*c*) it makes reference to innate structures which determine the relevance of experience rather than deriving development in a linear way from the environment.

This third point reminds us of the controversy which rages between the heirs of "Cartesianism" and "empiricism" in linguistics and the philosophy of language; and the use of the word "transformational" seems to point out the connection.

The idea underlying transformational grammar is that a grasp of deep structures and their relation to surface structures is part of a human being's cognitive repertoire, in this case his linguistic competence. Lenneberg suggests that this capacity to operate with deep and surface structures goes far beyond the lingustic domain and is at work also in our recognition of objects (see Lenneberg, 1967, pp. 296–299). But in the above we were talking about transformations between different stages of the repertoire, rather than those which are part of this repertoire at a given stage. These two levels of discourse have to be distinguished, but in fact they are closely related—so much so that it is often easy to confuse them.

The only way we can characterize a given repertoire, that is, a structure of intelligence and learning, is in terms of the characterizations and discriminations which a subject with this repertoire can make, and the inferences and connections he can establish from them. The picture of a given stage of cognitive development is simply a picture of things as characterized and discriminated and linked together, or inferred to, in a certain way. This poses a number of problems for genetic psychology which I shall try to touch on later, notably the difficulty of constructing this picture of competence from performance, and that of describing a stage of the repertoire which for us is "illogical" in some way.

For the moment, the point I would like to bring out is this: The repertoire at a given stage is characterized in terms of a number of related skills and capacities to manipulate, describe, make inferences about the world; the repertoire thus is defined by the picture of the world which the subject of this repertoire generates. Transformations between stages of the repertoire are thus transformations from one such complex of interlocking skills to another, and hence from one picture of the world (that is, the world characterized and inferred about in certain ways) to another. But then it is not surprising if the repertoire beyond a certain stage includes the capacity to manipulate, describe, and infer about the world in more than one way, and further the capacity to relate one picture to another and hence to make transformations. Thus, the concept of structures of competence, which include the capacity to grasp things intellectually by means of transformations, goes well with a theory which posits transformational relations between these structures.

But is there a connection between the debate in linguistics and that concerning genetic psychology in relation to the issue of innateness? I have already tried to show how I believe that genetic psychology must make reference to innate structures, and hence that it must, unlike traditional learning theory, focus study not only on stage differences, but also on species differences. In addition, the difference between the notion of innateness that Chomsky and his associates defend, and that which has been the traditional target of empiricists, is reminiscent of the gap in outlook between genetic and traditional learning psychology. Empiricists have always focused their attack on "innate ideas" as specific contents existing in the mind in abstraction from experience (the analog in behavior would be rigid patterns of instinct which owe nothing to learning). But what Chomsky defends, along with most defenders of innateness in history, is rather the existence of innate schemas which not only require external stimulation to be activated, but whose content must, in an important sense, be determined by experience. What is innate is not contents, but ways of dealing with contents. One has a strong impression, reviewing this debate in history, that the fundamental issue is not so much nature versus nurture, but rather an atomistic incremental notion of intelligence versus a structural cluster-of-skills conception. If one accepts the first view, then innateness must be a matter of specific contents, and if one takes the second line, the issue is about structures. Thus, the two sides can never really join issue in this debate because of their different notions of the mind. But these rival notions also divide genetic psychology from traditional learning theory.

There is thus a close relation between the two debates, but not necessarily a perfect overlap between the corresponding positions. The reason is that the exact role of innate structures can be an important issue in genetic psychology. For instance, without being able to be entirely sure, I would tend to believe that Chomsky and Piaget would be in disagreement on this matter. A genetic psychology requires some innate structures at the start; but there are a wide number of options concerning the role which later maturing innate structures play in the subsequent transformations. Piaget, on the whole, seems not to give these much importance, whereas Chomsky postulates a highly selective innate structure underlying language learning. Because of their different concerns, the two positions do not meet head-on, but there is an important difference of emphasis here, or so it seems to me. It might, perhaps, better be put by saying that Piaget seems relatively uninterested in the role of innate structures, other than those which provide starting points for development in babyhood. Maturation certainly makes certain transformations possible, but the further development of schemas is understood almost entirely in terms of earlier schemas and experience. Piaget seems to offer little room for late-developing innate schemas of a highly elaborate kind. Maturation is a necessary condition for development, but it does nothing to determine its direction.

Genetic psychology thus can be characterized as holistic, transformational, and (to a greater or lesser degree) innatist. But there are two other, very non-Cartesian, properties which follow from this. In showing the development of intelligence, from its most primitive forms to its most advanced, (*d*) genetic psychology leads almost inexorably into an attempt to show the link between intelligence and biological function in general. No comment is needed on the importance of this theme in Piaget's work. And related with this is (*e*) a view of mature consciousness as evolved out of lower forms and out of the other processes of life. I do not mean here simply a view about its origin, as against one which touches its present nature in the mature adult; for on the principles outline above, these two cannot be separated. The mature form is the product of a series of transformations on more primitive forms, and cannot be fully understood without a grasp of these primitive forms.

We can see this in relation to one of the major issues of traditional epistemology. The theory of "ideas" of both traditional Cartesianism and empiricism, which has survived into our century in the form of the sense-datum theory, provides us with an example of a theory of consciousness which is not compatible with the notions about its genesis that we have been describing. From the point of view of genetic psychology, this theory takes our awareness of the world, which can only be seen as the functioning of schemas of perception, and construes it falsely as a set of quasi-objects, tableaux which are assembled out of smaller elements. If we see our perception of objects, space, causality, and so on, as skills which we have to acquire, and which we acquire in part through our commerce with objects, as beings capable of manipulating things and being affected by them, then the very idea of a basic building block of perception makes no sense. Perception is transferred from the category of something that happens to us to that of action; it is the exercise of a skill, and the pathologies from which it can suffer are to be understood accordingly. What is immediately seen can no longer be distinguished as something separable from the interpretation a subject brings with him because of his knowledge, understanding, and culture; and hence the idea of a percept identical through changes of interpretation has no application outside of its ordinary everyday application.[1]

[1] This notion of perception as a cluster of skills, which have themselves developed in relation to the motor skills by which we deal with the objects around us, makes comprehensible a conception of our knowledge of the world which is not entirely explicit. This is the view which has been explored in modern phenomenology (for example, by Heidegger and Merleau-Ponty) and by Polanyi (1958, 1966). A motor skill has no sharp boundary; rather it is a capacity for dealing with a relatively indefinite range of objects in a relatively indefinite range of ways. An awareness of things grounded in such skills is thus one in which the explicit focus can be surrounded and influenced by an implicit grasp of the situation, which resists reduction to a definite catalog. This conception of knowledge, of course, also flies in the face of the philosophical tradition—at this point common to both Cartesianism and empiricism—which underlies most modern attempts to develop a science of psychology.

We can see from this example how, on a very general level, our concept of consciousness is inextricably bound up with our idea of how it develops. But this connection is of relevance within the bounds of genetic psychology as well. If we describe mature consciousness in terms of certain capacities to describe and make inferences about things, it is impossible to define these capacities without reference to the less adequate clusters which they replace; for the capacities of maturity are defined partly in terms of the ability to go beyond the less adequate ways of generating a picture of things which precede it. In other words, if the description of the mature mind is that of a pattern of achieved skill, we cannot characterize it without reference to that the surmounting of which represents the achievement.

In this sense a genetic psychology can be said to deserve its name, in the strong sense that the mature present can only be understood in terms of the ontogenetic past. In this broad sense, of course, psychoanalysis must be considered a genetic psychology, and the ultimately adequate genetic psychology would englobe what is valid in the theories both of Piaget and of Freud. In the meantime, we live with the risk that any partial theory—one that deals only with cognition, or emotional development, or whatever—may be incapacitated by its terms of reference, as it were, from discovering the really fruitful connections.

If we define genetic psychology by the three basic properties above and the two corollaries just discussed, then it seems to me to be plainly preferable to the traditional learning theory which is its principal rival. Indeed, the attempt to find a simple universal mechanism at work in learning, which would allow us to abstract from structure, seems to me not far short of a dismal failure. At every turn, we come across undeniable evidence of heterogeneity in intelligence and learning repertoire, for which no coherent explanation in associative terms has been given. The ones that have, turn on appalling equivocations on such crucial notions as "stimulus" and "response." This case has been relatively well documented (see Chomsky, 1959).

Indeed, one might be tempted to believe that the argument is over and that the associationist position has been finally abandoned. Certainly in its original simple form it seems to be on the wane (although the growing production of Skinner-inspired teaching machines may make one nervous). But, even though most psychologists of a behavioral persuasion seem to be turning to some version of "centralist" theory and to look for models in automata demonstrating artificial intelligence, the gap between the two positions is far from closed. The search for a digital computer model of the mind is certainly compatible with a nonincrementalist learning theory in that it allows us to conceive of qualitative shifts in intelligence and learning mediated by changes in the underlying computing "machine." But the actual practice of much contemporary academic psychology remains in the intellectual grip of traditional theory.

Let us accept for the sake of argument that our ultimate aim is to find a mechanical model of the human organism. Then the approach of genetic psychology would still be to discover the shape of the structures of given stages and species, in order to discover what we want a machine analog, and ultimately a mechanistic explanation, for. It really should not concern us that this first stage of theory will inevitably be in "mentalistic" terms and will refer to innate schemas, even if we are convinced mechanists. In short, genetic psychology as such has nothing to say on the issue of the possibility or conceivability of mechanistic explanations. What it does deny is the possibility of a mechanistic shortcut via an atomistic incremental approach which could bypass cognitive structures in the explanation it offered. The issue of whether these cognitive structures can be "reduced" in terms of an underlying mechanistic theory is not prejudged.

The research strategy that follows from this is clear: first find the structures underlying intelligence, and then develop from this end whatever language is adequate, no matter how "mentalistic." But the deep-lying and widespread prejudices abroad in academic psychology rule out this approach for many. Any dalliance with mentalism or innate ideas seems like sacrilege. But if one must, at all costs, produce nothing but mechanistic explanations, then one cannot engage properly in the attempt to map competence. All one can do is return to the piecemeal approach, and try to devise good mechanical analogs for particular intelligent behaviors, like pattern recognition, for instance, without any assurance that this particular behavior, as we have circumscribed it, is relevant to the question of mechanical models of human intelligence—whether, for instance, it is not part of a more general skill which might require a quite different mechanism to explain it, if it can be explained mechanistically at all.

This kind of approach is in danger, to use the image of Dreyfus, of falling into the error of the man who climbed a tree and congratulated himself on having taken the first step to the moon (Dreyfus, 1971).[2] The

[2] Dreyfus also shows the powerful hold on workers in the field of artificial intelligence of the assumption that all knowledge is ultimately explicit—an assumption, as I mentioned above (footnote 1), which is common to both the empiricist and rationalist traditions. Indeed, Dreyfus' argument goes further, and tends to show that a model of the mind drawn from the digital computer cannot free itself from this assumption—cannot cope, in other words, with our implicit grasp of our situation. And this raises severe doubts about the capacity of this model to cope with our basic motor skills and the development from them of our mature consciousness of things; about whether, in short, this model can really come to grips with the subject matter of genetic psychology. Linked with this fixation on the explicit, the digital computer model also involves its own kind of atomism, that of discrete "bits" of information.

belief that a model adequate to reproduce a partial behavior is a step towards the explanation of human behavior, only makes sense if we accept atomist and incrementalist premises. A machine that will translate for an artificially restricted and simplified vocabulary may have no relevance to the problems of translation of natural languages; we cannot tell until we know something about the kind of structure that language competence is. To plunge on, regardless, in the certain faith of relevance is to say, in effect, that knowledge of the structure has no relevance for research, which is equivalent to an incrementalist position.

The issue is, thus, far from resolved in psychology today; and the approach which I would like to call the more fruitful one is far from being generally allowed. The reasons for this reluctance may have much to do with prejudice, but in fact the path of a genetic psychology is far from being without difficulty and uncertainty, and it is these which I would now like to look at more closely.

II. The Symbolic Function

Once we have accepted the approach of genetic psychology, a number of questions remain unresolved and difficult to resolve. The first concerns the innate schemas which are at work. Among these are obviously certain infantile reflexes and reactions, like sucking, grasping, looking at certain objects, smiling, cooing and later babbling, and so on. These, unlike the fixed patterns of some lower species, undergo transformations and develop into coordinated motor skills, while at the same time, the child learns to perceive and deal with a world of people and objects in three-dimensional space. This development has been studied in (what to this layman is) an admirable way by Piaget (1952, 1954).

It is the role of innate schemas in later transformations which is difficult to determine. The growth of language is a case in point. Obviously, the infant's innate tendency to babble plays a role here, as does the tendency to imitate. But it is clearly inadequate to try to account for language by these two tendencies; human language learning is not like superior, more flexible parroting. We have to try to determine what the skills are which underlie this achievement, which is in a way definitive of human intelligence.

For Piaget, the important thing seems to be the development of a symbolic function, that is, the ability to use signifiers (*signifiants*) to refer to significates (*signifiés*). Being able to produce or respond to signifiers is quite different from recognizing signals or cues (*indices*), whereby we recognize a whole through one of its parts or recognize a motor schema through some concomitant. This kind of achievement is entirely within the reach of higher animals, as is also an understanding of their environment which is largely "interiorized" (that is, higher mammals can often grasp solutions to problems by "insight").

Signifiers, on the other hand, refer to their significates not in virtue of a part–whole relation or of some close relationship of schemas, but are in a sense artificial. The symbolic function is thus in a real sense representational: One thing stands for another from which it is clearly separate. This is the case even though for the child (and also primitive peoples) things and their names inextricably belong together, the name *is* in a sense the nature of the thing. For, however unconscious the symbolic function is, the putting together of name and thing occurs here entirely out of the activity of naming, referring to, talking about, or representing things, whereas the relation of a signal to what it points to arises for the subject in, and is sustained by, any of a whole host of other activities in which animals also can engage; and the same goes for cues. Thus, animals can learn to operate with signals and cues, as when a dog gets ready to go out when he sees his master put on his hat; they can learn to make use of a large range of concomitances in their environment insofar as these are relevant to their activity. In these cases, in other words, the putting together of sign and thing (to use the term "sign" as a genus term for signals, cues, and symbols) comes from the shape of things as relevant to some motor activity; whereas the relation of signifier to significate can only be accounted for in terms of an activity which we can call (rather vaguely and inadequately) representational.

This holds even when we take account of the distinction which Piaget marks between symbols and signs in a narrow sense: whereas the latter can be thought of as "arbitrary," in that there is nothing in the signifier which evokes the significate, the true symbol is *motivé*; it resembles or in some way recalls what it signifies. Apart from certain elements of onomatopoeia, most of our vocabulary is sign in this sense, although we can certainly build powerful "images," hence symbols, with words. But even the symbol in the latter, secondary sense is a signifier; it arises out of the activity of representation and in no other way, however much its resemblance to the significate may add to its power.

For Piaget, the symbolic function arises out of the activities of imitation and play jointly; but it is hard to evaluate this theory without some greater understanding of the symbolic function itself, and we are as yet far from having a clearly articulated idea of this at the moment. It is not an easy matter to define what kind of activities are involved in the use of language. We have just seen that to think of language just as a relation set up for the subject between signs (in some general sense) and things is no use at all. This gives us no way of distinguishing language from other ways of operating with signs, for example, signals and cues in Piaget's sense. This kind of oversimplification is what underlies the facile but quite unilluminating comparisons of human and animal "language." It is a matter of looking at the result without looking at the activity which underlies it; and this leads to the same kind of distortion which we saw above in the sense-datum theory. Somehow in the course of developing or learning language, "chair" becomes linked to chairs and "walk" is linked to walking, but this is utterly different from the way the slap of a beaver's tail on the water is linked to flight behavior on the part of his companions. In order to understand language, we have to come closer to grips with the complex of activities vaguely subsumed under the cover term "representational" above.

For the same reason we cannot think of language just as a classification system, for animals also "classify" in the sense of reacting differentially to different types of things—even though man's classification is obviously infinitely more developed.

Perhaps one way of approaching this question of the nature of representational activity might be this: To be able to talk about things is to be potentially aware of them outside of any particular transaction with them; it is to be potentially aware of them not just in their behavioral relevance to some activity we are now engaged in, but also in a "disengaged" way. Language is the major vehicle of this capacity to grasp things in a disengaged way, but language users are also capable of using a number of other vehicles with the same effect: mime, acting out, depiction by drawing, probably nonverbal mental images.

To approach representational activity by seeing it as disengaged awareness is not, of course, to say that language users are always engaged in pure contemplation when they talk, though something like contemplation seems to become possible quite early. Obviously, language is used throughout the gamut of "engaged" human activity. The child who says "up, up" wanting to be picked up by his mother is deploying this lingustic expression very much as his younger brother deploys the gesture of holding up his arms and/or crying. Indeed, very little may have changed at the stage where the child has only a few words, of which "up" would be one in the case of the child above. What is crucial is that linguistic capacity, once it attains a certain level, permits an awareness of something like being picked up outside of the sole context of wanting to be picked up, that this "disengaged" awareness then becomes available in general to figure in new operations which require it, such as telling and hearing stories about being picked up, play acting the whole drama of being (or not being) picked up with a doll; and, much later on, in explicit verbal grasp of geometric and topological relations, and so on. Of course, all these activities are in a very real sense "engaged" in their own way—the term "disengaged" is in this sense unfortunate, even though it is hard to find another one which would create no misunderstanding. But, however passionate—and we know how deep the tensions can be which are discharged in children's play acting—these activities are all founded on an awareness of the object concerned which is disintricated from its original setting in some behavioral transaction.

But language permits us to do more than achieve disengaged awareness of a particular set of contents; it is a general capacity which makes us capable of describing (and hence disengaging our awareness of) new things, of describing and hence evoking awareness of things that are not present or that may not exist. Language is a capacity which permits us to put finite means to infinite ends, to paraphrase von Humboldt.

This open-endedness of language can be seen in two dimensions. Within a given language and way of talking about things, which a child picks up from his surroundings, he can make or understand an indefinite number of descriptions, either in talking about things around him or in telling or hearing stories. But this particular way of talking about things will have particular limitations; certain ways of grasping things will be facilitated, others will be difficult, still others inaccessible. The disengagement of awareness which comes from learning the language will thus be unlimited in one sense—it does not apply to a particular set of contents only—but limited in another, for it allows only certain kinds of descriptions.

The thing about linguistic capacity, however, is that it is not only unlimited in this sense, but also in the stronger one that a language user can in principle transcend the bounds of a particular language and conceptual structure; either by invention of new concepts, or by learning a new language, either a new natural language or a new terminology. I say "in principle," because not every innovation is accessible to everyone, or we would all be geniuses; there are important differences in intelligence and flexibility of mind which determine the limits of each one of us. But the potentiality for this kind of transcendence is implicit in linguistic capacity in this sense; it is the fundamental ability to disengage our awareness of things which, whatever the concepts which mediate this disengagement in the first case, allows us to examine these things in such a way that we discover new more adequate modes of description. In other words, it is our language, however impoverished in the first place, through which things become objects of disengaged awareness, and thus susceptible of being examined, compared, or related in such a way that new more powerful descriptions can come to light in proportion to our inclination and capacity. This "discovery," of course, may be entirely our own, or more usually we will be led to it by others, in school, university, or whatever; but in either case, it is the same "disengaging" feature of linguistic capacity which makes the achievement possible, whatever other conditions it may require (and plainly there are others, as is evident from interpersonal differences in intelligence). This type of transcendence is not achieved only in those comparatively rare cases where we shift cultures or study in some taxing discipline. Something of the same relation that holds between languages, or between ordinary and specialist terminology, also holds between different stages of a child's vocabulary and conceptual and reasoning capacities as he grows up. Transcendence is, in this sense, a commonplace.

Linguistic capacity is thus doubly unlimited. It is a general capacity for disengaged awareness which is not restricted as to level; that is, it can operate on what it has already generated, as we scrutinize more closely what we have already learned to conceptualize and find how to talk about it differently; and it can operate on itself, as we come, at a higher level of sophistication, to examine our conceptual nets themselves. But this general capacity, spiritual and disembodied as it appears to us, is mediated by our ability to deploy and hear articulated sound in a certain way. This statement is, of course, not quite true as it stands; we can transpose sounds into marks on paper, from aural into visual signs, or else into hand movements, as in sign language, or into tactile signs, as with braille. And people who lack sight and/or hearing can learn language in the first place in these other media. But the learning and exercise of linguistic capacity requires some medium of this kind. It involves a certain kind of deployment of the signs of the medium, and hence our linguistic awareness, however unlimited in principle, is always in fact limited in certain ways.

If we think of the "symbolic function" as a capacity for disengaged awareness, unrestricted as to level, which we exercise by the deployment of signs, in the normal case articulated sounds, what do we have to postulate as innate background to the acquisition of language? Clearly, the tendency to make sounds and to imitate are not enough, although in some description these are necessary. Clearly, the signs themselves are not innately determined, as one can see from the diversity of languages, nor are the types of descriptions (though certain divisions of semantic "space" may be easier and hence more "natural" for men than others, for example, certain shape and color distinctions). The innate tendency specific to man is just that to deploy signs in such a way as to achieve this disengagement of awareness. Of course, if this is all that we can say about it, talking about the innate background of language acquisition will not help us much; all we have here is a vague delineation of the area of search there must be.

We are easily led to overlook the need to look for the innate background to language learning because the most obvious fact about language is its diversity; the language a child will speak is a function of his social surroundings. But once we have discovered that the child surrounded by anglophones will speak English, we have not begun to penetrate the mystery of language learning; and we have no reason to think so unless we believe that the mechanism of language acquisition is some very simple one (for example, of the associationist type) which we already fully understand. But this is far from being the case. We still do not understand why the child will learn English and the baby chimpanzee will not. We have ultimately to understand how the child grasps our articulated sound as being *about* something, and can thus take it up himself as a vehicle of his disengaged awareness of these things, and then go on to make new descriptions of his own.

Perhaps what we are looking for here is the implicit attunedness to the categories of universal grammar which Chomsky holds the child must have to learn language; and we can then express the innate background in terms of certain fundamental grammatical structures and certain sets of rules governing transformations on these. But these structures would have to be seen in a genetic perspective as well. The child does not learn the whole language and its correct grammar at once; he passes through a number of stages, and at the most primitive ones, the vocabulary is very restricted, and the deployment of words follows a few simple patterns (that is, the syntax is rudimentary); and this regardless of how well and grammatically the parents talk to him. The structures which underlie his grasp and reproduction of speech are still relatively simple. They then undergo successive transformations until, in late childhood, he speaks pretty well like an adult.

If we could delineate the successive structures, then perhaps we could come closer to seeing what is required for the transformations which link them. Is it just a matter of slowly maturing capacity, so that the same speech surrounding produces more and more adequate grammar in the child's talk as he grows? Or are certain achievements in understanding necessary to pass from one stage to the next? Or certain developments of the ego? And what does this genesis show about the relation between these basic grammatical structures and the fact that the deployments of language they govern are the vehicles of disengaged awareness of things?

Alongside these general grammatical structures and transformations the innate background of language acquisition also includes man's particular type of gregariousness. The child learns language from within a relationship of communication with others, and this in turn puts the relationship on a new footing. At first the child not only speaks with the words, accent, mannerisms, and so on borrowed from his surroundings, he also does not have a very articulated idea of himself as a subject of thought, over against the others. This is what Piaget calls "egocentrism," constantly stressing himself that the word may mislead, because what is meant here is rather relative lack of dissociation between points of view, that of self and others, and thus "egocentrisms" can come out as much in overcompliancy as in self-centered behavior. It may be that the ability to learn language as a child does, that is, learn a first language (and even learn several languages as "first" ones), which seems to be restricted to the period before puberty, may be connected with the susceptibility to this type of relation of communication where the subject is as yet relatively undissociated. The child "resonates," to use Lenneberg's term, to the speech of his surroundings, and in this way the very general structures referred to earlier are embodied in the grasp of a particular language; whereas later we are incapable of resonating in this way; our linguistic style is fixed, and we have, alas, to work hard to acquire a new language.

III. The Concept of Maturity

The discussion of language Section II shows the difficulty of defining the innate structures which underlie ontogenesis. But an even more difficult set of questions arise concerning the direction of the transformations they undergo. It is possible to test the child's capabilities at different ages in terms of the problems he can or cannot solve and the inferences he can or cannot make, as Piaget and his associates have done. Piaget has also attempted to abstract from these experiments certain general structures of reasoning. Some of these abstractions seem very well founded. Thus it seems that it is only in his early teens that a child can generate hypotheses by a systematic combination of elements (see Inhelder & Piaget, 1958); and it is around the same time that he begins to coordinate movements in different reference systems, and grasp the idea of compensating movements in equilibrium systems.

The step from these to the postulation of a general group-lattice structure, which Piaget characterizes by the initials INRC, is much more problematical. Similar questions arise in connection with some of the "group" structures which Piaget holds underlie the child's thinking in the period of "concrete operations." The difficulty is one of interpretation. In the case of some supposed structures and procedures, there is little problem, because the subject himself is explicitly aware of them, or can easily recognize them as his when they are described. This is the case with the generation of all possible hypotheses through combination when the problem is, for instance, to assess the effect of several different factors on a single result. But the case is very different with the INRC structure.

As physically embodied in a system in equilibrium, we can perhaps accept it as a general description of the subject's understanding; but here it means no more than that he understands the relation between countering a movement by reversing it and countering it by compensation. As a general structure accounting for a whole range of achievements in problem solution and reasoning, INRC is much more open to question.

What we require here is an interpretation which goes well beyond what the subject is able to avow. In a way, we are in a similar position to that of psychoanalysis: we take a number of protocols, and reconstruct a chain of reasoning which we claim was that of the subject. In the nature of things, the plausibility of this interpretation is bound to repose in part on general hypotheses about how this subject, or subjects of this kind, usually reason; and these in turn will be strengthened or undermined by the plausibility of other interpretations that we make following these hypotheses.

Genetic psychology in this way is "hermeneutical," that is, it reposes on interpretations, as does psychoanalysis and—I believe—the sciences of man in general; and it suffers the corresponding limitations in exactitude and certainty. But this is a long and complex story, and the point I wanted to pursue here is rather this: Since our interpretations repose on general propositions about reasoning at a given stage, we cannot separate them from our general notions of the direction of development, that is, of what is involved in the transformations that take us from one stage to the next.

But our notion of the direction of development is itself bound up with our idea of what mature human life and intelligence are, so that, distressing as this may be to many, we are operating implicitly with a concept of the *terminus ad quem* of human development, a concept of successful maturity. In Piaget's case, for instance, there seem to be two very important directing ideas concerning the path of development: The subject moves away from egocentricity, and his thinking about things becomes more and more reversible. Egocentricity was already mentioned above, and is understood by Piaget as relative indissociation of points of view. Although it is not easy to be sure of the exact meaning of this term (and a concept whose exact meaning cannot be finally pinned down is not surprising in a science which makes use of interpretation), it would seem that overcoming egocentrism is a matter of gradually distinguishing oneself as a subject and coordinating one's point of view with others, and consequently being able to "decenter" one's grasp of things; being able, in other words, to grasp things not just in relation to oneself, or in the aspects that most strike one, but in terms of the inner articulations of the object itself.

This, in turn, is closely related to the growth of reversibility. This term is even harder to characterize in general; but it seems to involve something like this: thought is "reversible" when it can operate transformations and still recover its point of departure. Now, properly to understand something is to be able to follow the changes it undergoes or could undergo, and to grasp well enough what is involved in these changes so that one can say what would be required to return the object to its initial state; and this either by simple reversal, or by compensating operations of some kind whose relation to the original one understands. Irreversible thought is thus thought which is unconscious of its implications, which cannot operate with the transformations that things undergo, and grasp what they involve and how they are related to each other. It is a form of thinking which is focused on static conditions of things without being able to understand their relations.

Reversibility is thus a certain concept of objectivity; it is a concept of objectivity which naturally goes with a picture of the real as a system which can undergo a coherent set of transformations. The growth away from egocentrism and towards reversibility thus can be seen as a growth in objectivity, from a view of the world as it impinges on me to a grasp of it as it is "in itself." And to see the world objectively is to see it as a coherent set of transformations, as something which would ideally be manipulable in a coherent way.

These are among the ideas which underlie Piaget's particular formulas for intellectual development and performance at given stages. But it is not the only view compatible with his voluminous findings or with certain of his general ideas which no one would challenge.

It might appear that this picture of development dovetails perfectly with the theory of language developed above. Language as the capacity for disengaged awareness must surely set us on a path by which we overcome egocentrism and attain greater objectivity. But when we examine the matter more closely, we can see that this is not necessarily the case.

Play acting, or pretending, is an important activity that children start engaging in about the time that they start to talk. Piaget, as we saw, assigns this a role in the development of the symbolic function. Play represents the supremacy of assimilation over accommodation; it is "*la pensée égocentrique à l'état pur*" (Piaget, 1968, p. 175). It arises because the subject cannot yet make a balanced adaptation to reality, where accommodation and assimilation are in equilibrium, and hence his grasp on things is an objective one. It is destined to merge more and more into constructive activity, on the one hand, and socialized competitive games with rules, on the other, as the child matures. But it has its importance in preparing the assimilative side of the eventual mature intelligence, that deductive reasoning power which can place the real in a matrix of possibles and which is an essential complement to empirical examination of things.

It is possible to take another view of the nature and function of this kind of symbolic play. Piaget sees it in the context of a growth towards objectivity which is itself defined in terms of reversibility. But we can see it in another light. Make-believe can be seen as a function which is complementary to language. If speech is the vehicle of a disengaged awareness of what surrounds us, pretending or make-believe is a way of disengaging in another sense, by lifting oneself out of one's situation. It is a way of transcending one's predicament, which can also alter this predicament; either because we may come to see and feel it in a different way, or because play acting and its adult derivatives may allow us to work through the predicament and come to terms with it.

This latter is very clearly a frequent function which playacting has for children. A child may act out with her doll a dramatic scene she has just had with her mother. In this context, pretending can be seen as a necessary concomitant to speech. For language, in facilitating disengaged awareness, is also at the root of human feeling. Not only is there a great range of human emotions like indignation or admiration which are "thought-dependent" in the sense that they can only be attributed to language users; but it also seems plausible to say that even the common core which animals also feel, like fear and anger, are qualitatively different with man in that they are linked with an awareness of their objects which is open only to beings with language. That is why we can feel some reluctance to admit that animals have emotions in the human sense—an animal's fear or anger is confined to the context of provocation, we only use these terms to speak about a quality of his response in this context—and why we can think of human feeling as a mode of effective awareness of an object (even though this awareness may sometimes be repressed). [For a further discussion and defense of this view of emotion, see Taylor (1970).]

The experience of a strong emotion is thus the experience of a situation which moves us, which rouses strong affect in us, affect which can be unbearable. It is tremendously valuable to be able to step out of the situation, not in the sense of escapism (though this, too, may be a relief) but in order to be able to live it from another vantage point; not, in other words, to remain inextricably trapped in the primary experience. And this stepping out of our situation may help us to come to terms with it, to see it as something different, and hence to live it in a different way. This is how I would interpret the behavior of the child who reenacts the emotional scene with her mother with her doll. The powerful emotion is worked through again in the make-believe situation in which the little girl even takes the other role, and in this way the child can come to terms with it.

The general notion of play acting that I am putting forward here is that it is a kind of complement to language, in that it is a way of stepping out of our situation which allows us to live it in a different way. It allows us to see our predicament from a different vantage point, and it builds up a capacity to live on several levels, which the adult normally has. The adult acts, in fact, in reference to a situation which has many levels beyond that of his immediate spatial or interpersonal predicament; he also lives in relation to social, political, professional, religious, or ideological realities. The life of the imagination is thus in part the successor activity in adult life of the playacting of the child; it continues to feed this ability to extend the situation in which we live.

Now, this view of playacting may or may not be right. It certainly is not without rivals; plenty of theories of play have been put forward in our intellectual tradition; in connection with the above example we have only to think of Freud's analysis of the child's game of "Fort! da!" But my purpose in putting it forward was not just to add another one (if indeed this one is new), but rather to show how a different and no less defensible view of play can alter our view of Piaget's conception of development.

In this view, playacting is not an early inadequate substitute for objectivity in Piaget's sense; it is not a deforming assimilation destined to be replaced by a properly balanced one. On the contrary, it may help us to come nearer to an objective understanding of our emotions and our relations with others. But this kind of objectivity is not to be understood in terms of reversibility. Our consciousness of what moves us, of our feelings in relation to it, and of our relations with others is always likely to be clouded over with self-induced illusion. In this sense, our consciousness tends to be "egocentric," and one of the achievements of maturity can be that we are able to overcome this. Now, pretending and symbolic play, as a way of stepping out of our predicament, can help this process along (but there is no necessity in this; it can also feed our egocentric fantasies). It can also help the child to achieve the articulated understanding of distinct points of view on a common world, that is, to overcome egocentrism in Piaget's sense.

But the objectivity in question here is not Piaget's. Reversibility implies a grasp of things as systems which can undergo a coherent set of transformations as ideally manipulable entities; and connected with this it implies that we abstract from their significance for us in so coming to grips with them. But an objective understanding of our feelings or our relations with others can have neither of these features. Properly to understand one's own motivation, for instance, is not to grasp oneself as the locus of a set of coherent transformations; it is to be able to see one's feelings, desires, and situation in a certain perspective. Our understanding of potential transformations may be very uncertain and fragmentary, and may be far from the coherent systematic interrelatedness which is the essence of reversibility. It may be, indeed, that the findings of a science whose aim is objective understanding of man as a system of reversible transformations will help us to understand ourselves in this way; but the two enterprises are distinct.

If the first feature of reversibility is not appropriate here, the second feature is not either; There is no question of abstracting from the significance for us of what we are examining when we are trying to understand our own feelings. Rather, we are trying to get a balanced view of this significance. The same point can be made even more strongly about understanding our relations with others. It is, after all, intimately bound up with understanding our feelings. As we come to see the hidden sources of tension in a relationship, for instance, we can put it in perspective; and with this we alter the relationship in some degree, so that its past form can become unrecoverable in its entirety; and by this I mean not just that we cannot return to it in fact, but that we cannot even get a clear grasp intellectually of a return path; in other words, our thought here is "irreversible." Here, of course, the significance of what we are trying to put in perspective is a shared significance. To attempt to treat it as an object, which can be examined in abstraction from our involvement in it, is itself to stand back from this sharing, and hence alter the relationship.

We are dealing here with situations of involvement, to give them a general name, in which the strategy of seeking objectivity in the sense defined by reversibility is not available to us. We cannot abstract from their significance to us without shifting our object of study, and hence very possibly failing to come to grips with the original problem; and any substantial gain in our understanding of them, changes them in ways which are often irreversible both factually and intellectually. We cannot become disintricated enough from them to dominate them as manipulable objects, and hence objectivity here has to mean something else; it can only mean that we come to put them in perspective.

By contrast, the type of objectivity appropriate in other contexts, such as when we are examining a physical system, is very much the kind which Piaget seems to designate by the term "reversibility," the two aspects of which are closely connected. We attain reversibility when we grasp our object as a system of coherent potential transformations, and hence as an ideally manipulable object whose operations we therefore dominate, intellectually if not in act. And in order to attain this dominance, we have to abstract from our involvement with the object in order to grasp it "as it is in itself." Disinvolvement is thus the condition of a gain in intellectual dominance.

The hypothesis I am developing here is that mature intelligence involves the achievement of two different though related types of objectivity; one entails disenvolvement, and leads to reversibility and greater manipulative power; the other cannot achieve disinvolvement, and strives rather to achieve a truer perspective on the predicament concerned. The first can be seen as an advanced development of the basic capacity for disengaged awareness which is implicit in linguistic competence; whereas the second is built up more through our capacity to step out of our situation and "play it back" from a different vantage point, which in the child takes the form of symbolic play. In other words, where we cannot loosen the affective link with our situation, we can still live it through play in another perspective.

This hypothesis may or may not have validity. I introduce it only to show the scope of potential theories here, among which the choice is not yet foreclosed. Piaget's concept of development is, thus, far from being the only possible one compatible with his data and consonant with some of his basic ideas, such as that growth is away from egocentrism and towards objectivity in some sense. Rather, in contrast to the hypothesis developed here, Piaget would be said to give a privileged position to one form of objectivity, and to have neglected the other. Thus, he sees symbolic play only in the context of the growth towards disinvolved objectivity, and hence simply as a one-sided assimilation unbalanced by accommodation, and not also as a stepping out of our predicament which develops our capacity to alter our perspective and hence achieve the other type of objectivity. (Of course, symbolic play and its successor activities facilitate objectivity without necessarily engendering it; they can just as well serve to entrench egocentric fantasy.)

There is thus a gamut of theories here which have to be weighed and tested. Each determines research paths which diverge at some point from the others. Thus, the hypothesis introduced above would examine childhood play from a different perspective, would try to chart the development in patterns of imaginative stepping out of the predicament as the child grows, would attempt to correlate these with the successive stages of the child's dissociation and articulation of his point of view with that of others, and the consequent development of his ego. Research of this kind would also show the extent to which different theories were compatible. For instance, the form in which our above hypothesis might be eventually validated would have a great deal of overlap with Piaget's theory. Divergences would come in the notions of play, in the gamut of skills which constitute a given stage, and at other points, but there would be a substantial common area.

But these different theories each determine a view of what I have called above the *terminus ad quem* of human development, a concept of successful maturity. In this way, genetic psychology cannot avoid entering one of the domains traditionally written off by academic psychology as "philosophical," and cannot be thought of in the traditional sense as a "value-free" science. Concepts of successful maturity are the basis of arguments concerning how we should live. For instance, the opposition between different concepts of objectivity adumbrated above is obviously related to potential differences about the value of "objective" behavior in one or the other sense in certain circumstances, about objectivity as an ideal, and so on.

But this need not lead us to write off genetic psychology as "unscientific." The fact that it impinges on the domain of concepts of maturity, and hence value, does not mean that it must proceed with any less regard for empirical fact or care in formulation and testing of theories. Genetic psychology is in fact the area where notions of maturity can be brought to empirical confrontation with each other. While the important place of interpretation in this science may make a final definitive and universally accepted selection difficult if not impossible, this does not make the enterprise any the less rational or subject to scientific canons. The fact that a science is not value-free does not mean that dispassionate and (largely in Piaget's sense) objective research is not required.

IV. Conclusion

The upshot of the discussion in Sections II and III seems thus to be: Genetic psychology operates with two major ranges of basic theoretical notions, those which touch on the nature of maturity—the *terminus ad quem* of development—and those which define innate structures—the *terminus a quo*. The study is, as it were, suspended between these two ranges which determine both its strategy of research and the interpretations it makes of the transformations which the child's intelligence, behavior, and feelings undergo, including, of course, the definition of the stages of growth. Now, theory of this high level may make many dizzy; and if so, it is always possible to remain on the lower slopes and collect facts about the solution or nonsolution of problems and the avowed reasoning of the subject. But only at a certain price: first, of parasitism, since the experiments which have now been made fashionable were themselves designed out of a theoretical approach which they have helped to define further—indeed, in Piaget's case a very far-reaching one which sees intelligence in its biological context. Second, one would be unable to generalize beyond the performance record for different types of problems, and the avowed reasoning of different stages; one would be debarred from seeking the underlying structures. This would mean, third, that one would be condemned to a kind of sterility in which no new frontiers of experimentation would be opened, and the field of study itself would stagnate.

In order to map effectively the transformations of ontogenesis, genetic psychology has to operate with notions of these two ranges, to devise research strategies from them, and to confirm, refute, or refine them in the light of the resultant findings. It is this rich theoretical component, perhaps as much as its rejection of incremental and environmental approaches, which makes genetic psychology appear still foreign and slightly discreditable among many academic psychologists in the Anglo-Saxon world. It is still too often the case in this world that theory seems to be the more valued, the less conscious it is. But this moratorium on basic theory seems now to be coming to a close, and genetic psychology will in the future arouse the interest it merits.

References

Chomsky, N. Review of Skinner's "Verbal behavior." *Language* 1959, **35**(1), 26–58.

Chomsky, N. *Aspects of the theory of syntax.* Cambridge, Massachusetts: M.I.T. Press, 1965.

Dreyfus, H. L. *What computers can't do.* New York: Harper, 1971.

Inhelder, B., & Piaget, J. *The growth of logical thinking from childhood to adolescence.* New York: Basic Books, 1958.

Lenneberg, E. H. *Biological foundations of language.* New York: Wiley, 1967.

Piaget, J. *The origins of intelligence in children.* New York: International Univ. Press, 1952.

Piaget, J. *The construction of reality in the child.* New York: Basic Books, 1954.

Piaget, J. *La formation du symbole chez l'enfant.* Neuchâtel: Delachaux et Nestlé, 1968.

Polanyi, M. *Personal knowledge.* Chicago, Illinois: Univ. of Chicago Press, 1958.

Polanyi, M. *The tacit dimension.* Garden City, New York: Doubleday, 1966.

Taylor, C. Explaining action. *Inquiry,* 1970, 1970, **13**, 1–2.

Author Index

Numbers in italics refer to the pages on which the complete references is listed.

Subject Index

L

M

N

P

S

T

5 6 7 8 9 0 1 2 3 4
C D E F G H I J